*The ICSA Handbook of*
# Good Boardroom Practice

*The ICSA Handbook of*

# Good Boardroom Practice

## BARBARA COOPER
BA, MSc, FCIS

Published by ICSA Publishing Limited
16 Park Crescent
London W1B 1AH

Designed and typeset in Minion by Paul Barrett Book Production, Cambridge

Printed and bound in Great Britain by TJ International, Padstow, Cornwall

*British Library Catalguing in Publication Data*
A catalogue record for this book is available from the British Library

ISBN: 1 86072 185 0

# Contents

# Introduction

For more than a decade, standards of boardroom practice in UK listed companies have attracted intense political, regulatory and public scrutiny.

In part, this reflects the enormous economic and social significance of such companies. In his report *Institutional Investment in the United Kingdom*, published in March 2001, Paul Myners estimated that around 80 per cent of shares in UK listed companies are held on behalf of individual savers and investors by insurance companies, pension funds and other financial institutions. UK listed companies thus represent a pool of assets comprising the savings and pensions investments of millions of individuals, and their management and control is therefore a matter of the highest relevance for public policy. In part, however, the continuing high level of debate has been fuelled by corporate failures and scandals – from Maxwell to Enron and beyond – which have undermined investor and wider public confidence in the quality, integrity and effectiveness of company boards.

As in any other kind of organisation, the function of the board in a listed company is to take responsibility for managing the company's business on behalf of its members or shareholders. Separation between membership and management has many advantages, not least that decision-making can be entrusted to those with the necessary skills and capacities, leaving the members to enjoy the benefits of their association with the organisation without needing to involve themselves in matters of detail. In a listed company, the separation of membership and management facilitates efficient aggregation and use of capital, by enabling the possessors of capital to invest in enterprise without requiring them to become involved in its operation. At the same time, it allows responsibility for the strategic direction and control of business to be delegated to professional managers who (it is assumed) possess the required entrepreneurial skills and management expertise.

However, separation between membership and management may also create tensions between the interests of the parties. In listed companies, these tensions are known collectively as the 'problem of agency' – essentially, the special potential for conflicts of interest between shareholders, as the company's owners, and its directors, as their agents. According to agency theory, the managers of the company, as rational beings, will seek to maximise their own well-being through their control of the company's resources. As a result, they are likely to pursue self-serving objectives, which will not necessarily be in the best interests of the shareholders.

The problem of agency is not a new phenomenon. In *The Wealth of Nations*, published in 1776, Adam Smith famously warned that 'negligence and profusion' were inevitable where owners did not themselves attend to the needs of the business, but instead appointed managers as their agents. In contemporary terms, the problem of agency may manifest itself in board decisions that promote the interests of the directors, but do not necessarily enhance the value of the company for the shareholders. Examples of such decisions might include:

> pursuit of short-term share price growth, where sustained investment in the company's asset base might produce greater long-term benefits for shareholders;
> inappropriate expansion or diversification of the company's activities into areas which involve unwarranted risks to shareholders' investments; or
> resistance by managers to mergers or takeovers which might threaten their own job security, but which may be in the best interests of the company's shareholders.

In some cases, the potential for conflict of interest between owners and managers may be exacerbated by the company's executive remuneration arrangements. As shown by recent highly publicised events in companies such Marconi, GlaxoSmithKline and Railtrack, remuneration and incentive arrangements may be intended to align the interests of directors and shareholders but may, in practice, reward the pursuit of inappropriate objectives, while failing to punish poor management performance.

The problem of agency in listed companies can be exacerbated by the board's ability to control the supply of information to shareholders about the company's position and performance. In extreme cases, this may result in shareholders and others being seriously misled. A recent notorious example concerns the US energy corporation Enron, whose directors systematically overstated profits, failed to inform shareholders about risky financing arrangements and continued to declare the corporation's financial soundness until days before its filing for bankruptcy protection.

In any organisation in which the management of activities is separated from the membership, the governing body must be provided with the powers and authorities needed to enable it to manage the organisation's activities effectively. At the same time, however, there must be sufficient checks and balances on the governing body's actions to assure the members that the organisation will be run in their interests. In any organisation, therefore, a system of good boardroom practice is essential, comprising as its generic components:

> a definition of the role and responsibilities of the governing body, including its membership, the limits on its powers of management and rules for the proper conduct of its business;
> a requirement for the governing body to account for its actions through timely reporting of compete and accurate information; and
> the retention by the organisation's members of powers to appoint and remove the governing body and to ratify key decisions affecting their interests.

## About this Handbook

Good boardroom practice in any organisation is therefore concerned with the relationship between managers and owners – in other words, it relates essentially to the *internal* governance of the organisation. But many organisations, including listed companies, also exist and operate within an external framework of laws, regulations and public expectations.

Part One examines the external environment in which listed companies operate, taking into account legal and regulatory requirements, international developments and changing public attitudes to the way in which companies conduct their activities and account to society for their impacts. To this end:

> Chapter 1 briefly describes the framework of current company law in the UK and considers the extent to which provides an appropriate context for good boardroom practice;
> Chapter 2 traces the development of non-statutory codes of corporate governance in the UK, from the Cadbury Report of 1992 up to and including the July 2003 version of the Combined Code of Corporate Governance;
> Chapter 3 examines issues of good boardroom practice in other economies worldwide and assesses the evidence for an emerging international consensus on key issues of corporate governance; and
> Chapter 4 discusses contemporary challenges to traditional ideas about corporate purpose and accountability and describes the growing need for companies to demonstrate high standards of social, ethical and environmental responsibility.

Part Two is devoted to a detailed examination of the origins, content and practical implications of the main provisions of the July 2003 Combined Code of Corporate Governance. This is longest and most detailed such code promulgated in the UK to date, comprising some 16 Main Principles, 24 Supporting Principles and nearly 50 detailed provisions. It introduces a number of new concepts and principles, including the recommendation that boards should undertake formal and rigorous evaluation of their own performance. At the same time, it introduces a new clarity into previously nebulous areas, such as the independence of non-executive directors (NEDs) and the composition of board committees.

The increased length and specificity of the revised Combined Code has been greeted with dismay in some boardrooms. It is important to bear in mind, however, that like its predecessors, the Combined Code is not mandatory and has no statutory force. Listed companies are not required to comply with its provisions, but are required by the Listing Rules to disclose in their annual reports whether or not they have complied with Code recommendations and, to extent that they have not, to give their reasons for non-compliance.

At the same time, it should be noted that the increasing degree of detail in the Combined Code's provisions is not a reflection of regulatory ambition. Rather, it is a response to *real* events and their consequences – that is, to scandals, failures and unprincipled actions which have undermined investor and public confidence in the quality, integrity and effectiveness of boardroom conduct.

The four main themes of the Combined Code are addressed in Part Two as follows:

## A Directors

> Chapter 5 considers the collective role of the board of directors in UK listed companies.
> Chapter 6 addresses the composition of the board, including the role of non-executive directors and the division of power and authority at the top of the company.

> Chapter 7 examines the new emphasis on the effectiveness of the board of directors, with particular reference to the need for the board to evaluate its own performance and that of its committees.
> Chapter 8 describes the processes for the selection and appointment of directors.

## B Remuneration

> Chapter 9 outlines the role and composition of the remuneration committee and considers current issues of regulatory and public concern, including the perceived problem of 'rewards for failure'.

## C Accountability and audit

> Chapter 10 describes the current formal requirements for reporting to shareholders and explores current concerns about the adequacy of both financial and non-financial reporting by listed companies.
> Chapter 11 examines the measures taken to clarify and improve the effectiveness of the audit committee and the external auditors following the Enron scandal; and
> Chapter 12 outlines the board's responsibility for the establishment of an effective system of internal control and risk management.

## D Relations with shareholders

> Chapter 13 considers the responsibilities of companies and their boards for fostering positive relationships with institutional shareholders and the reciprocal obligations of institutional shareholders to make considered use of their powers of ownership.
> Chapter 14 describes current best practice for the open and constructive conduct of business at the AGM.

This Handbook is intended to help directors and those who advise them to explore how the principles of good governance can be translated into sustainable good practice in the boardroom. Although it focuses on UK listed companies, it is now widely accepted that organisation of all kinds face similar challenges and can learn from each other. As a result, there is growing evidence that good practice is readily transferable between different sectors of the economy. Examples are the now widespread use in the public and not-for-profit sectors of the audit committee concept first developed in the corporate sector, and the increasing emphasis on the need for governing bodies of all kinds to include a strong independent element. Conversely, there is growing recognition that management skills developed in running large public and charitable bodies may be equally valuable on company boards. While it is expected that this Handbook will find much of its audience amongst the directors and secretaries of listed companies, it is hoped that it will also be of use to those involved in the management of public bodies, charities and non-listed companies.

# Abbreviations

| | |
|---|---|
| ABI | Association of British Insurers |
| AGM | annual general meeting |
| APB | Auditing Practices Board |
| ASB | Accounting Standards Board |
| CA 1985 | Companies Act 1985 |
| CA 1989 | Companies Act 1989 |
| CDDA 1986 | Company Directors Disqualification Act 1986 |
| CEO | chief executive officer |
| CFO | chief financial officer |
| CSR | corporate social responsibility |
| DTI | Department of Trade and Industry |
| EC | European Commission |
| EEA | European Economic Area |
| EU | European Union |
| FRC | Financial Reporting Council |
| FRRP | Financial Reporting Review Panel |
| FSA | Financial Services Authority |
| FSMA 2000 | Financial Services and Markets Act 2000 |
| ICAEW | Institute of Chartered Accountants in England and Wales |
| ICSA | Institute of Chartered Secretaries and Administrators |
| IoD | Institute of Directors |
| ISC | Institutional Shareholders Committee |
| NAPF | National Association of Pension Funds |
| NED | non-executive director |
| NYSE | New York Stock Exchange |
| OECD | Organisation for Economic Co-operation and Development |
| OFR | Operating and Financial Review |
| PIDA 1998 | Public Interest Disclosure Act 1998 |
| PIRC | Pensions Investments Research Consultants Ltd |
| SEC | Securities and Exchange Commission |
| SRI | socially responsible investment |
| TSR | Total Shareholder Return |
| UKLA | United Kingdom Listing Authority |

# Listed companies and their operating environment

Part One examines the *external* environment in which listed companies operate, taking into account legal and regulatory requirements, international developments and changing public attitudes to the way in which companies conduct their activities and account to society for their impacts. To this end:

- Chapter 1 briefly describes the framework of current company law in the UK and considers the extent to which this provides an appropriate context for good boardroom practice.

- Chapter 2 traces the development of non-statutory codes of corporate governance in the UK, from the Cadbury Report of 1992 up to and including the July 2003 version of the Combined Code of Corporate Governance.

- Chapter 3 examines issues of good boardroom practice in other economies worldwide and assesses the evidence for an emerging international consensus on key issues of corporate governance.

- Chapter 4 discusses contemporary challenges to traditional ideas about corporate purpose and accountability and describes the growing need for companies to demonstrate high standards of social, ethical and environmental responsibility.

# The Legal Framework

> Company legislation has two main functions: (i) enabling and (ii) regulatory. The enabling function empowers people to do what they could not otherwise achieve – namely, to create a body with a distinct corporate personality. The regulatory function prescribes the conditions which have to be complied with to obtain incorporation and the rules that thereafter have to be observed to protect members, creditors and the public against the dangers inherent in such a body.
>
> *Gower's Principles of Modern Company Law*

This chapter explores the legal environment within which UK listed companies are established and operated, with particular reference to those statutory and regulatory provisions which impact on their governance. As such, it considers:

> ❯ the methods by which companies are formed and the various advantages of incorporation;
> ❯ the principal legal provisions governing the operation of listed companies in the UK;
> ❯ the extent to which UK company law, in its present form, provides a framework for good boardroom practice; and
> ❯ the prospects for changes to current statutory provisions to strengthen accounting and auditing practices in the light of the Enron scandal and to implement proposals arising from the fundamental review of company law initiated by the Government in 1998.

It is not possible within the scope of this chapter to provide a comprehensive guide to the detailed technical requirements of UK companies legislation in respect of registration, filing and other administrative obligations. (For suggested sources of information on these matters, see the bibliography.)

## The formation of companies

When a company is formed, a legal distinction is created between the existence and identity (or 'personality') of the company itself and those of its members or shareholders. This distinction gives incorporated form significant advantages as a means of establishing and carrying on business:

> As a legal person in its own right, a company can possess rights and privileges not available to its shareholders, and can take action to enforce these rights.
> Only the company not its shareholders, can be sued for breach of its legal duties.
> Property owned by the company is distinct from the property of its shareholders, with the result that shareholders' property is unaffected by the claims of creditors in the event that the company becomes insolvent.
> Unless a fixed lifetime is specified in its constitution, the company can continue in business indefinitely, undisturbed by changes in its shareholder base.

Under UK law, companies may be formed in three different ways:

1 Registered companies are formed under the Companies Acts and are the most common type of company, with an estimated 1.5 million registered companies currently active in Great Britain. As discussed below, the registered company form is extremely versatile and is capable of adaptation to a wide range of commercial and other purposes.
2 Statutory corporations are formed under specific statutory provisions. There are currently fewer than 10,000 statutory corporations, of which the majority are co-operative societies formed under the Industrial and Provident Societies Act.
3 Chartered companies are formed pursuant to letters patent issued under Royal Prerogative or special statutory powers. There are currently about 750 chartered companies in the UK, consisting mainly of organisations established for charitable or quasi-charitable purposes, but also including a small number of long-established trading companies.

While all three types of company provide the benefits of separate legal personality, registered company form has the advantage that members are able to limit their liability for the company's debts. Limited liability can be achieved in one of two ways: by guarantee or by shares. In guarantee companies, the liability of members to subscribe to the company's debts in the event of liquidation is limited to an amount agreed in advance, but there is no provision for the distribution of any profits to members. For this reason, guarantee company form is generally used for social or charitable purposes only.

In registered companies limited by shares, profits can be distributed to shareholders in proportion to their holdings in the company. At the same time, the potential liability of each shareholder to contribute towards the company's debts in the event of insolvency is limited to the nominal value of their shares. Registration with liability limited by shares thus provides a convenient way of allocating profit among the shareholders of a commercial enterprise, while enabling them to know in advance the extent of the risk to their investment.

Registration with liability limited by shares is the most common method of incorporation: according to the Department of Trade and Industry, this type represents approximately 95 per cent of all companies currently constituted in Great Britain.

Registration with liability limited by shares is available to private companies, in which shares cannot be offered for sale to the general public, and public companies, in which shares can be offered for sale to the general public under regulated conditions. Public companies account for less than 1 per cent of all registered companies in Great

Britain, while fewer than 1,500 public companies have their shares listed for trading on the London Stock Exchange. Despite their small number, UK listed companies are of major economic significance: their total market value in August 2003 was more than £1,200 billion, of which 80 per cent was represented by fewer than 100 companies.

A key objective of company law is to ensure that the advantages of incorporation are readily available by ensuring that companies can be formed quickly, easily and relatively cheaply. At the same time, it seeks to manage the consequences of separate personality and limited liability by:

> establishing minimum standards for the proper conduct of business by companies, in particular by establishing model constitutional arrangements;
> providing for the appointment of directors and obliging them to deal fairly with the company;
> requiring the disclosure of key information; and
> creating enforceable rights for shareholders and (to a lesser extent) creditors of the company.

## The principal UK legal provisions

Until comparatively recently, all the main legal provisions relevant to the formation and operation of listed companies were contained in single Acts of Parliament. Since the mid-1980s, however, separate branches of specialised legislation have been established to deal with different aspects of company operation. As a result:

> requirements for the formation and operation of companies are specified in the Companies Act 1985, the Companies Act 1989 and associated secondary legislation (recent additions to secondary legislation include the Directors' Remuneration Regulations 2002 and are discussed further in *Chapter 9*);
> the regulation of the securities markets is contained in specific financial services legislation, currently the Financial Services and Markets Act 2000;
> arrangements for the disqualification of delinquent directors are set out in the Company Directors Disqualification Act 1986; and
> corporate insolvency and personal bankruptcy are covered by a distinct legislative regime under the Insolvency Act 1986.

In addition to these statutory provisions, there is a large body of sometimes difficult and obscure case law, particularly in the areas of directors' duties and the rights and legal remedies available to shareholders.

### The Companies Acts

*The Companies Act 1985*

The Companies Act 1985 (CA 1985) sets out the basic statutory provisions governing the formation and registration of companies, including the requirement for key documents relating to the purpose, ownership and management of the company to be lodged with the Registrar of Companies and regularly updated.

Provisions of particular relevance to the governance of the company and the protection of shareholders' interests are:

> *Directors:* disclosure of directors' interests in the company's shares (CA 1985 Part VI); the qualifications, duties and responsibilities of directors (Part IX); and the enforcement of fair dealing by directors, in particular to restrict the ability of directors to take unfair financial advantage of their position (Part X).
> *Accountability:* the requirements for preparation of annual accounts (Part VII) and the appointment of external auditors (Part XI).
> *Shareholders' powers and entitlements:* arrangements for the allotment of shares (Part IV) and limitations on the company's ability to vary the voting rights attaching to shares (Part V); shareholders' entitlements to participate in distributions of profits and other assets (Part VIII); and the requirements for general meetings of shareholders (Part XI).

Regulations made under CA 1985 set out, in a series of tables, model Memoranda of Association and Articles of Association for companies of different types.

Taken together, a company's Memorandum and Articles of Association comprise its constitution and define the relationship between the shareholders and the directors. Broadly speaking, the Memorandum of Association defines the company's identity, in terms of its name, the jurisdiction in which it is registered, the amount of its authorised share capital and its division into shares of a fixed amount, and, in the 'objects clause', the purpose and scope of the company's intended activities. The Articles of Association give further details of the company's share capital, including the transferability of shares, shareholders' pre-emptive rights to purchase shares offered in a rights issue and arrangements for the declaration and payment of dividends. The Articles set out internal aspects of the company's constitution, including arrangements for the appointment, retirement and removal of directors.

Model Articles for public and private companies limited by shares are set out in Table A to CA 1985. While it is for the company itself to decide whether to adopt a model Memorandum or model Articles, in whole or in part, its Memorandum (and its Articles, unless it adopts the format prescribed in Table A) must be delivered to the Registrar of Companies and appear on the public register.

### The Companies Act 1989

The main purpose of the Companies Act 1989 (CA 1989) was to take account of the UK's membership of the European Union (EU) by implementing the requirements of the Seventh Company Law Directive, dealing with consolidated accounts, and the Eighth Company Law Directive, dealing with audit. In addition, the opportunity was taken to introduce many new and reformed domestic provisions, including the establishment of the Financial Reporting Council (FRC), the Accounting Standards Board (ASB) and the Financial Reporting Review Panel (FRRP) to monitor standards of financial reporting by UK companies and to make, amend and withdraw accounting standards as necessary.

## The Financial Services and Markets Act 2000

The provisions of company law are supplemented for listed companies by the requirements of the Financial Services and Markets Act 2000 (FSMA 2000). This appoints the

Financial Services Authority (FSA), in its capacity as the United Kingdom Listing Authority (UKLA), as the competent authority in the UK for the listing of company shares and other securities for trading on public stock exchanges.

As the competent authority for listing, the UKLA promulgates Listing Rules intended to ensure that investors have access to relevant and accurate financial information to enable them to make informed investment decisions. To this end, the Listing Rules require that, as a condition of access to the markets for listed securities, companies must prepare detailed prospectuses or listing particulars setting out the nature of their business, their management and financing arrangements and potential material risks to potential investors. Once a company's securities have been listed for trading, it is required by the Listing Rules to fulfil a number of ongoing obligations, which in many cases amplify existing duties under the Companies Acts. These include:

> financial reporting in accordance with the accounting standards set and monitored by the FRC;
> full and timely disclosure of other information relevant to the interests of existing shareholders, such as related party transactions, directors' dealings in the company's shares and changes in major shareholdings; and
> the provision of adequate opportunity for shareholders to consider and vote on proposals for major changes in the business operations of the company and other matters of importance concerning the company's management and constitution.

In addition, the Listing Rules require the directors of listed companies to report to shareholders on whether they are complying with the recommendations of the Combined Code of Corporate Governance appended to the Listing Rules and to explain their reasons for any departures from the Code. In this way, the Listing Rules give effect to the 'comply or explain' regime for corporate governance discussed in more detail in *Chapter 2*.

The Listing Rules also give effect to the Model Code. The purpose of the Model Code is to regulate share dealing and other activities by directors and key officers and employees of a listed company, especially during the period leading up to the announcement of the company's financial results or other significant announcements of price-sensitive information. More broadly, FSMA 2000 gives the FSA power to impose penalties for market abuse, defined as the use of information not generally available to market users to give a false or misleading impression about the price or availability of listed securities. The market abuse provisions create a new civil offence, additional to the criminal offence of insider dealing under the Criminal Justice Act 1993, and are of special relevance to company directors and senior managers who have access to 'inside' information about their company's performance and prospects.

## The Company Directors Disqualification Act 1986

The Company Directors Disqualification Act 1986 (CDDA 1986) protects shareholders and the general public by preventing the involvement in company management of persons who are considered by the courts to be unfit for such involvement because of their previous conduct. CDDA 1986 applies to both solvent and insolvent companies and empowers the courts to disqualify individuals, for periods of between two and fifteen years, from acting as directors or being concerned in the management of companies. It therefore regulates who may act as a director, and applies to all persons directly or indirectly involved in the promotion, formation and management of a company.

## The Insolvency Act 1986

Under the Insolvency Act 1986 (IA 1986), directors and other officers of an insolvent company may be required to contribute to the assets of the company if they have acted negligently or in breach of their fiduciary duties, which include a duty to consider the interests of the company's creditors. In addition, a director who knew or should have known that there was no reasonable prospect of avoiding insolvent liquidation may be liable for wrongful trading if he or she failed to take every step which could have been taken to minimise losses to creditors.

# Company law and good boardroom practice

This section considers the treatment in UK company law of the three elements of good boardroom practice, namely the definition of the role and responsibilities of the board of directors; the requirement for the board to account for its actions to the company's shareholders; and the retention by the shareholders of powers to appoint and remove the directors and to ratify key decisions affecting their interests.

## The role of directors

There is no formal legal definition of a director, but the term is generally understood to mean one of a group of individuals at the top of the company who have been duly appointed by the shareholders to direct and control the business, formulate its strategy and supervise its management. Despite the emphasis in corporate governance on the need for a balance of executive and non-executive directors on the board, no such distinction is made in law. Consequently, all directors who have been formally appointed are considered to have the same duties, powers, obligations and liabilities as set out in statute, regulation and common law.

### Directors' duties

There is currently no definitive statement in law of the duties owed by directors to the company. Although some statutory guidance is available (for example in Part X of CA 1985), the principles on which directors' duties are currently based derive mainly from common law. In this context, the directors are agents of the company, to which they owe the fiduciary duties of loyalty and good faith expected of trustees. Unlike trustees, however, directors are expected to take entrepreneurial risks on behalf of the company and in doing so are expected to exercise care and skill.

The fiduciary duties of directors entail the obligation to behave loyally towards the company and act in good faith in its best interests, where necessary by balancing long-term objectives against the short-term interests of present shareholders. Directors are required to maintain independence of judgement and to avoid putting themselves in a position where their duties to the company conflict, actually or potentially, with their personal interests. In addition, directors must obey the company's constitution, as laid down in its Memorandum and Articles, and must act fairly as between shareholders. Directors must not use their powers under the company's constitution for purposes for which they were not intended: where the directors use their powers for an improper purpose (for example, to issue additional shares in order to defeat a possible takeover bid), it is not enough that they honestly and reasonably believed that their actions were in the best interests of company.

Directors are also expected to apply reasonable care and skill in the exercise of their functions. The standards of care and skill expected of directors have been developed through case law, such that directors' performance is expected to meet both:

> An objective test applicable to directors generally: did the director concerned have, and exercise, the general knowledge, skill and experience reasonably to be expected of a person carrying out the functions carried out by that director in relation to the company?
> A more demanding subjective test applicable to each director personally: did the director concerned exercise the particular knowledge, skill and experience that he or she actually possessed?

## Directors' powers

A company's Articles will usually entrust the directors to manage the business of the company and exercise all the company's legal powers. In exercising these powers, the directors must have regard to the limits on the company's corporate capacity, as set out in the objects clause of its Memorandum.

In principle, any transaction outside the objects clause is void, although CA 1985 provides that the validity of a transaction cannot be called into question on the grounds that the company lacks capacity because of a gap in its objects clause. None the less, it is technically possible for shareholders to bring proceedings to stop any transaction not permitted by the objects clause, provided that they obtain an injunction before the transaction becomes legally binding. Moreover, the directors may be personally liable if they exceed their powers under Memorandum, unless the shareholders have approved a special resolution relieving the directors of liability.

Directors must observe the limits placed on their authority by provisions of CA 1985, which prohibit certain transactions or require them to be approved in advance by shareholders in general meeting. The transactions affected include:

> *Substantial property transactions*: except in limited circumstances, a director is not permitted to enter into an arrangement to acquire from the company or transfer to the company any non-cash asset without first obtaining the approval of shareholders in general meeting – a provision which is intended to ensure that directors cannot sell property to the company at an inflated price or acquire property from the company at less than its full value.

> *Loans to directors*: subject to specific exemptions, a company is not permitted to make loans to directors or connected persons, to provide guarantees or security for such loans or to assume responsibility to a third party for a loan entered into by a director or a connected person.

> *Service contracts*: while the board has general authority to negotiate the terms and conditions of directors' service contracts, it must seek shareholders' approval in certain circumstances, for example, where the proposed contract is for a term of more than five years.

> *Takeovers and mergers:* when considering or recommending to shareholders an offer for a takeover or merger, the directors must observe their fiduciary duties and act honestly in the interests of the company and its shareholders as a whole. Accordingly, any payment received by a director in compensation for loss of office as consequence of the transaction must be disclosed to and approved by the shareholders. In addition, the directors of listed companies must observe the requirements of the Listing Rules and the Takeover Code in respect of the information to be provided to shareholders, the equal treatment of shareholders and the protection of minority interests.

> *Capital maintenance:* directors must observe statutory rules intended to ensure that the company receives full value on the initial issue of its shares and thereafter maintains its paid-up share capital. The rules specify the conditions on which the directors may take actions which might involve the diminution of its paid-up share capital, including the allotment and issue of shares at less than nominal value; distributions to shareholders in the form of dividends or returns of capital; the purchase and redemption of the company's own shares; and the provision of financial assistance for the purchase of the company's shares.

### Directors' obligations

In keeping with the obligation on directors not to put themselves in a position where there is a conflict between their personal interests and their duty to the company, CA 1985 requires directors to disclose certain information both to the company and to the shareholders. This includes:

> *Interests in contracts and transactions:* a director who has a direct or indirect material interest in a contract or proposed contract, transaction or other arrangement with the company must disclose it at a board meeting at the earliest opportunity. The director's interest must be formally recorded by the company and must be disclosed to shareholders in the annual report and accounts.

> *Interests in shares*: directors must notify the company of their own and connected persons' interests in the company's shares or debentures. A listed company must record directors' interests in shares and share options in its register of directors' interests, disclose them to shareholders in the annual report and accounts and promptly announce any changes in directors' interests.

### Directors' liabilities

As explained in the foregoing sections, directors may incur personal liabilities in a variety of circumstances, for example if they fail to exercise the necessary care and skill in the performance of their functions or are otherwise in breach of their duty to the company. Except in limited circumstances (for example, where an application for relief from liability is granted by the courts on the grounds that the director has acted honestly and reasonably) companies are not permitted to undertake to indemnify or exempt directors against any liability arising from negligence, default, breach of duty or breach of trust relating to the company. However, companies may purchase and maintain insurance for directors and officers against liability for negligence, default, breach of duty or breach of trust in relation to the company. Further discussion on directors' personal liabilities and their mitigation is set out in *Chapter 6*.

## Accountability to shareholders

Directors of listed companies are required to disclose information on such matters as the company's financial position and performance, proposed transactions affecting the future of the company, and the interests of directors and connected persons in the company's shares. Although disclosure is required in the interests of prospective investors and the general public, its primary purpose is to enable existing shareholders to understand the company's position and performance and to facilitate the exercise their authority. The principal means by which information must be disclosed include:

> *Circulation to shareholders:* directors of listed companies are required to prepare and approve annual reports and accounts setting out the contents prescribed in CA 1985 and CA 1989 and to ensure that copies are sent to all shareholders and other parties entitled to receive them. The annual report and accounts must be laid before the shareholders in general meeting, notice of which, giving details of the resolutions to be proposed, must also be circulated to shareholders and other entitled parties in accordance with the prescribed notice periods. As required by statute and the Listing Rules, appropriate notice of any extraordinary general meeting (EGM) must also be given to shareholders and others, together with full details (including a prospectus or other circular) of any significant transaction for which the shareholders' approval is required.

> *Filing of returns with the Registrar of Companies:* the directors are responsible for notifying to the Registrar of Companies key information relating to the company's location, structure and management and for updating this information as necessary. Matters on which filings are required include changes in the company's registered office or in the identity of the directors or the company secretary; the creation of any charge over the company's assets; allotments of shares; any increase in the authorised share capital; any consolidation, conversion or subdivision of the company's shares and any purchase by the company of its own shares; and details of resolutions approved by the shareholders, including all special, extraordinary and elective resolutions and certain ordinary resolutions.

> *Availability of statutory records for inspection:* the directors are responsible for making sure that the statutory books and records of the company are complete and up-to-date and for making them available for inspection at the company's registered office or any other place as notified to the Registrar of Companies. The records required include registers containing details of the company's shareholders; directors' interests in the company's shares and debentures; other sig-

nificant interests in the company's securities and any changes in such interests; and details of any mortgages and charges over the assets of the company.

## The retained powers of shareholders

The retained powers of shareholders to control and influence the actions of the directors are of two main sorts, known to economists as 'voice' and 'exit'.

The power of 'voice' consists of the shareholders' ability to exercise the voting powers attaching to shares. As explained above, significant decisions of the company, including the appointment and reappointment of directors, proposed dividend payments and other substantial transactions must be disclosed to shareholders and considered at general meetings. The shareholders have the power, to give or withhold approval for any of the resolutions proposed by the directors, and ultimately to dismiss the directors. The shareholders' power of 'voice' is preserved in UK law by the disclosure obligations outlined above, by the requirement for listed companies to hold general meetings of all shareholders and by the limits imposed by CA 1985 on the ability of companies to vary the voting and other rights attaching to shares.

The power of 'exit' consists of the choice available to the shareholders to maintain, increase or dispose of their shares in the company according to their opinion of the performance of the business and the quality of the directors. Widespread dissatisfaction with the company's performance, particularly on the part of large institutional shareholders, could potentially result in the disposal of large numbers of the company's shares, adversely impacting on its share price and ultimately on the bonuses and career prospects of the directors. The power of 'exit' is safeguarded principally through the provisions of FSMA 2000, which ensure the maintenance of transparent markets in listed companies' shares.

Beyond their powers of exit and voice, shareholders have only limited ability to seek legal remedies, on an individual basis, against careless, delinquent or under-performing directors. In most circumstances, there is a general presumption that, where directors' performance or conduct is considered to be unsatisfactory, it is for the company as a whole, rather than for shareholders individually, to take action, for example by bringing legal action against directors who are considered to be in breach of their duties. That said, there are limited circumstances in which individual shareholders, who consider that the company's affairs have been conducted in an oppressive or unfairly prejudicial manner, can bring claims against directors on behalf of or instead of the company. Remedies available to shareholders in these circumstances include:

> applying to the Secretary of State to investigate the company's affairs;
> seeking a court order to regulate the future conduct of the business or to prevent an unfairly prejudicial act or omission to be remedied; or
> as a last resort, petitioning the court for a 'just and equitable' winding up on the grounds that the management of the company has irretrievably broken down.

## The prospects for legal reform

A fundamental review of UK company law was established by the Government in early 1998 with the intention of improving the consistency, transparency and predictability of company law. In discharging this remit, the Company Law Review Steering Group established for the purpose was invited to take into account the increasing globalisation of business, contemporary developments in information technology and the need for a more sophisticated approach to corporate governance. Following the publication of the Steering Group's final report and recommendations, the Government issued the White Paper *Modernising Company Law* (Cm 5553) for consultation in July 2002.

Despite widespread support for the reforms outlined in the White Paper, the Government announced in mid-2003 that it had reassessed its legislative programme to take account of the need to restore investor and wider public confidence in the light of the Enron scandal described in *Chapter 2* below. As a result, priority is being given to the implementation of legal changes designed to tighten independent regulation of the audit profession and strengthen the enforcement of company accounting.

The Companies (Audit, Investigations and Community Enterprise) Bill introduced into the House of Lords in December 2003 is intended to improve the reliability of financial reporting and the independence of auditors by:

› requiring directors to state that they have not withheld any relevant information from their auditors;
› requiring companies to publish details of non-audit services provided by their auditors;
› imposing independent auditing standards, monitoring and disciplinary procedures on the professional accountancy bodies;
› strengthening the role of the FRRP in enforcing good accounting and reporting, by giving it new powers to require documents and broadening its scope; and
› allowing the Inland Revenue to pass information about suspect accounts to the FRRP.

In addition, the Bill proposes to increase the ability of DTI inspectors to investigate companies, for example by widening their document-gathering powers and enabling them to require entry to, and remain on, premises without obtaining a warrant.

The proposals set out in the Companies (Audit, Investigations and Community Enterprise) Bill represent the final element of a package of measures aimed at restoring investor confidence in corporate governance, company accounting and auditing practices in the UK. The other components of this package are:

› the revision of the Combined Code of Corporate Governance to incorporate recommendations from the Higgs and Smith Reviews, as described in *Chapter 2* and discussed in detail in *Chapters 5 to 14*; and
› changes in the arrangements for the oversight of accounting and financial reporting, as discussed in *Chapter 11*.

While there is general agreement that action is needed to restore investor and wider public confidence in the wake of the Enron scandal, the decision to prioritise Enron-related legislation has created some uncertainty regarding the Government's intentions in respect of the more broadly-based proposals arising from the Company Law Review and outlined in the July 2002 White Paper. These included a number of proposals designed to promote improved standards of boardroom conduct in listed companies, notably:

> A new, definitive, statement of directors' duties to replace the current loose assembly of common law duties. The proposed legislative statement of directors' duties is discussed further in *Chapter 4*.

> A requirement for listed and other economically significant companies to incorporate within their annual reports and accounts an Operating and Financial Review (OFR) designed to enhance the quality of non-financial and forward-looking information provided to shareholders: further consideration of the OFR format is contained in *Chapter 10*.

> A revised timetable, further considered in *Chapter 14*, for the publication by listed companies of their annual reports and notices of annual general meeting in order to improve the effectiveness of the AGM as a forum for debate between shareholders and directors.

In her speech to the ICSA Annual Conference on 16 October 2003 Jacqui Smith MP, the Minister of State for Company Law and Related Matters, indicated that the statutory OFR for large companies was likely be introduced under existing Ministerial powers and that draft regulations for this purpose would be published for consultation in due course. Similarly, the DTI consultative document *Director and Auditor Liability*, published in December 2003, reaffirmed the Government's acceptance of the case for a statutory statement of directors' duties, including a statutory standard of care, skill and diligence.

However, no timetable has been given for the legislative programme required to implement these or other recommendations of the Company Law Review and it now seems unlikely that a comprehensive new Companies Act will reach the statute book before 2008.

## Conclusion

Existing UK company law and its proposed development address external aspects of corporate governance, particularly in respect of accountability and the reserved powers of shareholders. However, the law does not attempt to regulate matters of internal governance, such as the composition, conduct and effectiveness of the board of directors, reflecting a traditional assumption that these are essentially private issues for resolution at the company's own discretion. As *Chapter 2* explains, however, company failures and continuing controversy over issues such as executive remuneration have challenged the concept of companies as self-regulating entities and have prompted the development of voluntary codes of corporate governance designed to raise standards of boardroom practice.

# 2

# Codes of Corporate Governance

> Corporate governance is the system by which companies are directed and controlled. Boards of directors are responsible for the governance of their companies. The shareholders' role in governance is to appoint the directors and the auditors and to satisfy themselves that an appropriate governance structure is in place.
>
> Cadbury Committee (1992)
> *Report on the Financial Aspects of Corporate Governance*

This chapter explains the 'comply or explain' approach to corporate governance which has been adopted in the UK, and traces the evolution of successive codes of corporate governance. It also examines the UK's response to the corporate governance issues raised by the Enron scandal.

As we have seen in the Introduction, it has long been recognised that the separation of ownership and control in all but the most closely held companies entails a risk that the directors, as the managers of the business, will exploit the powers delegated to them to serve their own interests at the expense of those of the shareholders. As a result, the interests of shareholders and directors may diverge on a wide range of issues, including the strategic direction of the company, its response to takeover and merger proposals, the composition of the board and the remuneration of directors. In these and other areas, the ability of the shareholders to detect and censure unsatisfactory performance or improper conduct may be severely curtailed by the directors' control of information. The legal provisions described in *Chapter 1* seek to redress the imbalance between directors and shareholders by requiring companies to report externally on their ownership, financing arrangements and performance and by reserving to shareholders powers to appoint and dismiss the company's directors and to ratify key decisions affecting their interests.

In addition, there is widespread debate about issues of corporate governance and standards of boardroom conduct which are not regulated by law. In the UK, this debate was prompted by a series of unexpected company failures and other corporate scandals in the late 1980s and early 1990s, including BCCI, Polly Peck and the Maxwell Communications Group. These events aroused widespread public concern about the standards of business conduct and the credibility of company reporting. In addition, they highlighted the difficulties experienced by boards, external auditors and shareholders in controlling the actions of dominant chairmen and chief executives.

These concerns led to the adoption in 1993 of the UK's first code of corporate governance: the Cadbury Code of Best Practice. Through a continuing process of revision and amendment, subsequent codes have addressed the structure and numerical balance of the board, focusing in particular on the role of non-executive directors (NEDs) in ensuring that executive directors are now unable to exercise unfettered power over critical decisions. Although the Cadbury Code and its successors were addressed to listed companies, they have been widely influential on other types of company and on organisations outside the corporate sector.

The collapse of Enron in late 2001, followed by other major corporate crises in the US and elsewhere, have called into question the effectiveness of many of the established concepts of corporate governance. As a result, the adequacy of corporate governance arrangements in the US, the UK and internationally have come under close scrutiny. In the UK, this process has involved wide-ranging review, focusing in particular on the role and effectiveness of NEDs and the arrangements for audit committees and leading to the introduction of a revised Combined Code of Corporate Governance.

## The 'comply or explain' regime

A key feature of the UK's approach to corporate governance, from the Cadbury Code onwards, has been the avoidance of prescriptive rules. This reflects the view that different governance approaches will be appropriate for different companies, depending on their size, business activity, operating environment and ownership structure. In consequence, successive Codes have had no statutory force, but have been appended to the Listing Rules, with a requirement on listed companies to disclose in their annual reports whether or not they have complied with Code recommendations and, to the extent that they have not, to give reasons for the areas of non-compliance. Companies' statements of compliance are reviewed by their external auditors, who are required to report their findings to shareholders.

Under the resulting 'comply or explain' regime, a company is under no formal obligation to comply with the best practice recommendations enshrined in the Code. However, the disclosure obligation ensures that the company's shareholders are able to monitor the extent of its compliance, consider the explanations provided by the directors for any areas of non-compliance and, if dissatisfied, express their concerns through their voting behaviour at the AGM. At the same time, shareholders are urged to avoid a 'box-ticking' approach when evaluating companies' corporate governance arrangements, by showing flexibility in the interpretation of Code recommendations and judging directors' explanations on their merits.

## From Cadbury to the Combined Code of 1998

### The Cadbury Committee on the Financial Aspects of Corporate Governance

In response to concerns about the low level of public confidence in financial reporting and in the safeguards provided by external auditors, the Cadbury Committee on the Financial Aspects of Corporate Governance was set up in 1991 by the FRC, the London Stock Exchange (then the listing authority in the UK) and the accountancy profession.

At the time of the committee's establishment, it was commonplace for the offices of chairman and CEO to be combined in one powerful individual (as, for example, in the case of Robert Maxwell). Some company boards had no NEDs at all and, where NEDs were appointed, they were usually outnumbered by executive directors. Further, in many cases, the independence of NEDs was in doubt because of their status as former executive directors of the same company, close connections with major shareholders or external advisers, or personal relationships with the chairman. Reflecting developments in the US, about 75 per cent of the top 250 companies in the UK had audit committees, but formally constituted remuneration and nomination committees were the exception rather than the rule.

The Code of Best Practice resulting from the Cadbury Committee's investigations was appended to the Listing Rules in 1993. The Cadbury Code identified generic themes of abiding concern and has had a major impact on thinking about corporate governance across the corporate, public and not-for-profit sectors within and beyond the UK.

The key recommendations of the Cadbury Code were in four main areas:

### 1. The board of directors

To ensure that the board functions as an authoritative decision-making body, rather than as a formal rubber stamp for executive decisions, the Code recommended that the full board should meet regularly. In addition, it should establish a formal schedule of matters (including material acquisitions and disposals, capital projects and treasury and risk management policies) specifically reserved for its collective decision. The board should monitor the performance of executive management and should agree formal procedures for the taking of material decisions between meetings of the full board.

The board should have access to professional advice, from independent external sources and internally from the company secretary. Importantly, the responsibilities of the company secretary for procedural and corporate governance matters were explicitly recognised by the Code, which recommended that any proposals for the removal of the company secretary should be a matter for the full board.

The Cadbury Code contained a numbers of recommendations on the composition and balance of the board. It expressed a clear preference for a formal separation between the roles of chairman and CEO. Recognising, however, that some companies would be reluctant to abandon the practice of appointing the same person as chairman and CEO, it recommended that, where the posts were combined, there should be strong and independent NEDs, including a recognised senior NED. The Code made no formal recommendation on the number of NEDs required, but suggested that in most cases a minimum of three would be needed, one of whom might also be non-executive chairman.

## 2. Non-executive directors

The Cadbury Code provided the first formal definition of the role of NEDs. It suggested that, in addition to their share in the strategic responsibilities of the board, they have explicit control and monitoring functions which are distinct from the day-to-day managerial responsibilities of their executive colleagues. Accordingly, a majority of the NEDs should be 'independent of management and free from any business or other relationship which could materially interfere with the exercise of their independent judgement, apart from their fees and shareholding'. In addition, the Code recommended that the interests of NEDs should be disclosed in the annual report and accounts to enable shareholders to make informed judgements on their independence.

To preserve the independent status of NEDs, the Code recommended that NEDs should be appointed for specified terms by means of a formal selection and appointment process and that their reappointment to the board should not be automatic. Although the Code contained no absolute requirement for the establishment of nomination committees, it commended this as good practice and suggested that, where nomination committees were set up, they should have majority of NEDs and be chaired by the chairman or a NED.

## 3. Executive directors

The Cadbury Code's treatment of executive remuneration issues was sparse by later standards, but did acknowledge the potential for conflicts of interest between shareholders and directors on matters of pay, performance and job security. Accordingly, it recommended that shareholder approval should be obtained for new service contracts in excess of three years (compared with the five-year contracts permitted by statute) and stated that executive pay should be subject to the recommendations of a remuneration committee made up wholly or mainly of NEDs. In addition, the annual report and accounts should contain full and clear disclosure on directors' remuneration, including basic salary, performance-related pay, pension contributions and share options.

## 4. Reporting and controls

The Cadbury Code emphasised the board's obligation to present to shareholders a balanced and understandable assessment of the company's position. This should include a coherent narrative explanation of its performance and prospects, with details of setbacks as well as successes. In order to discourage incomplete and potentially misleading reporting, it recommended that the directors should acknowledge publicly their responsibilities for preparing the accounts and should report to shareholders that the business is a going concern, with supporting assumptions and qualifications as necessary.

Recognising the need for independent validation of the company's disclosures, the Code also recommended the establishment of audit committees of at least three NEDs, the majority of whom should be independent. Further, it emphasised the need for the board to ensure that an objective and professional relationship was maintained with the external auditors, who should review the company's compliance with Code recommendations and report to shareholders on their findings.

The Cadbury Committee recommended that the directors should report to shareholders on the effectiveness of the company's system of internal control. Although it made clear in its report that it intended that the directors' responsibilities should encompass a systematic approach to risks of all kinds, this proposition was not generally accepted in consultation. As a result, the guidance for directors eventually produced by the accounting profession (in the form of the Rutteman Report issued in 1994) concluded that directors should limit their review to internal financial controls only. Further, they should report only that they had carried out such a review, giving no opinion on whether or not the controls were effective.

## The Greenbury Study Group on Directors' Remuneration

The Greenbury Study Group on Directors' Remuneration was established in 1995 in response to public concern over apparently unjustified increases in the level of directors' remuneration, particularly in recently privatised utilities. The Study Group's remit was to establish good practice in determining directors' remuneration, particularly in the hitherto neglected area of performance-related pay. The resulting Code of Best Practice for directors' remuneration was appended to the Listing Rules in October 1995.

The Greenbury Code had as its principal objectives to:

> *Prevent executive directors from setting or influencing their own remuneration.* To this end, it recommended that responsibility for determining executive remuneration should be formally delegated to a remuneration committee, rather than merely inviting the remuneration committee to make recommendations to the board, as envisaged by Cadbury. To ensure their objectivity, the Greenbury Code recommended that remuneration committees should consist exclusively of NEDs with no personal financial interests other than as shareholders, no cross-directorships and no day-to-day involvement in running the business.

> *Introduce greater rigour into the design of executive remuneration packages,* particularly in respect of performance incentives and rewards. To this end, the Greenbury Code contained an explicit recommendation that executive rewards should be linked to the performance of the company and of the individual director. In addition, it established as recognised good practice that executive directors' services contracts should not contain notice periods in excess of one year or provide for termination payments in excess of one year's salary and benefits.

> *Improve accountability to shareholders.* For this purpose, it recommended that explicit statements should be included in the annual report and accounts on the remuneration of each director and on the company's remuneration policy, including performance criteria and measurement and compensation commitments for early termination of executive directors' service contracts.

The recommendations of the Greenbury Code were reflected, largely unchanged, in the Combined Code, which was introduced in 1998. However, executive remuneration and, in particular, the link between company and individual performance and pay have remained highly contentious. In 2002, the government introduced secondary legislation, in the form of the Directors' Remuneration Report Regulations 2002, to enforce improved accountability to shareholders by quoted companies. A more detailed discussion on remuneration issues is set out in *Chapter 9.*

## The Hampel Committee and the Combined Code of 1998

The Cadbury and Greenbury Codes operated concurrently until June 1998, when a new Combined Code of Best Practice was appended to the Listing Rules. The Combined Code was based on the recommendations of a Committee on Corporate Governance established in 1995 under the chairmanship of Sir Ronald Hampel. Although intended primarily as an updating and consolidation of the two earlier codes, the Combined Code represented a considerable broadening of the scope and detail of directors' obligations, particularly in the areas of internal control and risk management, accountability to shareholders and the company's relations with institutional investors.

The 1998 version of the Combined Code consisted of 17 Principles of Good Governance, 14 of which were addressed to listed companies and the remainder to institutional investors. Each principle was amplified by a number of more detailed provisions, and the Code also contained schedules on the design of executive remuneration packages and their disclosure to shareholders. The principles and provisions applicable to companies were divided into the following broad areas:

> *Directors:* the Combined Code confirmed the principle first established in the Cadbury Code that listed companies should be led by an effective board, with a balance of executive and non-executive directors and a clear division of responsibilities between the chairman and the CEO. However, it placed much greater emphasis on the personal competencies of the directors, through a recommendation that directors should receive appropriate training on first appointment and subsequently as necessary. In addition, the Combined Code recommended that the board should establish a formal and transparent procedure for appointing new directors, and that all directors should stand for re-election by the shareholders at least every three years.

> *Directors' remuneration:* the Combined Code broadly endorsed the principles established in the Greenbury Code. It emphasised that directors' remuneration should not be higher than necessary to recruit and retain directors of the right calibre. Further, it recommended that some element of executive pay should be performance-related to encourage the achievement of corporate objectives and to reward individual performance. No director should be involved in determining his or her own remuneration and details of the company's remuneration policy and the remuneration of each director should be stated in the annual report and accounts.

> *Relations with shareholders:* the Combined Code emphasised the need for companies to be prepared to enter into a dialogue with institutional investors and to

encourage the active participation of private investors in the annual general meeting.

> *Accountability and audit:* the Combined Code endorsed the Cadbury Code's recommendations in respect of the board's responsibility for presenting a balanced and understandable assessment of the company's financial position and prospects. In addition, it emphasised the central role of the audit committee in considering how to apply the principles of financial reporting and internal control, and in safeguarding the independence and objectivity of internal and external auditors.

### The Turnbull guidance on internal control

Perhaps the most significant innovation introduced by the 1998 Combined Code was the extension of the directors' responsibilities not merely for financial control, but for the effectiveness of all internal controls, including financial, operational and compliance controls and risk management. Responsibility for producing formal guidance for directors on the interpretation and implementation of this recommendation was given to a working party appointed by the Institute of Chartered Accountants in England and Wales (ICAEW) and chaired by Nigel Turnbull. The final report of the working party was published in September 1999.

The Turnbull guidance encourages companies to embed their internal control systems in the day-to-day management of the business in order that the control measures adopted can evolve over time to meet changes in the company's business environment. To this end, it advocates the development of a risk-based approach to internal control and the review of its effectiveness. In addition, it provides guidance on the respective roles of the board, the audit and other committees and the company's management in designing and maintaining effective internal controls and sets out questions to assist the board in its ongoing and annual review of the effectiveness of the company's system of internal controls. A more detailed discussion on internal control and risk management is set out in *Chapter 12*.

## Corporate governance after Enron

Despite increasing levels of compliance with the recommendations of the Combined Code, investor and public confidence in standards of corporate governance, in the UK and other countries was severely shaken by the collapse in late 2001 of the US energy trader Enron, at that time one of the largest companies in the world.

Briefly, Enron announced in October 2001 that it was taking a $544 million charge to its reported earnings after tax in respect of transactions with an off-balance sheet entity owned by Enron, but created and controlled by its chief financial officer (CFO); in addition, shareholders' equity was being reduced by $1.2 billion. Less than one month later, the company announced that it was restating its accounts for the years 1997–2001 because of accounting errors in relation to off-balance sheet entities controlled by the CFO and other senior managers. The restatements involved reductions of between 10 per cent and 28 per cent in reported net income in each of the years affected, with substantial reductions in shareholders' equity and increases in the reported levels of indebtedness. The company also revealed for the first time that the CFO had received personal payments from off-balance sheet entities he controlled: these were originally estimated at $30 million, but were subsequently shown to be much larger. Following these announcements, investor confidence in Enron's ability to recover its position collapsed and the company filed for bankruptcy in protection December 2001.

Subsequent investigations by independent consultants, regulators and the US courts indicated that the destruction of Enron had been brought about by a complex series of events in which individual officers, the board of directors and its sub-committees and the company's external auditors were all implicated. Specific findings of failures and weaknesses in corporate governance included:

> The waiver by Enron's board of directors of the company's rules on conflict of interest. This permitted the CFO and other senior managers to set up and control limited partnerships whose purpose was to hold assets and liabilities separate from the balance sheet.

> The subsequent failure of both the board and the audit committee to demand information about transactions between Enron and the off-balance sheet partnerships, despite the explicit recognition that these transactions involved very high levels of risk.

> Lack of independence of Enron's external directors, some of whom had financial and other ties with the company, for example through consultancy fees.

> The failure of the board and audit committee to prevent the exploitation of accounting rules to present a better picture of the company's financial position and performance than was justified. As a result, very large energy trading losses were systematically hidden from investors and the capital market through improper reporting of transactions with off-balance sheet entities, creating a false impression that Enron's exposures were hedged through contracts with third parties.

> The failure of Enron's external auditors, Arthur Andersen, to provide the objective and professional scrutiny required to ensure that shareholders received an accurate account of the company's financial position.

The collapse of Enron was the catalyst for increased scrutiny of other major companies in the US, the UK and internationally, leading to further corporate bankruptcies, notably that of the US telecommunications company WorldCom. While the initial concerns related to the credibility of financial reporting, the events surrounding Enron have triggered a wide-ranging debate on issues including the operation of capital markets, the adequacy of auditing standards and regulatory arrangements, and the quality and integrity of those involved in the governance of major companies. In response to these concerns, governments and regulators around the world have undertaken urgent reviews of their accounting, auditing and corporate governance arrangements. *Chapter 3* provides a brief survey of the international response to the issues raised by Enron.

In the UK, the Government established a Co-ordinating Group on Audit and Accounting Issues (CGAA) with responsibility for reviewing the existing arrangements for regulation of the accounting and auditing profession and oversight of financial reporting. *Chapter 1* describes proposed legislative measures to improve the reliability of financial reporting and reinforce audit independence; *Chapter 11* outlines ongoing changes in the regulatory regime .

In addition, the UK's corporate governance arrangements have been the subject of two major independent reviews: the Higgs Review on the role and effectiveness of NEDs; and the Smith Report on audit committees – both published in January 2003. Following a period of consultation with listed companies and major investors, the Combined Code of Corporate Governance has been revised to take into account the recommendations of the Higgs and Smith Reports.

The text of the revised Combined Code, which is applicable to UK listed companies for reporting years beginning on or after 1 November 2003, is set out in *Appendix 1*. The detailed recommendations of the revised Combined Code and their implications for good boardroom practice are discussed in *Chapters 5–14*.

# 3

# The International Dimension

> ... there is no single model of good corporate governance. Different legal systems, institutional frameworks and traditions mean that a range of different approaches have developed around the world. Common to all good corporate governance regimes, however, is a high degree of priority placed on the interests of shareholders, who place their trust in corporations to use their investment funds wisely and effectively. In addition, the best-run corporations recognise that business ethics and corporate awareness of the environmental and societal interest of the communities in which they operate can have an impact on the reputation and long-term performance of corporations.
>
> OECD (1999) *Principles of Corporate Governance*

This chapter describes the key characteristics of outsider and insider systems of company ownership and their implications for corporate governance. It also examines the development of national codes of corporate governance and the emerging international consensus on key corporate governance principles. The impact of Enron and other recent corporate crises on existing national and international approaches to corporate governance are also explored.

Within the legal and regulatory environment of the UK, ownership of listed companies is typically widely dispersed among numerous shareholders, who delegate to professional managers responsibility for the day-to-day conduct of the business. In this respect, the UK's legal and regulatory environment is similar to those of the US, the Republic of Ireland and certain Commonwealth countries, notably Australia, Canada and New Zealand. While no two countries have identical patterns of company ownership and control, these environments are, for the purposes of this discussion, broadly characterised as 'outsider' systems, because shareholders, as the owners of the company, are generally excluded from direct involvement in the management of the business.

In other legal and regulatory environments world-wide, including those of continental Europe, most Asian and South American countries and the emerging economies of the former Soviet bloc, the ownership of companies is typically more concentrated. As a result, the majority of shares may be held by one owner, or by a small number of connected owners. Again, no two countries are identical, but such environments are here described as 'insider' systems, because majority shareholders typically have direct involvement in or influence over the conduct of the business.

The factors leading to the development of the outsider and insider systems are not currently well understood, but may be related to underlying differences in legal system, history and culture. Importantly, there is no evidence to suggest that either system favours superior company performance: of the world's leading economies over the past half-century, the US is perceived as having an outsider environment, while Germany and Japan have historically been dominated by companies of the insider model. Conversely, neither system is immune from failure at the company or market level. Recent scandals (Enron, WorldCom, Equitable Life) affecting companies in the outsider environment of the US and UK have their counterparts in the insider model in the failures of continental European companies (e.g. Ahold, Vivendi, Parmalat).

The rapid globalisation of business activity means that there is increasing interaction between economies with outsider and insider systems of company ownership and control. This has many different contributing factors, including:

> cross-border takeovers, mergers and joint ventures, which bring companies from different systems into close contact with each other;
> the need for companies in insider systems to demonstrate acceptable standards of corporate governance in order to access the equity markets located in outsider economies, particularly those in the US and the UK;
> financial crises and scandals which prompt international action to rebuild investor confidence by improving overall standards of transparency and accountability; and
> formal programmes of legal harmonisation between countries with contrasting systems – notably that currently in progress within the European Union (EU).

While it would be going too far to suggest that this interaction is likely to produce a single global code of corporate governance in the foreseeable future, there is some evidence of an emerging consensus between outsider and insider systems on certain key corporate governance principles. These include the need for effective internal and external scrutiny, board and auditor independence, shareholder voting rights and transparency of information.

## Characteristics of outsider and insider systems

### Outsider systems

Certain generic features characterise outsider systems of company ownership and control. These include:

> *dispersal of ownership:* company ownership is widely dispersed amongst numerous shareholders, including both investment institutions and private individuals;
> *separation of ownership and control:* shareholders, as the owners of the company, generally do not participate in the management of the business, but delegate responsibility to professional managers who act as their agents; and

> *cash flow and voting rights:* all shareholders have rights, strictly protected in law, to receive part of the cash flows of the company in proportion to their shareholdings and to vote on major corporate decisions on a 'one-share-one-vote' basis.

Consistent with these features, outsider systems typically include liquid stock markets on which company shares can readily be traded, with strict disclosure requirements in respect of price-sensitive and other information of relevance to investment decisions. In most cases, there are active markets for corporate control, but mergers and takeovers are typically subject to tight regulatory controls which effectively prevent the accumulation of controlling interests in listed companies.

Despite these shared characteristics, there are significant differences among outsider systems. These differences are most apparent in the contrasting legal and regulatory approaches of the two most influential outsider systems, namely those of the UK and the US.

In the UK, the preferred approach to company law and matters of internal governance has been to avoid prescriptive rules, relying instead on the definition of general principles and outcomes which require companies and individuals to assume wide responsibilities and exercise professional judgement. By contrast, legislators and regulators in the US have typically adopted a more legalistic, rules-based approach, which seeks to define clear boundaries within which companies and individuals are free to act. The contrast between the two approaches is visible in the case of accounting standards. US accounting standards typically prescribe detailed accounting treatment according to the legal form of transactions, while UK standards generally permit the exercise of discretion to enable a 'true and fair' view of the substance of a transaction to be reflected.

Although a Model Business Corporation Act is maintained by a committee of the American Bar Association, the US has no nationally applicable company law: instead, it is left to individual states to produce their own legislation. Companies are able to incorporate in the state jurisdiction of their choice, leading to inter-state competition for company incorporation. The development of the outsider system in the US has been greatly influenced by this competition, which has led to a trend towards company laws which are, on balance, attractive to company management and unfavourable to shareholders. A key example is the relative tolerance in US law for 'poison pill' defences and similar measures designed to enable managers to protect their own positions by resisting takeover. As result, the managers of US companies typically have a greater degree of security than their counterparts in the UK (where such measures are illegal), while legal protections for shareholders are arguably less robust in the US than in the UK.

So far as other outsider systems are concerned, the framework of company law and corporate governance in the Republic of Ireland is broadly similar to that of the UK. Commonwealth countries such as Australia, Canada and New Zealand initially adopted UK-style legal and regulatory systems, but are now increasingly influenced by the US pattern.

Within the outsider model, there are also important differences in corporate governance and boardroom practice. Again, these stand out most clearly in the UK and the US and include contrasting approaches to:

> *Combined chairman/CEO appointments:* the posts of chairman and CEO are now generally separate in UK, but this is still uncommon in the US.
> *Board composition:* while executive directors are still numerically dominant on UK boards, the boards of US companies are dominated by outside (i.e. non-executive) directors. In US companies, the CEO is often the only member of the company's executive management team with a seat on the board.
> *Independence:* although most US boards have a majority of outside directors, the directors concerned may not be independent because of prior connections with the company or length of tenure, thus reducing the effective independence of the audit and other key board committees.
> *Executive remuneration:* executive pay is much higher in US than in the UK and typically includes a higher proportion of share options, giving rise to greater share ownership by directors in the US than in the UK.

## Insider systems

The most cited examples of insider systems are Japan and the countries of continental Europe. While company law and governance practices vary widely in these countries, there are strong similarities in the following areas:

> *Concentration of ownership:* company ownership is typically much more concentrated than in outsider systems.
> *Use of group structures:* group and pyramid structures based on cross-shareholdings are typical of insider systems. In many cases, these structures reinforce the influence of large shareholders by enabling them to exercise a degree of control which is disproportionate to their actual investment in the company.
> *Use of non-voting shares:* insider systems have traditionally permitted large shareholders to consolidate their control rights, either by acquiring shares that carry disproportionately high numbers of votes or by constraining the voting powers of minority shareholders.
> *Involvement of controlling shareholders in management:* controlling shareholders (who may be individuals, family members, banks, other corporations or governments) can exert influence over company decisions through their equity holdings and may also be able to exert control more directly, for example through their own membership of the board or through the ability to appoint directors.
> *Cash flow and voting rights:* although all shareholders (including minority shareholders) are generally entitled to receive dividends in proportion to their shareholdings, shareholder voting arrangements in insider systems do not necessarily conform to the one-share-one-vote principle typical of outsider systems. The exercise of minority voting rights may be limited in insider systems through the issue of dual-class shares or through voting caps, proxy voting mechanisms and ownership chains which enable controlling shareholders to exercise disproportionate voting rights, while the rights of minority shareholders to ask questions or table resolutions may be limited and/or difficult to exercise.

In insider systems, bank lending has traditionally been more important than shareholders' equity as a source of company financing. In addition, stock markets are often illiquid, making it difficult for dissatisfied shareholders to dispose of their holdings. In some cases, legal provisions make takeovers very difficult, rendering takeover ineffective as a means of disciplining under-performing managers. Reflecting their relative lack of importance, equity markets and associated disclosure requirements may be lightly regulated compared to those in outsider systems. Conversely, company law in insider systems will often contain more prescriptive rules than in outsider systems on matters such as the composition of the board.

Despite these generic similarities, there are some significant differences in the company law and corporate governance of different insider economies.

The most frequently cited examples of insider systems are those in mature economies, such as Japan and the countries of continental Europe. In these countries, the legal and regulatory environments relating to the operation of companies are sophisticated and well established. However, insider systems also include examples of emerging economies, including many Asian countries, together with economies – notably China and the republics of the former Soviet bloc – where the company concept is itself relatively new. Understandably in such systems, company law and corporate governance are often relatively undeveloped. In these circumstances, the concentration of ownership typical of insider systems may be a defence against weakly entrenched property rights and unreliable law enforcement.

There are also marked differences between different insider systems in the identity of controlling shareholders:

> *Family control* is prevalent in many developing economies, particularly in Asia, where the company may be affiliated with a business group also controlled by the same family. However, family control is also found in developed economies such as Sweden and Italy.
> *Other corporations* are the predominant shareholders in economies as diverse as Germany, Korea, Taiwan and Brazil.
> *Banks and other financial institutions* are the most important shareholders in Japan, typically exercising control through the *keiretsu* system whereby networks of companies are connected by cross-holdings around a major bank. Banks are also significant shareholders in Israel, while German banks have historically exercised voting powers in excess of their investments through their control of proxies on behalf of individual shareholders.
> *Governments* are still significant shareholders in some countries, ranging from transitional economies, such as China and South Africa, to developed economies such as Singapore and Austria.

Perhaps the most striking variation between insider systems relates to the organisational structure of the board, as reflected by the use in certain developed economies of a 'two-tier' structure. In such structures, the supervisory and management functions of the board are formally separated between:

> a *supervisory board*, composed of outside directors, with responsibility for advising and supervising management and monitoring the performance of the company; and

> ❭ a *management or executive board*, composed entirely of executives, with delegated authority for the day-to-day operation of the business.

The two-tier board structure is required by law, for certain types of company or for companies of specified size, in four European countries: Germany, the Netherlands, Denmark and Austria. In France, Finland and Portugal, listed companies are able to choose between a unitary and a two-tier board structure. In France, the optional two-tier structure is similar to that used in Germany and provides scope for employee representation. However, the two-tier option is relatively little used and most French companies have unitary boards.

The two-tier board model, particularly in its German manifestation, is frequently invoked as a solution to many of the corporate governance problems discussed elsewhere in this Handbook, primarily because it creates a clear separation between the management and monitoring functions of the board. The independence of the supervisory board is assured by excluding executive managers from membership, so conferring on the members of the supervisory board some of the characteristics of independent NEDs in the unitary board structure.

It is important to note, therefore, that the two-tier board structure is currently confined to a small number of mature continental European economies. It has not been adopted elsewhere, although it is proposed to make it available as an option for all listed companies within the EU as part of the ongoing company law harmonisation process. Moreover, the two-tier structure is not without its disadvantages. In particular, members of the supervisory board may have more limited access to information than do NEDs in a unitary board, reducing both their understanding of the business and their ability to contribute effectively to its strategic direction.

## The codification of corporate governance

### Issues for corporate governance

In both the outsider and the insider systems, conflicts of interest can arise between the controllers of the business and those who invest in it, but are excluded from involvement in its operation.

In outsider systems, the separation of ownership and control of listed companies means that potential conflicts of interest can arise between the directors as the managers of the business, and shareholders as its owners. In outsider systems, therefore the primary objective of corporate governance is to ensure effective scrutiny of executive management.

In insider systems, by contrast, a controlling shareholder, or group of connected shareholders, may be able to influence and control the company's management. Conversely, minority shareholders may have poor access to information about the company's performance and may therefore lack the resources needed to monitor the conduct of the managers and controlling shareholders. In insider systems, then, conflicts of interest are likely to arise, not between the directors and the majority of shareholders, but between controlling owners and minority shareholders. The aim of corporate governance in these circumstances is to secure fair treatment of minority shareholders and to ensure that controlling shareholders are not able to exercise a disproportionate influence over the company's supervision and management.

Although the issues for corporate governance in the outsider and insider systems arise at different locations, the issues of principle involved are remarkably similar across the two systems. Thus, there is concern in both systems about the role and composition of the board of directors, the availability to shareholders of timely and accurate information and the ability of shareholders in general to monitor effectively the actions of management. These concerns are increasingly being reflected in both outsider and insider systems, and at the national and international level.

## The development of national codes of corporate governance

In historical terms, outsider systems were the first to develop codes of corporate governance, driven primarily by shareholder concerns about the perceived lack of effective board oversight over company performance. Key examples, both from the early 1990s, are the UK Cadbury Code and the Dey Report in Canada, both of which have been influential as sources for the development of guidelines and codes in other countries.

Although compliance with corporate governance guidelines in outsider systems has not generally been required by law, it has been enforced as a condition of listing on relevant stock exchanges. Thus, outsider systems such as the UK, Ireland, Canada and Australia have very similar 'comply or explain' regimes whereby listed companies need not follow code recommendations, but must disclose whether they do so and provide an explanation of any divergent practices. The main exception to this is the US: although many voluntary codes have been issued by organisations such as the Business Roundtable, the Council of Institutional Investors and the National Association of Corporate Directors, these are essentially voluntary. In the absence of a national code of corporate governance, disclosure and other requirements are specified in legislation by the Securities and Exchange Commission and reflected in the listing rules promulgated by, for example, the New York Stock Exchange (NYSE) and Nasdaq.

Insider systems have generally been slower to develop codes of corporate governance, presumably because of the privileged access to management enjoyed by controlling shareholders. Where voluntary codes have been developed, they have tended to be promulgated by employers' and trade associations rather than by stock exchanges. Examples include codes published in France by the Viénot Committee in 1995 and 1999 at the behest of employers' federations, supported by leading private sector companies.

Similarly, codes of best practice have been promulgated in developing economies as diverse as Brazil, Mexico, India and Thailand, but have been designed to build awareness of governance best practice and have not been linked to listing requirements. Exceptions are the Malaysian Code on Corporate Governance, the Code of Best Practice issued by the Hong Kong Stock Exchange and the King Commission Report on Corporate Governance in South Africa, all of which contemplate mandatory disclosures by listed companies on their compliance with code recommendations.

Despite the underlying economic, legal and cultural differences between outsider and insider systems and between mature and developing economies, there is evidence of broad agreement amongst national codes of corporate governance on a range of key issues. These include:

> *Obligations owed to the generality of shareholders:* it is generally accepted that the board's duty to protect and enhance shareholders' investment is owed to all shareholders, not just to controlling shareholders.

> *Board responsibilities:* codes generally assert the responsibility of the board for the stewardship of the company, with heavy emphasis on the board's financial reporting obligations and responsibility for oversight of the audit function.

> *Directors' qualifications:* while codes vary in the extent to which they specify the qualifications of directors, most emphasise the need for appropriate experience, personal independence and the ability to make an adequate time commitment.

> *Directors' appointments:* codes tend to emphasise the need for a formal and transparent process for appointing new directors, with some codes recommending the use of nomination committees as a means of reducing the CEO's influence over directors' appointments.

> *The requirement for independent directors:* most codes agree that some degree of director independence – or at a minimum the ability to exercise objective judgement – is needed to ensure that the board is able to monitor management performance effectively. Further, a broad consensus is emerging among systems of all types that boards should include at least some non-executive members who are free of significant family and business relationships with management.

> *Independent board leadership:* many codes recommend a clear division of responsibilities between the chairman and the CEO, in particular where the board does not contain a majority of independent directors.

> *Board committees:* there is general agreement across codes about the need for an audit committee, with many codes including specific recommendations on the size of the committee, the extra time requirements demanded of members and the need for the audit committee to have written terms of reference. Codes in developed economies, including Australia, Belgium, France, Japan, the Netherlands, Sweden, the UK and the US, typically go further, recommending that boards should also establish nomination and remuneration committees. While the recommended composition of these committees varies, it is generally recognised that independent non-executive directors have a key role.

> *Disclosure of information:* in most countries, codes of corporate governance augment the existing legal requirements for disclosure, emphasising the obligation of directors for ensuring that timely, accurate and meaningful information is available to all shareholders.

### International principles of corporate governance

The emergence of a broad international consensus on key corporate governance issues is reflected in the Principles of Corporate Governance issued in 1999 by the Organisation for Economic Cooperation and Development (OECD).

The members of the OECD include both the major outsider economies (the UK, Ireland, the US, Canada, Australia and New Zealand) and insider systems, ranging from mature economies such as France, Germany and Japan to developing economies such as Mexico, the Czech Republic, Hungary and Poland. In issuing the Principles of

Corporate Governance, the OECD recognised this diversity, noting that different legal systems, institutional frameworks and traditions had contributed to the development of a wide range of different approaches around the world. For these reasons, the OECD concluded that it is not possible to specify a single international model of good corporate governance. The Principles aim instead to embrace and build on the common elements of good corporate governance identified in the various national codes in order to provide a reference point for the future development of legal and regulatory frameworks for corporate governance.

The OECD Principles of Corporate Governance, the full text of which is included at *Appendix 2*, recommend that member states should include in their national corporate governance frameworks the following key principles:

**Principle I:** *The rights of shareholders:* each corporate governance framework should protect shareholders' rights, including right to obtain relevant information on the corporation on a timely and regular basis; participate and vote in general shareholder meetings; and share in the profits of the corporation.

**Principle II:** *The equitable treatment of shareholders:* each corporate governance framework should ensure the equitable treatment of all shareholders, including minority and foreign shareholders. All shareholders should have the opportunity to obtain effective redress for violation of their rights.

**Principle III:** *The role of stakeholders in corporate governance:* each corporate governance framework should recognise the rights of stakeholders as established by law and encourage active co-operation between corporations and stakeholders in creating wealth, jobs, and the sustainability of financially sound enterprises.

**Principle IV:** *Disclosure and transparency:* each corporate governance framework should ensure that timely and accurate disclosure is made on all material matters regarding the corporation, including its financial situation, performance, ownership, and governance.

**Principle V:** *The responsibilities of the board:* each corporate governance framework should ensure the strategic guidance of the company, the effective monitoring of management by the board, and the board's accountability to the company and the shareholders.

## The impact of Enron

The collapse of Enron and other major corporate crises have challenged investor and public confidence, leading to close examination of the adequacy of national and international approaches to corporate governance.

### National codes of corporate governance

At the national level, the most radical reforms are those implemented in US itself under terms of the Public Company Accounting Reform and Investor Protection Act of 2002 (less formally known as the 'Sarbanes-Oxley' Act.). Significant provisions of the Act include:

> *Integrity and completeness of company financial reports:* the CEO and CFO of a listed company are required to assume personal responsibility for its financial reports by certifying that these do not contain any untrue statement of material facts, do not omit to state any material fact necessary to ensure that the statements are not misleading in the light of the circumstances in which they are made, and fairly present in all material respects the financial condition and results of operation of the company.

> *Non-interference in the audit process:* company directors and officers are explicitly prohibited from interfering with accounting firms in the performance of an audit: civil penalties are provided against directors and officers, and anyone acting at their direction, who attempt to influence an audit for the purpose of rendering the company's financial statements materially misleading.

> *Audit regulation:* the Act establishes a Public Company Accounting Oversight Board (PCAOB) with responsibility for registration, inspection and discipline of public accounting firms, including the establishment of auditing, quality control, ethical, independence and other standards relating to the preparation of audit reports.

> *Audit independence:* the lead audit or coordinating partner and the reviewing partner responsible for the audit of a company must rotate at least every five years. The Act also makes it unlawful for a registered public accounting firm to provide specified non-audit services to an audit client, including bookkeeping or other services; design and implementation of financial information systems; appraisal or valuation services; actuarial services; outsourced internal audit services; human resources or other management functions; broker or dealer, investment adviser, or investment banking services; legal services and expert services unrelated to the audit; and any other service determined by PCAOB to be impermissible.

> *Company records:* the Act makes it a criminal offence for anyone knowingly to alter, destroy or falsify a document or to shred, hide or alter a document or other object in order to impede or attempt to impede an official investigation.

> *Whistleblower protection:* audit committees are required to establish procedures for the treatment of complaints regarding accounting, internal accounting controls or auditing matters; at the same time, employees who raise concerns about questionable accounting or auditing matters are protected against dismissal, demotion, suspension, harassment and other forms of discrimination.

> *Codes of ethics:* companies are required to disclose whether they have adopted a code of ethics for senior financial officers and, if not, to explain their reasons. For this purpose, codes of ethics must set out the standards necessary to promote honest and ethical conduct, including the ethical handling of actual or apparent conflicts of interest between personal and professional relationships; full, fair, accurate, timely and understandable disclosure of information; and compliance with applicable governmental rules and regulations.

In addition, changes to the listing rules of the NYSE and Nasdaq have introduced a number of recommendations which are new to the US environment, including a mandatory vote on remuneration policy; a requirement for the majority of the board to be independent; and separation of the positions of the chairman and the CEO.

Outside the US, more than 20 countries have adopted their first codes of corporate governance following the Enron scandal, while many companies with established codes have modified or added to their provisions. In the vast majority of cases, the prescriptive approach adopted by US legislators has been avoided, with most new and revised codes relying for their effectiveness on 'comply or explain' regimes of the type already established in the UK.

Despite continuing disparities between outsider and insider systems on matters such as shareholder voting rights and board structure, new and modified national codes assign priority to a broadly similar range of objectives, including:

> reinforcement of shareholder rights;
> increased transparency and improved disclosure of information;
> making boards more independent; and
> clarifying the responsibilities of institutional shareholders in respect of the exercise of their voting powers on matters of corporate governance.

As noted in the previous chapter, the UK's corporate governance framework has been revised in accordance with the Higgs and Smith Reports and the detailed provisions of the July 2003 Combined Code of Corporate Governance are addressed in Part Two of this Handbook.

Other examples of Code revisions in the light of the Enron crisis include:

> The Bouton Report, which recommends that one-third of the boards of French companies should be independent and should have audit committees composed exclusively of independent directors; in addition, it recommends that boards should undertake an evaluation of their own performance every three years.
> The Cromme Kodex of best practice for the conduct of German supervisory and management boards: this places restrictions on number of executive directors on boards, seeks improved disclosure, particularly on remuneration matters, and defines the role of external auditors.

## International principles of corporate governance

To date, the most complete response at the international level to the governance issues arising from the collapse of Enron is contained in the Action Plans on company law modernisation and audit adopted by the European Commission in May 2003.

The Action Plans are intended to apply to all existing EU Member States, encompassing the insider systems of Austria, Belgium, Denmark, Finland, France, Germany, Greece, Italy, Luxembourg, Portugal, Spain, Sweden and the Netherlands and the outsider systems of the UK and Ireland. In addition, they will cover new Member States, including the developing insider economies of the Czech Republic, Estonia, Hungary, Latvia, Lithuania, Poland, Slovakia and Slovenia, as these countries accede to membership of the EU. Recognising the underlying differences amongst existing Member States, and between existing and prospective Member States, in terms of legal and regulatory approaches to corporate governance, the European Commission has concluded that it should not attempt to design a single European code of corporate governance, but should instead identify a common approach and ensure an appropriate measure of co-ordination between national corporate governance codes. For this purpose, it is proposed to establish a European Corporate Governance Forum to promote coordination and convergence among national codes and encourage consistency of monitoring and enforcement.

In common with the US Sarbanes-Oxley Act, the EU Action Plans prioritise accounting, financial report and audit issues. However, the intention is to eschew the prescriptive, rules-based approach adopted in the US in favour of a principles-based approach. In this context, the Action Plans identify the following key issues:

> *Audit regulation:* the audit Action Plan proposes the creation of an Audit Regulatory Committee to provide independent oversight of the auditing profession, together with the development of a comprehensive legal basis for all statutory audits conducted within the EU.

> *Auditor independence:* the Action Plan establishes that, as a matter of principle, statutory auditors should not carry out a statutory audit if they have any financial, business, employment or other relationships with the audit client (including the provision of non-audit services) that might, in the view of a reasonable and informed third party, compromise the statutory auditor's independence. The need for a more restrictive approach to the provision of non-audit services will also be investigated.

> *Requirement for audit committees:* to ensure that statutory auditors are able to maintain an appropriate degree of independence from audit clients, the audit Action Plan recommends the development of consistent principles, applicable across the EU, for the appointment, dismissal and remuneration of statutory auditors, including provisions dealing with the independence, competence and terms of reference of the audit committee or its equivalent.

> *Adoption of International Standards on Auditing:* it is intended to adopt International Standards on Auditing (ISAs) for all statutory audits from 2005 within the EU, subject to the satisfactory development of a framework for the assessment of ISAs, the evaluation of possible endorsement systems and the development of a common audit report for use in the annual reports of listed companies across the EU.

More broadly, the EU Action Plans propose a series of measures designed to achieve consistency of approach on the disclosure of financial and non-financial information; the required standards of independence for NEDs and members of supervisory boards; the composition and role of nomination and remuneration committees; and the enhancement of shareholder influence over directors' remuneration, supported by greater transparency of individual remuneration packages.

The Action Plan on company law modernisation also addresses key issues of relevance to the interests of minority shareholders in insider systems. It proposes a number of measures designed to give effect to the principle of proportionality between capital and control, including:

> *Shareholders' rights:* the Action Plan envisages the development of a legislative framework to facilitate the exercise by all shareholders of their rights to ask questions, table resolutions, vote by proxy and participate in general meetings by electronic means; it also proposes to address current problems relating to cross-border voting in order to ensure that these facilities are available to shareholders across the EU.

> *Groups and pyramids:* the Action Plan acknowledges the legitimacy of the group structures typical of insider systems, but notes that these involve risks to the interests of minority shareholders: in order to mitigate these risks, it recommends greater transparency in the financial and non-financial information disclosed by groups, including improved disclosures on group structures and intra-group relations and on the financial situation of the various parts of a group.

> *Corporate restructuring and mobility:* in order to enhance the transfer and exit rights of minority shareholders, the Action Plan proposes the implementation of 'sell-out' rights to allow minority shareholders to compel holders of a large majority of the capital to purchase their securities at a fair price; in return, 'squeeze-out' rights would also be provided to permit the holder of a large majority of a company's securities to compel minority shareholders to sell their stock at a fair price.

# 4

# Emerging Expectations

> ❝ ... business plays an increasingly prominent role in modern society, at every level from the local community to the international stage. This brings new opportunities, such as private sector involvement in areas like education and health which have previously been the preserve of the state. But it also introduces new risks as politics increasingly invades the corporate world. This blurring of the boundaries between public and private has introduced new elements into the business equation, which carry added potency because of the changing nature of business itself. Society expects more of business, in every sense. The quid pro quo for companies becoming more embedded in society is that they behave in ways which society regards as more responsible. And if the standard for corporate responsibility is not met, society bites back, often in the form of a campaign or exposé by one of the growing number of increasingly powerful campaign groups ... In short, corporate social responsibility is a serious business issue, with serious implications for shareholders.
>
> Association of British Insurers (2001) *Investing in Social Responsibility* ❞

*Chapters 1–3* have addressed the role of company law and codes of corporate governance in promoting good boardroom practice and facilitating the accountability of directors, as the managers of the business, to the shareholders as its owners. This chapter examines the growing debate about the purposes of the company, involving fundamental questions of principle concerning the definition of shareholders' interests; the period over which these interests are to be satisfied; and, crucially, whether the interests of shareholders must always take precedence over the interests of other stakeholders in the company. To investigate these questions, it:

> ❯ examines the traditional assumption that the purpose of the company is to maximise its profits on behalf of shareholders;
> ❯ describes the contrasting definitions of corporate purpose considered by the Company Law Review and outlines the resulting proposals for statutory reform to clarify directors' duties and improve disclosure on environmental and social issues;
> ❯ examines the growing interest of institutional investors and other external observers in matters of corporate social responsibility; and

❯ draws attention to the implications of the Enron scandal for corporate culture, values and ethical practices.

## The profit maximisation objective

The traditional view of corporate purpose and accountability, particularly in the outsider economies described in *Chapter 3*, can be described as a 'profit maximisation' model. This assumes that the objective of the company is to maximise financial returns to its owners. Company success can therefore be measured in terms of increased profitability, enabling larger dividends to be paid to shareholders and leading, in principle at least, to share price growth.

Consistent with this view, the directors of the company have overriding obligations to the shareholders to maximise the company's profits. As such, they should not take any actions which might reduce returns to shareholders, other than to the extent needed to comply with external laws and regulations in areas such as employment, health and safety, product safety and the environment.

The assumption that shareholders have overriding claims is based on the view that, as the ultimate owners of the business, they are uniquely exposed to the risk of financial losses if the company's business fails. While it is now generally acknowledged that other stakeholders, such as employees and suppliers, may invest in developing skills and processes in connection with the company's business, proponents of the profit maximisation model argue that because their skills and processes might well be transferable in the market in the event of the company's failure, these stakeholders are not exposed to the same degree of risk as shareholders.

Supporters of the profit maximisation model argue that, while the claims of the shareholders are paramount, this does not require directors to take a short-term view of the shareholders' interests or to act irresponsibly or unethically in the pursuit of profits. Accordingly, it may be permissible for the directors to risk or forgo profits at the margin in the interests of, for example, product safety, pollution control and fair dealing with other parties, even where there are no explicit external requirements.

Similarly, it is argued that profit maximisation is consistent with social welfare objectives, on the grounds that the returns generated by companies on behalf of their shareholders contribute to an overall increase in wealth. From this perspective, it is unnecessary – and indeed undesirable – for companies to acknowledge broader social responsibilities: as stated by the American economist Milton Friedman:

> 'In [a free] economy there is one and only one social responsibility of business – to use its resources and engage in activities designed to increase its profits so long as it stays within the rules of the game, which is to say, engages in open and free competition without deception or fraud.'

The profit maximisation model is, on a strict interpretation, consistent with directors' duties as currently formulated in UK company law. However, it is increasingly criticised from a broad range of economic, social and political perspectives on the grounds that it fails to maximise overall prosperity and welfare. Specific challenges to the profit maximisation model include:

> *Short-termism:* despite the argument, noted above, that UK company law as currently formulated does not oblige directors to take a short-term view of their responsibilities, there is concern that a narrow focus on dividends and share price appreciation may discourage investment in longer-term projects, even though these might well be in the ultimate best interests of shareholders.
> *The claims of non-shareholder stakeholders:* the traditional view that shareholders' claims are overriding ignores the value to the company of the contributions made by other stakeholders and inhibits the development of cooperative long-term relationships which would benefit the company as a whole.
> *Externalisation of costs and impacts:* reliance on external laws and regulations, which are slow to adapt to changing circumstances, may allow profit-maximising companies to evade responsibility for the adverse impacts of their activities by exploiting gaps and loopholes in legal provision.
> *Social injustice:* unmodified profit-maximising behaviour by companies may result in environmental damage and/or violations of human rights, especially in the context of emerging economies where legal and regulatory frameworks may be relatively undeveloped.

## Contrasting models of corporate purpose and accountability

In the course of its fundamental review of UK company law, the Company Law Review Steering Group considered the need for statutory change to:

> facilitate competitiveness and efficient creation of wealth and other benefits for all participants in the company's activities;
> minimise the negative impacts of corporate activity; and
> foster harmonious long-term relationships between companies and stakeholders and promote recognition of the wider interests of the community.

For this purpose, it identified two alternatives to the traditional profit maximisation model. These were the 'social welfare' (or pluralist) model and the 'enlightened shareholder value' model.

### The social welfare model

In contrast to the profit maximisation model, supporters of the social welfare model argue that a company's business should be managed so as to advance the interests of all participants, without the interests of any single group, such as shareholders, having overriding priority.

The social welfare model assumes that parties other than shareholders, including employees, suppliers of goods and services, customers and local communities, make commitments which contribute to the value of the company and represent part of its assets; accordingly, these parties have a stake in the business and thus have claims, equivalent to those of owners, to have their interests taken into account in the formulation of business strategies. From this perspective, the company cannot be regarded as synonymous with its shareholders, but includes all other stakeholders who make commitments to it. By recognising that the commitments of such stakeholders are assets of the company and deserve equal consideration alongside shareholders' investments, it is argued that the company's ability to develop and maintain long-term cooperative relationships will be enhanced, to the benefit of all participants.

The main problem with the social welfare model is that it replaces the single goal of profit maximisation, with a clear channel of accountability to shareholders, with a broader but unspecific requirement to achieve a balance between the interests of shareholders and other stakeholders (and indeed between the interests of different stakeholder groups). In practical terms, this would require the company's directors to trade off the competing claims, for example of economic and social goals, the interests of shareholders and the interests of the wider community, but without providing them with objective and consistent criteria against which corporate decisions could be made and company performance measured.

In its investigation, the Company Law Review Steering Committee concluded that (except where their Articles so provided) UK companies could not adopt an explicit social welfare objective in the context of company law as currently formulated. As a minimum, directors' duties would need to be revised to permit or, more radically, to require the directors to promote the success of the company in the interests of all stakeholders, with none of the participants, including the shareholders, being regarded as having overriding claims. In order to provide the directors with the necessary wide range of discretion, directors' duties would need to be expressed subjectively, involving a risk that there would then be no enforceable remedy for abuse of the directors' powers.

In addition to the reformulation of directors' duties, the Company Law Review Steering Group suggested that the implementation of the social welfare model in the UK might require changes to the existing rights of shareholders, particularly to appoint and dismiss directors, in order to enable constituencies other than shareholders to nominate directors to represent their interests.

Against this background, the Company Law Review Steering Committee expressed some doubt as to whether desirable reform might not be more satisfactorily achieved through improved information flows and greater disclosure, within the framework of an enlightened shareholder value model.

## The enlightened shareholder value model

Unlike the social welfare model, the enlightened shareholder value model assumes that corporate purpose and accountability as currently envisaged in UK company law – that is, the generation of value for shareholders – is correct and, moreover, is the best means of securing overall prosperity and welfare. It differs from the profit maximisation model, however, in that it acknowledges the duty of the directors to take proper account of wider objectives, including the company's health and safety, employment and contracting practices and its impact on the environment. It argues further that well-managed companies with long-term strategic objectives will recognise that the acceptance of wider responsibilities is in their own enlightened self-interest. This recognition will be reinforced by external influences, including increased scrutiny by governments, regulators, the media, pressure groups and local communities and the growing importance of corporate reputation.

Within this perspective, the recognition by the company of social responsibilities is not only consistent with its obligations to shareholders, but may positively help it to discharge these obligations. Thus, it is argued that a business case can be made for corporate social responsibility (CSR), based on:

> the management of downside risks, particularly to corporate reputation, arising from, for example, poor management of supply chain issues; inadequate environmental standards; human rights abuses; and poor treatment of workers, customers and suppliers; and

> the creation of potential competitive advantages through the alignment of business practices with stakeholder expectations resulting in, for example, reduced regulatory interventions; higher sales and increased customer loyalty; more supportive communities; the ability to attract and retain more talented employees; and better productivity, quality and innovation.

The Company Law Review Steering Group concluded that the enlightened shareholder value model was fully compatible with the existing formulation of directors' duties, which in no way required directors to take an unduly narrow or short-term view of their functions. It commented, however, that the existing law is widely misunderstood, with the result that directors often do not recognise their obligation to have regard to the need to build long-term and trusting relationships with employees, suppliers, customers and others, as appropriate, in order to secure the success of the enterprise over time. It noted in addition that proper and meaningful company reporting was essential to enable shareholders, other stakeholders and the general public to evaluate performance and, where necessary, to bring pressure on the company to satisfy broader social requirements. It found, however, that current statutory reporting requirements pay little regard to the need to account for 'soft' assets and resources, such as the level of skills and the stability of the company's work force, its relationships with its key suppliers or the value of its reputation and brands.

## Proposals for statutory change

### Statement of directors' duties

In its final report, the Company Law Review Steering Committee proposed the adoption of a new statutory statement of directors' duties designed, among other things, to clarify the nature, scope and duration of the duties owed to shareholders. The proposed statement makes clear that, while the directors must promote the success of the company for the benefit of the shareholders as a whole, they must take into account all the material factors that it is practicable in the circumstances for them to identify, including:

> the likely consequences, short- and long-term, of the actions open to them; and

> all other relevant factors, such as the company's need to foster its business relationships, including those with its employees and suppliers and the customers

for its products and services; its need to have regard to the impact of its operations on the communities affected and on the environment; its need to maintain a reputation for high standards of business conduct; and its need to achieve outcomes that are fair as between its shareholders.

The proposal for a definitive statement of directors' duties, the text of which can be found at *Appendix 3*, has been accepted by the Government and was incorporated in the White Paper *Modernising Company Law*, published in July 2002. As explained in *Chapter 1*, however, it is not clear when, and in what form, legislation will be brought forward to implement this and other recommendations of the Company Law Review.

*Disclosure of information*

Reflecting its criticisms of the narrow range of information currently required in company reports, the Company Law Review Steering Committee recommended that 'economically significant companies' should be placed under a new statutory obligation to publish an annual Operating and Financial Review (OFR). In addition to a description of the company's business, objectives and development, this would require an account of the dynamics of the business, including risks and uncertainties arising from factors such as dependencies on customers and suppliers; health, safety and environmental costs and liabilities; and programmes to maintain and enhance tangible and intellectual capital, including employee training.

In addition, the companies covered by the OFR obligation would be required to report on other matters, to the extent that the directors considered that these were material to an understanding of the business. These additional matters would include, for example, the company's key relationships with its employees, customers, suppliers and others, and its environmental, community, social, ethical and reputation policies. Further discussion on the OFR proposal can be found in *Chapter 10*.

## The demand for corporate social responsibility

In the course of its investigation, the Company Law Review Steering Committee noted the increasing demand from institutional investors for companies to provide information not currently required by company law which will give evidence of their policies and practices on non-financial matters. An example is the publication by the Association of British Insurers (ABI) of guidelines on socially responsible investment. These set out the disclosures on social, environmental and ethical matters that institutional investors now expect to be included in the annual reports of listed companies. The text of the ABI guidelines is given in *Appendix 4*, while further discussion on relations with institutional shareholders is contained in *Chapter 13*.

## Corporate culture, values and ethics after Enron

The above discussion demonstrates that there is increasing focus on the responsibility of companies for managing the external impacts of their activities and for fostering positive long-term relationships with external stakeholders. Until recently, however, less attention has been paid to the internal culture of the company, as represented by the values, ethical principles and standards of business conduct practised by employees at all levels. The significance of these issues was vividly demonstrated by the collapse of Enron and other major US corporations amidst allegations of unethical practices on the part of corporate managers, independent auditors and other market participants.

As discussed in *Chapter 3*, the Enron scandal has caused governments and regulators, in the US and world-wide, to re-examine their legal frameworks, accounting and auditing standards and codes of corporate governance with the aim of restoring investor confidence in the integrity of company management and the wider financial markets. Reforms introduced in the US under the provisions of the Sarbanes–Oxley Act have been widely influential and include measures specifically intended to raise standards of business conduct within listed companies. These include:

> the requirement for listed companies to disclose in their annual reports whether they have adopted codes of ethics applicable to the CEO, the CFO and other senior managers with accounting and financial functions and, if not, to explain their reasons; and

> the obligation of audit committees to establish procedures for the receipt, retention and treatment of 'whistleblower' reports regarding accounting, internal accounting controls and auditing matters.

While these and related measures reflect an understandable determination to avoid any repetition of the events at Enron, there is no evidence that those events were attributable to a lack of formal rules. Enron had a published statement of corporate values and maintained a confidential helpline for internal whistleblowers. Further, it required new employees to sign a written code of ethics, in line with the US Federal Sentencing Guidelines, which provide for mitigation of sentence for corporate defendants if it can be demonstrated that reasonable steps were taken by the company to prevent unethical conduct on the part of employees. This approach is designed to protect the company's legal position after something has gone wrong. As the example of Enron suggests, however, it does little to prevent ethical failures from occurring in the first place.

If Enron did not lack ethical rules, the evidence suggests that it did lack a corporate culture in which such rules were respected. At best, Enron appears to have had a compliance-based culture, in which it was considered sufficient to obey rules and regulations to the letter, while ignoring their intention. At worst, rules appear to have been regarded as an obstacle to creativity and enterprise, to be sidestepped or changed as necessary. This disrespect for rules was reinforced by the cultivation of aggressive business practices and by the prioritisation of profitability and share price performance, to the exclusion of almost any other consideration.

Increased scrutiny of companies in the US and the UK since the collapse of Enron has suggested that if that company's problems were extreme, they were not unique. As result, there is now a failure of trust in business, characterised by concerns about the quality of corporate governance, the credibility of financial and auditing standards, the effectiveness of regulatory arrangements and the integrity of capital markets.

In the task of restoring confidence, formal requirements for companies to have codes of ethics and to establish processes for the receipt and investigation of whistle-blower reports have a useful, if limited, part to play.

On the positive side, written codes of ethics can provide helpful guidance, triggering reflection about appropriate standards of business conduct and prompting employees to modify their behaviour. Similarly, provided that confidentiality is assured and protection is provided against retaliation, whistleblower helplines can help to demonstrate that the company is serious in its commitment to ethical principles. The collective responsibility of the board of directors for standards of conduct within the company is outlined in *Chapter 5*, while *Chapter 12* discusses the need for whistleblower protection in the context of the company's system of internal control and reputational risk management.

## PART 2

# Application of the Combined Code

Part Two of this Handbook is devoted to a detailed examination of the origins, content and practical implications of the main provisions of the July 2003 Combined Code of Corporate Governance.

The four main themes of the Combined Code are addressed as follows:

## Directors

- Chapter 5 considers the collective role of the board of directors in UK listed companies;
- Chapter 6 addresses the composition of the board, including the role of non-executive directors and the division of power and authority at the top of the company;
- Chapter 7 examines the new emphasis on the effectiveness of the board of directors, with particular reference to the need for the board to evaluate its own performance and that of its committees; and
- Chapter 8 describes the processes for the selection and appointment of directors.

## Remuneration

- Chapter 9 outlines the role and composition of the remuneration committee and considers current issues of regulatory and public concern, including the perceived problem of 'rewards for failure'.

## Accountability and audit

- Chapter 10 describes the current formal requirements for reporting to shareholders and explores current concerns about the adequacy of both financial and non-financial reporting by listed companies.
- Chapter 11 examines the measures taken to clarify and improve the effectiveness of the audit committee and the external auditors following the Enron scandal.
- Chapter 12 outlines the board's responsibility for the establishment of an effective system of internal control and risk management.

## Relations with shareholders

- Chapter 13 considers the responsibilities of companies and their boards for fostering positive relationships with institutional shareholders and the reciprocal obligations of institutional shareholders to make considered use of their powers of ownership.
- Chapter 14 describes current best practice for the open and constructive conduct of business at the AGM.

References at the beginning of each chapter are extracted from the text of the July 2003 Combined Code of Corporate Governannce.

# 5

# The Collective Role of the Board

> Every company should be headed by an effective board, which is collectively responsible for the success of the company.
>
> Main Principle A.1: The Board

This chapter examines the key responsibilities of the board as defined in the Combined Code of Corporate Governance, taking into account:

> - the need for the board to reserve certain important matters for its collective decision;
> - the board's responsibility for ensuring that the company's strategic objectives and policies are communicated;
> - the board's responsibility for setting and demonstrating appropriate standards of business conduct;
> - the conditions on which the board can properly delegate its collective decision-making powers.

In principle, the supreme decision-making body in a listed company is the general meeting of shareholders: the Companies Act, the Articles and the Listing Rules all specify particular circumstances in which the approval of shareholders must be obtained for decisions affecting their interests. In practice, however, the company's Articles generally entrust the directors, as the agents of the shareholders, to manage the company and its activities. Thus, Table A Articles (Regulation 70) provide that 'the business of the company shall be managed by the directors who may exercise all the powers of the company'.

The conferment on the directors of largely unconstrained authority to act on behalf of the company raises two interrelated issues for good boardroom practice. The first of these arises from the nature and composition of the board itself. As discussed in *Chapter 3*, boards have both supervisory and management functions, which in two-tier boards are formally allocated to separate boards. In the UK's unitary board system, however, these functions are the responsibility of a single board consisting of both executive directors, who are directly involved in management of company's activities, and NEDs, who have no such involvement.

Although, as discussed in *Chapter 6*, executive directors and NEDs make different contributions to governance, for the purposes of the current discussion there is no distinction between directors in terms of their collective responsibility for the supervisory and management functions of the board: all directors are equally responsible in law for the conduct of the business and the stewardship of shareholders' assets. None the less, recent corporate failures – notably Marconi in the UK and Enron in the US – have revealed a lack of clarity on the part of some boards about the nature of their collective responsibilities. Specifically, there is some uncertainty about the extent to which the board as a whole is empowered (and where necessary required) to intervene actively in the company's activities in order to monitor and control the actions of the CEO and other executive directors.

The second issue for good boardroom practice arises from the practical limitations on the board's ability to involve itself directly in the company's business. Although the board is ultimately responsible to shareholders for all aspects of the company's activities and performance, it is clearly impractical in complex businesses for the board to have hands-on involvement in every area of the company's business. This again raises the question of balance between the supervisory and management functions of the board – in particular, to what extent and on what terms can the board delegate some aspects of management, while retaining the ability to control the business and account to shareholders for its stewardship?

## The key responsibilities of the board

In the absence of a definitive statutory summary of the role of the board, successive codes of corporate governance have offered their own definitions. Of these, the most recent is the July 2003 Combined Code of Corporate Governance, Supporting Principle A.1 of which states:

> 'The board's role is to provide entrepreneurial leadership of the company within a framework of prudent and effective controls which enables risk to be assessed and managed. The board should set the company's strategic aims, ensure that the necessary financial and human resources are in place for the company to meet its objectives and review management performance. The board should set the company's values and standards and ensure that its obligations to its shareholders and others are understood and met.'

According to this definition, the key responsibilities of the board are:

> ❭ *Strategy:* setting the company's strategic aims, determining its strategic objectives and policies and providing clear definitions of responsibility.
> ❭ *Resources:* ensuring that the necessary financial and human resources, including key appointments, are in place to enable the company to meet its objectives.
> ❭ *Performance:* reviewing management performance and monitoring progress towards objectives.
> ❭ *Values and standards:* setting the company's values and standards and ensuring that all employees know what standards of conduct are expected of them, in par-

ticular by drawing up codes of ethics or statements of business practice and publishing them internally and externally.

> *Communication:* ensuring that the company's strategic objectives and obligations to shareholders and other stakeholders are clearly understood within the organisation and that all employees know what targets and standards are to be met.

The revised Combined Code makes clear that the board has active responsibility for the conduct of the company's business. Although the board, and in particular its non-executive members, may be able to fulfil a valuable advisory role, the collective purpose of the board is not to advise management, but to account directly to shareholders for the performance of the company.

The board derives its collective authority by direct delegation from the shareholders and must therefore exercise it in interests of shareholders. If the board fails to exercise its delegated authority effectively, the interests of shareholders will be unrepresented in the governance of the company and may become subordinated to the interests of other parties, including those of current company management. Within the context of the unitary board structure, this means that the role of the board as a whole, including NEDs, is to lead and direct the company's activities. Conversely the whole board, including the CEO and other executive directors, is responsible for monitoring the conduct and performance of management.

## Matters reserved to the board

In order to discharge effectively its collective duties of management and supervision of the company's business, the board must determine the scope of its own activities and the areas of the business to which it will assign high priority.

The Cadbury Code recommended that, in order to ensure that the direction and control of the company remained firmly in its hands, the board should specifically reserve certain important matters for its collective decision: in the view of the Cadbury Committee, such matters were likely to include, as a minimum, material acquisitions and disposals of assets and decisions concerning investments, capital projects, authority levels and the company's policies on treasury and risk management. As a safeguard against misjudgements and possible illegal or unethical practices, the matters reserved to the board should be set out in a formal written schedule, thus making it more difficult for the company's executive management to usurp the authority of the board.

The requirement for a formal schedule of matters specifically reserved for the collective decision of the board has been confirmed in subsequent codes of corporate governance, with the addition, in the July 2003 Combined Code, that the company should state in its annual report how the board operates, with a high-level description of the types of decisions to be taken by the board or delegated to management.

In its Guidance Note on the schedule of matters reserved for the board, the ICSA points out that the precise content of the schedule will vary from company to company according to the size and nature of the company's activities, its operating and regulatory environment and the board's assessment of the risks and opportunities faced by the business. Further, every board will need to establish its own view on the materiality of particular categories of decision, including, for example, the financial limits for transactions which should be referred to the board for approval. The full text of this Guidance Note is set out in *Appendix 5*.

With this proviso, it is likely that the boards of most listed companies will wish, in the light of the recent revisions to the Combined Code, to reserve the following matters for their collective decision.

## Companies Act and other legal requirements

> approval of interim and final financial statements;
> approval of the annual report and accounts;
> approval of the interim dividend and recommendation of the final dividend;
> approval of any significant changes in accounting policies or practices;
> appointment or removal of the company secretary;
> remuneration of the auditors and recommendations for the appointment or removal of auditors (subject in each case to the recommendations of the audit committee);
> the calling of any meeting of shareholders;
> resolutions and corresponding documentation to be put forward to shareholders at a general meeting;
> policy regarding charitable and political donations;
> environmental policy.

## Listing requirements

> approval of all circulars and listing particulars requiring to be submitted to the London Stock Exchange prior to despatch to shareholders;
> approval of regulatory announcements and press releases concerning matters decided by the board;
> major changes in employee share schemes and the allocation of executive share options;
> application of the Model Code on share dealing.

## Board membership and board committees

> approval of all board appointments and removals (subject to the recommendations of the nomination committee);
> approval of any recommendation to shareholders to re-elect a director on retirement by rotation (subject to the recommendations of the nomination committee);
> terms and conditions of directors and senior executives (subject to the recommendations of the remuneration committee);
> approval of any special terms and conditions attached to the proposed appointment of a director (subject to the recommendations of the remuneration committee);

> terms of reference of chairman, chief executive and other executive directors;
> terms of reference and membership of board committees;
> minutes, reports and referrals from committees of the board;
> appointments to the boards of subsidiary companies.

## Management

> approval of the group's long-term objectives and commercial strategy;
> approval of the annual operating and capital expenditure budgets;
> changes relating to the group's capital structure or its status as a PLC;
> changes to the group's management and control structure.

## Corporate governance

> review of the company's overall corporate governance arrangements;
> internal control arrangements, including changes to the company's/group's management and control structure;
> risk management strategy;
> appointment or removal of the head of internal audit;
> amendments to the schedule of matters reserved for board decisions;
> Directors' and officers' liability insurance.

## Employment

> pay and human resource policy;
> major changes in the rules of the company pension scheme, or changes of trustees or (where this is subject to the approval of the company) changes in the fund management arrangements;
> health and safety policy and reports on significant incidents and 'near-misses'.

## Financial

> delegations of authority to executive directors;
> subject to delegations of authority approved and in force:
  – major capital projects;
  – contracts of the company (or, where relevant, of any subsidiary (in the ordinary course of business, e.g. bank borrowings and acquisition or disposal of fixed assets which are material, contracts of the company (or, where relevant, of any subsidiary) not in the ordinary course of business, e.g. loans and repayments; foreign currency transactions; major acquisitions or disposals; in each case where the value exceeds the level predetermined by the board;
  – major investments, including the acquisition or disposal of material interests in the voting shares of any company or the making of any takeover bid.
> treasury policies, including foreign currency exposure and the use of derivatives and similar financial instruments;
> any significant change in accounting policies or practices.

### Miscellaneous

> ❯ approval of the company's principal professional advisers;
> ❯ prosecution, defence or settlement of litigation which is material by reason of size or strategic significance.

The schedule of matters reserved to the board effectively constitutes the board's 'job description', reflecting its priorities and determining the extent of its intended direct involvement in particular areas of the business. Conversely, the schedule delineates the areas which the board considers it appropriate to delegate authority to others, including board committees, the CEO and other executive directors. It is therefore of fundamental importance to the board's ability to control and direct the activities of the company in the interests of the shareholders and demands both careful analysis and regular review.

## Communicating strategic objectives and policies

The board is responsible for ensuring that the powers of the company, whether exercised by itself collectively or by committees and individuals to whom it has delegated authority, are used in the interests of shareholders:

> ❯ it must take account of shareholders' objectives in order to define the purposes for which the company's powers are to be used, in terms of long-term strategic objectives and target returns on shareholders' investment; and
> ❯ it must then prescribe the methods by which the company's objectives are to be achieved, in terms of its operating procedures and standards of business behaviour, taking into account legal, regulatory and ethical requirements and the need to avoid unacceptable risk exposure.

In addition to defining its own job description and agenda, the board must therefore ensure that the company's strategic aims and objectives are understood throughout the organisation.

The formulation of business strategy is the subject of unending theoretical debate and is beyond the scope of this Handbook. The concern for corporate governance is to ensure that the strategic objectives and methods determined by the board in the interests of shareholders are translated into clear, binding guidance for the conduct of the company's business.

Although there is no formal requirement for this, many boards of large companies find it helpful, in the interests of internal and external accountability, transparency and audit, to document their strategic objectives and prescribed methods and standards in formal business policies. These may be communicated to company employees in written form or electronically via the company's intranet. They are also increasingly made publicly available, in whole or in part, on the company's external web-site: a leading example is BP, the business policies of which can be found at www.bp.com/company_overview/business_pol/index.asp.

**GOOD PRACTICE POINT**

## Preparing the schedule of matters reserved for the board

The preparation of the schedule of matters reserved to the board is too important to be regarded as a purely administrative exercise. The content of the schedule reflects the board's priorities and the matters in which it intends to be actively involved, and thus represents the board's collective 'job description' and the perpetual agenda for its meetings. The following issues are therefore of critical significance to the board's ability to lead and control the company in the interests of shareholders:

### Ownership of the schedule

- The board must 'own' the schedule of matters reserved for its collective decision and must be fully involved in and responsible for defining and controlling its own job.
- The company secretary has a key role in assisting the board in the preparation of the schedule, but should not be left with sole responsibility.
- The contents of the schedule must be determined by the board collectively, not by any individual or group of directors – whether the chairman, the CEO, the senior independent director, the executive directors or the non-executive directors.

### Strategic content of the schedule

- The schedule of matters reserved to the board must be an accurate reflection of the strategic issues of greatest importance to the company, having regard to its business activities, its current position and performance, its operating and regulatory environment, its risk profile and its long-term objectives.
- As the board's 'job description' however, the schedule must not focus exclusively on what is going on in the organisation, but must reflect the board's primary responsibility for determining the strategic direction of the company.
- The schedule must therefore distinguish clearly between the role of the board for defining the direction and objectives of the company and the responsibilities of management for realising the outcomes identified by the board.

### Relevance of the schedule:

- The schedule must be reviewed regularly in the light of business developments to ensure that the board is devoting its attention to the strategic issues of most significance to the interests of shareholders.

### The board's commitment:

- The board as a whole must commit itself to active involvement in the matters it reserves to itself, taking into account its accountability to shareholders for its own actions and omissions.
- However, if particular matters so reserved prove to be an inappropriate use of the board's time and attention, the schedule must be amended promptly and responsibility for the matters concerned must be delegated elsewhere, subject to appropriate reporting arrangements and other guidance as necessary.

Company business policies are typically prefaced by a short mission or vision statement describing the company's identity and key objectives, such as customer satisfaction, market share, product development or territorial expansion. Other components typically include policies and procedures designed to provide guidance for company employees on specific areas of business activity and a statement of the company's values.

The number of policy and procedural documents will vary widely from company to company according to business complexity, regulatory and operating environment and management style. None the less, a degree of formality is usually considered necessary in key areas of the business to ensure that the board is well informed about the company's position and performance and can account fully to shareholders for its conduct of the business.

The typical elements of policy and procedural documentation can thus be broadly categorised as follows:

> *Internal transparency and accountability:* the schedule of matters reserved for the collective decision of the board (see above); a schedule of the primary delegations of authority to committees and individual directors and officers, including details of approval limits and the need for multiple signatures; the terms of reference of all committees established by the board; arrangements for periodic reporting by business units, including where appropriate guidance on the content and format of reports to be submitted.

> *External accountability and communications:* protection and dissemination of price-sensitive information in accordance with listing requirements; relations with the media; corporate identity and brands.

> *Financial control and reporting:* accounting procedures; treasury; taxation; pensions policy and administration; procurement practices.

> *Strategy and planning:* business planning methodology and guidance; criteria for investment in new businesses and/or criteria for investment in new territories; establishment of joint ventures.

> *Safeguarding of assets:* internal control and risk management processes; insurance; IT security; physical security of plant and buildings; disaster recovery and business continuity; information security and confidentiality; document retention; data protection; intellectual property.

> *Health, safety and environment:* safeguarding of employees; accident reporting; environmental protection policies, taking account of any special hazards posed by the company's activities.

> *Employment:* remuneration; human resources; employment policies, including equal opportunities; employee communications; succession planning.

> *Business ethics and conduct:* share dealing code; fraud and malpractice; whistleblowing; anti-corruption and money laundering procedures; human rights.

## Standards of business conduct

The Combined Code recommendation that the board should set the company's values and standards reflects growing recognition that the board's duty to safeguard company assets on behalf of shareholders extends to the company's reputation. Good reputation promotes confidence in the quality of the board's leadership and governance and enhances the company's credibility in the eyes of the investment community, with a positive influence on its value and share price. Conversely, a poor or damaged reputation may reduce the company's market value and can threaten or even destroy its business: a key example is the accounting firm Arthur Andersen, which was destroyed by its perceived complicity in the Enron scandal.

Although the company's financial performance and record of compliance with laws and regulations are important considerations, they are insufficient by themselves to guarantee the company's reputation. Other factors of critical importance include the company's values, comprising a complex mix of corporate culture, the quality of the company's dealings with shareholders and other stakeholders and its attitude towards the environment and the communities affected by its operations.

The preparation by the board of an explicit statement of the values and standards of conduct expected of all employees can play a key role in upholding and enhancing the company's reputation. Key elements of such a statement include:

> openness and transparency of information, including the provision to shareholders and other stakeholders of timely, accurate and meaningful information about the company's position and significant developments in its affairs;
> compliance with the spirit, rather than merely the letter, of all applicable laws, regulations and corporate governance requirements;
> the conduct of the company's relationships with shareholders and other stakeholders;
> the ethical conduct of business.

The company's statement of values will often incorporate or be supported by an employee code of conduct or code of ethics. As a result of regulatory changes in the US following the Enron scandal, such codes are now mandatory in the US for certain employees of listed corporations. Although there is no equivalent formal requirement in the UK, it is increasingly the practice of well-regarded companies in the UK to produce written codes for the guidance of all employees.

Employee codes of conduct typically emphasise the personal responsibilities of individual employees for:

> honest and ethical conduct, including the avoidance of real or apparent conflicts of interest between personal and professional relationships;
> mutual respect in dealings with colleagues at all levels;
> full, fair, accurate, timely and understandable disclosure of information in company reports, documents and other public communications;
> fair dealing with customers, suppliers, employees and competitors;
> compliance with laws, regulations and other applicable requirements;
> reporting illegal and unethical behaviour through the company's established whistleblower procedure.

A further discussion on the need for companies to establish whistleblowing procedures is given in *Chapter 12*.

## THE GOODCORPORATION CHARTER

The GoodCorporation charter is intended to provide a framework for socially responsible behaviour in organisations of all types. It is an open standard on which organisations are encouraged to draw, acknowledging that their activities are based on or adapted from the standard. However, organisations wishing to state compliance with the charter participate in a formal verification and benchmarking process and provide evidence to demonstrate that they meet the charter principles in practice. Further information on the GoodCorporation charter can be found on www.goodcorporation.com.

### Employees

The organisation respects the dignity and rights of all employees. It –

- provides clear and fair terms of employment;
- provides clean, healthy and safe working conditions;
- has a fair remuneration policy everywhere it operates;
- strives for equal opportunities for all present and potential employees;
- encourages employees to develop skills and progress in their careers;
- does not tolerate any sexual, physical or mental harassment of its employees;
- does not discriminate on grounds of colour, ethnic origin, gender, age, religion, political or other opinion, disability or sexual orientation;
- does not employ underage staff.

### Customers

The organisation treats its customers with respect. It –

- seeks to be honest and fair in its relationships with its customers;
- provides the standards of products and services that have been agreed;
- takes all reasonable steps to ensure the safety and quality of the goods and services it provides.

Written codes of conduct can provide guidance, trigger reflection about appropriate standards of business conduct and prompt individuals to modify their behaviour. It cannot be overemphasised, however, that a code of conduct in isolation cannot have a decisive influence on corporate behaviour. If an employee code of conduct is to succeed in promoting the company's values and reputation, it must be seen to apply to all employees, including the directors themselves, and must have the visible support and leadership of senior management. Further, it must be integrated within a corporate culture in which ethical conduct is expected from all employees, irrespective of position or seniority, and in which ethical decision-making is seen to be practised at all levels, from the board down.

Moreover, no written code can anticipate every situation likely to be encountered by employees, or provide specific guidance on all conceivable ethical dilemmas. Instead, the company must seek to develop its employees as individuals, and equip them with the skills and confidence to recognise and resolve ethical issues for themselves, in a manner consistent with the principles upheld by the company. To this end, the company must consistently demonstrate its belief that ethical behaviour is compatible with, and supports the achievement of, its business objectives. Further, it must ensure that its decision-making processes enable business issues to be framed and discussed in

### Suppliers

The organisation treats its suppliers and subcontractors with respect. It –

- seeks to be honest and fair in its relationships with its suppliers and subcontractors;
- has a policy not to offer, pay or accept bribes or substantial favours;
- pays suppliers and subcontractors in accordance with agreed terms;
- encourages suppliers and subcontractors to abide by the principles of this Charter.

### Community and environment

The organisation seeks to be a good corporate citizen respecting the laws of the countries in which it operates. It –

- aims to make the communities in which it works better places to live and do business;
- aims to be sensitive to the local community's cultural, social and economic needs;

- endeavours to protect and preserve the environment where it operates.

### Shareholders and providers of finance

The organisation is responsible to those who provide its funding. It –

- is accountable to its shareholders for financial reports that are accurate and timely;
- communicates to shareholders all matters that are material to an understanding of the future prospects of the organisation;
- aims to protect shareholders' funds, manage risks and ensure that funds are used as agreed.

### Management commitment

The management of the organisation will do all in its power to conform to the letter and spirit of this Charter.

ethical terms, with full weight being given to the long-term consequences of business decisions, including the impacts on the company's stakeholders.

Within this framework:

> Directors and senior managers must give leadership by demonstrating their commitment to the company's ethical standards through their own behaviour and values, and by upholding compliance with the intention, as well as the letter, of internal rules and external laws and regulations.

> The company's performance management system must reward ethical behaviour and punish unethical behaviour by reflecting not just results, but the manner in which results have been achieved.

> Employee training programmes must include focus on realistic ethical dilemmas likely to be encountered in the workplace and promote open discussion of controversial ethical issues.

## The delegation of authority

No board, however effective, can have hands-on involvement in every area of the company's business. Some further degree of delegation of the authorities granted to the board by the shareholders is therefore inevitable.

Having defined its own role and responsibilities through the preparation of the schedule of matters reserved for its collective decision, the board must decide what authority and accountability it is appropriate to delegate to others. At the board's discretion, authority may be delegated to committees or to individuals, including the CEO and other executive directors. In either case, however, the board as a whole remains fully responsible for the exercise of the powers granted to it by the shareholders. Shareholders should therefore be able to assess the actions of the board, its committees and others to whom it has delegated authority and should have the opportunity at the AGM to question the directors about the processes adopted and the decisions reached.

## Delegation to committees

In most companies, the board is empowered under the Articles (Table A Regulation 72) to delegate its powers to committees consisting of one or more directors. The board can impose regulations by which such committees operate and can also revoke any delegation of authority, whether to a committee to or an individual, at any time by recording its decision in the board minutes.

Under the terms of the July 2003 Combined Code, the board of a listed company is required to establish:

> a nomination committee, a majority of the members of which should be independent non-executive directors, to lead the process for board appointments and to make recommendations to the board (see also *Chapter 8*);

> a remuneration committee of at least three (or, in the case of smaller companies, two) independent non-executive directors with delegated responsibility for developing policy on executive remuneration and for setting remuneration for all executive directors and the chairman (see also *Chapter 9*);

> an audit committee of at least three (or, in the case of smaller companies, two) independent non-executive directors to monitor the integrity of the company's financial statements of the company, oversee its relationships with its external auditors and monitor the effectiveness of the internal audit function (see also *Chapter 11*).

The board may set up further committees as necessary to deal with specific issues or to assist it with defined aspects of its own responsibilities. These may include:

> temporary committees, with membership drawn from the board and appropriate members of the company's senior management team, with delegated authority to deal with specific matters such as major acquisitions and mergers or to give final approval for the annual report and accounts and similar documents;

> board committees, often consisting wholly or mainly of independent non-executive directors, with responsibility for advising the board as a whole on matters such as risk management, environmental and community responsibility and corporate ethics;

> executive committees, consisting of the CEO and the other executive directors, with defined powers to take decisions between scheduled meetings of the full board.

In each case, it is important to bear in mind that committees are creations of the board: their powers to act are derived from the board, and ultimately from the shareholders, and they must therefore always remain under the board's control. For these reasons, the board as a whole is responsible for ensuring that each committee's status and functions are clearly specified in advance in its terms of reference. These should set out the committee's membership and key tasks, including where appropriate the time-scale within which it is required to complete its activities, and should define its authority and any limitations on the powers delegated to it by the board. Each committee's terms of reference should also set out the frequency with which it is required to report to the board on its activities, including the exercise of its delegated powers. Where appropriate, the minutes of committees should be circulated to all directors prior to the next board meeting to give them an opportunity to raise questions about the committee's activities at that meeting.

### Delegation to individuals

The Articles of most companies permit the board to delegate such of their powers as they see fit and desirable to the CEO or any other director holding executive office (Table A Regulations 84 and 72). Executive directors can therefore be given authority to take decisions on behalf of the board and to enter into contracts or agreements on behalf of the company. Such delegated authorities may be general or may be limited to certain types of transactions or to transactions up to a specified financial value. In addition, authority may be delegated, either directly by the board or indirectly by executive directors, to other members of the company's senior management team, including the company secretary.

As with the delegation of authority to committees, the board retains ultimate responsibility to shareholders for the activities of individual directors and officers of to whom it has delegated authority. The board must therefore ensure that individuals to whom it delegates powers are fully accountable for their decisions and actions, for example, by requiring them to report periodically to the full board on decisions taken.

## Chapter summary

> In the UK's unitary board system, all directors – both executive directors and NEDs – participate equally in the collective management and supervisory functions of the board.

> Accordingly, the board as a whole is actively responsible to shareholders for setting the company's strategic aims, ensuring that the necessary financial and human resources are in place, reviewing performance and monitoring progress towards objectives, setting the company's values and standards and ensuring that the company's strategic objectives and obligations to shareholders and other stakeholders are understood and met.

> In order to discharge its obligations to shareholders, the board must first define its own 'job description' and priorities by preparing a schedule of the key business decisions it intends to reserve to its collective decision. The schedule of matters reserved to the board is of the highest importance to the board's ability to control and direct the activities of the company and demands both careful analysis and regular review.

> The board must also ensure that the company's strategic aims and objectives are understood throughout the organisation and are translated into clear, binding guidance for the conduct of the company's business.

> In order to protect the company's reputational assets, the board must set the company's values and standards of business conduct and must demonstrate leadership through its own commitment to ethical standards.

> Finally, the board must define the conditions on which its collective decision-making powers are to be delegated to others, taking into account its ultimate responsibility for the exercise of the powers granted to it by the shareholders.

# 6

# The Composition of the Board

> There should be a clear division of responsibilities at the head of the company between the running of the board and the executive responsibility for the running of the company's business. No one individual should have unfettered powers of decision.
>
> Main Principle A.2 Chairman and chief executive

> The board should include a balance of executive and non-executive directors (and in particular independent non-executive directors) such that no individual or small group of individuals can dominate the board's decision-taking.
>
> Main Principle A.3 Board balance and independence

This chapter considers the division of power between the chairman and the CEO and the role of non-executive directors in preserving the balance of influence on the board. It also looks at the developing concept of independence, together with the potential liabilities faced by individual directors and the role of insurance and due diligence in mitigating these.

As described in *Chapter 5*, the board is collectively responsible to the shareholders for the management of the company's business (encompassing entrepreneurial leadership, strategic direction, the assessment and management of risk and the decisions about the required level of resources) as well as for the review of management performance.

Although there is no distinction in law between directors, the UK's system of corporate governance is increasingly recognising that in practice the boards of listed companies are composed of directors of two distinct types. Executive directors, including the CEO, are full-time employees of the company, with direct involvement in and delegated responsibility for the executive management of a defined area of the business. Non-executive directors, by contrast, are not employees of company, have no involvement in its management and may spend no more than 15-30 days a year on its business. None the less, all directors, irrespective of type, are equally responsible for both management and supervision. Thus, non-executive directors are responsible, as members of the collective board, for the leadership and direction of the company's activities, despite their lack of involvement in its management. Similarly, the CEO and other executive directors share the board's collective responsibility for supervising manage-ment conduct and performance, despite their own direct involvement and responsibil-ity as managers.

Participation in the collective responsibilities of the board therefore involves ten-sions for both types of director, raising significant issues for good boardroom practice. Most obviously, there is an inherent tension for executive directors between their responsibilities as members of the board and as managers of the company's business. Executive directors are in a powerful position, especially because of their privileged access to information about the business, to evade effective oversight and to influence board decision-making to serve their own interests, rather than those of shareholders, in areas such as executive remuneration and job security. Conversely, the ability of non-executive directors to counteract the influence of the executive directors may be limited by lack of information about the company's activities and insufficient time spent with the company.

Concerns about the ability of the unitary board to represent and further the inter-ests of shareholders have led to provisions in successive codes of corporate governance designed to dilute the influence of executive management over board decisions, and in certain cases – notably executive remuneration – to exclude executive directors from decision-making entirely. In addition, there is an increasing focus on the composition of the board and the balance of power and influence over its decision-making, accom-panied by an increasing differentiation between the roles and qualifications of differ-ent members of the board.

## The division of power

The approach of corporate governance to the problems arising from an excessive con-centration of power and authority at the top of the company has evolved in two distinct stages. The first has been characterised by a strengthening presumption that the posts of chairman and CEO should not be held by the same individual. In the second, on-going, stage, attention has turned from structural to qualitative issues, including the distinctive role of the chairman, the need for the chairman to be independent on first appointment and the method of nominating and appointing the chairman.

### The chairman and the CEO

The chairman and CEO are the most powerful members of the board of directors.

The chairman is responsible for the functioning of the board, calling board meetings, setting the agenda and leading the meeting. As such, he or she is not the 'boss' of the board, but is accountable to the board for facilitating the discharge of its collective responsi-bility to shareholders for the governance of the company. As chairman of the company, he or she also presides at general meetings of shareholders and is therefore the public representative of the company in its dealings with institutional and private investors.

The CEO is responsible for the executive management of the company's operations. As the senior executive in charge of the management team, the CEO is accountable to the board as a whole for implementing its collective decisions in the conduct of the company's business. While other executive managers may also be directors of the company, they will normally report to the CEO rather than to the board direct.

Although the two offices thus entail different, and arguably irreconcilable, roles and responsibilities, there is no legal or constitutional prohibition on both offices being held by the same person. Table A Articles (Regulation 91) provide that the directors may appoint one of their number to be chairman of the company, but give no further guidance on which of the directors is eligible to be so appointed. Indeed, when the Cadbury Committee was established in 1991, it was still common for the offices of chairman and CEO to be combined on the boards of UK listed companies.

## The chairman/CEO split

In its report, the Cadbury Committee emphasised the need for the chairman to be able to stand back from the day-to-day running of the business in order to ensure that the board as a whole is in full control of the company's affairs and is mindful of the interests of shareholders. It pointed out that the proper discharge of this role requires the chairman to ensure that all directors, whether executive or non-executive, accept their full share of responsibility for the governance of the company and that non-executives in particular are kept properly informed.

The Cadbury Committee concluded that, given the importance and special nature of the chairman's role, it should, as a matter of principle, be separated from that of the chief executive. However, the ensuing Cadbury Code stopped short of requiring a formal separation in listed companies, conceding that some companies might wish to continue to combine the roles of chairman and chief executive. Where this was done, it recommended that there should be strong and independent element on the board as a safeguard against an excessive concentration of power in the hands of one individual.

The presumption against the appointment of a combined chairman and CEO was reinforced by the Hampel Committee in the 1998 version of the Combined Code. This recommended that any decision to combine the two posts should be publicly justified and that, whether or not the posts were held by different people, the board should contain a strong and independent non-executive element.

Research carried out in 2002 on behalf of the Higgs Review of the role and effectiveness of non-executive directors found that the principle of separation between the positions of chairman and CEO is now generally accepted, with around 90 per cent of listed companies splitting the roles. The Review concluded that the benefits of separation, in terms of the dispersal of authority and power and differentiation between leadership of the board and the running of the business, were so well established that there should now be a categorical presumption that the roles of chairman and chief executive should be separated. Accordingly, the July 2003 Combined Code provides that the functions of chairman and CEO should not be exercised by the same individual. Further, the division of responsibilities between the chairman and CEO should be clearly established, set out in writing and agreed by the full board (Code Provision A.2.1).

## The role of the chairman

In addition to its conclusions on the separation of the roles of chairman and chief executive, the Higgs Review identified a need for definitive guidance on the distinctive responsibilities of the chairman within the unitary board structure. Following the recommendations of the Review, the July 2003 Combined Code states that:

> '*The chairman is responsible for leadership of the board, ensuring its effectiveness on all aspects of its role and setting its agenda. The chairman is also responsible for ensuring that the directors receive accurate, timely and clear information. The chairman should ensure effective communication with shareholders. The chairman should also facilitate the effective contribution of non-executive directors in particular and ensure constructive relations between executive and non-executive directors.*'

Supporting Principle A.2

Expanding on this principle, Higgs indicates that the chairman has responsibility for managing the business of the board, in particular to ensure that sufficient time is allowed for discussion of complex or contentious issues. To this end, the chairman must ensure that the board's agenda is forward-looking and focuses on strategic, rather than management, issues and takes full account of the concerns of all board members. In addition, the chairman is responsible for creating the conditions for the effective performance of non-executive directors, in particular by ensuring that they receive accurate and meaningful information and have sufficient time to consider critical issues.

In the view of Higgs (Annex D), the effective chairman:

> ❯ upholds the highest standards of integrity and probity;
> ❯ sets the agenda, style and tone of board discussions to promote effective decision-making and constructive debate;
> ❯ promotes effective relationships and open communication, both inside and outside the boardroom, between non-executive directors and the executive team;
> ❯ builds an effective and complementary board, initiating change and planning succession in board appointments, subject to board and shareholders' approval;
> ❯ promotes the highest standards of corporate governance and seeks compliance with the provisions of the Code wherever possible;
> ❯ ensures a clear structure for and the effective running of board committees;
> ❯ ensures effective implementation of board decisions;
> ❯ establishes a close relationship of trust with the chief executive, providing support and advice while respecting executive responsibility;
> ❯ provides coherent leadership of the company, including representing the company and understanding the views of shareholders.

## The independence of the chairman

In most companies in which the roles of chairman and CEO are already separated, the chairman is typically part-time and is often described as a non-executive director. In its examination of the functions of the chairman, however, the Higgs Review noted that, while the chairman needed to foster relationships of trust with both the executive and non-executive directors, he or she would inevitably have a much greater degree of involvement with the executive team than would the non-executive directors. For this reason, the Review concluded that the role differed significantly from that of either the non-executive directors or the executive directors.

In line with these considerations, the Review concluded that, at the time of his or her first appointment to the board, the chairman should meet the restated test of independence applicable to the non-executive directors (see 'The Concept of Independence', below). It recognised, however, that, once appointed, the chairman's independence would inevitably be reduced by the degree of his or her involvement with the executive directors; the test of continued independence could not therefore be applied to the chairman's reappointment.

The review also highlighted the difficulties that might arise from the common practice of appointing a former CEO to the chairmanship of the same company. In these circumstances, the individual's history of direct responsibility for the day-to-day management of the business could make it difficult for him or her to establish an appropriate relationship with the new CEO, while their familiarity with the company's affairs could reduce their sensitivity to the information needs of the non-executive directors.

Reflecting the recommendations of Higgs, Provision A.2.2 of the revised Combined Code provides that:

> on first appointment, the chairman should meet the restated independence criteria for non-executive directors;
> a chief executive should not go on to be chairman of the same company;
> if, exceptionally, a board decides that a chief executive should become chairman, the board should consult major shareholders in advance and should set out its reasons to shareholders at the time of the appointment and in the next annual report.

## The nomination and appointment of the chairman

In view of the particular sensitivities surrounding the post of chairman, the Higgs Review concluded that special arrangements were required for the nomination and appointment of the chairman. It therefore recommended that the following principles should be observed when a board is appointing a new chairman:

> The nomination and appointment process should be led, not by the incumbent chairman, but by the senior independent director (see 'Senior independent director', below) or by the deputy chairman (provided that the latter is independent).
> Any existing director who is putting him- or herself forward as a candidate for the chairmanship should be excluded from involvement in the appointment process.
> The nomination committee or another group comprising a majority of independent non-executive directors should lead the process and make a recommendation to the board as a whole.

> ❭ A systematic approach should be taken to identify the skills and expertise required for the role of chairman and a job specification should be prepared.
> ❭ Rather than possible individuals being considered in isolation, a shortlist of potential candidates should be considered, preferably with the benefit of external advice.

Further information on selection and appointment and the role of the nomination committee is set out in *Chapter 8*.

## Board balance: the role of non-executive directors

The widespread presence of non-executive directors on the boards of listed companies is a comparatively recent phenomenon. The Cadbury Committee found in the early 1990s that some company boards had no non-executive directors at all, and that in many cases where non-executives had been appointed, they were outnumbered by executive directors. Further, the independence of many non-executive directors was in doubt because of pre-existing links with the company or its major shareholders or external advisers.

The initial focus of corporate governance was therefore to reinforce the presence of non-executive directors as a numerical counterweight to the powers of the CEO and executive management. More recently, in the light of concerns about the effectiveness of non-executive directors aroused by Enron and other corporate scandals, attention has focused on the quality of the contribution made by non-executive directors, both as individuals and – more controversially – as a distinct group with a recognised senior member.

### Non-executive directors

As noted in the introduction to this chapter, all directors, whether executive or non-executive, participate equally in the management and management oversight responsibilities of the collective board. As result, non-executive directors typically play a dual role on the board:

> ❭ Although they have no direct involvement in the management of the company's activities, non-executive directors may provide skills and experience not possessed by the executive directors, particularly in areas such as strategy and business development. In addition, they are expected to contribute to the quality of the board's decision-making through objective and constructive challenge to proposals brought forward by management.
> ❭ At same time, non-executive directors are expected to help maintain a proper balance of power on the board and to scrutinise management performance and reporting, in particular as members of the audit, remuneration and nomination committees of the board.

More information on the involvement of non-executive directors in the scrutiny of management performance can be found in *Chapters 8, 9 and 11*.

The desirability of appointing non-executive directors to the boards of listed companies was first formally advanced in the Cadbury Code, which recommended that non-executive directors should bring independent judgement to bear on issues of strategy, performance, resources (including key appointments) and standards of conduct. It gave no firm guidance on the proportion of the board that should be made up of non-executive directors, stating only that they should be '*of sufficient calibre and number for their views to carry significant weight in the board's decisions*'. It did emphasise, however, that where the posts of chairman and CEO were combined, a strong and independent element on the board was essential.

More specific guidance was provided in the 1998 version of the Combined Code, which followed the Hampel Committee's deliberations. This recommended that, in order to ensure that no individual or small group of individuals could dominate the board's decision-taking, a least one third of the board should be made up of non-executive directors, of whom the majority should be independent.

## The effectiveness of non-executive directors

Despite the reinforcement in successive codes of corporate governance of the role and required proportion of non-executive directors on the board, there has been continuing criticism of the real value of their contribution to effective corporate governance. These criticisms have suggested that:

> Non-executive directors lack knowledge about the business of the company and their contribution is therefore constrained, not only by their own lack of capacity, but by the ability of executive management to withhold or manipulate information.

> Non-executive directors are unable or unwilling to devote sufficient time to the company's affairs, particularly because of the competing demands of other directorships.

> Non-executive directors are often reluctant to question and challenge management, whether because of the dominant position of the CEOs or because cross-directorships create a mutual interest in not 'rocking the boat'.

A further possible constraint on the effectiveness of non-executive directors was identified by Paul Myners in his 2001 review of institutional investment in the UK, which suggested that they were the 'missing link' in the chain of company accountability to shareholders. In Myners' view, although non-executive directors were supposed to represent shareholders' interests, the dominant position of executive directors meant that institutional shareholders had little opportunity to communicate their concerns to non-executives. A further discussion on the need for involvement of non-executive directors in discussions with institutional shareholders can be found in *Chapter 13*.

Doubts about the contribution of non-executive directors have been reinforced by the failure of the board of Enron – which, like many US boards, was predominantly made up of outside directors – to intervene in the management decisions which led ultimately to the collapse of the company.

The Higgs Review of the role and effectiveness of non-executive directors was established by the UK government in direct response to the issues highlighted by Enron. The

Review's recommendations and the subsequent revision of the Combined Code in July 2003 have sought to strengthen the contribution of non-executive directors in the areas summarised below.

### Numerical balance of the board

The Higgs Review endorsed the principle of the unitary board, emphasising the need for the board to be of an appropriate size and to contain strong executive and non-executive representation. Reflecting the recommendations of the Review, the July 2003 Combined Code provides that:

> ❭ except for smaller companies (defined for this purpose as listed companies below the FTSE 350) at least half the board, excluding the chairman, should be made up of independent executive directors; while
> ❭ the boards of smaller companies should contain at least two independent non-executive directors.

### The role and responsibilities of individual non-executive directors

Identifying a need for more explicit guidance than previously available, the Higgs Review suggested that the role of the non-executive director should encompass four key areas:

> ❭ *Strategy:* non-executive directors should constructively challenge and contribute to the development of strategy.
> ❭ *Performance:* non-executive directors should scrutinise the performance of management in meeting agreed goals and objectives and monitor the reporting of performance.
> ❭ *Risk:* non-executive directors should satisfy themselves that financial information is accurate and that financial controls and systems of risk management are robust and defensible.
> ❭ *People:* non-executive directors are responsible for determining appropriate levels of remuneration of executive directors and have a prime role in appointing, and where necessary removing, senior management and in succession planning.

The Higgs Review also offered guidance on the behaviours and personal attributes of the effective non-executive director, suggesting that in the course of their activities non-executives should:

> ❭ uphold the highest ethical standards of integrity and probity;
> ❭ support executives in their leadership of the business while monitoring their conduct;
> ❭ question intelligently, debate constructively, challenge rigorously and decide dispassionately;
> ❭ listen sensitively to the views of others, inside and outside the board;
> ❭ gain the trust and respect of other board members;
> ❭ promote the highest standards of corporate governance and seek compliance with the provisions of the Combined Code wherever possible.

The recommendations of the Higgs Review are reflected in the July 2003 Combined Code, Supporting Principle A.1 of which states that:

'As part of their role as members of a unitary board, non-executive directors should constructively challenge and help develop proposals on strategy. Non-executive directors should scrutinise the performance of management in meeting agreed goals and objectives and monitor the reporting of performance. They should satisfy themselves on the integrity of financial information and that financial controls and systems of risk management are robust and defensible. They are responsible for determining appropriate levels of remuneration of executive directors and have a prime role in appointing, and where necessary removing, executive directors, and in succession planning.'

The Combined Code also emphasises the need for non-executive directors to be pro-active in the exercise of their responsibilities, stating that:

> where they have concerns which cannot be resolved about the running of the company or a proposed action, they should ensure that their concerns are recorded in the board minutes; and
> on resignation, a non-executive director should provide a written statement to the chairman, for circulation to the board, if they have any such concerns.

### Non-executive directors as a distinct contingent on the board

Among the more contentious of the Higgs Review's proposals is that the non-executive directors should represent a distinct contingent of the board.

Noting the recently introduced requirement, under the listing rules of the New York Stock Exchange, for the independent directors of US listed corporations to meet regularly at scheduled sessions without management present, the Review suggested that this could help to increase the effectiveness of non-executive directors by allowing more organised discussion of issues of governance and performance in areas such as the provision of information or succession planning. Such discussions should be informal and should not replace other discussions between the board as a whole.

Reflecting Higgs' findings, Provision A.1.3 of the July 2003 Combined Code recommends that:

> the chairman should hold meetings with the non-executive directors without the executives present; and
> for the purpose of appraising the chairman's performance, the non-executive directors led by the senior independent director, should meet without the chairman present at least annually, and additionally as necessary.

### The senior independent director

The role of senior independent director highlighted in the Higgs Review and July 2003 Combined Code originated in the recommendation of the Cadbury Code in 1991 that, where the posts of chairman and CEO were combined, there should be a strong and independent element on the board, with a recognised senior member. This recommendation was taken further in the 1998 Combined Code, which recommended that, whether or not the posts of chairman and CEO were combined, the non-executive element on the board should have a recognised senior member other than the chairman. A particular function envisaged for the senior independent director is to provide a channel of communication for shareholders who have concerns about the company's performance or proposed developments, but who have been unable to resolve these in discussion with the chairman or the CEO.

As the Higgs Review acknowledged, the need for a senior non-executive director has not hitherto been accepted by all listed companies, some of which have suggested that the role may be both unnecessary and divisive given the ability of shareholders to raise concerns with any of the non-executive directors, including the chairmen of board committees. Despite these concerns, the July 2003 Combined Code has adopted the proposals set out in the Review and recommends that:

> the board should appoint one of the independent non-executive directors to be the senior independent director (Provision A.3.3);
> the senior independent director should be available to shareholders if they have concerns which contact through the normal channels of chairman, chief executive or finance director has failed to resolve or for which such contact is inappropriate (Provision A.3.3);
> the senior independent director should lead meetings of the non-executive directors which it is inappropriate for the chairman to attend (Provision A.1.3);
> the senior independent director, together with the chairman, the deputy chairman (where there is one), the chief executive, and the chairmen and members of the nomination, audit and remuneration committees, should be identified in the annual report (Provision A.1.2).

## The concept of independence

As explained in the introduction to this chapter, the collective nature of the unitary board means that all directors, whether executive or non-executive, have responsibility for management oversight. Thus, the task of monitoring management conduct and performance is not restricted to the non-executive directors, but applies equally to the CEO and other executive directors, despite their direct involvement and responsibility as managers.

For this reason, the 1998 Combined Code emphasised that all directors, without exception, should bring an independent judgement to bear on issues of strategy, performance, resources (including key appointments) and standards of conduct. The point is reinforced in the Higgs Review, which draws attention to the need for all directors, whether executive or non-executive, to be 'independent of mind and willing and able to challenge, question and speak up'.

It is now broadly accepted, however, that for the purposes of corporate governance, at least a proportion of non-executive directors need to be independent in a stricter technical sense, in particular to ensure that they are free of potential conflicts of interest over issues such as remuneration, appointment and audit. This principle was established in the UK by the Cadbury Code and has been widely adopted elsewhere in post-Enron corporate governance reforms.

The requirement for a strong independent element on the board does not constitute a prohibition on the appointment as non-executive directors of individuals who have a recent or existing connection with the company. Indeed, it is recognised that such individuals, who may include former executive directors, representatives of major shareholders and senior external advisers to the company, may contribute skills and expertise of great value in the board's decision-making. However, there is general acceptance that such individuals may be less willing to question the views of the company's executive management and cannot therefore be regarded as truly independent.

## The definition of independence

The standard of strict technical independence considered necessary for at least a proportion of non-executive directors on the board has evolved over time. Both the Cadbury Code and the 1998 version of the Combined Code stated that '*the majority non-executive directors should be independent of management and free from any business or other relationship which could materially interfere with the exercise of their independent judgement*', leaving it to the discretion of the board to determine which of its members met this test.

The Higgs Review expressed concern that, in the absence of definitive guidance, both boards and shareholders were uncertain as to what the test of independence should entail. As a result, institutional investors and their representatives had developed their own, mutually inconsistent, definitions for use in determining their voting intentions: according to the Review, by 2002 there were over a dozen such definitions in the UK, all with different criteria. It therefore recommended that a new, definitive test of independence should be adopted, emphasising that this should address not only those relationships or circumstances that would impair a non-executive director's objectivity, but also those that could appear to an outside observer to do so.

According to the Higgs Review, a non-executive director can be regarded as independent in a technical sense only if there are no relationships or circumstances which could affect, or appear to affect, his or her judgement. The more stringent definition of independence proposed by Higgs has been adopted in the July 2003 Combined Code, Provision A.3.1 of which states that the board of a listed company should:

> identify in the annual report each non-executive director it considers to be independent;
> for this purpose, determine whether the director is independent in character and judgement and whether there are relationships or circumstances which are likely to affect, or could appear to affect, the director's judgement; and
> state its reasons if it determines that a particular director is independent notwithstanding the existence of relationships or circumstances which may appear relevant to its determination, including if the director:
> – has been an employee of the company or group within the last five years;
> – has, or has had within the last three years, a material business relationship with the company either directly, or as a partner, shareholder, director or senior employee of a body that has such a relationship with the company;

- has received or receives additional remuneration from the company apart from a director's fee, participates in the company's share option or a performance-related pay scheme, or is a member of the company's pension scheme;
- has close family ties with any of the company's advisers, directors or senior employees;
- holds cross-directorships or has significant links with other directors through involvement in other companies or bodies;
- represents a significant shareholder; or
- has served on the board for more than nine years from the date of their first election.

## Directors and their risk exposure

All directors, whether executive or non-executive, are exposed to litigation and other personal risks and liabilities as a consequence of their duties as directors. These risks arise from two principal sources: directors may be exposed to personal financial liabilities and other sanctions under statutory and other legal provisions, and may also incur reputational harm as a result of their association with a discredited company. While the Higgs Review has suggested that these risks are of particular relevance to the position of non-executive directors, they apply equally to all directors.

### Legal risks and their mitigation

*Statutory provisions*

The Companies Act identifies more than 200 offences for which directors may be punished on conviction, including failure to keep proper accounting records and making loans on uncommercial terms to an associated company. The directors and officers of a company may also face claims arising from areas such as employment law, health and safety, takeovers and mergers, misrepresentation, liability under the Environmental Protection Act 1990 and the Financial Services and Markets Act 2000.

In addition, the Company Directors Disqualification Act 1986 and insolvency legislation provide for the disqualification and personal liability of directors who have permitted a company to continue to trade when they were, or should have been, aware that it had gone (or would soon go) into insolvent liquidation and thus negligently failed to act to minimise potential losses to creditors. Directors may also be convicted of the more serious criminal offence of fraudulent trading if it can be shown that they allowed the company to continue trading when insolvent, with the intent of defrauding creditors or for some other fraudulent purpose.

### Breach of directors' duties

All directors owe a duty to the company to act in its best interests, to avoid conflicts between their own personal interests and those of the company and to carry out their duties with care, skill and diligence. In consequence, all directors, whether executive or non-executive, are potentially exposed to claims for damages in respect of:

> *Breach of fiduciary duties*: directors may be held personally liable for breach of fiduciary duties and may be sued by the company for recovery of benefits wrongly obtained from such breaches.

> *Breach of duties of care and skill*: claims for damages may be brought, usually by the company, against directors who are considered to have breached their duties of care and skill. Traditionally, a director's actions have been judged by reference to a subjective standard – that is, the particular director's actual knowledge and experience – such that a non-executive director would be less likely to be held personally liable for error because of his or her lack of direct involvement in the management of the business. However, it is expected that the courts will increasingly impose an objective standard, whereby a director's actions are judged by the standard of care and skill to be expected of a reasonably competent director.

Although companies are permitted by company law to insure their directors against actions by the company or by third parties and to indemnify directors in respect of third party claims where the directors are not in breach of duty or obligation to the company, these measures do not (and arguably should not) represent a complete mitigation of the personal risks faced by directors. In particular, section 310 of CA 1985 invalidates any provision exempting any director, officer or auditor from, or indemnifying them against, any liability for negligence, default, breach of duty or breach of trust in relation to the company. Further, it provides that a commitment made by the company in advance to indemnify a director against his or her legal costs will be invalid unless it is made contingent upon a successful defence by the director: as a result, directors might not be covered to the full extent of their potential liabilities and might also be required to meet their own legal expenses.

Concern was expressed by the Higgs Review that, as result of the increasing scope and likelihood of litigation, the perceived risks associated with being a director were growing and that this might deter potential candidates from coming forward, especially for non-executive appointments. In line with the Review's recommendations, the July 2003 Combined Code recommends that companies arrange appropriate insurance cover in respect of legal action against their directors.

At the request of the Higgs Review, guidance on directors' and officers' insurance has been prepared by the ICSA in collaboration with the City of London Law Society, the Association of British Insurers and the British Insurance Brokers Association. The resulting Guidance Note on Directors' and Officers' Insurance was published by the ICSA in October 2003 and is reproduced in full as *Appendix 7*.

In its consultative document, *Director and Audit Liability* (December 2003), the DTI invited comments on whether further steps are needed to define the position in civil law on the liabilities and indemnification of directors, to ensure that qualified candidates are not deterred by uncertainty. See www.dti.gov.uk/cld/condocs.htm.

## Reputational risk and due diligence

In addition to their potential exposure to financial liabilities and other legal sanctions, all directors encounter reputational risks arising from their association with the company. These risks are likely to be particularly acute for new directors, whether executive or non-executive, who are recruited from outside the company on the basis of their past achievements. Such individuals will have established reputations for their business ability, sound judgement and personal probity and will want to preserve their reputational assets, both as matter of personal pride and as the basis on which they hope to advance their careers.

The Higgs Review urged that, prior to appointment, potential new non-executive directors should carry out due diligence on the board and the company to satisfy themselves that they have the knowledge, skills, experience and time to make a positive contribution to the board.

At the request of the Review, guidance has been prepared by the ICSA on the due diligence process to be undertaken by prospective directors before joining a company. The due diligence process is equally relevant to new executive and non-executive directors, given that their reputations and future career prospects are equally likely to be impaired if the company runs into financial difficulties or engages in illegal or unethical behaviour.

Guidance on the due diligence process to be undertaken by prospective directors before joining a company is provided in the ICSA's Guidance Note on Due Diligence for Directors, the full text of which is given in *Appendix 6*.

## Chapter summary

> Although there is no distinction in law between directors, there is an increasing focus for corporate governance purposes on the composition and balance of the board, involving a growing differentiation between the roles and contributions of executive and non-executive directors.

> This is reflected in the strengthening presumption that the posts of chairman and CEO should not be held by the same individual and in new Combined Code recommendations relating to the role, independence and method of appointment of the chairman.

> In addition, recent corporate failures have led to close scrutiny of the role and effectiveness of non-executive directors, leading to a more stringent definition of independence and a firm recommendation that the boards of listed companies should appoint one of their independent non-executive directors to be the senior independent director.

> Recent corporate failures have increased the perceived risks associated with being a director, leading to renewed emphasis on the need for both companies and individuals to satisfy themselves that prospective new directors have the knowledge, skills, experience and time to make a positive contribution to the board.

# 7

# Board Effectiveness

> The board should be supplied in a timely manner with information in a form and of a quality appropriate to enable it to discharge its duties. All directors should receive induction on joining the board and should regularly update and refresh their skills and knowledge.
>
> Main Principle A.5 Information and professional development
>
> The board should undertake a formal and rigorous annual evaluation of its own performance and that of its committees and individual directors.
>
> Main Principle A.6 Performance evaluation

This chapter explores company and individual responsibilities for the induction of new directors and the professional development of directors in service. The operation of the board, including the roles of the chairman and the company secretary in ensuring the effectiveness of its decision-making processes, is also examined, together with the emerging expectation that boards and individual directors should undertake regular, formal evaluation of their own performance and the evolution of techniques and processes for that purpose.

The ability of the board to lead and control the company in the interests of shareholders is critically dependent on the quality of its decision-making. This in turn is determined by the skills and capacities of individual directors, by the existence of an open and constructive boardroom culture and by the availability to the board of accurate, timely and meaningful information.

While these factors have long been recognised, the traditional assumption has been that the board collectively, and directors individually, are merely the recipients and consumers of information and that responsibility for ensuring that the board is well informed lies primarily with the company's management.

Recent corporate failures demonstrate that this assumption is no longer tenable. The increased technological complexity and geographical dispersal of business activity mean that serious problems may materialise very quickly and that boards cannot rely passively on information provided by management (who may have their own reasons for preferring not to draw the board's attention to potential problems). Given the potential legal and reputational risks involved, directors cannot afford to adopt a passive attitude to information, but must instead be ready to define their information requirements and to ask searching and, if necessary, repeated questions.

Current developments in corporate governance in the UK are designed to increase board effectiveness through an increased emphasis on the need for directors, individually and collectively, to take responsibility for their own professional development and ability to contribute to the work of the board. In addition, there is a growing recognition of the board's obligation regularly and objectively to re-evaluate the mix of skills and experience it needs and to change its membership in an orderly manner over time.

## Directors' induction and professional development

### The induction of new directors

Newly appointed directors need to familiarise themselves quickly with the company's activities so that the skills and experience for which they have been appointed can be used for the benefit of the company and its shareholders. The need for a proper induction process for this purpose has long been recognised: the Cadbury Report made clear in 1992 that newly appointed board members are entitled to expect proper induction into the company's affairs.

Despite this recognition, research carried out in 2002 for the Higgs Review found that half of all newly appointed chairmen, and nearly one-fifth of newly appointed non-executive directors, received no induction at all for their roles, while less than a quarter of non-executive directors received formal briefing or induction after appointment. In many cases, it is left to new non-executive directors to take the initiative in seeking an induction programme and to ask the right questions in order to receive the information they need.

Commenting that the current position is not acceptable, the Higgs Review concluded that companies must set aside adequate resources and ensure that sufficient time is available for a thorough induction for new directors. It recommended that the chairman should take the lead in providing a properly constructed induction programme, which should be facilitated by the company secretary.

The Higgs Review suggested that induction programmes should consist of a combination of written briefing material, together with presentations and activities such as meetings and site visits, and should be designed to develop the new director's understanding in the following main areas:

> the company's business and the markets in which it operates, including its products and services; its principal assets, liabilities and significant contracts; major competitors; significant risks and risk management strategy; key performance indicators; and regulatory constraints;

> the culture of the company and the board, including the company's constitution; board procedures and matters reserved for the board; the behaviours needed for effective board performance; and, for foreign directors, the working of the UK unitary board;

> the company's people, including fellow directors, the senior management team and employees, through visits to company locations, attending company events and other informal contacts; and

> the company's external relationships with, for example, its auditors; major customers; major suppliers; and principal shareholders.

At the request of the Higgs Review, the ICSA has developed a checklist of written material that should be considered for inclusion in an induction pack to be provided to all new directors. The full text of the ICSA Guidance Note on the Induction of Directors can be found at *Appendix 7*.

## Professional development of existing directors

The Higgs Review found that few directors currently receive any structured training or development: two-thirds of non-executive directors and chairmen received no formal training beyond the experience acquired through their involvement in the company's business and participation in board discussions. Questioning whether this experience alone was sufficient to ensure the effectiveness of the board, Higgs called on companies to provide the resources needed to develop and update the knowledge and skills of their directors. To this end, the chairman should address the development needs of the board as a whole, and should also take the lead in identifying the development needs of individual directors, with the company secretary playing a key role in facilitating provision.

The Higgs Review acknowledged, however, that there are significant barriers to the effective professional development of directors. In particular:

> existing directors may be encouraged by an entrenched boardroom culture to assume – not necessarily correctly – that they already have all the skills and knowledge needed to carry out their role, and they may therefore be unable or unwilling to recognise their own development needs; while

> externally available training programmes for directors may not be suited to the needs of boards and individual directors, as reflected in the relatively low take-up of the Chartered Director qualification and other training offered by business schools and similar providers.

To overcome these barriers, professional development for existing directors needs to be tailored closely to company and individual requirements, with an emphasis on practical lessons drawn from real events and situations rather than formal lectures and presentations.

Company-specific needs are likely to include updating and expanding the knowledge of directors in strategic areas, including technological developments, new and potential markets and changes in the company's legal and regulatory environment. Individual development needs may include personal behaviours and competencies, such as influencing and negotiating skills, conflict resolution, chairing skills and board dynamics.

In addition, non-executive directors may have specific needs for technical education and development to enable them to evaluate the strategic proposals brought forward by the executive management team and to fulfil their roles as members of the audit, remuneration or nomination committees. For these purposes, development may be needed in areas such as, for example, risk management, the company's treasury policies, including its use of new and complex financial instruments, recruitment and evaluation methodologies and developments in the design of performance incentives.

In the light of concerns identified by the Higgs Review about the limited range of development opportunities available for directors, a task force of business leaders chaired by Laura D'Andrea Tyson, Dean of London Business School, has examined the external provision of training programmes. In its report, published in June 2003, the task force noted that the following types of training were available externally:

> introductory seminars and courses offered by bodies such as the Institute of Directors (IoD), the Confederation of British Industry (CBI), business schools and consultancies, alone or in partnership;
> general training on board effectiveness and specific training in areas such as financial accounting delivered via open enrolment courses by business schools and consultancies independently or in conjunction with entities such as the IoD and the CBI; and
> customised training and evaluation programmes developed for specific companies by business schools or consultancies in consultation with senior company management.

Despite the variety of ways in which board training is currently available, the Tyson Report identified a continuing mismatch between the programmes available and the needs of companies and individual directors. It therefore recommended that a group of training providers and companies should be convened by the Financial Reporting Council or the London Stock Exchange to establish guidelines for practical board training programmes for directors and to collect and provide information about available programmes.

## The operation of the board

However well qualified for their roles, individual directors can only make an effective contribution to the leadership of the company in the context of a well-organised and supportive board culture. Key considerations include:

> the size of the board and the frequency and duration of its meetings;
> the clarity of the board's role and the quality and timeliness of the information provided by management to support the board's decision-making;
> the conduct of board meetings and the extent to which full and open discussion is promoted; and
> the contributions of the chairman and the company secretary.

### The size of the board

Research carried out in 2002 for the Higgs Review found that the average size of the board of a UK listed company was seven, typically comprising three executive directors, three non-executive directors and a chairman. A FTSE 100 board was generally bigger, with an average of 12 members, of whom six were non-executive directors, five executive directors and one the chairman. Nearly half FTSE 100 boards had 12 or more members.

While the July 2003 Combined Code cautions that the board should not be so large as to be unwieldy, there are indications that some smaller boards may need to increase in size in order to ensure that they can comply with corporate governance requirements on the balance and composition of the board and its committees. In particular, the Combined Code recommends that the audit and remuneration committees of smaller companies should consist of at least two independent non-executive directors, increasing to three for larger companies, and that all nomination committees should have a majority of independent non-executives. In combination with guidance from the ICSA that, to avoid potential conflict, there should be no overlap of membership between the remuneration and nomination committees, this would seem to imply a minimum requirement, even for smaller companies, of four non-executive directors.

There are suggestions also that the size of the board may affect the quality of its decision-making. In particular, excessively small boards may lack diversity in terms of skills, experience, education, attitudes and background and may therefore be less well equipped than a larger board to control and direct the company in the interests of shareholders.

## The frequency of board meetings

The July 2003 Combined Code gives no specific recommendation on the frequency of board meetings, stating only that the board should meet sufficiently regularly to discharge its duties effectively. The frequency of meetings of the full board will therefore depend on the internal and external circumstances of the business and on any specific issues the company needs to deal with at a given time. The typical pattern for listed company boards appears to be around eight meetings a year, often supplemented by strategy 'away days', with additional meetings as necessary at times of rapid change.

The July 2003 Combined Code does, however, place a new emphasis on the expectation that all directors will attend meetings and devote the time needed for proper debate. To enable shareholders to monitor the extent of directors' participation in the board's activities, Provision A.1.2 recommends that the annual report disclose the number of meetings of the board and its committees and individual attendance by directors.

## The duration of board meetings

The length of board meetings should be sufficient to enable directors give appropriate attention to the issues at hand, while still representing a sensible investment of the time of individual directors. While excessively long meetings devoted to routine business are clearly a waste of time, care is equally needed to ensure that important issues are not being missed or that discussions on potentially contentious matters are not being unduly curtailed.

# Planning board meetings

## Annual calendar

It was suggested in *Chapter 5* that the schedule of matters reserved for collective decision by directors effectively constitutes the board's 'job description' and will to a large extent determine the business of a cyclical nature which is to be transacted by the board at its meetings. Such business will clearly vary from company to company, but is likely to include:

> approval of, for example, the annual report and accounts and other financial statements, proposed dividends, the calling of the AGM and the despatch of notices and other documentation to shareholders;

> consideration of periodic reports from board committees, the CEO and executive management and business units; and

> consideration of the company's business plan, annual operating and capital expenditure budgets and review of the effectiveness of its internal control and risk management arrangements.

To assist in the planning of meetings and help maximise the attendance of individual directors, it is generally desirable for the chairman, assisted by the company secretary, to draw up an annual calendar of meetings, with an outline of the cyclical business to be considered at each meeting, and to present this for advance agreement by the full board.

## The quality and timeliness of information

As a matter of principle, all directors should receive the same information at the same time and should be given sufficient time in which to consider such information.

In most companies, normal practice is to assemble and circulate the following documents to directors a week to ten days before each board meeting:

> an agenda listing the items to be covered during the meeting, with cross references to the relevant board papers;

> the minutes of the previous meeting, together with the minutes or action notes of board committees (including any executive committee) which have taken place since the last board meeting; and

> papers relating to agenda items, including regular financial and other business reports and specific proposals for board approval: where appropriate, these should specify the wording of any formal resolution which the board is being asked to approve.

In addition, advance copies of the company's annual report and accounts and any other significant external publications would usually be sent to all directors as soon as available, even if not intended for discussion at a scheduled board meeting.

In practice, the preparation of the agenda for board meetings and the collation and circulation of papers are generally the responsibility of the company secretary, subject

### The well-informed board

The board as a whole should be proactive in determining what information it needs to do its job, how often it wants this information and in what form. It should provide regular feedback to the chairman and company secretary on the following questions:

- Is information communicated to the board as concisely as it should be?
- Is it clear why information presented to the board is important?
- Could information be more clearly presented – for example, graphically rather than in words?
- Is it generally clear how information presented to the board relates to goals set by the board, past performance, or comparative data?
- Is information presented in a timely manner relative to the board's current agenda?

- Does the information help the board or board committee discharge its responsibilities?
- Is the information the best available indicator of the situation or condition being described? Could better information be provided?
- Is a correct balance being achieved between monitoring information, decision information and general background intelligence? Would the board prefer to receive more or less of any category of information?

Given regular and appropriate feedback by the board, the chairman and the company secretary can establish the content, format and frequency of information required by the board and brief the senior management team accordingly.

to the approval of the chairman. As in the case of the schedule of matters reserved for the collective decision of directors, however, it is essential that the board should 'own' its agenda and be actively involved in and responsible for defining and controlling its own role and information requirements.

## The conduct of board meetings

### Board meeting management and procedures

The board should establish written procedures for the formal conduct of its business and should ensure that a copy is given to each director. These should include:

- ❭ the role, functions and powers of the chairman and arrangements for the nomination of a person to preside over board meetings if the chairman is not present;
- ❭ the quorum of the board and board committees and the consequences of lack of an adequate quorum;
- ❭ arrangements for the disclosure and recording of individual directors' interests in items proposed for discussion;
- ❭ the general order of business for board meetings, including the recording of apologies for absence; confirmation and approval of the minutes of the last

meeting; any matters arising or deferred from previous minutes; receipt and consideration of reports from the CEO and board committees; and consideration of matters requiring the express approval of the board;

> the procedure for consideration of business without notice; and
> the rules of debate and procedures for voting on formal resolutions of the board.

Further guidance on the conduct of board meetings is given in the ICSA Code of Good Boardroom Practice, the full text of which is set out in *Appendix 9*.

While it is clearly essential that the business of the board should be conducted and recorded with an appropriate degree of formality, it is equally important for the effectiveness of the board that open and constructive dialogue should be facilitated in an environment of trust and mutual respect.

The central challenge for effective governance is to ensure that the full range of opinions represented by the directors individually are brought out, discussed and resolved into a single position which can command the collective support of the board. To enable this to be achieved, all directors, including new or inexperienced directors, must be able to express divergent views.

Once a clear policy position has been reached, it is the duty of the board to ensure that it is clearly stated: vagueness in this area will merely lead to uncertainty and hence to waste of the company's resources. Further, there must be agreement from the outset that any position arising from a fair and open process represents the collective position of the board: individual directors who continue to disagree must uphold any collective position which has been reached correctly and must not seek to undermine it.

## The role of the chairman

As pointed out by the Higgs Review, the chairman has a pivotal role in creating the conditions in which the board collectively and directors individually can perform effectively. In addition to the strategic role outlined in the previous chapter, the chairman is accountable to the board for the management of its business and must therefore ensure that:

> the board's agenda takes full account of the issues and concerns of all directors and focuses on strategic issues;
> sufficient time is available for the consideration of complex or contentious issues;
> all directors have the necessary time and information to consider critical issues and are not faced with unrealistic deadlines for decision-making; and
> where appropriate, informal discussions are held before the meetings of the full board to facilitate thorough preparation for the board discussion.

## The role of the company secretary

The company secretary should be accountable to the board as a whole, through the chairman, for the proper administration of the meetings of the board and its committees. To carry out this responsibility, the company secretary should be entitled to be present, or represented, at all such meetings and should be responsible for preparing, or arranging for the preparation of, the minutes of the meetings. In addition to ensuring that the board's deliberations and decisions reached are correctly recorded in the minutes, the company secretary has a key responsibility for ensuring that actions placed by the board are communicated to the appropriate responsible officers and carried out on a timely basis.

The Higgs Review emphasises the need for the company secretary to be independent in order to provide impartial information and guidance on board procedures, legal requirements and corporate governance, together with best practice developments. The company secretary should also support the chairman in assessing the information required by the board and in facilitating the induction of new directors and the professional development of existing directors.

In addition to these responsibilities, the ICSA considers that the company secretary has a distinctive role in relation to corporate governance and wider issues of accountability and corporate social responsibility, as described in the specimen job description.

## Board performance evaluation

### The need for board performance evaluation

As described above, the July 2003 Combined Code places heightened emphasis on the induction and professional development of directors and the effectiveness of the board as a whole. In addition, it introduces for the first time a formal expectation that the boards of UK listed companies will undertake regular evaluation of their own performance and, where necessary, will act on the results by changing their membership.

As noted by the ICSA in its pamphlet *Board performance evaluation*, it is now extremely rare for organisations not to review periodically the performance of their key contributors, whether individual employees, work teams, business units or senior managers. Moreover, well-publicised increases in executive remuneration have reinforced shareholder and wider public expectations that rewards will be linked to measurable performance. Research carried out for the Higgs Review indicated, however, that more than one-third of boards never formally evaluate their own performance, while over three-quarters of non-executive directors and over half of chairmen never have a formal personal performance review.

The Higgs Review concluded that listed company boards could benefit significantly from formal performance evaluation, encompassing both individual and collective board performance, including committees. Review of individual performance could assist directors in identifying and addressing their own development needs. Additionally, it would enable the chairman to identify problems and take appropriate action, if necessary by seeking the resignation of under-performing directors and proposing new appointments to the board. At the same time, appraisal of the collective performance of the board would facilitate the chairman's management and development of the board by helping to identify and address its strengths and weaknesses.

## ICSA GUIDANCE NOTE: SPECIMEN JOB DESCRIPTION FOR THE CORPORATE GOVERNANCE ROLE OF THE COMPANY SECRETARY

- Ensuring the smooth running of the board's and board committees' activities by helping the chairman to set agendas, preparing papers and presenting papers to the board and board committees, advising on board procedures and ensuring the board follows them.
- Keeping under close review all legislative, regulatory and corporate governance developments that might affect the company's operations, and ensuring the board is fully briefed on these and that it has regard to them when taking decisions.
- Ensuring that the concept of stakeholders (particularly employees – see section 309 Companies Act 1985) is in the board's mind when important business decisions are being taken. Keeping in touch with the debate on corporate social responsibility and stakeholders, and monitoring all developments in this area and advising the board in relation to its policy and practices with regard to corporate social responsibility and its reporting on that matter.

- To act as a confidential sounding board to the chairman, non-executive directors and executive directors on points that may concern them, and to take a lead role in managing difficult inter-personal issues on the board, e.g. the exit of the directors from the business.
- To act as a primary point of contact and source of advice and guidance for, particularly, non-executive directors as regards the company and its activities in order to support the decision making process.
- To act as an additional enquiring voice in relation to board decisions which particularly affect the company, drawing on his/her experience and knowledge of the practical aspects of management including law, tax and business finance. To act as the 'conscience of the company'.
- To ensure, where applicable, that the standards and/or disclosures required by the Combined Code annexed to the UK Listing Rules are observed and, where required, reflected in the annual report of the

In line with the Higgs Review's conclusions, the July 2003 Combined Code recommends that there should be a formal and rigorous annual evaluation of the performance of the board and its committees and of individual directors and that:

> The aim of the individual evaluation process should be to show whether each director continues to contribute effectively and to demonstrate commitment to the role (including commitment of time for board and committee meetings and any other duties).
> The chairman should lead the evaluation process and should act on its results by recognising the strengths and addressing the weaknesses of the board and, where appropriate, proposing new members be appointed to the board or seeking the resignation of directors.
> The chairman's own performance should be evaluated by the non-executive directors, led by the senior independent director, and should take into account the views of the executive directors.

directors – the secretary usually takes the lead role in drafting the annual report, including the remuneration disclosures and agreeing these with the board and board committee.

- Compliance with the continuing obligations of the Listing Rules, e.g. ensuring publication and dissemination of the report and accounts and interim reports within the periods laid down in the Listing Rules; dissemination of regulatory news announcements such as trading statements to the market; ensuring that proper notification is made of directors' dealings and the acquisition of interests in the company's incentive arrangements.
- Managing relations with investors, particularly institutional investors, with regard to corporate governance issues and the board's practices in relation to corporate governance.
- To induct new directors into the business and their roles and responsibilities;
- As regards offences under the Financial Services and Markets Act (e.g. s. 395), ensuring that the board is fully aware of its responsibility to ensure that it does not mislead the market by putting out or allowing the release of misleading information about its financial performance or trading condition, or by omitting to state information which it should state, or by engaging in a course of conduct which could amount to misleading the market.
- Ensuring compliance with all statutory filings, e.g. Forms 288, 88(2), annual returns, filing of resolutions adopted at annual general meetings/new Articles of Association and any other filings required to be made with Companies House.
- Making arrangements for and managing the whole process of the annual general meeting and establishing, with the board's agreement, the items to be considered at the AGM, including resolutions dealing with governance type matters, eg the vote on the remuneration report and votes on special incentive schemes involving directors. Information about proxy votes, etc.

> ❯ The board should disclose in the annual report how the performance evaluation of the board, its committees and its individual directors has been conducted.

## Introducing a board performance evaluation process

The Higgs Review acknowledges that the concept of formal board evaluation is relatively new and that methodologies are still evolving. While this is certainly the case, boards and individual directors may also be reluctant for internal reasons to reflect on their own performance. Thus, the underlying culture of the board may make it difficult for directors to challenge each other, while senior individuals may be sensitive about having their personal capabilities and contributions evaluated.

In view of these methodological and cultural barriers, is seems likely that, where regular board performance evaluation does not already take place, it may need to be introduced gradually – perhaps over two to three years – to ensure that the purpose of the evaluation is understood and accepted and that all directors have confidence in the objectivity of the process.

Each company will need to develop its own board performance evaluation process, taking into account the nature of its business, the concerns of its shareholders and other stakeholders and the current composition of its board. However, the following generic considerations are likely to be relevant in most cases.

### Phased introduction

Where the performance evaluation process needs to be introduced in phases, the first phase should focus on high-level, impersonal review of the collective performance and effectiveness of the board, with attention turning to the performance of individual directors only when confidence has been established in the process. Successive stages might involve:

1  Review of the functioning of the board: at least once a year, the board as a whole should evaluate, for itself and its principal committees, whether the necessary frameworks are in place to support effective decision-making. This should focus on the key elements of the board and committee functions, including:
    a) the structure, development and operation of the board and its committees;
    b) timeliness and quality of information provided by the management team and any improvements required; and
    c) review of the principal decisions taken in the past year: did the discussion at the time address the main issues? were the relevant risks identified? were decisions followed up appropriately?

2  Review of the chairman's performance as the manager and facilitator of the board's business, including:
    a) the relevance of board agendas to the concerns of directors and the strategic issues facing the company;
    b) the running of meetings to ensure informed level of debate with sufficient time for the consideration of complex or contentious issues; and
    c) the chairman's management of board change and the induction and professional development of directors.

3  Review of the performance of individual directors, including each director's:
    a) attendance at and quality of contributions to board discussions;
    b) acceptance of collective responsibility and boardroom confidentiality; relationships with other directors, senior managers and employees and shareholders; and
    c) understanding and promotion of high standards of independence and ethical judgement.

### Methodologies

To ensure that evaluations are carried out on an objective basis and produce transparent and comparable information, it is generally recommended that consistent checklists are used as a basis for self-evaluation and to provide a framework for wider discussion.

A model framework for board and individual director performance evaluation has been developed by the Commonwealth Association for Corporate Governance and can be found at *Appendix 10.*

*Confidentiality*

To enable the evaluation process to be carried out in a way that is supportive of the board, it must be seen to be objective and fair. As far as possible, directors should be assured that any opinions they give about their own or other directors' performance will be received on a confidential basis. Consistent with this, the summarised results of board evaluation as a whole should be shared with the board, but the results of individual assessments should remain confidential between the chairman and the individual director concerned.

*External facilitation*

It is widely recognised that the use of an external third party can help to ensure the objectivity of the evaluation process, and in particular to the review of the chairman's performance.

Experience from the US suggests, however, that consultants with existing client and interpersonal relationships with the board should not be asked to facilitate the evaluation process. Specialist evaluation services are available in the UK from the ICSA, the Institute of Directors and a small number of commercial providers.

## Chapter summary

> Recent corporate failures have led investors, regulators and the general public to question the effectiveness of company boards, focusing on both the quality of collective decision-making and the competence, skills and capacities of individual directors.

> The response of corporate governance has been to emphasise a need for better induction of new directors and for more focused attention to be paid to the professional development of directors already in service, who may assume – not necessarily correctly – that they have all the skills and knowledge needed to carry out their role.

> There is also increased recognition of the need for a well-organised, open and supportive board culture, including the timely availability of high-quality information, to enable individual directors to make an effective contribution to the leadership of the company.

> At the same time, there is emphasis on the responsibilities of directors themselves undertake regular, formal and objective evaluation of their own performance and on the obligation of the board as a whole to re-evaluate the mix of skills and experience it needs and to change its membership in an orderly manner over time.

# 8

# The Appointment of Directors

❝ There should be a formal, rigorous and transparent procedure for the appointment of new directors to the board.

Main Principle A.4 Appointments to the Board ❞

❝ All directors should be submitted for re-election at regular intervals, subject to continued satisfactory performance. The board should ensure planned and progressive refreshing of the board.

Main Principle A.7 Re-election ❞

This chapter examines:

> the extent of shareholders' influence over the appointment, reappointment and removal of directors, as reflected in the powers of the general meeting;
> the evolving role and responsibilities of the nomination committee, as reflected in the successive codes of corporate governance from Cadbury to the July 2003 Combined Code; and
> the strategic and qualitative issues identified by the Higgs Review in relation to succession planning, the terms of directors' appointments and the diversity of the board.

According to the report of the Cadbury Committee (1992):

*'The formal relationship between the shareholders and the board of directors is that the shareholders elect the directors, the directors report on their stewardship to the shareholders and the shareholders appoint the auditors to provide an external check on the directors' financial statements. Thus, the shareholders as owners of the company elect the directors to run the business on their behalf and hold them accountable for its progress. The issue for corporate governance is how to strengthen the accountability of boards of directors to shareholders.'*

In principle, then, the directors as the managers of the company are the agents of its owners and can be appointed, reappointed or dismissed by them at any time. In widely owned companies, however, there are practical limitations on the scope for shareholder involvement in matters relating to the appointment and removal of directors: in consequence, the powers of appointment and removal vested in the general meeting are essentially symbolic. This is not to say that these powers are without value in corporate governance terms. On the contrary, they serve to remind directors who appoint them and in whose interests they are required to manage the company's affairs, but they do not confer on shareholders the right to be directly involved in decisions affecting the composition and quality of the board.

In reality, the selection and appointment of new directors are determined by the existing board, without reference to the generality of shareholders. As a result, there is increasing concern that, in many cases, the chairman and/or the CEO exercise undue influence over the system of board nomination and appointments, reducing its objectivity and independence. Other criticisms suggest that many boards are self-perpetuating, limiting their recruitment searches to individuals of similar outlook and experience and thus protecting themselves from unwelcome challenge; and that the resulting tendency for individuals to hold several directorships leads to an unhealthy concentration of influence and reduces the likelihood that individuals with multiple appointments are doing all of their jobs properly.

In response to these perceived problems, the traditional aim of corporate governance has been to ensure that the interests of shareholders are properly observed in the conduct of processes in which they have no direct involvement. Accordingly, successive codes of corporate governance have focused on increasing the transparency of the nomination and appointment processes. More recently, however, the deficiencies in board effectiveness revealed by Enron and other corporate failures have underlined the importance of longer-term strategic and qualitative issues in the selection and appointment of directors. Thus, the Higgs Review emphasises the need to ensure that the selection and appointment of directors is regarded as a continuous process, to be carried out objectively and with close attention to the independence and effectiveness of the board as a whole.

## Shareholders' powers

### Statutory provisions

Company law provides shareholders with limited and uneven powers in respect of directors' appointments.

#### *Removal of a director*

Under CA 1985, shareholders who are dissatisfied with the performance of a director have the right to remove him or her from office by ordinary resolution in general meeting. Shareholders may requisition an appropriate resolution at a scheduled general meeting of shareholders, or they can requisition a general meeting for the specific purpose of considering the proposed removal, provided that they represent at least 5 per cent of the company's voting share capital. The ability of shareholders in general meeting to appoint and remove directors is discussed in *Chapter 14*.

While the board cannot refuse to call a general meeting which has been properly requisitioned for the purpose of removing a director, other board members may well be opposed to any attempt to remove one of their colleagues and are likely to recommend that shareholders vote against the resolution. Moreover, it is likely in these circumstances that the board will have the support of the company's institutional shareholders: where such shareholders are unhappy with the performance of a particular director, they are likely to raise their concerns privately rather than to support a general meeting resolution. For these reasons, an ordinary resolution to remove a director is unlikely to succeed, and in practice shareholder initiatives of this kind are very rare.

*Election and re-election*

Other than the provisions, described above, for the removal of a director, company law makes little formal provision for shareholder involvement. There are no formal statutory requirements for election or re-election of directors by the shareholders in general meeting, although the standard form of Articles set out in Table A to CA 1985 provides that, at each AGM:

> ❭ one-third of the directors who are subject to retirement by rotation should step down and submit themselves for re-election by the shareholders; and
> ❭ any director who has been appointed by the board since the company's last AGM should step down and submit him or herself for re-election.

## Corporate governance developments

While the Cadbury Report noted that it was in the shareholders' interests to see that the boards of companies were properly constituted and were not dominated by any one individual, it made no specific proposals to reinforce shareholders' powers of influence over the appointment of directors. Thus, the Hampel Committee on Corporate Governance found in 1998 that the uneven character of the statutory requirements on directors' appointments had led to widely divergent practices amongst UK listed companies. The principle that newly appointed directors should be re-elected by the shareholders at the next AGM had been incorporated into the Listing Rules and was therefore generally observed. However, not all companies complied with the principle of retirement by rotation. Even where Table A Articles had been adopted, some companies specifically exempted certain directors – usually the chairman and/or the CEO – from this requirement, thus enabling them to occupy entrenched positions until they chose (or were forced) to resign.

Hampel therefore proposed as a principle of good governance that all directors, without exception, should be required to submit themselves for re-election at regular intervals of no more than three years. This recommendation was incorporated into the 1998 version of the Combined Code, which provided that:

> ❭ new directors appointed by the board should retire at the annual general meeting following their appointment and seek re-election by the shareholders;
> ❭ all directors should submit themselves for re-election at the AGM at least every three years; and

> non-executive directors should be appointed for a specific term, subject to re-election, and their reappointment at the end of the period should not be automatic.

Hampel recommended in addition that those companies that did not already conform to the principle of retirement by rotation should make the necessary changes to their Articles as soon as possible and that, to enable shareholders to take an informed decision whether to support the re-election of directors, all names submitted for election or re-election as directors should be accompanied by biographical details indicating their relevant qualifications and experience. This is taken further in the July 2003 Combined Code, which emphasises that the re-election of directors retiring by rotation should not be automatic, but should be subject to continued satisfactory performance. Further, the Higgs Report recommended that, in order to ensure that shareholders have sufficient information on which to base their approval of appointments, the board should explain why they believe a proposed director should be appointed and how the individual concerned meets the requirements of their prospective role as a director.

Although the Combined Code provisions offer shareholders the theoretical opportunity to vote a director out of office, it would be very difficult in practice for dissatisfied shareholders to command a sufficient voting majority to remove a director at the AGM. However, the provisions may still serve a useful purpose, by enabling shareholders to signal their dissatisfaction to the board through a high level of combined votes against and abstentions on the proposed re-election of a particular director. Voting signals can be used to communicate concerns over the performance of the director concerned, or to express disagreement with an aspect of company policy with which the director is closely associated. A typical example is a high level of votes against the re-election of a non-executive director who, as chairman of the remuneration committee, is considered by shareholders to have presided over an unacceptably high level of executive pay and bonuses.

A problem here is that, because only one-third of the board retires at each AGM, shareholders may lack a timely opportunity to register dissatisfaction with a particular director, with the result that the intended message to the board is blurred or lost. This has led some observers, such as Pensions Investments Research Consultants (PIRC), to call for compulsory annual re-election of directors. This proposal was rejected by Higgs on the grounds that annual re-election of all directors could be potentially damaging to a company, encouraging the board to take an excessively short-term view or leaving a vacuum at the top of the company in the unlikely event that an entire board were voted out.

## The nomination committee

It is well established as a principle of corporate governance that power over appointments to the board should not rest exclusively with the chairman and/or the CEO, but should be a matter for the full board. Reflecting this principle, review committees from Cadbury onwards have recommended that the appointment process should be formal and transparent. In the absence of definitive guidance, however, there is still a measure of inconsistency and informality in the selection and appointment of new directors to the boards of listed companies.

One problem has been that successive codes of corporate governance have provided companies with a degree of latitude in the choice of arrangement for the selection and appointment of new directors. Thus, the Cadbury Code identified the establishment of nomination committees as best practice, but did not formally recommend that all listed companies should establish such committees. Similarly, the 1998 version of the Combined Code endorsed the use of nomination committees, but continued to accept that in some circumstances, particularly for smaller boards, it might be appropriate for the full board to be involved in the selection process.

Anecdotal evidence suggests that, in many companies where nomination committees have been established, the committee is convened only when necessary to fill a vacancy and as a result has no consistent role or membership. This is confirmed by the research carried out on behalf of the Higgs Review in 2002, which found that although almost all FTSE 100 companies had nomination committees, these were the least developed of all committees of the board in terms of defined role and responsibilities: nomination committees usually met irregularly and often had no clear understanding of the extent of their role in the appointment process. In some cases, directors who were not members of the nomination committee were present at committee discussions, effectively making the committee indistinguishable from the board as a whole.

Reflecting the findings of the Higgs Review, the July 2003 Combined Code makes clear that all listed companies should have a nomination committee. Further, it clarifies the required membership of such committees and provides more explicit guidance than was previously available on the committee's role and responsibilities.

## Membership of the nomination committee

The July 2003 Combined Code recommends that a majority of the members of the nomination committee should be non-executive directors who are independent on the new, more stringent definition (see *Chapter 6*). The controversial proposal made by Higgs that the chairman of the company should not chair the nomination committee has not been adopted, however, with the result that the July 2003 Combined Code provides that the committee may be chaired by either the chairman or an independent non-executive director. It states explicitly, however, that the company chairman should not chair the nomination committee when it is dealing with the appointment of a successor to the chairmanship.

In its guidance note on the terms of reference of the nomination committee, the ICSA makes further specific recommendations designed to minimise the risk of conflicts of interest in the selection and appointment of directors. In particular, it recommends that the chairman and members of the committee should be rotated on a regular basis and that, as far as possible, overlaps between the membership of the nomination committee and other committees of the board should be avoided. Detailed guidance on the composition and terms of reference of the nomination committee can be found in ICSA's Guidance Note which is reproduced at *Appendix 11*.

## Frequency of meetings

The July 2003 Combined Code envisages that the nomination committee should play a key strategic role in the ongoing development of the board, in particular by supporting a continuous process of succession planning and by keeping under review the leadership needs of the organisation. Reflecting this, the ICSA's Guidance Note recommends that the committee should not wait until a board vacancy occurs, but should meet at least once a year, close to the end of financial year, if only to consider whether or not directors retiring by rotation or reaching a predetermined age limit should be put forward for reappointment at the next AGM. It further recommends that, to maximise attendance, meetings of the nomination committee should take place on the same day as meetings of the full board.

## The role and responsibilities of the nomination committee

The revised Combined Code (Provision A.4.1) states that the nomination committee should lead the process for board appointments, evaluating the balance of skills, knowledge and experience of the existing directors and, in the light of this evaluation, preparing a description of the role and capabilities required for a particular appointment. It should make recommendations to the board on proposed new appointments, except in the case of the appointment of a new chairman: the appointment of a new chairman should be a matter for the full board, but the nomination committee should prepare a job specification, including an assessment of the time commitment expected, recognising that the chairman will normally not be full-time but will need to be available in the event of crises.

## Reporting to shareholders

Following the recommendations of the Higgs Review, the July 2003 Combined Code requires that the nomination committee should make a statement about its activities in a separate section of the annual report. This should identify the chairman and members of the committee, give the number of committee meetings held during the year and the attendance of individual members, and describe the process used for the selection and appointment of directors, with an explanation, if external advice or open advertising has not been used in making in the appointment of a new chairman or a non-executive director.

In addition, the terms of reference of the nomination committee are to be made publicly available, for example, through publication on the company's web-site. The terms of reference must explain clearly the role of the nomination committee and the nature and extent of the authority delegated to it by the board.

## Strategic and qualitative issues relating to board appointments

The provisions of the July 2003 Combined Code reflect the findings of the Higgs Review, which recommended that the nomination committee should conduct the process for board appointments, with responsibility for identifying and nominating

## SUMMARY OF THE DUTIES OF THE NOMINATION COMMITTEE

Key duties of the nomination committee, as set out in the ICSA's guidance note on the committee's terms of reference, include:

- regularly reviewing the structure, size and composition of the board and making recommendations to the board with regard to any adjustments deemed necessary;
- preparing a description of the role and capabilities required for a particular appointment;
- taking responsible for identifying and nominating for the approval of candidates to fill board vacancies as and when they arise;
- satisfying itself with regard to succession planning that appropriate processes and plans are in place with regard to both board and senior appointments;
- assessing and articulating the time needed to fulfil the role of chairman, senior independent director and non-executive director, and undertaking an annual performance evaluation to ensure that the all members of the board have devoted sufficient time to their duties;
- ensuring on appointment that a candidate has sufficient time to undertake the role and review his or her commitments, ensuring that if he/she is

an executive of another company this will be his/her sole non-executive appointment;
- ensuring that a candidate for chairman will not be considered if he/she is already chairman of a FTSE 100 company or equivalent;
- ensuring that the company secretary, on behalf of the board, formally advises appointees to the board of the expected role and time commitments and proposes an induction plan produced in conjunction with the chairman;
- assessing, at least every three years, whether the incumbent chairman should continue in post, taking into account the needs of continuity versus freshness of approach, and making appropriate recommendations to the board;
- making recommendations to the board on the re-appointment of any non-executive director at the conclusion of his or her specified term of office, especially where the director has concluded a second term;
- recommending whether directors retiring by rotation in accordance with the company's Articles should be proposed for re-election by the shareholders.

candidates and making recommendations as necessary for approval by the full board. In Higgs' view, however, the role of the nomination committee should not be limited to filling board vacancies as and when they arise, but should include ongoing responsibility for the effectiveness of the board through oversight of succession planning, the terms of directors' appointments and the diversity of the board.

## Succession planning

Higgs recommends that the nomination committee should play a key role in succession planning for both executive and non-executive directors, taking into account the challenges and opportunities facing the company and the skills, expertise and leadership needed in the future. To this end, the committee should ensure that plans are in place for orderly succession to appointments within the company, to both the board and to other senior management positions, and should satisfy itself that the company has a programme of recruitment and retirement for board members and has adequate management development and succession planning.

## The terms of directors' appointments

In addition to its role in planning for the development of the board as a whole, Higgs suggests that the nomination committee should pay increased attention in the selection and appointment process to the personal capacities and qualities of candidates and the ability of existing and new directors to provide the level of commitment demanded from them. To this end, Higgs recommends that the nomination committee should take responsibility for the terms of directors' appointments, including the permitted number of external directorships and, for non-executive directors, the duration of appointments, the required degree of independence and advance specification of the time commitment required from each director.

### External directorships

Although the Higgs Review found that less than one-fifth of non-executive directors hold more than one non-executive directorship in a UK listed company, it recognised the need to ensure that all directors are able to devote the time and effort required to do their jobs properly. Accordingly, it recommended that:

> *Full-time executive directors* should not take on more than one non-executive directorship, nor become chairman, of a major company, defined in this context as a company included, or likely to be included shortly, in the FTSE 100. Further, where companies release executive directors to serve as a non-executive director elsewhere, they should include in their remuneration policy reports whether or not the director will retain such earnings and, if so, what the remuneration is.

> *The chairman* of a major company has what is close to a full-time engagement and has ultimate responsibility for the conduct of the board; accordingly, no individual should chair the board of more than one major company. In addition, the July 2003 Combined Code recommends that a prospective chairman's other significant commitments should be disclosed to the board before appointment and included in the annual report. Changes to such commitments should be reported to the board as they arise, and included in the next annual report.

> *Non-executive directors* are not in full-time employment with the company, and the Higgs Review therefore concluded that it would be arbitrary and unrealistic to set a prescriptive limit on the number of non-executive directorships any individual may hold. None the less, the Review recommended that non-executive directors should disclose to the chairman the nature and extent of their other appointments and confirm that they will have available the time required for their role. During their period of office, non-executive directors should

inform the chairman of any other appointments they take up (including the amount of time they will need to devote to them), and make the chairman aware of any changes to their other commitments which might impact on the time they can devote to the company's affairs. Once reported to the chairman, such matters should be formally recorded by the company secretary at the next board meeting.

## Duration of appointments

The planned development of the board over time is dependent on the board's ability to change its membership in an orderly manner, while maintaining a proper balance between experience and continuity on the one hand, and the benefits of independence and freshness of approach on the other.

To this end, the Higgs Review recommended that the terms of appointment of the chairman and non-executive directors should be of appropriate duration: initial appointments should be not for less than three years (subject to satisfactory performance), while most non-executive directors should be expected to serve a second term of three years. While there might be circumstances in which it is appropriate for a non-executive director to serve for more than two three-year terms, this should be by exception only and the reasons for it should be explained to shareholders. Where, exceptionally, a non-executive director serves more than nine years, their appointment should be subject to annual re-election by the shareholders. In addition, the Higgs Review points out that a systematic process of induction, training and professional development is needed to accelerate the learning curve for individual non-executive directors and so ensure that each is able to contribute effectively to the board's activities from an early stage in his or her term of appointment.

## Independence

The Higgs Review emphasises that, in considering the personal qualities required of prospective directors, nomination committees must take account of the legal requirement for all directors, whether executive or non-executive, to take decisions objectively in the interests of the company as a whole. Accordingly, nomination committees must ensure that all directors, without exception, demonstrate independence of mind and the willingness and ability to challenge, question and speak up.

At the same time, it is well established in the UK that at least a proportion of non-executive directors should be independent in a stricter sense, in order to provide assurance that objective scrutiny is being carried out in areas of potential conflict of interest between management and shareholders, notably remuneration, audit and the selection and appointment of new directors.

Since Cadbury, codes of corporate governance have adopted a loose definition of independence, comprising independence of management and freedom from any business or other relationship which could materially interfere with the exercise of their independent judgement, and have made it the responsibility of company boards to determine which of their non-executive directors meet this definition. In line with the recommendations of Higgs Review, however, a more explicit definition of independence has been incorporated into the July 2003 Combined Code. This is intended to identify relationships and circumstances which might compromise, or appear to compromise, a director's objectivity and will, it is hoped, avoid the need for institutional shareholder bodies to draw up their own definitions against which to assess proposed appointments. The revised definition of independence included in the July 2003 Combined Code of Corporate Governance is set out in full in *Chapter 6*.

### Time commitment and other expectations

According to the Higgs Review, failure to devote sufficient time to the role is widely considered to be the most significant barrier to the greater effectiveness of non-executive directors. The Review therefore concluded that non-executive directors must commit the necessary time, taking into account the time required for induction and professional development, developing an understanding of the company's affairs, participating in succession planning, involvement in discussions with shareholders and availability at short notice to deal with major issues as they arise. This is reflected in the recommendations of the July 2003 Combined Code, which requires non-executive directors, on appointment, to undertake that they will have sufficient time to do what is expected of them and to disclose to the board their other significant commitments and any subsequent changes.

The nomination committee is also given specific responsibilities in respect of the time commitments required from non-executive directors, including:

> before appointment, articulating the time and responsibility envisaged in the appointment of a non-executive director, including any additional commitments as chairman, senior independent director or board committee member;
> on appointment, ensuring that each non-executive director's letter of appointment specifies the expected time commitment; and
> following appointment, evaluating at least annually the performance of each non-executive director and assessing whether the individual is committing enough time to fulfil his or her duties.

## Diversity

It was explicitly recognised by the Higgs Review that the increased demands on non-executive directors, as reflected in its own proposals in respect of the duration of appointments, the definition of independence and the required level of personal commitment, might make it more difficult for companies to recruit non-executive directors. At the same time, the Review pointed out that the current population of non-executive directors is drawn from a very narrow base (dubbed by Higgs 'the usual suspects'): research carried out for the Review showed that non-executives are typically white males nearing retirement age with previous experience as directors of public limited companies. Specifically, in 2002:

> only 4 per cent of executive director posts and 6 per cent of non-executive director posts were held by women, while fewer than 1 per cent of listed company boards were chaired by women;

> only 7 per cent of non-executive directors were non-British and only 61 per cent were from black and ethnic minority groups;
> the average age of a non-executive director in the FTSE 100 were 59, with over three-quarters 55 or over; conversely, fewer than 20 non-executive directors of FTSE 100 companies were under the age of 45; and
> the average age of a FTSE 100 chairman was 62, and almost 40 per cent were 65 or over.

The Higgs Review warned that difficulties in recruiting new directors would be exacerbated if companies continued to restrict their selection and recruitment processes to the existing narrow pool of candidates. Consideration of candidates from a wider range of backgrounds was therefore needed to ensure that the best available people are recruited to the boards of listed companies to demonstrate the reality of companies' commitment to the principle of equal opportunity. As the Review points out, the motivational value of such commitments will be severely undermined if it is apparent to employees that the board does not comply with its own policies in this respect.

Higgs attributed the present narrow range of the non-executive director population to the assumption on the part of many boards that the required skills can be found only among individuals with previous experience as board members in listed companies. Higgs challenged this view, pointing out that the necessary commercial and management strengths can be found in a wide range of other organisations, and recommended that listed companies should:

> appoint individuals from wider and more diverse backgrounds to the boards of subsidiary companies as a possible stepping-stone to the full board;
> encourage senior managers just below board level to take a non-executive director position on a non-competitor board;
> consider private companies and the non-commercial sector, including major charitable or public sector bodies, as potential sources of non-executive directors with strong commercial and market understanding as well as breadth and diversity of experience; and
> where the company operates in international markets, consider the appointment of at least one international non-executive director with relevant skills and experience, providing training as necessary.

In support of these objectives, nomination committees should insist that any executive search or recruitment consultants employed by the company should look beyond the 'usual suspects' to find candidates who would make good board members.

### The Tyson Report

Following on from the recommendations of Higgs in respect of board diversity, the Tyson task force of business leaders chaired by Laura D'Andrea Tyson, Dean of London Business School was invited by the Department of Trade and Industry to propose ways in which companies might draw on broader pools of talent with varied and complementary skills, experiences and perspectives to enhance board effectiveness.

The Tyson Report on the recruitment and development of non-executive directors was published in June 2003. Its principal conclusions were in the following three areas:

*Vigorous and transparent non-executive director selection processes*

> The selection process for each non-executive appointment should rest on a careful assessment of the needs and challenges of the particular company and on a broad, transparent and rigorous search that reflects this assessment.

> To demonstrate that it is committed to a vigorous and transparent selection process and to foster greater trust in its non-executive appointments, the company should share information with shareholders, employees and others.

> Companies should broaden their searches for new non-executive directors to include sources of talent that they have tended to overlook in the past, including the so-called 'marzipan layer' of corporate management just below board level in plc companies; professional services firms; unlisted companies and private equity firms; the non-commercial sector; and the commercial and non-commercial sectors in foreign countries.

*More and better evaluation and training for board members*

> Companies should invest more in programmes to train and evaluate the members of their boards.

> Training should encompass both a thorough induction programme for new board members and training and development opportunities for ongoing board members and should be linked to regular processes to evaluate board performance.

> As boards become more diverse, formal training and evaluation for board members will become even more important to foster trust, cohesion and communication among board members.

> Guidelines should be established for practical board training programmes for directors.

> Information should be collected and provided about available programmes for companies seeking board training services.

In response to the Higgs and the Tyson Reports, the Institute of Chartered Accountants in England and Wales (ICAEW) announced in November 2003 that it was launching an online register of suitably qualified chartered accountants as potential candidates for appointment as NEDs. The register seeks to promote greater diversity in UK boardrooms by focusing on women and chartered accountants working overseas and is targeted at individuals in the 'marzipan layer' of senior managers who have the requisite experience and expertise to serve on boards, but who have not previously been brought to the attention of those involved in recruiting for NED vacancies. The ICAEW register is available at www.icaew.co.uk/idregister.

*Research and measurement to encourage greater board diversity*

> A high-visibility initiative should be developed to provide regular and reliable measures of board composition for individual companies and to monitor

progress on achieving rigorous and transparent processes for appointments and building more diverse boards.

> In addition, this initiative should disseminate best practice examples of how individual companies can build more meritocratic and diverse boards and should foster research on the business benefits of greater board diversity.

> To maximise its effectiveness, the initiative should receive a substantial share of its funding from the business community and be independent of government, although it may need to be jump-started by government.

## Chapter summary

> The need for transparent processes for the nomination and appointment of directors is well established as a principle of corporate governance in the UK.

> However, Enron and other corporate failures have underlined the importance of longer-term strategic and qualitative issues in the selection and appointment of directors, leading to wider recognition that these should be regarded as a continuous process, to be carried out objectively and with close attention to the independence and effectiveness of the board as a whole.

> As part of this process, there is now greater emphasis on the evolving role and responsibilities of the nomination committee, especially in relation to appointment of the chairman and the evaluation of the performance of individual directors and the board as a whole.

> More radically, there is growing pressure on boards and nomination committees to look beyond the 'usual suspects' in making appointments, in particular by seeking well-qualified candidates from the public and not-for-profit sectors and other potential sources beyond the limited sphere of listed companies.

# 9

# Directors' Remuneration

> Levels of remuneration should be sufficient to attract, retain and motivate directors of the quality required to run the company successfully, but a company should avoid paying more than is necessary for this purpose. A significant proportion of executive directors' remuneration should be structured so as to link rewards to corporate and individual performance.
>
> Main Principle B.1: The Level and Make-up of Remuneration

> There should be a formal and transparent procedure for developing policy on executive remuneration and for fixing the remuneration packages of individual directors. No director should be involved in deciding his or her own remuneration.
>
> Main Principle B.2: Procedure

This chapter examines current practice, issues of continuing shareholder and public concern and proposed corporate governance developments in each of the four key areas identified by the Greenbury Study Group, namely:

1. the role and composition of the remuneration committee;
2. remuneration policy and the level and make-up of executive remuneration, including the use of performance-related incentives designed to align directors' interests with those of shareholders;
3. the disclosure of remuneration policy and individual directors' remuneration and the circumstances in which shareholder approval must be obtained; and
4. directors' service contracts, particularly in respect of notice periods and the provisions for termination or compensation payments in event of a director's dismissal for unsatisfactory performance.

Of all the issues dealt with by codes of corporate governance, executive remuneration is at once the most visible and most contentious. The combination of mandatory disclosure and newsworthiness guarantees that executive pay awards will be highly publicised and dissected in detail in the media. The issues involved become particularly stark at times of economic uncertainty, when the rewards received by directors are seen against the background of falling share prices, profits warnings and employee redundancies.

Adverse investor and public reactions to apparently unjustified levels of executive pay can inflict serious reputational damage, on both the company and the individual directors concerned. Recent changes to the law to provide for an automatic share-holder vote on the remuneration reports of listed companies have enlivened debate at many AGMs, and in some cases have resulted in humiliating defeats for board resolutions.

Although the potential for conflicts of interest between shareholders and directors over matters of pay, performance and job security have long been recognised in princi-ple, it was not until the early 1990s that executive remuneration was addressed as specific issue for corporate governance. The Cadbury Code of 1993 recommended that executive pay should be determined by the board as whole on the basis of the recommendations of a remuneration committee made up wholly or mainly of non-executive directors, but gave no guidance on the level or composition of executive remuneration.

Following public controversy over seemingly undeserved increases in the level of directors' remuneration, particularly in recently privatised utilities, the Greenbury Study Group on Directors' Remuneration carried out the first formal investigation into executive pay in the UK. As a result, the Listing Rules were amended in 1995 to require detailed disclosure on remuneration policy and the actual remuneration of individual directors. In addition, a Code of Best Practice on directors' remuneration was appended to the Listing Rules and subsequently incorporated into the Combined Code. Although many areas of the Greenbury Code have been superseded in the July 2003 Combined Code, it has been widely influential on the subsequent debate.

The Greenbury Code's attempt to persuade companies to undertake voluntary reform of their remuneration practices has achieved some successes. The majority of UK listed companies now have remuneration committees consisting exclusively of independent non-executive directors and, as recommended by Greenbury, most exec-utive directors' service contracts now have notice periods of no more than 12 months. In addition, a much greater volume of information on remuneration matters is now available to shareholders and the general public, although the complexity of much of this makes it uncertain whether there has been an equivalent increase in transparency and accountability.

Despite these advances, it is widely held that the Greenbury recommendations have failed to curb executive remuneration, which in some cases is still felt to be excessive in both absolute terms and in comparison to average salaries. Other criticisms are that the recommendations did not do enough to reinforce the link between pay and perform-ance or to provide shareholders with an appropriate degree of influence. In addition, concerns not addressed or only partly addressed by Greenbury have recently come to the fore, including 'rewards for failure' in the form of over-generous compensation payments to departing executives. In the light of these concerns, major institutional shareholders are increasingly seeking to influence company practices on remunera-tion, through both direct contact with boards and the issue of explicit guidelines.

There are indications, however, that the Government is becoming less inclined to rely on companies' willingness to undertake voluntary reform of their remuneration practices. Secondary legislation, in the form of the Directors' Remuneration Report

Regulations 2002, has already been used to introduce an automatic shareholder vote on the remuneration report and further legislation to improve the ability of shareholders to scrutinise compensation and severance payments is under consideration.

## The role and composition of the remuneration committee

### The Greenbury principles

A fundamental concern for the governance of widely held companies is that the separation between ownership and day-to-day control may provide direct opportunities for unscrupulous managers to enrich themselves at the expense of the owners by appropriating or misusing the company's assets.

To counter this risk, the Greenbury Code established as a basic principle that no director should be involved in determining his or her own remuneration. It recommended instead that the board of every UK listed company should delegate authority for determining executive remuneration to a remuneration committee, which should consist exclusively of non-executive directors with no personal financial interests other than as shareholders, no cross-directorships and no day-to-day involvement in running the business. The remuneration committees should be responsible for determining the company's overall policy on executive remuneration and the specific remuneration package of each executive director, including pension entitlements and compensation or termination payments in event of early termination.

Greenbury recommended that the remuneration committee should be directly accountable to shareholders through a separate remuneration report in the company's annual report and accounts, the detailed content of which was prescribed in the Listing Rules. In addition, the chairman of the remuneration committee should attend the AGM in order to answer shareholders' questions on remuneration matters and should also be responsible for keeping the company's main institutional shareholders informed on remuneration issues.

In order to preserve the independence of the remuneration committee, the Greenbury Code stated explicitly that the remuneration of non-executive directors should be determined by the board as a whole, not by the remuneration committee. The remuneration of a non-executive director is usually in the form of a fixed annual fee, with an additional sum for chairing a committee. As a general principle, non-executive directors should not participate in any bonus, share option or pension arrangements operated by the company, nor should they receive payments from the company for consultancy or other services or otherwise enter into relationships with the company that might impair their ability to make independent judgements.

### Developments since Greenbury

*The effectiveness of non-executive directors*

The principles established by Greenbury have done much to reassure shareholders and the general public that executive directors are not directly involved in or able to influence the setting of their own remuneration. However, confidence in remuneration committees has been affected by wider concerns about the independence and effectiveness of non-executive directors. These concerns have been addressed by the Higgs Review, with the result (see *Chapter 6*) that a more stringent definition of non-executive independence has now been incorporated into the July 2003 Combined Code. In keeping with this definition, remuneration committees must in future consist exclusively of non-executive directors who are independent in character and judgement and free from relationships or circumstances which are likely to affect, or could appear to affect, their judgement.

The independence of the remuneration committee is also addressed in the Guidance Note on the terms of reference of the remuneration committee prepared by the ICSA in conjunction with the Higgs Review (see *Appendix 12*). This recommends that, in order to minimise the risk of any conflict of interest that might be seen to give rise to an unacceptable influence on the remuneration committee or its members:

> the chairman and members of the remuneration committee should be rotated on a regular basis;

> so that no conflict of interest can arise at the time of appointment of a new director, no member of the remuneration committee should also be a member of the nomination committee; and

> (except for small companies which do not have sufficient non-executive directors) no member of the remuneration committee should also be a member of both the audit and nomination committee.

### The role of remuneration consultants

The Greenbury Code recommended that, in addition to consulting the company chairman and/or the CEO about their proposals, remuneration committees should have access to professional advice inside and outside the company. The use of external consultants was intended to provide remuneration committees with access to independent and objective professional advice on market rates of remuneration for executive directors in comparable companies and on the design of remuneration packages, including long-term incentive schemes.

There is increasing concern, however, that remuneration consultants may have contributed to an upward spiral in remuneration levels by failing to challenge excessive demands and thus creating an assumption that companies need to match or exceed the remuneration paid by other similar companies, irrespective of individual circumstances. In addition, the involvement of remuneration consultants in the design of long-term incentive schemes may have resulted indirectly in an increased level of technical complexity, making it more difficult for shareholders to evaluate the link between performance and anticipated rewards.

Quoted companies are already required by the Directors' Remuneration Report Regulations 2002 (SI 2002/1986) to disclose in their annual reports the name of any person, other than a director, who has provided material advice or other services to the remuneration committee during the year. Given the current level of interest, however, it seems likely that the role of remuneration consultants will come under continued scrutiny by shareholders.

# Remuneration policy

## The Greenbury principles

The Greenbury Code recognised that executive remuneration packages must be sufficient to attract, retain and motivate directors of the quality required by the company. It emphasised, however, that the total rewards available to directors should not be excessive, and that the company should avoid paying more than necessary. To this end, it recommended that remuneration committees should be aware of what other comparable companies are paying, taking into account their own company's performance relative to that of comparable companies. Remuneration committees should also be sensitive to the wider scene, including pay and employment conditions elsewhere in the company.

Greenbury identified the following as the typical components of executive remuneration packages and recommended that the level and cost of each component should be disclosed separately to shareholders:

> basic annual salary;
> benefits in kind, such as car and medical insurance;
> pension contributions on behalf individual directors under defined benefit or defined contribution pension schemes; and
> performance-related remuneration, in the form of annual bonus payments and/or participation in longer-term arrangements such as executive share option schemes.

Performance-related remuneration was identified by Greenbury as the most complex, and potentially the most contentious, component of executive remuneration, reflecting shareholder and wider public concerns that many schemes were excessively generous, providing very high rewards for mediocre performance. The Code emphasised that all performance-related remuneration, whether annual or longer-term, should be designed to align the interests of directors and shareholders and to give directors incentives to perform at the highest levels. Performance conditions should therefore be relevant, stretching and designed to enhance the business. To minimise the risk of directors receiving undeserved windfalls, remuneration committees should consider the need for an upper limit to be placed on potential gains, and should also consider ways in which executive directors could be encouraged to retain meaningful long-term shareholdings in the company.

So far as annual bonuses are concerned, Greenbury recommended that eligibility for annual bonuses should not be automatic and that remuneration committees should consider whether individual directors should receive bonuses. Awards to directors under longer-term performance arrangements should be subject to challenging performance conditions, and should preferably measure the company's performance against that of a group of comparator companies in key variables such as Total Shareholder Return (TSR). To ensure that performance conditions were sufficiently challenging over a sustained period, remuneration committees should consider the use of long-term incentive plans (LTIPs) as alternatives to traditional share option schemes.

## SHARE-BASED INCENTIVES 1

### Executive share options

Prior to the Greenbury Report in 1995, share options were the most common form of long-term incentive arrangement for executive directors. Share options:

- give the holder the right (but not the obligation) to 'exercise' by purchasing shares in the company at a predetermined option price at a specified future period;
- executive share options cannot normally be exercised before the third anniversary of the date of grant, and lapse if not exercised by the tenth anniversary of the date of grant;
- if the company's share price has risen between the date of grant and the exercise period, the director can make a gain equal to the difference between the option price set at grant and the price for which the shares can be sold after exercise;
- if the share price has fallen or remained the same, there is no benefit to the director and the options are said to be 'under water'.

### Problems with share options

Although share options are intended to align the interests of directors with those of shareholders by linking part of the directors' future rewards to the company's share price, Greenbury found that the grant of share options could encourage behaviour which was not necessarily in the shareholders' interests, for example:

- the linkage to share price could create an incentive for directors to overstate the company's profits to meet or exceed market expectations in the hope of boosting the share price;

- the practice of granting share options in large blocks could encourage directors to focus on the company's share price performance in a narrow window of time, at the expense of long-term development;
- the potential for large personal profits motivated directors to sell their shares immediately after exercise, frustrating the intention that share options should align directors' and shareholders' interests;
- in rising market conditions, an increase in the company's share price might not necessarily reflect the efforts of the directors, so share options could reward indifferent performance; and
- in falling market conditions, the practice of re-pricing share options to ensure that they remained exercisable insulated directors from the financial risks faced by directors.

### Current practices

The design of executive share options has evolved in response to the Greenbury criticisms such that, for example:

- it is now usual practice to grant options in relatively small annual tranches rather than in large blocks in order to ensure that directors have the incentive to improve performance over a sustained period;
- options can no longer be exercised simply on the basis of increased share price at the time of exercise, but become exercisable only if other predetermined performance criteria have been met over a longer period; and
- the practice of re-pricing share options is now strongly discouraged.

## Developments since Greenbury

An important effect of the Greenbury Code has been that many companies have now introduced LTIPs. These vary widely in design and degree of complexity, but most involve some requirement for shares to be retained for minimum period – usually three years – and make the potential gains receivable by executive directors conditional on the achievement of performance conditions.

Despite these developments, there are continuing concerns that executive remuneration and 'perks' are excessive and that performance-related awards are still insufficiently related to the long-term interests of shareholders. Reflecting these concerns, institutional investors are increasingly publishing statements which set out the conditions on which they will be prepared to endorse companies' remuneration policies.

The most influential of these statements is the guidance on executive remuneration issued by the Association of British Insurers (ABI). Originally published in December 2002, a revised version was issued in December 2003 (see *Appendix 13*). This urges remuneration committees to take proper account of market requirements, including the competitive forces applicable to the sector in which the company operates and the

---

### SHARE-BASED INCENTIVES 2

**Performance measurement**

Following the Greenbury Report, more demanding performance measures were introduced to ensure that executive options could no longer be exercised simply on the basis of increased share price at the time of exercise. For some years, the most common measure used was a requirement that the company's earnings per share (EPS) should outperform the Retail Price Index (RPI) by a certain percentage – usually 2–3 per cent – over three or more years.

More recently, Total Shareholder Return (TSR) has increasingly been used as a performance measure in executive option schemes and other long-term share-based incentive arrangements. TSR also forms the basis of the comparative performance chart required under the Directors' Remuneration Report Regulations 2002.

TSR is preferred to other performance measures because it is believed to provide a more balanced evaluation of the total benefits received by shareholders over time. It measures the percentage increase in the value of a given holding of the company's shares over a specified period, based on the change in the market share price and assuming that all dividends received on the holding are reinvested in the company's shares.

Where TSR is used, a director's right to exercise of share options may be conditional on the achievement of further performance conditions: for example, exercise may be subject to the company's TSR equalling, or outperforming, the median TSR of a comparator group consisting of companies of similar size and business activity. Additionally, in some companies, the number of shares over which the director is permitted to exercise options may increase on a sliding scale related to the extent to the company's TSR has outperformed the TSR of the comparator group.

## SHARE-BASED INCENTIVES 3

### Long-term incentive plans

Following the Greenbury criticisms of share options, various forms of long-term incentive plan (LTIP) have been devised. The purpose of LTIPs is to link rewards more closely to the achievement of demanding performance conditions and to encourage executive directors to build up and retain meaningful holdings of shares in their company.

There is no single form of LTIP, each company designing its own according to its circumstances and the views of its shareholders. Some typical variations include:

- *Restricted shares:* legal ownership of a given number of shares is vested in the executive director, but the shares themselves are placed in trust, typically for three years. The release of the shares from trust at the end of the retention period is linked to the achievement of specific performance conditions, with the proportion of shares released varying according to how the company has performed. The shares may also be forfeited if performance targets are not met or if the director leaves the company.

- *Matching shares:* executive directors purchase shares in the company, at the current market price and with their own money, and hold them for an agreed period (typically three years). At the end of the holding period, the company provides matching shares, the number of which will vary according to the performance of the company during the holding period.

- *Deferred bonus plans:* executive directors are required by the company to use a proportion of any performance-related annual bonus to purchase shares in the company at the current market price. The shares are held in trust for an agreed period (typically three years), at the end of which the company provides an equivalent number of matching shares.

particular challenges faced by the company. In so doing, remuneration committees should not automatically assume that they must match or exceed pay levels in comparator companies, but should consider a policy of setting salary levels below the comparator group median. More generally, remuneration committees should have regard to pay and conditions elsewhere in the company and should encourage executive directors to build up meaningful long-term shareholdings.

Specific recommendations of the ABI guidelines include:

> *Basic annual salary:* the fixed component of annual salary should be set at a modest level relative to the variable component in order to link remuneration more closely to performance.

> *Benefits in kind:* these should be closely scrutinised by remuneration committees to ensure that they are justified and appropriately valued.

> *Pension contributions:* the full economic costs of pension contributions and pension enhancements must be fully evaluated and, where potential liabilities are unfunded, remuneration committees must be able to demonstrate to shareholders that the approach adopted involves the least overall cost to the company.

> *Annual bonuses:* directors must not be automatically entitled to bonuses, which should be cut or eliminated when individual performance is poor; transaction bonuses which reward directors for completing transactions irrespective of the future financial consequences are not acceptable to shareholders.

> *Long-term incentive arrangements:* the vesting of awards under share incentive schemes must be conditional on the achievement of demanding performance targets over a sustained period; targets should be disclosed and transparent and shareholder approval should be obtained for any changes which make it easier to achieve performance targets; performance targets must not be subject to automatic waiver in the event of a change of control of the company or on the retirement of a director.

## Disclosure and shareholder approval

### Greenbury principles

The Cadbury Code established as a basic principle that shareholders are entitled to full and clear disclosure on directors' remuneration. This principle was expanded by the recommendations of the Greenbury Study Group, which defined in detail the required content of the remuneration report to be included in the annual report and accounts of every UK listed company. The resulting requirements, which for the first time included detailed disclosures on the actual remuneration and other benefits received by directors individually, were incorporated in the Listing Rules in October 1995 and remained in force until replaced by the Directors' Remuneration Report Regulations 2002 (see below).

Although the Greenbury recommendations substantially increased the amount of information available to shareholders, they did little to increase shareholder influence over companies' decisions regarding the level and make-up of executive directors' remuneration. The Greenbury Code concluded that formal shareholder approval was necessary only in the case of new long-term incentive schemes and similar arrangements which would potentially dilute the equity holdings of existing shareholders or commit shareholders' funds over more than one year. It explicitly rejected the suggestion that the company's remuneration policy or the packages provided for individual executive directors should be subject to shareholder approval as a matter of course. It did recommend, however, that the remuneration committee should formally consider each year whether changes in the company's circumstances or remuneration policy were such that the shareholders should be asked to approve the policy.

### Developments since Greenbury

Despite the increased volume of information made available by companies in response to the Greenbury recommendations, shareholders have continued to express concerns about the increasing levels of executive remuneration and, specifically, about the continuing opacity of the relationship between company performance and directors' bonuses and other incentive payments. In addition some (but by no means all) shareholders have voiced frustration about their limited ability to influence remuneration practices in the absence of a compulsory vote on the remuneration report.

Following a lengthy consultation period, the Government responded to these concerns by issuing the Directors' Remuneration Report Regulations 2002. The Regulations apply to company reports for financial years ending on or after 31 December 2002 and require the inclusion in the annual report and accounts of a detailed remuneration report. In addition, companies caught by the Regulations are required to put their remuneration reports to a vote of shareholders at their AGMs.

Although the Regulations retain and amplify the disclosure requirements previously set out in the Listing Rules, their application has been extended to all quoted companies: in addition to UK listed companies, this definition includes companies listed in any state of the EEA (the EU plus Iceland, Norway and Liechtenstein) and on the New York Stock Exchange and Nasdaq.

*New disclosure requirements*

Reflecting current shareholder concerns, the Regulations require the disclosure of significant new information in the areas of performance-related bonuses and other awards and on the company's liability to pay compensation to departing directors in the event of early contract termination following unsatisfactory performance. A summary of the disclosure requirements is given below for ease of reference. It should be

---

**DIRECTORS' REMUNERATION REPORT REGULATIONS 2002 (SI 2002/1986)**

**Summary content of the remuneration report for inclusion in the company's annual report and accounts***

*Information subject to review by the company's external auditors*

Remuneration of individual directors by name:

- total emoluments, including salary and fees; bonuses; expenses; estimated non-cash benefits; and compensation for loss of office and any other termination payments;
- share options awarded, exercised or lapsing during the year, including performance criteria and details of any options whose terms and conditions have been varied during the year;
- benefits received or potentially receivable from the director's participation in a long term incentive scheme, including the period within which performance conditions must be met;
- pension entitlements under defined benefit or money purchase schemes, including

excess retirement benefits paid to or receivable by directors and past directors.

*Information not subject to review by the company's external auditors*

The remuneration committee:

- the names of the remuneration committee members;
- any directors, other than remuneration committee members, who provided material advice to the committee during the year;
- any other person (such as a remuneration consultant) who advised the committee during the year, with details of any other services provided by that person to the company.

Statement of policy on directors' remuneration:

- the company's remuneration policy for future years;
- the performance criteria in respect of long-term incentive schemes and share options,

noted, however, that the drafting of the Regulations is extremely complex and should be studied in full before attempting to prepare the remuneration report.

*Shareholder voting on the remuneration report*

The introduction of the requirements for quoted companies to put their remuneration reports to a vote of shareholders at their AGMs has coincided with a period of considerable financial uncertainty, characterised by falling share prices, diminished company profits and reduced or passed dividends. In addition, a number of prominent companies have terminated executive directors' contracts for poor performance and have been obliged by the Regulations to disclose embarrassingly generous compensation arrangements.

Against this background, the mandatory vote on the remuneration report has produced some startling results, given that companies would typically expect AGM resolutions to be carried by majorities of around 95 per cent. In the most spectacular case, that of GlaxoSmithKline, over 50 per cent shareholders either voted against or abstained on the remuneration report as a means of registering their dissatisfaction with the lavish compensation and pension arrangements provided for the CEO. Severely reduced majorities have also been experienced by the boards of many other major companies, including Tesco, WPP, Barclays, Reckitt Benckiser and Cadbury

explaining why the performance conditions were chosen, use of comparator groups and other external factors, and how actual performance will be measured against the criteria;

- the division between basic and performance-related elements of pay and their relative importance;
- the company's policy on contract duration, notice periods and termination payments.

Comparative performance graph:

- a line graph comparing, for the year under review and the preceding four years, the Total Shareholder Return (TSR) on a holding of the company's listed shares to the TSR on a hypothetical holding of shares in a broad equity market index; and
- the name of the index selected for the purposes of the graph and the company's reasons for selecting that index.

Service contracts of directors and former directors:

- the date of the individual's service contract, the unexpired term and notice period;
- any provision for compensation payable on early termination of the contract;
- any other information needed to enable shareholders to estimate the company's liability in the event of early termination of the contract;
- an explanation of any significant award paid during the year on early termination of a director's service contract.

* Where the company publishes a short-form Annual Review/Summary Financial Statement in addition to its full annual report and accounts, the short-form document must contain the information on aggregate directors' emoluments required under the Companies Act 1985. The comparative performance graph described above and information on the company's remuneration policy should also be disclosed.

Schweppes. In all of these cases, the levels of votes against and abstentions cannot be attributed solely to dissatisfied private shareholders, but indicate clearly that institutional shareholders – normally loyal to the boards of investee companies – are unhappy about aspects of current remuneration practice.

It is difficult at this early stage to assess the real implications of the shareholder vote on the remuneration report. The Regulations make clear that, although it is intended that boards should take shareholders' views seriously, the vote has 'advisory' status only; moreover, it is stated explicitly that the contractual entitlements of individual directors are not subject to shareholder approval of the remuneration report.

The 'advisory' status of the vote may in itself have encouraged a high level of protest voting at recent AGMs, with institutional investors in particular using the opportunity to administer a salutary warning to boards in the knowledge that there would be no immediate adverse consequences. None the less, a number of major companies have indicated that they intend to review their remuneration policies, and all boards are now on notice that their policies and the rewards received by individual directors must be justifiable to shareholders and the wider public.

## Directors' service contracts

With the exception of long-term incentive arrangements, the most contentious issues currently arising in the area of directors' remuneration relate to potential payments to directors in the event of early termination of their service contracts for reasons of unsatisfactory performance.

Where a director leaves a company involuntarily, following inadequate personal performance or policy disagreements with the other directors, his or her service contract will normally require the company to provide a severance package. Such packages may include some or all of a lump sum termination payment; continuation of salary and other benefits, either for a defined period or until a new job is obtained; and pension enhancements. The period for which the company will be required to continue to pay the director's salary and other benefits will depend on the director's service contract:

> if the contract has a fixed term, the company may be required to pay throughout the unexpired term of the contract; or
> if the contract has a rolling notice period, the company may have to continue to pay for the entire duration of notice period.

### The Greenbury principles

The Greenbury Code emphasised the need for remuneration committees to consider the company's liability to pay compensation to directors in the event of early termination for unsatisfactory performance. In order to limit the potential liabilities, Greenbury recommended that:

> notice periods in executive directors' service contracts should be limited to 12 months or less under normal circumstances: longer notice periods (of two or,

exceptionally, three years) might be appropriate for new directors, but should reduce to 12 months or less after the initial period of employment;

> where performance has been unsatisfactory, remuneration committees should seek to keep compensation payments as low as possible, particularly by reducing compensation to reflect a departing director's obligation to mitigate his or her own loss by securing other employment; and

> any compensation should be paid in instalments rather than as one lump sum, and payments should be reduced or stopped when the former director takes on new employment.

## Developments since Greenbury

The Greenbury Code has had some success in limiting the duration of notice periods, in that 12-month notice periods are now standard for directors' service contracts. However, concern has been expressed by shareholders that 12 months is now regarded as a floor, although in many cases a shorter notice period would be preferable as a means of avoiding excessive severance payments.

The Greenbury Code was less successful in its attempt to moderate the level of potential termination payments. As a result, there is widespread shareholder and public perception that departing directors may be 'rewarded for failure' – that is, unfairly insulated from the consequences of their own incompetence – while shareholders suffer reduced investment values and employees potentially lose their jobs.

### Institutional guidelines

Institutional shareholders have attempted to promote improved practice in this area through the issue of guidance for remuneration committees. In a joint statement on executive contracts and severance initially published in December 2002 and revised in December 2003, the ABI and the National Association of Pension Funds (NAPF) made clear that, while executive directors were entitled to some protection against the risk of removal from office, executive remuneration is already at a level that allows for this risk.

The revised joint statement by the ABI and NAPF (reproduced in *Appendix 14*) suggests that remuneration committees should consider the inclusion in directors' service contracts of specific provisions for the reduction of severance payments. Techniques considered include:

> *Phased payments*, whereby the company would continue to pay a departing executive on a normal monthly basis for the outstanding term of his or her contract or until the director finds fresh employment, thus avoiding the need to pay a large lump sum which cannot be recovered.

> *Liquidated damages*, whereby the amount to be paid in the event of severance is agreed in advance with the director, thus providing certainty for the company (but also precluding the opportunity for the company to reduce the amount to take account of under-performance).

> *Reliance on mitigation*, whereby the departing executive is legally obliged to mitigate his or her own loss, for example by seeking other employment and thus reducing the need for compensation from the company.

*Prospective legislation*

Similar contractual devices are explored in the consultative document *Rewards For Failure: Directors' Remuneration – Contracts, Performance and Severance* issued by the Government in June 2003. This sought views on two alternative methods of improving shareholder scrutiny and accountability in relation to compensation and severance payments made to directors. These are:

> ❯ changes in best practice guidance (either through amendments to the Combined Code or through guidance issued by institutional shareholders) on the way in which compensation and severance payments are addressed in directors' service contracts; and
> ❯ legislative reform to achieve the same effect.

The consultative document outlined the options for best practice to include extension of the existing Code and investor guidance to secure further reductions in contract and notice periods. Measures might also be taken to promote the inclusion in contracts of provisions designed to reduce severance payments following poor performance, for example by capping the level of liquidated damages or by encouraging the use of phased payments.

Legislative reform options included possible amendments to CA 1985 to require boards, in agreeing executive directors' service contracts, to take into account under-performance in determining severance payments. Other measures could include a reduction in the statutory period for a director's contract to one year duration, or three years on first appointment; a prohibition on rolling contracts having a notice or contract period in excess of a specified statutory maximum length; or a statutory prohibition on covenants which provide for more compensation than would be available under a one-year or three-year contract, as appropriate.

## Chapter summary

> ❯ The widely publicised shareholder protests over executive pay at company AGMs during the summer of 2003 demonstrate that good governance in matters of executive remuneration is not achieved simply by complying with the rules on remuneration committees and disclosure.

> ❯ Boards, individual directors and their advisers need to be sensitive to shareholder and wider public concerns, taking into account company performance.

> ❯ Employment conditions in the company, including employee pension entitlements and job security; conditions in the wider economy; and broader concepts of what is fair and reasonable in the circumstances.

> ❯ In addition, all parties need to bear in mind the long-range nature of many remuneration and incentive measures and to ensure that current proposals will not produce unintended, costly and potentially damaging outcomes in the future.

❯ Boards and remuneration committee members should assume that they will be required to defend their proposals and their eventual outcomes in public at the company's AGM. Before finalising their proposals, they should therefore satisfy themselves that they can answer in good faith questions about whether:
   - the levels of executive remuneration provided for new directors are genuinely required to secure and retain the services of directors of appropriate calibre;
   - all possible steps been taken to ensure that the company is not paying too much;
   - employment conditions elsewhere in the company, including pay levels, pension entitlements and job security, have been taken fully into account in formulating proposals on executive directors' remuneration;
   - performance conditions are properly aligned to shareholders' interests, and do not create potential incentives for directors to pursue developments which are not in the interests of the company;
   - performance conditions are sufficiently challenging in terms of time scale and the selection of comparator groups of companies and do not produce potential 'rewards for failure'.

# 10

# Reporting to Shareholders

❝ The board should present a balanced and understandable assessment of the company's position and prospects.

Main Principle C.1 Financial Reporting ❞

This chapter outlines the current formal requirements for reporting to shareholders and examines the division of responsibility between the directors and the external auditors for ensuring that shareholders are given a true and fair view of the position and state of affairs of the company. Also considered are:

> the current concerns relating to the integrity of financial reporting and ongoing changes in the arrangements for regulatory supervision;
> the quality and effectiveness of non-financial reporting, proposals for reform of current reporting requirements and options for voluntary reporting by companies.

The board presents its assessment of the company's position and prospects primarily through the annual report and accounts, supplemented for listed companies by the interim report and the preliminary results announcement.

From the point of view of corporate governance, the annual report and accounts and other externally published reports are fundamental to ensuring that the directors are properly accountable to the generality of shareholders. Although institutional shareholders may have access to the directors in person, the information contained in the annual report and accounts is often the only direct means by which private shareholders can assess the stewardship of the directors and the state of the company. The annual report and accounts thus have important procedural links to the annual general meeting (AGM), where they provide the context by which shareholders can assess and vote on the proposals recommended by the directors for their approval.

Further discussion of the procedural links between the annual report and accounts and the AGM, together with an analysis of the proposals arising from the Company Law Review for changes to the timetable for publication of the annual report and accounts, can be found in *Chapter 14*.

The company's external reporting is also an important element in its relationship with other stakeholders, such as employees, customers, suppliers and local communities, whose decisions on whether to do business with the company or otherwise to support its activities may be influenced by its published information. In addition, the annual report and accounts may be widely circulated and commented on, and may therefore have a significant impact on the company's reputation among a wide range of external audiences, including politicians, the media, pressure groups and the general public.

Despite the importance of the annual report and accounts, there are significant concerns about whether information produced in compliance with current statutory and other formal rules can, in fact, provide the balanced and understandable assessment of the company's position and prospects required by the revised Combined Code. Some of these concerns have been reinforced by Enron and other corporate scandals and relate to the integrity and reliability of financial reporting. Other concerns address the adequacy of traditional financially based reporting and its ability to provide shareholders and other users with insights into the risks and opportunities facing the company, the quality of its management and the effectiveness of its key relationships.

## Current formal requirements

### Statutory requirements

The basic content of the annual report and accounts is determined by CA 1985 and the accounting standards issued by the Accounting Standards Board (ASB), and is heavily weighted towards financial disclosure.

#### Financial reporting

The annual report and accounts must contain accounting statements comprising:

> a profit and loss account setting out the financial performance of the company over the previous financial year and incorporating a statement of recognised gains and losses;

> a balance sheet describing its financial position at the end of that year; and

> notes setting out the assumptions and estimates necessary to support and explain the information in the accounting statements. The notes must also provide other specified information, including details of related undertakings and, unless a specific exemption has been granted, information on the aggregate emoluments of directors.

In preparing the accounting statements, the directors must adopt suitable accounting policies and apply them consistently from one financial year to the next. They must also observe the principles of prudence and conservatism, particularly in the recognition of income and the valuation of assets and liabilities. Where applicable, they must treat the company as a going concern – that is, as if it will continue in business and operations on its present scale for the foreseeable future.

#### Non-financial reporting

By comparison with the required financial content, the mandatory narrative content of the annual report is minimal and, in some respects, oddly assorted. The annual report and accounts of a public company is required by CA 1985 to include a directors' report setting out:

> the principal activities of the company and any subsidiaries during the year and any changes in these activities;
> the names of directors who held office during the year and details of their interests in the company's shares, including share options held or exercised during the year;
> particulars of any purchases of its own shares made by the company during the year;
> any political or charitable contribution made by the company in excess of £200; and
> where applicable, additional disclosures stipulated by statutory instrument, for example, on directors' remuneration and payments to the company's external auditors in respect of non-audit work.

The directors' report of a medium-sized or large company must also provide information including:

> a fair review of the business of the company and its subsidiaries during the year, the position at the end of the year and any likely future developments;
> the amount of any dividend recommended by the directors;
> important post-balance sheet events;
> details of research and development carried out by the company; and
> where the company is a public company or a subsidiary of a public company, its policy on the payment of trade creditors.

Where the average number of employees exceeds 250 during the year, the directors' report must also explain the company's policy on the employment of disabled people and set out a statement of employee involvement, including employee consultation procedures and arrangements for encouraging participation by employees in the company's performance, for example, through an employee share scheme.

## The Summary Financial Statement

Directors of listed companies are permitted to send a short-form version of the annual report and accounts, known as the Summary Financial Statement (SFS), to shareholders and other recipients who do not specifically elect to receive a copy of the full document.

The minimum content of the SFS is specified by the Companies (Summary Financial Statement) Regulations 1995 (SI 1995/2092) and includes summaries of the profit and loss account and balance sheet derived from the company's full accounting statements, together with a summary of the directors' report from that document. In practice, most companies taking advantage of the Regulations to produce a short-form document voluntarily include in it narrative sections similar to those included in the full annual report and accounts. In this case, the short-form document is often known as the annual review.

## THE SUMMARY FINANCIAL STATEMENT

The SFS option has been widely adopted by listed companies with large shareholder registers, notably the privatised utilities and former building societies. It can provide significant benefits for the company and its shareholders:

- the simplified format enables private shareholders in particular, who may lack the time or expertise to grapple with the full accounting statements, to monitor the progress of their investment; while
- the shorter length of the document provides savings for the company in terms of lower production and mailing costs.

However, great care must be taken to ensure that the SFS communicates properly and effectively with recipients without talking down or trivialising their concerns. The following points must also be observed:

- the SFS must be approved and signed by a director on behalf of the board;

- it must state in a prominent position that it does not contain sufficient information to allow as full an understanding of the results and state of affairs as would be provided by the full annual report and accounts;
- even where a shareholder has not previously objected to the receipt of an SFS, he or she is entitled at any time to receive a copy of the current annual report and accounts free of charge, and to elect to receive a copy of the full document in all future financial years; and
- even where an SFS is sent to the majority of the company's shareholders, the full annual report and accounts must be laid before the shareholders in general meeting.

*Source:* Companies (Summary Financial Statements) Regulations 1995 (SI 1995/2092)

## Requirements of the Listing Rules

### Annual report and accounts

The Listing Rules specify that a listed company must include in its annual report and accounts additional information designed to assist a proper understanding of the company's position and performance. The additional disclosures required for this purpose include:

> an explanation of any significant differences (that is, more than 10 per cent) between the company's actual results for the period under review and any published estimate or forecast;

> details of matters affecting the relative interests of shareholders in the company's securities, including any shareholdings in excess of 3 per cent of the company's issued share capital; and

> details of directors' interests (whether beneficial or non-beneficial) in the shares of the company and in significant contracts or other transactions involving the company.

The directors of a UK listed company must also include in the annual report and accounts an explicit statement, reviewed in advance with the company's external auditors, that the business is a going concern, with supporting assumptions and qualifications as necessary. This requirement has significant implications for the personal responsibilities and liabilities of the directors: if the company subsequently suffers a financial collapse, each director may be liable to any investor who has suffered a loss having relied on the going concern statement.

As explained in *Chapter 2*, the directors of a UK listed company are required by the Listing Rules to disclose in the annual report whether or not the company has complied with the recommendations of the revised Combined Code and, to the extent that it has not, to give reasons for the areas of non-compliance. The Listing Rules also give effect to the specific disclosure requirements contained within the revised Combined Code itself in respect of directors' remuneration and internal control. Further information on disclosure on internal control will be found in *Chapter 12*.

### Periodic reporting by listed companies

Under the Listing Rules, the directors of a listed company must publish two periodic financial statements in addition to the annual report and accounts. These are:

1   An *interim report* setting out the company's financial results in the first six months of its financial year, with the amount of any interim dividend to be paid to shareholders where applicable. The interim report (which need not be audited) must be published via one of the Regulatory Information Services designated by the Financial Services Authority (FSA) within 90 days of the end of the half-year period to which it relates. The company is not required to send a copy of the interim report to all shareholders, but can instead insert the report, as a paid advertisement, in at least one national newspaper.

2   A *preliminary results announcement* setting out the company's full-year results, including the profit and loss account, cash flow statement and balance sheet, in a format consistent with that adopted in the full annual report and accounts, together with details of any dividend or distribution recommended by the directors. The preliminary results announcement must be agreed in advance with the company's external auditors and must include any additional information necessary to enable shareholders and others to assess the significance of the reported position. The preliminary results announcement must be published via one of the Regulatory Information Services within 120 days of the year-end. The company is not required to send a copy of the preliminary results announcement to all shareholders.

## The responsibilities of the directors and the external auditors

The company's directors are responsible for preparing accounting statements which give a true and fair view of the position and state of affairs of the company, selecting and applying suitable accounting policies for this purpose.

In the case of a listed company, the revised Combined Code requires the directors to include in the annual report and accounts an explicit statement of their responsibilities. This should include:

> making prudent and reasonable judgements and estimates;
> following applicable accounting standards, subject to the disclosure and explanation of any material departures;
> preparing accounts on a going concern basis where appropriate;
> maintaining proper accounting records; and
> safeguarding the company's assets and taking reasonable steps to prevent and detect fraud or other irregularities by implementing an effective system of internal control.

The directors' statement of their responsibility for the preparation of the accounting statements is of great significance from the perspective of corporate governance. By this means, the directors acknowledge the nature and extent of their responsibilities and the potential liabilities which might arise from failure to carry them out.

In all but very limited circumstances, the annual report and accounts of a public company must also include a report to shareholders from the company's external auditors. The aim of the auditors' report is to give an expert and independent opinion about whether the accounting statements give a true and fair view of the company's financial position and performance during the year and comply with the relevant laws. It does not, however, diminish the directors' responsibilities for the preparation of the accounting statements; nor does it constitute an absolute guarantee that the accounting statements prepared by the directors are free from all fraud or error.

For a further discussion on the relationship between the directors and the external auditors, see *Chapter 11*.

## The reliability of financial reporting

In *Accounting for Growth: Stripping the Camouflage from Company Accounts* (1992), Terry Smith noted that during the recession of 1990–91, certain UK companies – among them Polly Peck, BCCI and Maxwell Communications – reported record profits but, almost simultaneously, went into administration.

Subsequent reforms, including the adoption in 1992 of the Cadbury Code of Best Practice on the financial aspects of corporate governance, have done much to assure investors about the quality and reliability of financial reporting. However, the sudden and spectacular collapse of major US corporations such as Enron and WorldCom, the part played in their demise by serious accounting irregularities and the failure of supposedly independent external auditors have again called into question the credibility of company accounting statements and the competence and integrity of those responsible for their preparation.

Published accounting statements can fail shareholders in various ways:

> They may fraudulently misrepresent the affairs of the company by deliberately presenting a false picture of the financial position and performance.
> They may use accounting policies that are just within permissible accounting practice, but which present a more favourable impression of its position and performance than would be the case if the principles of prudence and conservatism had been observed. Such 'aggressive' or 'creative' accounting policies

might involve, for example, the recognition of income at an early stage in a transaction process; deferred recognition of expenses; the use of separate companies as a means of avoiding the full disclosure of debts on the balance sheet; or the treatment of loans as operating income in order to increase reported cash flow from operating activities.

Aggressive accounting policies can improve the company's reported financial position, at least in the short term, and help to boost its share price. They may therefore be in the personal interests of the executive directors, for example by enabling them to fulfil their performance targets and increasing the value of their share options. However, the effect of such accounting policies is to hide the true financial position of the company and there is a significant risk that the real position will eventually emerge. In this event, the company will have to report declining financial performance and may have to issue unexpected profit warnings. This will have a negative impact on its share price and perhaps, ultimately, on the careers of the directors.

› Even in the absence of any deliberate intention to mislead users or conceal information, the accounting statements may lack transparency through over-complexity or the use of technical jargon, making it difficult for shareholders to understand the company's real position.

## The enforcement of reporting standards

The company's directors have ultimate responsibility for ensuring that the accounting statements are properly prepared, are free from deliberate fraud or unintended error and are presented to shareholders in an accessible and understandable form. Without diluting the responsibilities of the directors, external regulators, notably the Financial Reporting Council, its subsidiary bodies and the UKLA, also exercise influence over reporting techniques and standards.

The ASB is responsible for making accounting standards and, where necessary, for amending existing accounting standards in response to the use by companies of accounting techniques which might appear to violate the principles of prudence and conservatism. Thus, the ASB is currently revising FRS 5 'Reporting the Substance of Transactions' with the intention of curbing the use of aggressive accounting techniques, especially for revenue recognition, which were implicated in the collapse of Enron.

The Financial Reporting Review Panel (FRRP) and the UKLA have legal authority to review documents published by companies for compliance with reporting standards. Where necessary, the FRRP has powers to require the revision of defective accounts, while the UKLA has available a range of sanctions, including suspension from trading of the company's shares, a requirement for the company to announce additional information and the imposition of financial penalties or public censure on the company and its directors and sponsors.

In practical terms, however, the review processes carried out by these regulatory bodies have had significant limitations. The FRRP has not carried out sample checks of companies' published accounts, but has intervened only where there has been *prima facie* evidence that a particular set of accounts did not present a true and fair view.

Moreover, its powers have been confined to statutory accounts: it has not been able to consider the non-financial elements of the annual report, such as the chairman's statement, or to examine interim reports or preliminary results announcements published by listed companies. Similarly, the purpose of the UKLA's review has been limited to ensuring the completeness of companies' disclosures, but has not included any check on their veracity of the disclosures or any analysis of financial statements for compliance with relevant accounting standards.

The adequacy of the UK's arrangements for the enforcement of accounting and reporting standards has been examined by the Co-ordinating Group on Audit and Accounting Issues (CGAA) established by the Government following the collapse of Enron. Among other recommendations set out in its final report, published in January 2003, the CGAA concluded that there was an urgent need for greater proactivity in the review of companies' published reports, including more active engagement of regulators with reporting companies. The CGAA's proposals for regulatory reform has been accepted by the Government, and revised arrangements, including the development by the Financial Reporting Review Panel of a selective programme for review of company reports, is now being implemented.

A further description of the revised arrangements for professional and regulatory oversight of accounting and auditing in the UK can be found in *Chapter 11*.

## The adequacy of company reporting

In addition to concerns about the quality and reliability of financial reporting, there are questions as to whether current reporting requirements, with their heavy emphasis on the accounting statements, adequately address the information needs of shareholders and other stakeholders. Thus, it is increasingly being suggested that a balanced assessment of the company's performance and prospects demands a broader range of qualitative disclosures which can shed light on the credibility, consistency and integrity of directors and the quality of the company's strategic and risk management.

### The demand for non-financial information

The range of disclosures expected of listed companies has been significantly extended by the requirement, in the 1998 version of the Combined Code, for directors to report on their review of the effectiveness of the company's system of internal control. This requirement, together with the related guidance for directors in the Turnbull Report (1999), has made clear the extent of directors' responsibilities, emphasising that issues relevant to their review embrace a broad range of non-financial risks, including those arising from, for example, health and safety, the environment, corporate reputation and business probity. Similarly, appropriate internal control measures extend beyond audit and insurance to encompass human resource policies, performance management systems and codes of conduct designed to foster a climate of trust, competence and integrity within the company. Further information on the Turnbull guidance can be found in *Chapter 12*.

Beyond the Combined Code requirements, there is evidence of market demand for the publication by companies of a broader range of non-financial information. As noted in *Chapter 4*, there is growing market demand for qualitative information on the quality and strategic insight of company management, typified by the publication by the Association of British Insurance (ABI) of guidelines on the disclosures in respect of social, ethical and environmental issues which institutional shareholders would expect to see in the annual reports of listed companies.

## GOOD PRACTICE POINT

### Reporting on social, ethical and environmental issues

For each company, the method adopted for reporting on social, ethical and environmental issues must accurately reflect the nature of the business, the market in which it operates and the identity of its key external impact and stakeholders. The use of an externally developed reporting framework, however prestigious, may be inappropriate if the performance indicators and other criteria are not closely matched to the needs of the business.

If it is decided to report against an externally developed framework, the company should explain whether it has undertaken the full verification or other requirements associated the framework in collaboration with the organisation concerned, or if it is simply using the criteria established by the framework as a basis for its own reporting: if the latter, the company should make clear any departures from the external framework.

If the company decides to devise its own reporting methodology, it should seek to report to the same standards of objectivity as would be provided by an externally developed framework:

- Performance indicators and targets, whether qualitative or quantitative, should be relevant to the needs of the business and reflect the company's external impacts.

- Reporting against the targets and performance indicators should be consistent over time in order provide a basis for comparison of the performance of the company at different periods.

- As far as possible, the performance indicators should be developed collaboratively, through benchmarking with other companies in the same sector or industry, to provide users with a means of comparing the company's performance with that of others.

Whatever reporting framework is selected:

- The collection of data and internal reporting against the performance indicators selected should be integrated into the company's internal control and risk management processes to ensure consistency, avoid duplication of effort and communicate clear messages both inside and outside organisation.

- The company should recognise at the outset the need to report bad news – including failure to meet targets – as well as good.

- It is in the company's interests to be realistic about its starting position and avoid overstating its progress and achievements. Unfounded claims are likely to be exposed if – or more likely when – something goes wrong!

## Voluntary disclosures

In the absence of a formal statutory requirement, reporting by companies on non-financial issues is still largely voluntary.

Many public and listed companies recognise the importance of communicating effectively with their shareholders and include in their annual report and accounts significant narrative elements not formally required by statute and the Listing Rules. These typically include:

> ❭ a letter or statement by the company's chairman, and often also the chief executive officer;
> ❭ a discussion of the performance of different subsidiaries or divisions of the company;
> ❭ biographical information on the directors; and
> ❭ descriptions of the company's policies and performance with regard to the environment, health and safety and the community.

### Operating and Financial Review

Efforts have been made over a number of years to encourage companies to provide more systematic and objective information to assist shareholders and others in their assessment of the business. In particular, a Statement published by the ASB in July 1993 (revised January 2003) set out a proposed framework, the Operating and Financial Review (OFR), for the discussion and analysis by the directors of the factors underlying the company's results, financial position and future prospects. The text of the Statement is reproduced at *Appendix 14.*

The Statement emphasises the need for disclosures of a qualitative nature, including the directors' assessment of the key dependencies of the business, for example, on its relationships with customers, suppliers and employees, and for analysis of the factors and influences likely to affect future performance. Although the Statement does not have the authority of a formal Accounting Standard, many companies have adopted it voluntarily.

### Proposed legal reform: the statutory Operating and Financial Review

The Company Law Review Steering Group (CLRSG) recommended that the publication of an annual Operating and Financial Review (OFR) should be made mandatory for major companies, defined as any company which is not a subsidiary of a parent undertaking incorporated in an EEA state and which meets two out of three of the following size criteria:

> ❭ *Public company:* 1) turnover more than £50 million; 2) balance sheet total more than £25 million; 3) more than 500 employees.
> ❭ *Private company:* 1) turnover more than £500 million; 2) balance sheet total more than £250 million; 3) more than 5,000 employees.

The stated objective of the proposed mandatory OFR would be to enable the shareholders of a major company to make an informed assessment of the company's operations, financial position and future business strategies and prospects.

To this end, the directors of such companies would be required to ensure that the OFR contained at least the following compulsory elements:

> a statement of the company's business in the financial year to which the OFR relates;
> a fair review of performance during that financial year and of the position of the company at the end of that year; and
> a fair projection of the prospects for the company's business and of events which will, or are likely to, substantially affect the business.

The directors would also be required to consider whether, in order to achieve the review objective, the OFR should include information about any of the following matters:

> the company's management structure;
> receipts from, and returns to, shareholders during the financial year;
> the company's policies on employment, the environment and social and community issues;

## OPERATING AND FINANCIAL REVIEW WORKING GROUP

### Summary of Guidance for Directors on the Preparation of the OFR

*The concept of materiality in the context of the OFR*

- Directors should make in good faith honest judgements about what information is material for inclusion in the OFR and should bear in mind the objective of the OFR to enable users to assess the company's strategies and prospects.
- Information is material to the OFR if failure to disclose it might influence shareholders' assessments of the company and hence the decisions they take.
- Information material to the OFR may be quantitative or qualitative, and may relate to facts or probabilities and to past, present or future events and decisions.

*Principles to be applied by directors in arriving at their judgements on materiality*

- In making judgements about materiality, the directors should act collectively and should make well-informed, good faith, honest

judgements with the involvement of the full board.

- Where necessary (for example, in assessing wider environmental, community, social or ethical considerations), the directors may require access to specialist advice.
- Directors must base their consideration of materiality on the purpose and values of the business and the needs of prospective users of the OFR, including shareholders, customers, employees, suppliers, and local, national and international interest groups.
- The information contained in the OFR must be relevant to an assessment of the future as well as to the past and present, and must therefore include the directors' views on the trends and future events that will shape the prospects for the business.
- Directors should consider items for inclusion in the OFR in their wider context: the test should be whether information, if omitted, misstated or inadequately described, would change users' understanding and thus potentially change their decisions.

> the company's performance in carrying out these policies during the year; and
> any other matters which affect, or may affect, the company's reputation.

The OFR would have to be approved by the full board of directors and signed on its behalf by a director. In addition, the company's external auditors would be required to report to shareholders on the adequacy of the procedure adopted by the directors in preparing the OFR, drawing attention to any apparent inconsistency between the information contained in the OFR and the company's financial statements or any other information of which they are aware or if, in their opinion, the OFR did not comply with any applicable rules.

The Government's White Paper *Modernising Company Law*, published in July 2002, gave support for the proposed mandatory OFR. Although it would be for directors to decide what information was material to their particular business and should be published in their OFR, the White Paper indicated that detailed regulatory guidance would provided on the compilation of the OFR. As a first step, the Government set up an Operating and Financial Review Working Group, led by Rosemary Radcliffe, to develop broad principles and practical guidance on how directors might be able to

- Directors should not omit potentially material information from the OFR solely because it cannot be measured, although they will need to consider how best to describe it.
- Directors should be consistent from year to year in their approach to the OFR and should explain their reasons when an item hitherto included is omitted in subsequent years.
- Directors should ensure that the OFR is consistent with the disclosures in other reports issued by the company, including presentations to shareholders.
- All material information should be disclosed in the OFR unless the directors have satisfied themselves that disclosure would result in material prejudice to the company's interests.
- Information about future possibilities need not be disclosed in the OFR unless they are more likely to happen than not or unless failure to disclose might itself be misleading.

### The process for making materiality judgements

The directors' process for making their materiality judgements should:

- Be *transparent*, with clearly defined responsibilities for key tasks, a clear timetable and communication to all those involved, both with preparation and as users.
- *Provide for appropriate consultation* within the business and externally.
- *Take account of appropriate comparisons*, both within the business (prior years' OFRs, other published reports) and externally (best practice, industry guidance, etc).
- Be *comprehensive*: it should be applied across the whole business unless there are sound, documented reasons for not doing so.
- Be *consistent*: it should be applied the same way both across the business and from year to year, unless there are sound, documented reasons for not doing so.
- Be *subject to review*, internally and by the external auditors. This might include a review after each reporting cycle, with a major review perhaps every three to five years.

assess whether an item is material to their company and hence whether it must be included in an OFR. The Working Group's outline guidance was published for consultation in June 2003 and a summary is set out below. Since the Working Group published its consultation document, the Government has announced plans to introduce the statutory OFR using existing powers in CA 1985 and, as noted in *Chapter 1*, has indicated that it will be publishing draft regulations for comment in due course. The Working Group has stated that it will work closely with the DTI to ensure that the publication of its own final report is co-ordinated with the publication of the draft OFR regulations.

## Other voluntary reporting frameworks

In addition to investor demands for a wider range of non-financial disclosure, governments, non-governmental organisations (NGOs) and other stakeholders are increasingly calling for companies to publish information on their approach to corporate responsibility. This concept encompasses the management of the company's external risks and impacts; its social, environmental and ethical policies and performance; and the quality of its relationships with key stakeholders.

## GLOBAL AND SECTORAL FRAMEWORKS FOR SOCIAL RESPONSIBILITY REPORTING

The following are some of the main standards for social, ethical and environmental reporting currently in use internationally:

- The *AA1000* (www.accountability.org.uk) framework developed by the Institute of Social and Ethical Accountability provides a standard for social and ethical accounting, auditing and reporting, including mandatory external verification and stakeholder engagement.
- The *Sustainability Reporting Guidelines* (www.globalreporting.org) developed by the Global Reporting Initiative (GRI), a permanent institution of the UN. The *Guidelines* cover economic, environmental and social performance and aim to provide a universal structure for 'triple bottom line' reporting. They do not currently involve a requirement for external audit or verification, but this is likely to be added in future.
- The Social Accountability (www.cepaa.org)

*SA 8000* standard developed by an international coalition of businesses, trades unions and NGOs on the basis of International Labour Organisation (ILO) conventions, the Universal Declaration on Human Rights and the UN Convention on the Rights of the Child. SA 8000 seeks to provide transparent, measurable and verifiable performance standards in the areas of child labour; forced labour; health and safety; compensation; working hours; discrimination; discipline; free association and collective bargaining; and management systems.

- The *UN Global Compact* (www.unglobalcompact.org) developed in partnership between the UN, multinationals and NGOs on the basis of the Universal Declaration of Human Rights, the ILO labour conventions and the Earth Summit Agenda 21 environmental principles. The *Compact*

There is now a large number of competing performance standards and reporting frameworks for corporate responsibility. These differ widely in the issues and impacts covered, the extent to which external auditing, validation or verification are required and the expectations placed on companies in terms of direct dialogue with stakeholders: brief details of some of the main global and sectoral reporting frameworks now in use are set out below.

A more systematic approach to non-financial reporting is currently being explored through the Corporate Impact Reporting Initiative co-ordinated by Business in the Community: this is seeking to develop a standard, business-led framework for voluntary reporting against a range of impact indicators, including the marketplace, the environment, the workplace, the community and human rights. Further details of the project can be found at www.iosreporting.org.

## Chapter summary

> A balanced and understandable assessment of the company's position and prospects is fundamental to ensuring that the directors are properly accountable

covers human rights, labour and the environmental principles for multinationals in the developing world. Members of the *Compact* must publicly state their support for these principles and report annually on their performance, but there is no requirement for external verification.

- The *OECD Guidelines for Multinational Enterprises* (www.oecd.org/daf/ investment/guidelines) set out recommendations for responsible business conduct in employment and industrial relations; human rights; the environment; information disclosure; competition; taxation; science and technology; combating bribery; and protection of consumer interests. They are not legally binding and there is no requirement for reporting or external measurement.
- The *Ethical Trading Initiative* (www.ethicaltrade.org) Base Code has been developed by an alliance of retailers, trades unions and NGOs to promote ethical sourcing of products through a code of conduct covering business ethics and corporate responsibility; promotion of workers' rights; human rights; the ending of child labour, forced labour and sweatshops; and health and safety, labour conditions and labour rights. The Base Code is aligned to the ILO conventions, the Universal Declaration on Human Rights and the UN Convention on the Rights of the Child.

Sector-specific standards addressing issues relevant to particular business activities include the Responsible Care Scheme for the chemicals industry, the Green Globe audit and assurance scheme for hotels and the Green Alliance performance indicators for the waste management industry.

and that shareholders can assess the stewardship of the directors and the financial health of the company.

› The directors, not the external auditors, are responsible for the preparation of the financial statements in accordance with the Companies Act and applicable accounting standards and, where appropriate, the Listing Rules.

› The Enron débâcle has revived concerns about the quality and reliability of financial reporting, as a result of which the enforcement of accounting and reporting standards in the UK is expected to become much more interventionist.

› There are growing demands for improved reporting by companies on non-financial issues, including their social, ethical and environmental policies and performance, as a means of providing shareholders and other users with a more balanced assessment of the company's performance and prospects.

# The Audit Committee
# and the Auditors

 The board should establish formal and transparent arrangements for considering how they should apply the financial reporting and internal control principles and for maintaining an appropriate relationship with the company's auditors.

*Main Principle C.3: Audit Committee and Auditors*

This chapter considers the provisions of the revised Combined Code in relation to audit committees and auditors, with particular reference to:

> measures designed to reinforce audit committee membership and ensure that committees have sufficient resources available to them;

> changes to the audit committee's terms of reference to enhance and clarify their responsibilities and improve accountability to shareholders;

> the specific responsibilities of the audit committee in respect of financial reporting, internal control and risk management, internal audit and the appointment and independence of external auditors; and

> ongoing developments in the external regulation of the accountancy and auditing profession in the UK.

The Cadbury Code of Best Practice, introduced in 1992, created a general expectation that every listed company in the UK will have an audit committee made up of non-executive directors. This expectation has been reflected in all subsequent UK codes of corporate governance and is increasingly emulated in the codes adopted by other countries. In addition, it has progressively spread to other parts of the economy, with the result that many organisations in the public and not-for-profit sectors now have an audit committee.

Audit committees are considered to play a fundamental role in overseeing the financial reporting and audit process. By providing an effective counterbalance to executive management, audit committees uphold the independence of both internal and external auditors, thus helping to ensure that audits are carried out properly and that the accounting statements give a true and fair view of the organisation's financial position and performance.

In principle, therefore, the audit committees of listed companies should make a major contribution to the maintenance of shareholder and wider public confidence in the integrity of business practices and financial disclosures. However, the collapse of Enron in 2001, amid allegations of serious financial malpractice by senior executives and collusion by external auditors, has raised serious questions about the extent to which audit committees are able in practice to ensure the reliability of reporting and auditing processes.

As discussed in *Chapter 3*, governments and financial regulators in the US, the UK and internationally have responded to the Enron scandal by initiating wide-ranging programmes of legal and regulatory reform. These have been designed to strengthen the framework of corporate governance generally and, more particularly, to clarify and enhance the role of the audit committee. Leading examples are the US Sarbanes–Oxley Act 2002, associated changes to the listing rules of the Securities and Exchange Commission and New York Stock Exchange, and the Action Plans on company law modernisation and audit adopted by the European Commission in May 2003. Further information on the international response to the Enron scandal can be found in *Chapter 3*.

The response of the UK Government was to establish a Co-ordinating Group on Auditing and Accounting Issues (CGAA) to review existing regulatory arrangements for statutory audit and financial reporting. Following publication of the CGAA's interim report in July 2002, two further and more detailed investigations were initiated. The first of these, led jointly by the Treasury and the DTI, recommended far-reaching changes in the UK's regulatory regime for the accounting and auditing profession, which are in the course of implementation. The second, under the chairmanship of Sir Robert Smith, proposed amendments to the existing guidance in the Combined Code on the role and composition of listed companies' audit committees: together with changes arising from the closely related Higgs Review of the role and effectiveness of non-executive directors, these have now been incorporated into the July 2003 Combined Code.

The reviews carried out in the UK and internationally have confirmed the broad consensus that audit committees have a primary role in ensuring the integrity of financial reporting and auditing process, and so potentially represent a key part of companies' defences against corporate wrongdoing. They have concluded, however, that in order to fulfil this potential, more attention must be paid to the membership, qualifications and resources of audit committees. In addition, it must be made clear that in recommending the appointment and remuneration of auditors, monitoring audit quality and upholding auditor independence, audit committees act on behalf of and report to shareholders, rather than to executive management.

## Membership and resources of the audit committee

### The composition of the audit committee

Successive UK codes of corporate governance have recommended that the board of every listed company should establish an audit committee of non-executive directors, a majority of whom should be independent of management and free from any business or other relationship which could materially interfere with the exercise of their independent judgement.

In line with the findings of the Smith Report, the July 2003 Combined Code goes further. It recommends that the board of every listed company should establish an audit committee of at least three (or, in the case of smaller companies, two) non-executive directors, all of whom should be independent on the more stringent definition of independence introduced into the Combined Code at the instigation of the Higgs Review. See *Chapter 6* for the text of the revised definition of independence.

In addition, the Smith Guidance on Audit Committees (which is appended to, but does not form part of, the July 2003 Combined Code) recommends that, in order to preserve the collective independence of the audit committee, appointments to the audit committee should be for periods of no more than three years, extendable by no more than two additional three-year periods, and should terminate if a director ceases to be independent. Further, the Smith Guidance recommends that the chairman of the company should not be eligible for appointment as an audit committee member. The text of the Smith Guidance can be found at *Appendix 16*.

## The qualifications of audit committee members

Unlike earlier codes of corporate governance, which have offered no guidance on the qualifications of audit committee members, the July 2003 Combined Code makes the explicit recommendation that, in establishing the audit committee, the board should satisfy itself that at least one member of the committee has recent and relevant financial experience.

This recommendation is amplified in the Smith Guidance, which states that the audit committee member whom the board considers to have recent and relevant financial experience should have a professional qualification from one of the professional accountancy bodies. The Guidance further explains that the depth of financial know-how needed by other members of the audit committee will vary according to the nature of the company's business, but that experience of corporate financial matters will normally be required. Where the company's activities involve specialised financial activities, it will be particularly important for audit committee members to have appropriate financial expertise.

Despite this new emphasis on the qualifications required for audit committee membership, there is a general recognition that specialist financial expertise alone will not ensure that audit committees are able to operate effectively. The Smith Report drew attention to the importance of personal qualities, in particular the need for audit committee members to be 'tough, knowledgeable and independent-minded' and to be willing to ask challenging questions of executive colleagues, senior managers and internal and external auditors. In this regard, the Report suggested that an intelligent and independent audit committee member without significant financial experience might none the less contribute to the work of the committee by cutting through technicalities to ask relevant and straightforward questions. Like the Higgs Review, Smith highlighted the need for a more diverse pool of potential non-executive directors from which audit committee members can be drawn. For a discussion of the comments made by the Higgs Review on the need for increased diversity in the appointment of directors, see *Chapter 8*.

## The remuneration of audit committee members

Like the Higgs Review, the Smith Report clearly envisaged that the role and responsibilities of non-executive directors will become more onerous and that membership of the audit and other board committees will impose additional demands in terms of time and commitment. Accordingly, the Smith Guidance appended to the July 2003 Combined Code recommends that companies should consider the further remuneration that should be paid to members of the audit committee in recognition of their additional responsibilities, taking into account the commitment of time to audit committee business, the range of skills demanded and the nature of the responsibilities taken on by members. It suggests further that the level of remuneration paid to audit committee members should take account of the level of fees paid to other directors, and that the remuneration of the audit committee chairman should reflect the responsibilities and time demands involved in this role.

## Training

As explained in *Chapter 8*, the July 2003 Combined Code emphasises the need for all directors, whether executive or non-executive, to receive training, on first appointment and throughout their period of office. The Smith Guidance builds on this recommendation, identifying a need for the company to provide an induction programme for new audit committee members. This should cover the role of the audit committee, including its terms of reference and expected time commitment for members, and should also provide an overview of the company's main businesses and key financial dynamics and risks.

In addition, the Smith Guidance recommends that companies should provide ongoing and timely training for audit committee members, which should be designed to improve their understanding of the principles of and key developments in financial reporting and related company law. Where necessary, training should also include:

> understanding financial statements, applicable accounting standards and recommended practice;
> the regulatory framework for the company's business; and
> the role of internal and external auditing and risk management.

## The audit committee's access to information and other resources

The Smith Guidance emphasises the need for the audit committee to be provided with sufficient resources to undertake its duties.

The resources available to the audit committee should include access to the services of the company secretary and his or her staff, who should assist the chairman in:

> planning the audit committee's meeting agendas;
> preparing minutes;
> collecting and distributing information required by the audit committee;
> drafting the report on the audit committee's activities for inclusion in the annual report; and
> providing administrative, professional and other necessary practical support.

In addition, the board should make funds available to the audit committee to enable it to take independent legal, accounting or other advice when the audit committee reasonably considers it necessary to do so.

Most importantly, the Smith Guidance underlines the audit committee's need for access to information from the company's directors, managers and employees, and also from the external auditors. To this end, it recommends that the board should make clear to all directors and staff that they must cooperate with the audit committee and provide it with any information it requires.

## Terms of reference of the audit committee

Successive codes of corporate governance have recommended that audit committees should have written terms of reference, but have given little guidance on the required contents. As a result, the functions of the audit committees have varied from company to company. Core activities have typically included pre-publication review of the company's financial statements, receipt of reports from the internal and external auditors and consideration of issues related to defalcation, fraud and other irregularities. In the absence of other arrangements, some audit committees have also played a significant part in the review of effectiveness of the company's internal control and risk management systems.

In the light of the Smith Report's conclusions on the lessons arising from the Enron scandal, the July 2003 Combined Code is now much more explicit in its recommendations concerning the role and responsibilities of the audit committee. Thus, Code Provision C.3.2 recommends that the written terms of reference of the audit committee should state categorically the committee's responsibility for:

> monitoring the integrity of the financial statements of the company and any formal announcements relating to the company's financial performance and reviewing significant financial reporting judgements contained in them;

> reviewing the company's internal financial controls and, unless expressly addressed by a separate board risk committee composed of independent directors or by the board itself, reviewing the company's internal control and risk management systems;

> monitoring and reviewing the effectiveness of the company's internal audit function;

> making recommendations to the board, for it to put to the shareholders for their approval in general meeting, in relation to the appointment, re-appointment and removal of the external auditor and approving the remuneration and terms of engagement of the external auditor;

> reviewing and monitoring the external auditor's independence and objectivity and the effectiveness of the audit process, taking into consideration relevant UK professional and regulatory requirements;

> developing and implementing policy on the engagement of the external auditor to supply non-audit services, taking into account relevant ethical guidance regarding the provision of non-audit services by the external audit firm; and

> reporting to the board, identifying any matters in respect of which it considers that action or improvement is needed and making recommendations as to the steps to be taken.

The company should make the audit committee's terms of reference publicly available by publishing them on its web-site and by making copies available on request.

The Smith Guidance recommends in addition that the audit committee should review its terms of reference and assess its own performance and effectiveness annually, bringing forward any necessary changes for approval by the board. More detailed guidance on the membership and terms of reference of the audit committee in the light of the July 2003 Combined Code is set out in the ICSA's Guidance Note on the terms of reference of the audit committee, the full text of which can be found at *Appendix 17*.

In a significant departure from the provisions of earlier codes of corporate governance, the July 2003 Combined Code recommends that the audit committee should account directly to the company's shareholders on the discharge of its responsibilities in a separate section of the annual report and accounts. More specific suggestions on the content of the audit committee's report are given in the Smith Guidance (see *Appendix 16*), which recommends that the report should, as a minimum, provide:

> a summary of the role of the audit committee;
> the names and qualifications of all members of the audit committee during the period under review;
> the number of audit committee meetings held during the period;
> how the audit committee has discharged its responsibilities in the period under review, including an explanation of how auditor independence and objectivity are safeguarded in circumstances where non-audit services are provided by the company's external auditors.

The Smith Guidance also recommends that the chairman of the audit committee should be present at the AGM to answer questions, through the chairman of the board, on the report on the audit committee's activities and matters within the scope of audit committee's responsibilities.

## Specific responsibilities of the audit committee

### Financial reporting

Despite the emphasis in the July 2003 Combined Code on the importance of the audit committee's role in monitoring the integrity of the company's financial statements, it is clearly recognised that management, rather than the audit committee, is responsible for the preparation of financial disclosures and for compliance with applicable accounting standards and other relevant rules. The audit committee's role is therefore to satisfy itself that the executive directors are carrying out their responsibilities, rather than to duplicate the role of the executive directors by becoming too closely involved in matters of detail or making decisions on behalf of the company.

The audit committee is responsible for monitoring the integrity and completeness of the company's financial statements, and in particular for establishing whether management has adopted appropriate accounting policies and supported them with reasonable estimates and judgements. In discharging this duty, the Smith Guidance recommends that the audit committee should review all significant statements proposed for publication before they are submitted to the full board for approval. The audit committee's review should encompass the annual report and accounts, the interim report and preliminary results announcement and any other intended release of price-sensitive information. Scrutiny by the audit committee should not be confined to the accounting statements, however, but should extend to all relevant narrative information, including in the Operating and Financial Review and the company's statement of compliance with the July 2003 Combined Code.

For further discussion on the non-financial content of the annual report and accounts, including the Operating and Financial Review and the statement of compliance with the Combined Code, see *Chapter 10*.

In carrying out its review, the audit committee should evaluate the judgements and reporting decisions made by the executive directors, including changes in critical accounting policies, decisions requiring a major element of judgement, and the clarity and completeness of the proposed disclosures. It should receive explanations from management of the methods used to account for any significant or unusual transaction and should take into account the external auditor's views. The audit committee should also take into account any factors of which it is aware that might predispose management to present an incomplete or misleading picture of the company's financial position and performance. Such factors might include, for example, a perceived need to counter adverse market sentiment or to report the achievement of performance targets on which bonus payments depend.

The audit committee has clear responsibility for challenging inadequate accounting and auditing practices and for ensuring that weaknesses in these processes are not permitted to result in poor or misleading financial disclosures. While the Smith Guidance acknowledges the need for an open working relationship and a high level of mutual respect between the audit committee and the other directors of the company, particularly the chairman, the CEO and the finance director, it stresses that the audit committee must be prepared where necessary to take a robust stand on issues of principle.

## Internal control and risk management

In its examination of internal control and risk management issues, *Chapter 12* will explain that the collective responsibility of the board for ensuring that the effectiveness of the company's system of internal control extends to all controls, including financial, operational and compliance controls, and to all aspects of risk management, including risks arising from market, credit, liquidity, technological, legal, health, safety and environmental, reputational and business probity issues. So far as the role of the audit committee is concerned, the July 2003 Combined Code envisages that the audit committee should have primary responsibility, on behalf of the board, for the review of the company's internal financial control system. Where no alternative arrangements have

### ❯ Audit committee scrutiny of draft financial statements

The following issues warrant close scrutiny by the audit committee:

- the proposed adoption by executive management of accounting policies or treatment which are significantly different from those in normal use in the industry or sector;
- aggressive revenue recognition, such as recognition of income at a seemingly premature stage in a transaction process;
- under-statement of liabilities, for example through deferred recognition of expenses;
- significant asset write-downs or unusual credits;
- unexplained low depreciation charges and/or unduly long asset lives;
- establishing over-generous provisions to reduce declared profits, or releasing earlier provisions to smooth profits;
- off-balance sheet financing, including the use of separate companies as means of avoiding the full disclosure of debts on the balance sheet;
- unexpected trends, for example, rising profits against a background of static cash flow;
- concerns expressed by the external auditor and significant amendments to the draft accounting statements arising from the audit.

been made by the board, the audit committee may also be closely involved in reviewing the effectiveness of the company's systems for the control of financial, operational and compliance controls and risk management.

The precise scope of the audit committee's responsibility for reviewing the effectiveness of internal control and risk management is therefore likely to vary widely from company to company. In each case, however, operational management will be responsible for developing, operating and monitoring the system of internal control and for providing assurance that it has done so. The role of the audit committee, by contrast, will be to receive reports from those managers who are responsible for identifying and managing risks on the nature and effectiveness of the systems in place.

In addition, the audit committee will generally consider the results of reviews and investigations carried out by other assurance providers. Where the company's financial controls are under consideration, the audit committee may seek confirmation from the internal audit function and/or the company's external auditors on the adequacy and effectiveness of the controls. Where controls relate to non-financial matters, such as legal and regulatory compliance, health and safety and environmental protection, the audit committee may receive reports from the internal auditor or from other internal assurance providers, including the company secretary, with policy responsibilities for these areas of the company's activities.

### Whistleblowing

In addition to defining the formal responsibilities of the audit committee for internal control and risk management, the July 2003 Combined Code recommends that the audit committee should review arrangements made by the company to enable employee whistleblowers to report in confidence concerns about possible improprieties in matters of financial reporting or related issues. Specifically, the audit committee is enjoined to ensure that the company has appropriate arrangements in place for the proportionate and independent investigation of such reports and for taking any necessary follow-up action.

These recommendations of the July 2003 Combined Code reflect the failure of Enron, prior to its collapse, to take seriously the warnings of a senior employee who attempted to draw attention to the potential risks to the company's business of the unorthodox financial arrangements which contributed to its ultimate demise. Similar provisions are contained in the Sarbanes-Oxley Act and in other international responses to the Enron scandal. It is important to note, however, that improprieties and malpractice with potentially significant effects on the company's well-being are not limited to financial and accounting matters. Corporate failures in other areas, such as those relating to product quality, the safety of employees and the general public and the protection of the environment, may also inflict serious and long-lasting damage on the company's reputation and standing.

While it is clearly appropriate for the audit committee to satisfy itself that an appropriate whistleblowing procedure is in place, care should be taken to ensure that the scope of the procedure is wide enough to ensure that all matters of concern are surfaced and investigated. Further details on employee whistleblowing procedures can be found at *Chapter 12.*

## Internal audit

Previous UK codes of corporate governance have recognised the value of internal audit, but have recommended only that companies which do not have such a function should 'from time to time' review the need for one. The July 2003 Combined Code takes a much stronger line, recommending that where there is no internal audit function, the audit committee should consider annually whether there is a need for one and should make a recommendation to the board. It proposes also that the reasons for the absence of an internal audit function should be explained to shareholders in the audit committee section of the annual report and accounts.

Where the company has an internal audit function, the July 2003 Combined Code envisages that the audit committee should play a key role in ensuring that it is independent and has the necessary resources, standing and authority within the company to enable it to discharge its functions.

## The selection, appointment and remuneration of the external auditor

The primary role of the external auditors is to provide shareholders with an expert and independent opinion as to whether the accounting statements prepared by the company's directors give a true and fair view of its financial position and performance and comply with the relevant laws and regulations. For this reason, the external auditors are in principle appointed by the shareholders in general meeting and report directly to the shareholders through their statement in the annual report and accounts.

## The audit committee and the internal audit function

### Independence of the internal audit function

The audit committee should:

- approve any proposal to appoint or dismiss the head of the internal audit function;
- ensure that the head of internal audit has direct access to the board chairman and to the audit committee;
- meet the head of internal audit at least once a year without management;
- satisfy itself that the internal audit function carries out its activities in accordance with the professional standards of independence and objectivity appropriate for internal auditors.

### Internal audit resources

The audit committee should:

- keep under review the human resources of the internal audit function and ensure that these are of sufficient scale and quality to enable it to carry out its responsibilities;
- ensure that the internal audit function has proper access to information.

### Effectiveness of the internal audit function

The audit committee should:

- ensure that the internal audit function is directly accountable to the audit committee;
- review and approve the internal audit function's remit, having regard to the complementary roles of the internal and external auditors;
- assess and endorse the annual internal audit work plan;
- regularly consider reports on the outcome of the internal auditors' work and the effectiveness of any actions taken as a result of internal findings;
- monitor and assess the role and effectiveness of the internal audit function in the context of the company's internal control and risk management system.
- review and monitor management's responsiveness to the internal auditor's findings and recommendations

In practice, however, the external auditors' day-to-day contact with the company is with its executive directors, senior managers and other employees. Further, the views of executive management have typically shaped the recommendation on the appointment or reappointment of the external auditors put to the shareholders, who have thus been given little opportunity or encouragement to participate in the appointment process.

As the CGAA pointed out in its final report to the UK Government, the effect of this has been to relegate the shareholders to the role of little more than spectators in the appointment and reappointment of the external auditors. At the same time, it has put the independence of the external auditors at risk by making them reliant for future work on the views of the executive management whose financial statements it is their job to audit. The pitfalls inherent in this situation have been highlighted by the Enron affair, where there is evidence that the external auditors failed to challenge (or even colluded in) questionable accounting practices rather than jeopardise their ongoing relationship with management.

Reviews carried in the UK and elsewhere in the light of the Enron débâcle have considered how the risks arising from the over-involvement of management in the appointment and reappointment of external auditors can be reduced. Among the options proposed have been tighter rules on the rotation of lead audit partners and the introduction of requirements for the compulsory rotation of audit firms.

### Rotation of audit partners

It is well established in most jurisdictions that, in order to prevent the independence of the auditor from being compromised by a developing personal relationship with the client company, the same individual within an audit firm should not serve as the lead audit partner for a particular client for an excessive period of time. In the UK, the professional bodies within the accountancy and auditing profession have generally recommended to their members that lead audit partners should be rotated by their firms at intervals of not more than seven years. In the light of recommendations from the EU and the CGAA, however, it is now generally accepted that the maximum period before rotation of the lead audit partner should be reduced to five years. In addition, partner rotation should extend beyond the engagement partner to the other audit partners, who should be rotated by their firms at intervals of no more than seven years.

### Audit firm rotation and compulsory re-tendering

It has been suggested, however, that audit partner rotation may not be sufficient to prevent the development of too cosy a relationship between executive management and the external auditors, particularly where the client's business represents a high proportion of the audit firm's income. To counter this risk, it has been argued that there should be a formal requirement for rotation of audit firms, whereby companies would be required to change external auditors at prescribed intervals. Proposed methodologies have included a requirement for companies to undertake a formal assessment of the need for replacement of the external auditors every three years. Alternatively, as a 'backstop', companies might be required, at interval of no more than 10–15 years, to seek competitive bids from a number of firms, including the incumbent, for appointment as external auditor. The competing bids would then be assessed by the company, with the audit committee playing a leading role, and a recommendation made to shareholders.

It is argued that compulsory replacement of the external auditors after a defined period would enhance auditor independence because the incumbent firm, in the knowledge that its appointment was for a fixed period, would have nothing to gain from gaining favour with management by adopting an unchallenging approach to audit issues. Conversely, there are concerns that compulsory replacement might have negative effects on audit quality and effectiveness, particularly in the early years of a new appointment as the new auditors familiarise themselves with the client's business, financial and non-financial systems and recent history.

Accordingly, it has been concluded in the UK that companies should not be required to replace their external auditors at prescribed intervals. Instead, it is recommended that the audit committee should have an enhanced role in the appointment and monitoring of the external auditors' performance and relationship with management, with emphasis on independence where the auditors' appointment is of long duration.

### The role of the audit committee

Against this background, the July 2003 Combined Code recommends that the audit committee, rather than executive management, should have formal responsibility for recommending to shareholders, via the board, the appointment, reappointment and removal of external auditors. It suggests, moreover, that if the board does not accept the audit committee's recommendation, this should be drawn to the shareholders' attention through an explicit statement in the annual report and accounts, with an account of the audit committee's recommendation and an explanation of the board's reasons for taking a different position.

Where the audit committee recommends to shareholders that the incumbent firm should be reappointed as external auditor, its recommendation should be based on an assessment of the firm's qualifications, expertise and resources, effectiveness and independence. As part of this process, the audit committee should satisfy itself of the adequacy of the firm's quality control procedures and its compliance with relevant UK professional and regulatory requirements and ethical guidance. In this context, it should pay particular attention to the arrangements for the rotation of audit partners and the extent to which the firm is economically dependent, at the level of the firm, office or individual partner, on the fees paid by the client company.

If, on the basis of its assessment of the incumbent firm's performance, the audit committee proposes to the board that the firm should be replaced as the company's external auditors, it should oversee the selection process and make appropriate recommendations, through the board, for consideration by the shareholders in general meeting. In addition, the audit committee should approve the external auditors' terms of engagement and remuneration. In doing so, it should satisfy itself that the level of fee payable represents value for money, but is also sufficient to enable an effective audit to be conducted.

## Audit independence

The enhancement by the Combined Code of the audit committee's role in appointing, reappointing and remunerating the external auditors is designed to mitigate the risk to auditor independence arising from the reliance of the audit firm on executive management to secure continued business. Other sources of threat to the independence and objectivity of the external auditors may arise, for example from:

> the existence of a mutual business interest or close personal relationship between the audit firm or anyone closely associated with it (such as an audit partner) on the one hand, and the client company or any of its officers on the other;
> the appointment of former partners or senior employees of the audit firm to positions within the client companies; or
> non-audit work, for example, corporate finance advice, tax compliance and planning, information technology services and management consultancy, carried out for an audit client.

## UK PROFESSIONAL AND REGULATORY REQUIREMENTS FOR ACCOUNTING AND AUDITING

The Smith Guidance recommends that the audit committee should have procedures to ensure the independence and objectivity of the external auditor, taking into account relevant UK professional and regulatory requirements. These arrangements have been reviewed in the light of Enron and other financial accounting and reporting failures and a new regulatory structure is now being established.

The new regulatory structure will involve:

- The *Financial Reporting Council* will in future act as the independent regulator of the accountancy profession, with responsibility for promoting transparent and full reporting of relevant and reliable financial, governance and other information and effective and independent audit.
- The *Accounting Standards Board* will continue to have responsibility for issuing and amending accounting standards in response to evolving business practice and will also be responsible for liaison with the International Accounting Standards Board (IASB) on the intended adoption of international accounting standards by the EU in 2005.
- The *Auditing Practices Board* will continue to be responsible for establishing auditing standards with which external auditors are required to comply, setting ethical standards to ensure the independence, objectivity and integrity of external auditors and other assurance providers and working towards the intended implementation in the UK of international auditing standards in 2005.
- The *Financial Reporting Review Panel* will continue to be responsible for reviewing companies' published reports for compliance with reporting requirements, but will in future take a more proactive approach to this process by developing and operating a selective programme of review, based primarily on risk assessments, and by extending its review to relevant non-financial statements published by companies.
- A new *Professional Oversight Board for Accountancy* will be responsible for independent oversight of the regulation of the accountancy and auditing profession and will also have delegated statutory authority for the recognition of the supervisory bodies and qualifying bodies for the profession.
- A new *Accountancy Investigation and Discipline Board* will be responsible for providing a fair, independent and expert system for the investigation of significant public interest disciplinary cases involving the accountancy profession and for imposing appropriate sanctions.

*Threats to auditor independence and objectivity*

In its Guide to Professional Ethics, the Institute of Chartered Accountants in England and Wales (ICAEW) identifies several generic sources of threat, real and apparent, to the independence and objectivity of external auditors. These are:

> *The self-interest threat:* a threat to the auditor's objectivity stemming from a financial or other self-interest conflict. This could arise, for example, from a direct or indirect interest in a client or from a fear of losing a client.
> *The self-review threat:* difficulty in maintaining objectivity arising from a requirement, in reaching audit conclusions, to challenge or re-evaluate any product or judgement of a previous audit or consultancy assignment carried out by the same auditor or audit firm.
> *The advocacy threat:* the auditor's objectivity may be impaired if he or she becomes an advocate for (or against) the client's position in any adversarial proceedings or situations. While there is nothing inherently improper about a position of advocacy, if the auditor takes a strongly proactive stance or adopts an extreme position on a matter of professional judgement on the client's behalf, this may appear to be incompatible with the special objectivity that audit requires.
> *The familiarity threat:* an auditor who acts for the same client for a prolonged period of time or who is inadvertently drawn into the provision of management functions may become over-influenced by the personality and qualities of the directors and management, and consequently identify too closely with their interests. Alternatively, an auditor may fail to test management representations with sufficient rigour because of over-familiarity with the client or with the issues involved.
> *The intimidation threat:* an auditor may occasionally become intimidated by threats, by dominating personality, or by other pressures, actual or feared, from a director or manager of the client or by some other party.

To counter these threats, the July 2003 Combined Code recommends that, in addition to its involvement in the appointment and reappointment of the external auditors, the audit committee should have explicit responsibility for reviewing and monitoring the external auditor's independence and objectivity and the effectiveness of the audit process. For this purpose, the Smith Guidance appended to the Combined Code recommends that the audit committee should:

> seek reassurance that the audit firm, and individual partners and staff involved in the audit, have no family, financial, employment, investment or business relationship with the company;
> seek from the audit firm, on an annual basis, information about the firm's policies and processes for maintaining independence;
> monitor the audit firm's compliance with relevant requirements, including those relating to the rotation of audit partners and staff; and
> agree with the board and monitor the company's policy for the employment of former employees of the external auditor, paying particular attention to employees of the audit firm who were part of the audit team and moved directly to the company.

More broadly, the audit committee should oversee the activities of the external auditors, including the planning and execution of the annual audit cycle, and should monitor the external auditors' effectiveness and any risks to their independence arising from their relationships with the company's management.

### The audit committee's oversight of the audit cycle

While the audit committee must be careful not to duplicate the role of the external auditors, it should seek to satisfy itself, before the beginning of the annual audit cycle, that the intended scope of the audit is adequate and that the audit firm place appropriate quality control procedures and has taken proper steps to respond to changes in regulatory or other requirements. To this end, the audit committee should be involved in the planning of the annual audit. It should review and agree the engagement letter issued by the external auditor at the start of each audit and should establish that the auditor's work plan and resources, including the seniority, expertise and experience of the audit team, are consistent with the terms of the audit engagement. If the audit committee is not satisfied with the proposed scope of the audit, it should request that additional work be undertaken.

On completion of the audit, the audit committee should review with the external auditors, in the absence of executive management where appropriate, the findings of their work as reflected in the management letter or equivalent. The review should address the key accounting and auditing judgements encountered in the course of the audit and should consider, on the basis of the external auditors' opinion and the audit committee's own knowledge, whether the information provided by the company's management has been accurate and complete. In addition, the audit committee should review the level of errors and misstatements revealed during the audit and should establish, in discussion with management and the external auditors, whether adjustments recommended by the external auditors have been made and, if not, the reasons why not.

### Annual assessment

At the end of each annual audit cycle, the audit committee should review the quality and effectiveness of the audit process. It should assess whether the external auditors have performed the audit as planned and establish the reasons for any changes, obtaining feedback as necessary about the conduct of the audit from key members of the company's management, including the finance director and the head of internal audit.

In the course of its annual assessment, the audit committee should also consider the relationships between the company and the audit firm, including the provision of non-audit services, taking into account the views of the external auditor, the company's management and the internal audit function. Based on its assessment, the audit committee should determine whether any potential risks to the external auditors' judgement or independence arise from its relationships with management.

## Non-audit work

### The threat to auditor independence

Perhaps the most contentious source of potential risk to the independence and objectivity of the external auditors is the provision by audit firms of consultancy services which are outside the scope of the statutory audit but may none the less be closely associated with it.

It is generally acknowledged that the provision of such services by the external auditor can have significant advantages for the client company in terms of quality and cost, arising in particular from the auditors' understanding of the business and its management. As a result, the ratio of non-audit to audit services supplied to audit clients has increased rapidly in recent years, while the major audit and accountancy firms have built on their audit relationships in developing their consultancy businesses.

At the same time, however, the provision by the audit firm of non-audit services may constitute a significant threat to auditor independence, particularly where the firm's income from non-audit work for an audit client equals or exceeds the statutory audit fee. In these circumstances, the audit process may be less thorough than it should be because the audit firm is reluctant to challenge the company's executive management on whose goodwill it relies for its access to lucrative consultancy work. Additionally, a firm's ability to take an independent view may be inhibited in circumstances where it is required to audit the outcome of transactions recommended by its own consultancy arm.

Concerns about the risks to auditor independence represented by the provision of non-audit services are of long-standing, and it is well established in most jurisdictions that external auditors should not supply non-audit services which involve them in taking management decisions, auditing their own work or acting as an advocate for the client in an adversarial situation. However, events at Enron and WorldCom (where Andersen's consultancy income in the company's final year of trading was $12.4 million, compared with the statutory audit fee of $4.4 million), raised fresh concerns and prompted governments and regulators to consider whether tighter controls were needed on the extent to which audit firms should be permitted to carry out consultancy work for audit clients.

Suggested approaches to the regulation of non-audit services have ranged from a total ban on non-audit work for audit clients to various forms of partial prohibition, for example, through a defined limit on a firm's permitted consultancy income as a percentage of the client's statutory audit fee or through targeted restrictions on the type of consultancy work that a firm could undertake for an audit client. Services identified as representing a potentially unacceptable level of risk to auditor independence include involvement by the audit form in internal audit, the provision of valuation or other expert services relevant to the financial statements, taxation advice other than the application of established tax law, consultancy on IT and financial information technology systems and various legal services, including litigation support.

### The role of the audit committee

The Smith Report concluded that a prescriptive approach, though the imposition of specific restrictions on the auditor's supply of non-audit services, would be inappropriate. It therefore recommended that the audit committee of each listed company should develop its own policy on the supply by the auditor of non-audit services for board approval. The audit committee should explain to shareholders, in its statement in the annual report and accounts, how its policy on the provision of non-audit services by the external auditor provides adequate protection of auditor independence.

The fundamental principles underlying the audit committee's policy should be that external auditors should not audit their own firm's consultancy work, make management decisions for the company or assume the role of advocate for the company. In the light of these principles, the policy should specify the types of non-audit work from which, in the view of the audit committee, the external auditors should be totally excluded.

Where the audit committee considers that it may be permissible for the external auditors to carry out non-audit work, the policy should identify the types of non-audit work for which the external auditors can be engaged without referral to the audit committee and types of non-audit work for which a case-by-case decision by the audit committee is necessary. In the latter case, the audit committee should consider whether it is possible to give approval to individual items in advance; where this is not practicable, the audit committee may wish to give a general pre-approval for certain classes for work, subject to a fee limit determined by the audit committee and ratified by the board.

The Smith Guidance recommends that, in all cases where the procurement of non-audit services from the external auditor is under consideration, the audit committee must satisfy itself that the audit firm has the necessary skills and experience to provide the proposed non-audit service. In addition, it must ensure that adequate safeguards are in place to ensure that the provision of the proposed service does not threaten the objectivity and independence of the external audit. The audit committee should also consider the fees paid by the company for the provision of non-audit services by the external auditor, on a case-by-case basis and in aggregate, relative to the statutory audit fee.

## Chapter summary

> The collapse of Enron and other major US corporations amid allegations of serious financial malpractice by senior executives and collusion by external auditors has raised serious questions about the extent to which audit committees can ensure the reliability of reporting and auditing processes.

> Reviews undertaken by governments and financial regulators in the US, the UK and elsewhere have established a consensus on the need to strengthen the framework of corporate governance generally and, more particularly, to clarify and enhance the role of the audit committee.

> In the UK, changes to the Combined Code clearly envisage that the role and responsibilities of the audit committee will become more onerous in future, with significant implications for the composition and resources of the audit committee and the skills, personal qualities and remuneration of its members.

> Among its other responsibilities, it is envisaged that the audit committee should in future have primary responsibility for recommending to shareholders appoint-

ment, reappointment and removal of the external auditors and for safeguarding the independence and objectivity of both internal and external auditors.

> In keeping with its enhanced role, it is intended that the audit committee should in future account directly to shareholders for the effective discharge of its responsibilities.

# Internal Control and
# Risk Management

This chapter describes the allocation of responsibility for internal control and risk management between the board and its sub-committees; management and employees; and internal audit and other internal assurance providers. It also briefly outlines the elements of an embedded system of internal control and risk management; and examines the need, underlined by Enron, to incorporate within the company's internal control and risk management arrangements effective whistleblowing procedures designed to ensure that possible accounting irregularities and other failures of internal control can be reported and investigated.

It has long been recognised that directors have a primary responsibility for the stewardship of investors' assets and the protection of their investment. The company's system of internal control has as its main purpose the identification and management of risks which might impede the achievement of the company's business objectives and thereby reduce the value of shareholders' investments. Internal control and risk management are thus inextricably linked and are integral to the discharge of the directors' responsibilities.

The traditional assumption has been that internal control and risk management are concerned with financially quantifiable risks, whether arising directly (for example, from fraud, theft or error) or indirectly (for example, from fire or flood damage or from claims for personal injury or product liability). Broadly speaking, two forms of response have been considered appropriate, namely insurance and internal controls in the form of detailed rules and procedures designed to reduce the likelihood of fraud, theft, error and accident.

Both insurance and internal rules and procedures are essential elements of any company's system of internal control. At the same time, however, there is increasing recognition that traditional responses to risk may be insufficient by themselves to enable directors to discharge their obligations to shareholders. Exclusive focus on quantifiable financial and operational risks may result in failure to identify and manage more subtle and less quantifiable forms of risk, particularly those which may impact on the company's reputation. Equally, prescriptive rules and procedures may be effective in some situations and in the short term. When used on their own, particularly in the context of an authoritarian 'blame culture', such techniques are likely to fail to enlist the active participation of employees in risk management.

The limitations of traditional approaches to internal control were recognised by the Cadbury Committee on the Financial Aspects of Corporate Governance, whose report, published in 1992, suggested that directors' responsibilities should not be limited to the management of financial risks, but should encompass a systematic approach to risks of all kinds. This proposition was not generally accepted, however. The final version of the Cadbury Code and the subsequent guidance produced by the Rutteman Working Group recommended only that the board should have responsibility for the company's system of internal *financial* control, thus reinforcing the traditional view that risk management and internal control are top-down activities which are essentially concerned with the control of financial risks.

In its report, issued in 1998, the Hampel Committee on Corporate Governance returned to the holistic view taken by Cadbury, recommending that the board should be responsible for all aspects of internal control and risk management. This proposal was accepted and reflected in the 1998 Combined Code and has been retained in the July 2003 Combined Code, Provision C.2.1 states that:

> '*The board should, at least annually, conduct a review of the effectiveness of the group's system of internal control and should report to shareholders that they have done so. The review should cover all material controls, including financial, operational and compliance controls and risk management systems.*'

The broad conception of internal control and risk management introduced in the 1998 Combined Code is reflected and amplified in the report of the Turnbull working party published by the ICAEW in 1999. The Turnbull guidance is careful to recognise that profits are in part the reward for successful risk-taking. The purpose of a system of internal control is therefore to minimise the company's exposure to unnecessary risks, rather than to eliminate risk altogether. While even a sound system of internal control cannot exclude the possibility that company will incur losses, it should facilitate effective and efficient operation, enabling the company to manage significant known risks to the achievement of its business objectives and to respond quickly to new risks as they emerge.

The Turnbull guidance emphasises that, to be effective, the company's internal control and risk management arrangements must:

> ❯ be embedded in the company's day-to-day business processes, including its investment appraisal methodology, decision making structures, performance assessment and reward system and internal communication arrangements;
> ❯ be led by the directors through their demonstrable personal commitment to effective risk management and their own behaviour in terms of ethical conduct and decision-making;
> ❯ extend beyond quantifiable financial and physical risks to include risks arising from technological, legal, health and safety, environmental, reputational and business probity issues.

The report of the Turnbull Working Party, *Internal Control: Guidance for Directors on the Combined Code*, published by the ICAEW in September 1999, is reproduced in *Appendix 19*.

The case for an embedded system of internal control and risk management encompassing a broad range of financial and non-financial risks has been reinforced by the collapse of Enron. In that company, rules existed, but were held in low regard and were deliberately overridden by directors and senior managers. This vividly demonstrated that unless the company's system of internal control is embedded in a positive corporate culture, prescriptive rules and procedures alone may not be enough to prevent fraud and collusion between employees, up to and including directors. In such circumstances, ethical failures are not just a matter of personal morality, but are issues of wider corporate culture with potentially devastating effects on investors, employees, pensioners and local communities.

## Responsibilities for the company's system of internal control and risk management

As part of its accountability to shareholders for the strategic direction of the company and the safeguarding of its assets, the board of directors has ultimate responsibility for ensuring the existence of an appropriate system of internal control and risk management. In practice, however, the board will normally delegate to management many of the detailed activities involved and will also require employees in general to exercise personal responsibilities in respect of risk and control.

As a first step, the board must determine how it will fulfil its responsibilities for oversight. These may be discharged by the full board, by the audit committee or another committee of the board with specific responsibility for risk and control, or by a combination of these. In allocating responsibility, the board will need to consider the nature of the company's principal risks, the size, style and composition of the board and, in particular, the enhanced responsibilities of the audit committee under the provisions of the July 2003 Combined Code. Even if responsibilities are delegated to the audit committee or another appropriate committee, the board as a whole will still need form a collective view after due and careful enquiry. The enhanced role of the audit committee under the recommendations of the July 2003 Combined Code are discussed in detail in *Chapter 11*.

Having defined its own role, the board must assign responsibility for detailed identification, evaluation, monitoring and reporting on risk, allocating clear roles to managers and employees in the business units, risk management specialists and internal assurance providers, including the company's internal audit function.

### The role of the board

The board's responsibilities in respect of the company's system of internal control and risk management fall into four main categories:

1   oversight of the company's internal control and risk management arrangements to ensure that these promote the achievement of strategic objectives and safeguard shareholders' assets;

2   ongoing review of the effectiveness of the system of internal control and risk management;

3   annual review of the effectiveness of the system; and

4   formal confirmation to shareholders that the annual review of effectiveness has been carried out.

### The board's oversight of the system of internal control and risk management

In setting out its policies with regard to internal control and determining the elements of a sound system of internal control, the board should itself consider the following factors or should review the process by which they have been considered by management and formally endorse their conclusions:

> the nature and extent of the risks facing the company, with particular attention to risks which threaten the achievement of strategic objectives which are key to the success of the company;

> the company's risk appetite or risk tolerance, in terms of the extent and categories of risk which it is acceptable for the company to bear;

> the likelihood of risks concerned materialising;

> the company's ability to reduce the incidence and impact on the business of risks that do materialise; and

> the costs of operating particular controls relative to the benefit thereby obtained in managing the related risks.

Having done this, the board must publish a clear risk management policy covering its risk management philosophy and allocating responsibility for all aspects of risk and control. Consistent messages and priorities should be embodied in policy documents promulgated throughout the organisation, including the company's mission statement or corporate vision, its employee code of conduct and policy statements. Where necessary, the same messages and priorities should be cascaded to individual functions, divisions or operating units through detailed operating procedures and should be supported by appropriate staff training, performance management approaches and reward systems.

### The board's ongoing review of the effectiveness of internal control

Ongoing monitoring and reporting are essential components of a sound system of internal control and risk management. None the less, the board should not rely solely on these embedded processes, but should instead establish a defined process for its review of the system's effectiveness. In particular, it should ensure that it receives reports from management which comply with agreed procedures and provide a balanced assessment of the significant risks and the effectiveness of the system of internal control. To this end, the board must maintain a frank and open dialogue with management on matters of risk and control, and must ensure that there are no pressures on management to conceal control failures or weaknesses.

The Turnbull guidance (paragraph 31) recommends that, when reviewing reports from management, the board should:

> consider what are the significant risks and assess how they have been identified, evaluated and managed;

> assess the effectiveness of the related system of internal control in managing the significant risks, having regard, in particular, to any significant failings or weaknesses that have been reported;

> consider whether necessary actions are being taken promptly to remedy any significant failings or weaknesses; and

> consider whether the findings indicate a need for more extensive monitoring of the system of internal control.

Where appropriate, the board should commission more detailed reports on any areas of concern highlighted by management, including any reported issues which may be duplicated in other areas of business or otherwise appear to represent an unacceptable degree of risk.

### The board's annual review of the effectiveness of internal control

In addition to its ongoing review process, the board is required to undertake a specific annual assessment of the effectiveness of the company's system of internal control and risk management as a basis for its report to shareholders.

The board should specify in advance the process it intends to adopt for its annual review in order to ensure that it is provided by the company's management and internal assurance providers with information of the appropriate quality and detail to support for the statement to shareholders. This should revisit the issues raised in reports considered during the year, together with any additional information requested by the board.

The Turnbull guidance (paragraph 33) recommends that, in the course of its annual review, the board should consider:

> any changes since its last review in the nature and extent of significant risks and the company's ability to respond effectively to changes in its business and external environment;

> the scope and quality of management's ongoing monitoring of risks and the system of internal control, and, where applicable, the work of the company's internal audit function and other internal providers of assurance;

> the frequency with which the results of management monitoring have been communicated to the board or its committees and the extent to which this communication has enabled directors to build up a cumulative assessment of the state of control in the company and the effectiveness with which risk is being managed;

> the incidence of significant control failings or weaknesses that have been identified at any time during the period and the extent to which these have resulted in unforeseen outcomes or contingencies that have had, could have had, or may in the future have, a material impact on the company's financial performance or condition; and

> the effectiveness of the company's public reporting process.

*Reporting to shareholders on internal control*

Based on its annual review, the board is required to include in the annual report and accounts a statement in narrative form. This must acknowledge the board's responsibility for the company's system of internal control and for reviewing its effectiveness, while pointing out that no system of internal control can eliminate the possibility of failure to achieve business objectives.

The statement should confirm that the board has ensured the existence of an ongoing system for identifying, evaluating and managing the significant risks faced by the company, that this system has been in place for the year under review and up to the date of approval of the annual report and accounts, and that is regularly reviewed by the board in accordance with the Turnbull guidance. It should summarise the process applied by the board has applied in reviewing the effectiveness of the system and dealing with any significant problems revealed by its review. If the board is unable to make any of the required disclosures, it must identify the areas concerned and explain what it is doing to rectify the situation.

While the board is not required to give an opinion on the effectiveness of the company's system of internal control or to identify specific risk areas, is essential that its statement should provide meaningful, high-level information and does not give a misleading impression. To this end, the Turnbull guidance encourages the board to provide additional information to assist understanding of the company's risk management processes and system of internal control.

## The role of management

While the board has ultimate responsibility for ensuring the existence of an appropriate system of internal control and risk management, line managers in the company's business units will generally have delegated responsibility for:

> identifying and evaluating the significant risks faced by the company and presenting their conclusions to the board;
> designing and operating a system of internal control and risk management within the policies and parameters defined by the board; and
> monitoring the effectiveness of the system and reporting to the board.

*Risk identification and evaluation*

Risk identification and evaluation can be carried out by external consultants, but the process is more likely to be effective if it is conducted in-house with the direct involvement of business unit managers and employees. The business units will have immediate awareness of the significant risks affecting their area of responsibility, and will also be more committed to the resulting control measures if they have ownership of the risk management process.

There are numerous techniques and methodologies available for identifying and evaluating risk, including SWOT (Strengths, Weaknesses, Opportunities, Threats) and BPEST (Business, Political, Economic, Social, Technological) analyses and Hazard & Operability (HAZOP) studies. These could be used alone or in combination, and could be used to collect data by remote means (for example, through questionnaires) or directly through workshops or team meetings. Where workshops and meetings can be arranged, it may be helpful for discussions to be facilitated by the company's internal audit function or, where a dedicated resource exists, by internal risk management specialists.

The exact choice of methodology is probably less important than ensuring that the risk identification and evaluation process is well communicated and consistent. Regardless of the methodology chosen, the process should:

> assess both the probability of an identified risk occurring and its likely impact;
> identify the basic cause of each risk;
> analysis interdependencies between risks, bearing in mind that such interdependencies may have a critical effect on the potential impact of risks on the cost benefit analysis applied to proposed controls; and
> consider the reputational impact of risks as well as their financial or operational impact.

*Designing and operating the system of internal control and risk management*

Managers throughout the company are responsible for the integration of risk management objectives into the day-to-day activities of their operating areas and will therefore need to design and implement control measures in the form of operating and reporting procedures tailored to each type of activity for which they are accountable.

In addition, however, they must promote risk awareness on the part of employees so that all individuals within the company understand their ongoing responsibility for risk management. This is likely to involve a range of different techniques, including training and development, staff briefings and the use of the performance appraisal and reward structure, to encourage employees to participate actively in the risk management process.

*Monitoring the system of internal control and risk management*

Business unit managers are responsible for monitoring the system of internal control and risk management on an ongoing basis and for reporting promptly and systematically to the board on the system's effectiveness, drawing attention to new and emerging risks and to any weaknesses in existing control measures. To this end, they must develop self-assessment measures which enable them to monitor the key business and financial activities within their respective areas of operation and highlight significant variances from plan or other unexpected events casts at sufficient frequency to allow appropriate action to be taken.

## Internal audit and other internal assurance providers

Management monitoring is an important part of an embedded system of internal control and risk management, but is likely to be insufficiently objective to provide adequate assurance to the board of the effectiveness of the system. Independent assurance will therefore need to be provided by in-house specialists including:

> *The internal audit function:* the role of the internal audit function in respect of internal control and risk management will vary from one company to another

depending on the nature of the business, the legal and regulatory environment in which the company operates and the availability of other specialist resources in-house. Internal audit will certainly be responsible for providing assurance to the board on the adequacy of the internal controls relevant to significant financial and accounting risks, and in some circumstances may also take the lead in auditing all risk management processes across the company and in co-ordinating all risk reporting to the board.

> *The risk management function:* depending on its size, the company has no dedicated resource in the field of risk management; alternatively, it may have a single risk specialist, who may be full- or part-time, or a full risk management department. Where a specialist resource exists, its role is likely to include advising the board on the company's overall policy and strategy for risk management, building a culture of risk awareness within the company, with education and training where necessary, and reporting to the board on the adequacy of the company's internal control and risk management arrangements as a whole.

> *Other internal assurance providers:* assurance may also be provided to the board on specific aspects of the company's internal control and risk arrangements by functional specialists in areas such as legal and regulatory compliance, health and safety and environmental policy.

In each case, the purpose of independent review by internal audit and other assurance providers should be to challenge the outcome of management's self-assessment and to report to the board on the effectiveness of the company's system of internal control and risk management. Key areas for review will be the completeness of the strategic objectives covered by the system, the adequacy of the process adopted by management for the identification, assessment and management of the significant business risks and the transparency of reporting on control failures and weaknesses.

## Embedding internal control and risk management

The systems of internal control and risk management adopted by different companies will vary according to company-specific factors, including the nature of the business, the markets and regulatory environments in which the company operates and the attitudes of shareholders and directors towards risk-taking. In all cases, however, the board is responsible for ensuring the development and maintenance of an embedded system of internal control and risk management, based on a continuous cycle of activities encompassing the company's policies and procedures, the allocation of tasks and responsibilities, its communication processes and its cultural and behavioural norms. Typical key stages in the cycle are:

1  *Defining the company's strategic objectives and translating them into business plans, targets and budgets*

In order to identify and manage its significant risks, the board must first define the strategic objectives which are key to the company's long-term success, taking into account its main markets and the legal, social, political and cultural constraints on its activities. These strategic objectives must then be broken down into the detailed business plans, with associated targets and budgets, through which the company's key objectives will be delivered. Care must be taken to identify all business-critical objectives and plans, to ensure the inclusion of all significant business risks which might impact adversely on the company.

## 2 Evaluating the significant risks to the achievement of the company's objectives

Having defined the company's strategic objectives and the means by which they will be realised, the board must formally identify and analyse the risks to the achievement of objectives in order to establish a logical and systematic basis for determining how significant risks should be managed. A broad-ranging process is important, bearing in mind that risks may arise from wide variety of internal and external sources. The board, assisted as necessary by senior operational management and internal and external assurance providers, should assess the materiality of each of the identified risks, taking into account both the magnitude of the potential financial loss associated with each risk and the probability that the risk will actually occur. The identified risks can then be ranked in order of materiality to produce a risk profile, on the basis of which the board and senior management can begin to prioritise the company's internal control and risk management activities.

## 3 Determining the treatments of avoidable and transferable risks

When the risk analysis and ranking process has been completed, the resulting risk profile can be used to determine the risk treatments appropriate for different levels and types of risk. Depending on the attitude of the company and its investors towards risk-taking, the board may conclude that certain risks are unacceptable and may therefore decide to avoid them, either by discontinuing the activity from which the risk arises or by determining that the company will not enter into new high-risk activities. Other types of risk may be transferable, in whole or in part, for example, through insurance, hedging contracts, diversification or joint venture arrangements. After all practicable risk avoidance and risk transfer measures have been taken, the remaining risks or risk elements (known as 'residual risks') must be accepted and managed.

## 4 Designing or modifying internal controls

When the company's residual risks have been identified, internal controls must be designed (or existing controls modified) and implemented to ensure that they are managed to acceptable levels. Internal control activities occur throughout the organisation, at all levels and in all functions, and include a diverse range of measures: typical controls are delegations of authority, requirements for approvals and authorisations, segregation of duties, reporting procedures, accounting and other reconciliations, data protection, operating procedures, safety and environmental protection rules and physical security measures. In addition, contingency arrangements, in the form of a disaster recovery or business continuity plan, will need to be made and activated in the event of a serious interruption to business-critical activities. In designing its internal controls for the management of residual risks, the company should balance the costs and benefits of controlling risk and should also ensure that its control activities able to respond quickly to emerging risks arising from both internal and external change.

### 5   Establishing and maintaining an appropriate control environment

Importantly, the board must ensure that an appropriate control environment is established and maintained within which specific control activities can function effectively. This will depend not only on the extent to which internal control and risk management are aligned with day-to-day business activities, but also on less tangible factors such as the company's organisational culture, values, competencies and reward structures as manifested in the behaviour and attitudes of directors, managers and employees. Of particular importance is the avoidance of a 'blame culture' which encourages the concealment of breakdowns in control. The control environment must therefore include effective channels for communicating information down, across and up the organisation. All employees must receive a clear message from the directors that internal control and risk management are priority activities and must receive training on their own role and responsibilities and how these relate to the work of others and contribute to the achievement of the company's strategic objectives. Procedures must also be established for the immediate reporting to appropriate levels of management of control failings or weaknesses that are identified and for the careful aggregation and analysis of information that might indicate a need for preventative action.

### 6   Monitoring the effectiveness of the system of internal control

In addition to ongoing reporting arrangements, the company's system of internal control must be formally monitored in order to assess its quality and effectiveness over time. The monitoring process adopted should provide assurance that appropriate controls are in place and that the associated procedures and reporting arrangements are understood and followed and should identify any lessons for the assessment and management of risk in the future.

### 7   Adjusting strategic objectives, business plans and risk management activities

Experience with the operation and monitoring of the system of internal control and risk management should considered by the board in its discussions of the company's strategic objectives, business plan and risk profile. Where appropriate, these should be adjusted to take account of the significant financial and non-financial risks arising from internal sources and from changes in the external operating environment.

Detailed guidance on the design, operation and monitoring of internal control and risk management systems is given in the Risk Management Standard published in 2002 by the Institute of Risk Management (IRM), the Association of Insurance and Risk Managers (AIRMIC) and National Forum for Risk Management in the Public Sector (ALARM) can be found at www.airmic.com.

# The lessons of Enron

## The need for whistleblowing procedures

However well designed a company's system of internal control and risk management may be, it may still fail to protect shareholders' assets and promote the achievement of strategic objectives if it is not integrated within a principled corporate culture. As part of the process of integration, there is increasing emphasis on the need for companies to establish whistleblowing procedures so that employees who know or suspect that illegal or unethical practices are taking place within the company can report them to management for investigation without exposing themselves to victimisation or other forms of reprisal. The potential value of such procedures has been underlined by the Enron scandal, where some of the damage inflicted on the company's investors, employees and other stakeholders might have been averted had the company taken appropriate steps to investigate the concerns raised by an internal whistleblower, Sherron Watkins, about accounting irregularities.

In the US, the Sarbanes–Oxley Act requires quoted companies to make arrangements for the receipt and investigation of whistleblower reports on financial, accounting and auditing matters. The need for UK listed companies to establish effective whistleblowing procedures is recognised in the July 2003 Combined Code which (as explained in *Chapter 11*) assigns to the audit committee responsibility for reviewing the arrangements whereby employees can, in confidence, raise concerns about possible improprieties in matters of financial reporting or other matters. While the audit committee's objective is to ensure that arrangements are in place for the proper investigation of such matters and for appropriate follow-up action, care is necessary to ensure that the scope of any procedure is wide enough to ensure that matters of concern unrelated to financial and accounting matters can also be reported and investigated.

## The statutory position in the UK

In the UK, workers who report known or suspected wrongdoings in their organisations are protected from victimisation or discrimination by the Public Interest Disclosure Act 1998 (PIDA). The Act protects people who raise concerns about past, present and future malpractices in relation to criminal acts; failure to comply with legal duties (such as negligence or breach of contract); miscarriages of justice; danger to health and safety; damage to the environment; and deliberate cover-up of any of these.

PIDA provides protection for all disclosures made in good faith, even if it is subsequently shown that the whistleblower had misunderstood or misinterpreted the circumstances. However, anyone who deliberately makes false or malicious allegations about an individual or corporate body cannot avail themselves of PIDA protection and will be subject to their employer's normal disciplinary procedures.

PIDA encourages workers to raise their concerns with their employers in the first instance, but it also allows external disclosure, for instance to a regulatory body, the police or the media, as long as there are good reasons for doing so. The Act details four such good reasons:

1   the concern was raised internally or with a prescribed regulator, but has not been
    properly addressed; or
2   the concern was not raised internally or with a prescribed regulator because the
    whistleblower reasonably believed he would be victimised; or
3   the concern was not raised internally or with a prescribed regulator because the
    whistleblower reasonably believed a cover-up was likely and there was no pre-
    scribed regulator; or
4   the concern was exceptionally serious.

## Establishing a whistleblowing procedure

A whistleblowing procedure will work only if it has the confidence of the employees
who are its intended users. It must be established and implemented with the involvement of employee representatives and must also have the visible commitment of the
company's directors and management. It is also essential that the whistleblowing procedure be kept separate from the company's employee grievance procedure: employees
who raise concerns through the whistleblowing procedure should not be regarded as
'complainants', but should instead be recognised as responsible individuals who are
doing the company a service by bringing to its attention matters which could potentially damage its reputation.

The ICSA's Best Practice Guide on whistleblowing, published in 1999, recommends
that a copy of the whistleblower procedure should be distributed to every employee
and should:

> set out clearly all aspects of the procedure, including the identity of the person or
  persons to whom concerns should be addressed;
> emphasise that the company takes malpractice and misconduct seriously, is
  committed to investigating all allegations and will protect employees who report
  concerns in good faith from reprisals even if, on investigation, their concerns
  prove to be honest mistakes;
> give examples of the types of misconduct for which employees should use the
  procedures and the level of evidence needed, stressing that positive proof is not
  needed but that the reporter should be able to show good reasons;
> explain the process by which concerns will be investigated and the outcome
  reported to directors; and
> make clear that false and malicious allegations will result in disciplinary action
  against the person making them.

In rare circumstances, employees with genuine concerns may be reluctant to use the
company's internal whistleblower procedure, perhaps because of fears that the procedure will be insufficient to protect them from intimidation by immediate colleagues or
superiors. To ensure that all such concerns are reported, the company should offer an
external reporting route as an alternative to its internal arrangements. Information
and advice on external reporting processes can be provided by the registered charity
Public Concern at Work (www.pcaw.co.uk).

## Chapter summary

> Directors have a primary responsibility for the stewardship of investors' assets and the protection of their investment through the company's system of internal control and risk management.

> Contrary to the traditional assumption has been that internal control and risk management are primarily concerned with insurable risks, there is increasing recognition of the potential impact of more subtle and less readily quantifiable forms of risk, particularly those which may impact on the company's reputation.

> Alongside this recognition, there is strong emphasis on the need for internal control to be embedded in the company's day-to-day business processes, including its investment appraisal methodology, decision making structures, performance assessment and reward system and internal communication arrangements.

> The case for an embedded system of internal control and risk management has been reinforced by evidence that, while Enron had a full complement of rules and procedures, it lacked an ethical culture in which rules were respected and upheld.

# Relations with Institutional Investors

There should be a dialogue with shareholders based on the mutual understanding of objectives. The board as a whole has responsibility for ensuring that a satisfactory dialogue with shareholders takes place.
> Main Principle D.1 Dialogue with Institutional Shareholders

Institutional shareholders should enter into a dialogue with companies based on the mutual understanding of objectives.
> Main Principle E.1 Dialogue with companies

When evaluating companies' governance arrangements, particularly those relating to board structure and composition, institutional shareholders should give due weight to all relevant factors drawn to their attention.
> Main Principle E.2 Evaluation of Governance Disclosures

Institutional shareholders have a responsibility to make considered use of their votes.
> Main Principle E.3 Shareholder Voting

This chapter explores the responsibilities of companies and their boards for fostering positive relationships with institutional shareholders, taking into account their wider obligations in respect of the equal treatment of all shareholders and the protection of price-sensitive information. The reciprocal obligations of institutional shareholders to make considered use of their powers based on a balanced evaluation of company performance and governance arrangements is also examined.

Under UK law, shareholders in public companies delegate substantially all their powers as owners to the directors, who act as their agents. Having done so, shareholders effectively relinquish the right to be directly involved in the direction and management of company.

As explained in *Chapter 1*, however, shareholders do retain two forms of power over the actions of the directors, namely:

> ❯ 'Voice': shareholders in general meeting have right to exercise the voting powers attaching to their shares on significant decisions of the company, including the appointment and reappointment of directors, proposed dividend payments and other substantial transactions.
> ❯ 'Exit': shareholders can choose to maintain, increase or dispose of their shareholdings in the company according to their opinion of the performance of the business and the quality of the directors.

The focus of company law, and latterly of corporate governance, has been to facilitate the exercise of shareholders' powers, in particular by ensuring the availability of meaningful and reliable information about the position and prospects of the company, providing for independent scrutiny in areas such as directors' appointments, remuneration and audit, and promoting constructive use of the AGM.

At the same time, it has been assumed that it is for shareholders themselves to consult their self-interest in deciding how, and indeed whether, to exercise their powers. This assumption gave rise in turn to a long-standing belief that shareholders might be 'rationally apathetic' towards the use of their powers.

This view derives from the observation by Berle and Means in the 1930s that the wide dispersal of shareholdings in large publicly quoted companies may mean that it is not worthwhile for most shareholders to devote time, effort and resources to trying to change unacceptable management behaviour. Given the small size of most individual shareholdings, the potential benefits would be outweighed by the costs of the effort involved in seeking change, particularly in a large company where it may be difficult to achieve concerted action by shareholders. Even where successful action is possible, potential instigators are likely to be deterred by the prospect that shareholders who have not participated in the action will 'free ride' on their efforts. Moreover, the liquid market in listed company shares may mean that it is easier and cheaper for dissatisfied shareholders to exit by selling their shares or accepting a takeover offer than to seek to use their power of voice to effect a change of policy or management.

The view that 'rational apathy' is a legitimate position for all shareholders has been challenged in recent decades by the increasing concentration of share ownership in the hands of institutional investors, as a result of which a small number of institutions could in principle exert a decisive influence on company conduct. This was confirmed in 2001 by the Myners Review of Institutional Investment in the UK, which found that more than 50 per cent of the quoted equity markets in the UK were owned by institutional investors, dominated by pension funds, insurance companies and other collective investment vehicles.

It is increasingly argued that, as fiduciaries acting on behalf of millions of individual investors, institutional shareholders are under an obligation to make use of their powers as shareholders, where there is a reasonable prospect that the exercise of their powers will result in improved governance and enhanced performance for the benefit of the underlying beneficiaries. Accordingly, successive codes of corporate governance have placed reciprocal responsibilities on companies and institutional shareholders to enter into constructive dialogue based on the mutual understanding of objectives.

## The responsibilities of the company and the board

There is an implicit obligation on the directors, as the company's managers, to control and direct the business in the interests of the shareholders as a whole. As discussed in *Chapter 4*, the nature and scope of these interests is a matter of continuing debate and may evolve over time. None the less, there is no legal expectation that shareholders' views will be consulted in detail, except in so far as the consent of the shareholders in general meeting is needed for specific proposals of the board.

Moreover, principles enshrined in company law and the Listing Rules seek to protect the interests of all investors by achieving an orderly market in the shares of listed companies and ensuring that all market participants, whether actual or potential, have simultaneous access to information on companies' performance and prospects. The principles are reflected in the continuing obligations of listed companies, under Chapter 9 of the Listing Rules, to ensure that:

> all companies make timely disclosure of information relevant to investment decisions, including information which might affect the price of their listed securities; and
> all shareholders are given equal access to the same relevant information;

Against this background, the proposition in successive codes of corporate governance that the board should maintain direct contact with a limited number of major shareholders has significant legal, regulatory and procedural implications for companies. This was recognised in the Cadbury Report of 1991, which acknowledged that institutions would inevitably have greater access to boards than would individual shareholders: given that boards could not put all shareholders on equal footing, they must be careful to ensure that any significant statements are made publicly and so are available to all shareholders.

### Protection of price-sensitive information

The Listing Rules identify certain matters that a listed company must always announce to the market because they may lead to substantial movement in the price of the company's listed securities. These include:

> acquisitions and disposals above certain size criteria set out in the Listing Rules;
> interim and preliminary results and forthcoming and recommended dividends;
> board appointments and departures and details of share dealings by directors or substantial shareholders;
> profit warnings; and
> rights issues and other offers of securities.

In addition to the matters specifically identified in the Listing Rules, listed companies have a general obligation of disclosure to give sufficient and timely information to the market as a whole on any major new developments, including any changes in their financial condition or in the actual or expected performance of their businesses, which are not already public knowledge and which, if known, may lead to a substantial movement (whether up or down) in the prices of their listed securities. In fulfilment of this obligation, an announcement must be made without delay by the listed company concerned, via one of the Regulatory Information Services (RISs) designated by the UKLA.

There are two main areas of uncertainty for the company in deciding whether an announcement is needed:

1  *When is information already public knowledge?* Certain information, such as a change in UK interest rates, may be potentially price-sensitive information but will already be in the public domain. In these circumstances, the company would not normally be required to make an announcement unless the change could have an unusual or disproportionate effect on its business.

   The FSA has pointed out that just because it is possible for information to be obtained by the public it does not necessarily make it 'public knowledge': in particular, if a fee is required to obtain information, or if its availability is not generally known, the information is not 'public knowledge' and the company must make an announcement.

2  *What kinds of information are price-sensitive?* There is no definitive formula for determining what might constitute price-sensitive information: this will vary widely from company to company, depending on its size, developments in its recent past and activity in its sector. Major new developments, changes in the company's financial condition or business performance or changes in the its expectation of future performance could all trigger a significant movement – up or down – in the company's share price. There are therefore many events which may need to be announced: these could include, for example, the launch of a new product or service; the failure of a particular product or service to meet expectations; the winning or placing of a large contract; the initiation of a major internal restructuring; or the discovery of a major technical defect or health hazard associated with a particular product or process.

   In order to determine whether a particular item of information is potentially price sensitive, the company must be able to assess the likely impact of the information on the key factors which affect its share price, such as its reported earnings per share, pre-tax profits or borrowings. If the company believes that information may be price-sensitive, it must make an announcement to the market without delay.

## The management of investor relations

Given the constraints described above, any dialogue between a listed company and its institutional shareholders must be carefully planned, with clear objectives and procedures.

The directors have overall responsibility both for the control and dissemination of price sensitive information and for maintaining a constructive dialogue with institutional shareholders. In practice, day-to-day activities in these areas are usually delegated to designated investor relations staff. In addition, listed companies are generally advised by their brokers on external financing and investment matters, and may also use the services of specialist financial communications consultants. It is therefore essential for listed companies to establish consistent procedures for the management of their investor relations. Key items should include:

> *A clear allocation of responsibilities:* in order to control the dissemination of price-sensitive information and reduce the chance of unauthorised or inadvertent disclosure, the company should identify those employees who have responsibility for communicating with shareholders, analysts and the press and should ensure that all employees so designated are kept aware of the company's policy and relevant legal and regulatory requirements. It should be made clear to all employees that, unless they have been given specific responsibility, they are prohibited from communicating information to anyone outside the company. In addition, the company should notify external parties, including institutional shareholders, analysts and the press, of the identity of those employees who are responsible for communicating with them and of the company's policies on the treatment of price-sensitive information.

> *Consistent treatment of price-sensitive information:* the company should establish a consistent procedure for determining what information is sufficiently significant for it to be price-sensitive and for releasing that information to the market. For this purpose, the company should, with the assistance of its advisers, identify and keep under review the types of information that are likely to be price sensitive given the company's particular circumstances, and incorporating these in their communications policy;

> *Protection of price-sensitive information prior to announcement:* the company must make arrangements to keep price sensitive information confidential until the moment of announcement: in particular, it must not allow such information to 'seep' into the public domain. All employees, whether they have regular or occasional access to price sensitive information, must be made aware of the need at all times to observe the confidentiality of unpublished information given to them;

> *The content of announcements:* under the Listing Rules, a listed company must exercise a reasonable standard of care to ensure that its announcements are accurate and not misleading, present a balanced picture of its performance and prospects and that price sensitive information is given due prominence.

> *Making recipients of information 'insiders':* in some circumstances, the company may wish to disclose price-sensitive information in confidence to, for example, institutional shareholders or other parties with whom they are negotiating. Where this takes place, however, the recipient of the information will become 'insiders' and will be unable to deal in the company's shares until after the information has been announced to the market. For this reason, potential recipients will not necessarily wish to become 'insiders' and the company must therefore have an established procedure for obtaining the consent of potential recipients before any price-sensitive information is disclosed to them.

Detailed advice on the obligations of listed companies to protect price-sensitive information can be found on the FSA's web-site, www.fsa.gov.uk.

## The involvement of the board

In many listed companies, contact with institutional shareholders is currently regarded as the primary responsibility of the CEO and the finance director, with the support of the chairman and the other executive directors. This was confirmed in research carried out on behalf of the Higgs Review found that non-executive directors are rarely involved in discussions with major shareholders: there is therefore little communication under normal circumstances, and direct contact is likely to be made only when there is a serious problem. In consequence, there appears to be little mutual understanding on the roles of non-executive directors and institutional shareholders: non-executive directors perceive institutions as distant and disengaged, while institutions experience difficulty in making contact with non-executive directors and are keen to have better access to discuss issues in a timely manner.

To remedy the current deficiencies, the Higgs Review identified a need for closer relationships between non-executive directors and institutional shareholders, in particular through direct meetings designed to enable the non-executive directors to gain a proper understanding of the issues and concerns of major shareholders.

Although the proposition that non-executive directors should have closer contact with institutional shareholders has been the subject of much debate, the principle has now been generally accepted and is reflected in the July 2003 Combined Code. This acknowledges that most shareholder contact is with the chief executive and finance director, but emphasises that the board as a whole should keep in touch with shareholder opinion. To this end, it specifies in Code Provision D.1.1 that:

> ❭ *The chairman* should discuss governance and strategy with major shareholders and should ensure that the views of shareholders are communicated to the board as a whole.
> ❭ *Non-executive directors* should be offered the opportunity to attend meetings with major shareholders, and should expect to attend such meetings if requested to do so by major shareholders.
> ❭ *The senior independent director* should attend sufficient meetings with a range of major shareholders to develop a balanced understanding of their issues and concerns.

In addition, Provision D.1.2 requires the board to disclose in the annual report and accounts the steps taken to ensure that the board, and in particular the non-executive directors, are able to develop an understanding of the views of major shareholders about the company.

## The responsibilities of institutional shareholders

As noted in the introduction to this chapter, shareholders in general are under no obligation to inform themselves about the policies and performance of the companies in which they invest or to use the voting and other powers attached to their shares. The presumption in law is that it is for shareholders themselves to consult their own self-interest and decide accordingly how much involvement is appropriate.

The proposition in successive codes of corporate governance that institutional shareholders have positive responsibilities to engage with companies in which they invest and, where appropriate, seek to influence their business and governance policies, thus represents a departure from the accepted position: as such, it has significant implications for institutions in the management of their investment business.

## Institutional shareholders in the UK

Institutional shareholders are commercial organisations which aggregate and invest funds on behalf of the individual savers and investors who make up their client base. In the UK, the main institutional shareholders are pension funds, insurance companies and collective investment institutions such as unit trust funds and open-ended investment companies. The Myners Report estimated that in 2001 institutions owned more than £1,500 billion of assets, representing over half the UK's quoted equity markets.

Institutions' investment styles vary widely according to their income and capital growth objectives and the period over which they are contractually obliged to deliver returns to their clients. Although most institutions will seek to adopt a balanced approach, two broadly contrasting investment styles can be distinguished:

1 At one extreme, an institution may seek to achieve its target performance by actively buying and selling shares according to its judgement of the underlying strengths of companies in order to exploit possible short-term variations in share prices.

2 At the other extreme, an institution may adopt a passive strategy by matching its investment portfolio to the components of a share index such as the FTSE 100: this technique, known as 'index tracking', is intended to match the long-term results of the index as a whole, while avoiding some of the risks associated with an active trading policy.

## Institutional investor bodies in the UK

Institutional investors in the UK are represented by a number of bodies, each of which has its own constituency and makes recommendations to its members on engagement with investee companies on matters of policy and governance. The principal representative bodies are:

> The *Association of British Insurers* (ABI): the trade association for the UK insurance industry, the members of which account for approximately 20 per cent of shares listed on the London Stock Exchange. The ABI recommends responsible voting within the framework of a considered corporate governance policy. In 2001, it issued guidelines setting out the disclosures on social, environmental and ethical matters that institutional investors should expect to be included in the annual reports of listed companies. Unlike NAPF and PIRC, however, the ABI does not make specific recommendations on how its members should vote at company general meetings. The ABI's web-site can be found at www.abi.org.uk.

> The *National Association of Pension Funds* (NAPF): represents 75 per cent of occupational pension funds in the UK, accounting for some 20 per cent of shares listed on the London Stock Exchange. Through its Voting Issues Service (VIS), NAPF monitors the corporate governance practices of listed companies and makes recommendations to its members on the exercise of their voting powers at company general meetings. NAPF's web-site can be found at www.napf.co.uk.

> *Pensions Investment Research Consultants Ltd* (PIRC): produces advice and voting recommendations for its clients, mainly local authority and other public sector pension funds. PIRC is in some respects the most radical of the institutional investor bodies and is active in the public policy debate on issues of corporate governance and socially responsible investment. PIRC's web-site is www.pirc.co.uk.

> The *Institutional Shareholders' Committee* (ISC): an umbrella group comprising the ABI, NAPF; the Association of Investment Trust Companies; and the Investment Management Association. In October 2002, the ISC published a Statement of Principles on the responsibilities of institutional shareholders and agents (see below). The ISC's web-site is www.investmentuk.org.uk.

## Institutional engagement with investee companies

Until relatively recently, institutional investors have not generally regarded their investments in listed companies as long-term relationships. Accordingly, they have not voted their shares regularly and have tended to intervene directly with company management only in circumstances of crisis.

More recently, however, the ability of institutions to take a disengaged view has changed. This is partly for commercial reasons: because they now own a high proportion of the shares in listed companies, it is difficult for institutions simply to sell large numbers of shares in under-performing companies without depressing the market. Moreover, the adoption by many institutions of index tracking strategies means that they are committed to retaining substantial long-term holdings in all the listed companies in the selected index.

There is in addition a public policy interest in the conduct of institutional shareholders: as the Myners Report pointed out, the pool of assets controlled by institutions represents the savings of millions of people, whose economic well-being is dependent on the performance of the companies in which their funds are invested. There is therefore increasing pressure on institutions, as part of their fiduciary duties to their clients, to develop constructive relationships with the companies in which they invest and, where necessary, to intervene in their policies and governance practices.

The Myners Report found that although there was some evidence of increased institutional engagement with companies, there was still a lack of active intervention even where there was a reasonable expectation that this could enhance the value of investments. In particular, it found that fund managers acting on behalf of institutions argued that intervention was not part of their role or that there was no need for them to adopt such a strategy. The review concluded that this situation is a matter for concern and suggested legislative reform.

The Review recommended that UK law should be changed to require pension scheme managers to undertake active monitoring of investee companies, to communicate with the management of such companies and to exercise their voting rights where there is a reasonable expectation that such activities will enhance the value of an investment. The proposed duty is similar to one imposed on US pension funds under the Employment Retirement Income Security Act (ERISA)1974.

Following the publication of the Myners Report, the government has consulted on possible legislation to oblige institutions to promote their clients' interests through increased activism. In response, the Institutional Shareholders' Committee (ISC), which comprises representatives of the main investing institutions, has published a statement of principles on the responsibilities of institutional investors and their agents. Among its other recommendations, the statement of principles suggests that each institutional shareholder should have a clear statement of its policy on activism setting out:

> ❯ how investee companies will be monitored, including the institution's approach to active dialogue with the investee company's board and senior management;
> ❯ the institution's policy for requiring investee companies to comply with the core standards of the Combined Code;
> ❯ the policy for meetings with an investee company's board and senior management;
> ❯ how situations where the institution and/or its agent has a conflict of interest will be minimised or dealt with;
> ❯ the institution's strategy on intervention;
> ❯ an indication of the type of circumstances when the institution may take further action and details of the type of action that may be taken; and
> ❯ the institution's policy on voting.

The text of the Statement of Principles on the responsibilities of institutional shareholders and agents issued by the Institutional Shareholders' Committee is reproduced in *Appendix 20*.

Although the Government has indicated that it does not intend to place a statutory obligation on institutional investors to vote at general meetings, the possibility of legislation to promote institutional engagement with investee companies cannot be ruled out. In November 2003, the Secretary of State for Trade and Industry stated that provisions might be included in an eventual new Companies Act to require institutions account to underlying investors for their voting practices.

## Combined Code recommendations to institutional shareholders

In its recommendations to institutional shareholders, the July 2003 revision of the Combined Code reflects the increasing pressure for institutions to engage positively with the companies in which they invest on behalf of clients, but also takes into account the concerns of companies, in particular about the consistency of approach to be adopted by institutions.

The July 2003 Combined Code addresses concerns that some of the corporate governance policies adopted by individual institutions involve different, and sometimes mutually incompatible, provisions. In the interests of consistency, the Combined Code recommends (at Supporting Principle E.1) that institutional shareholders should adopt the ISC's Statement of Principles on the responsibilities of institutional shareholders and agents, in particular by publishing clear statements of their policies.

The Combined Code also takes into account the experience of companies that, despite the 'comply or explain' approach to corporate governance adopted in the Listing Rules, some institutions have tended in the past to adopt an inflexible stance where companies have not complied in full with the recommendations of the Combined Code. Responding to these concerns, the revised Combined Code emphasises, in Principle E.2, that institutional shareholders should:

> give due weight to all relevant factors drawn to their attention when evaluating companies' governance arrangements, particularly those relating to board structure and composition: in particular, they should consider carefully explanations given for departure from this Code and make reasoned judgements in each case, avoiding a 'box-ticking' approach to assessing a company's corporate governance; and

> give an explanation to the company, in writing where appropriate, and be prepared to enter a dialogue if they do not accept the company's position.

The Combined Code also stresses the obligations of institutional shareholders to account to their clients for the use of their voting powers, stating at Principle E2 that institutions should:

> on request, make available to their clients information on the proportion of resolutions on which votes were cast and non-discretionary proxies lodged; and

> attend AGMs where appropriate and practicable.

## The response of institutional shareholders

Following the publication of the revised Combined Code, there have been strong indications that institutional shareholders are increasingly ready to take an activist position on matters of corporate governance and that, where necessary, they are more willing than in the past to make their concerns public.

Best practice guidance issued by the ABI in October 2003 states as an overarching principle that institutional investors should aim to use their votes wherever practicable and should be prepared to vote against the board where companies have declined to address the legitimate concerns of shareholders. In addition, institutions should use their best efforts to ensure that votes cast are properly recorded and should collaborate with others as necessary to ensure that the voting process goes smoothly. The ABI's statement of policy on voting at general meetings is set out in *Appendix 21*.

In its corporate governance policy issued in December 2003, the NAPF emphasised its view that the informed use of votes is an obligation and implicit fiduciary duty of institutional investors. To this end, the NAPF will recommend active voting, and where appropriate will recommend a vote against management. In addition, the NAPF will facilitate collective action by institutional investors through confidential 'case committees' of its members where there are concerns about particular issues and/or about the strategic direction of investee companies.

## HERMES' STEWARDSHIP PROGRAMME

*In its response to the government's consultation document Encouraging Shareholder Activism, the UK pension fund manager, a prominent activist institution, gave a helpful account of its stewardship programme.*

Hermes' stewardship programme in the UK has three tiers.

At the most basic and regular level is proxy voting at company annual and extraordinary general meetings. In advance of deciding how to cast clients' votes at a company meeting, Hermes staff read the company's annual report from cover to cover, analysing the disclosures and the degree to which the company meets Hermes' corporate governance policy. If Hermes is content with the companies financial and governance performance and the resolutions proposed to the meeting, it will submit the votes in favour of management.

The next tier is what is now known as engagement. In effect, it has two separate aspects:

a) If Hermes has concerns about the disclosures made in the annual report its representatives will telephone the company secretary to discuss their position and explain that of Hermes. In light of that discussion, Hermes will decide whether it is willing to be pragmatic and accommodate the company's approach to a particular situation, or whether it will formally express opposition and vote against the management resolution. Generally, particularly if the issue is of an ongoing nature, Hermes will follow up with a letter to the board explaining its position in detail, outlining the action it would like the board to take, and proposing a timeframe in which it would like changes to be made. Hermes maintains a database of contact with companies and of voting decisions over time. In this way staff know in following years what was discussed with the company, what the company agreed to do, and whether there are any significant or irreconcilable differences in the respective positions of Hermes and the company.

b) The second aspect of engagement is where Hermes identifies companies that are not

## Chapter summary

> The expectation in codes of corporate governance that boards of listed companies should establish and maintain an active dialogue with major shareholders has significant legal, regulatory and procedural implications, given the presumption in law that all shareholders should be treated equally.

> Boards must therefore take care to ensure that any information disclosed to institutions and market intermediaries is also made available to shareholders as a whole.

> Dialogue between listed companies and their institutional shareholders must be carefully planned, with clear objectives and procedures and consistent treatment of price-sensitive information.

meeting its corporate governance policy but on an issue for which there is not a specific resolution to vote at the general meeting or where there has been a persistent problem. The issues that such engagement might cover include board composition, succession planning, directors' remuneration, strategy, financial performance, capital structure and the board's treatment of social ethical and environmental risks.

The process is graduated and the action Hermes takes will depend on the nature and perceived severity of the problem. Staff might speak to the company secretary, one of the senior executive directors or one of the non-executive directors. They may seek a meeting with one or more of the board directors in order to explain in more detail Hermes' concerns about the company. Hermes might confer with other institutional investors to assess the general level of concern and perhaps arrange a joint meeting with the company. Graduating along the spectrum towards intervention, Hermes might co-operate with other shareholders to propose a resolution for the annual general meeting agenda (say to remove or appoint a director) or to call an extraordinary meeting (EGM). Hermes has used the later avenue only once, but the threat of, and ability to call, an EGM is extremely powerful.

The third and final tier in Hermes' stewardship programme is proactive intervention in selected under-performing companies, involving direct contact with the directors (including the chairman and non-executive directors), external advisers and other major shareholders to discuss and secure agreement for change. In the absence of progress, Hermes would be prepared if necessary to call an EGM and to build shareholder and wider public support for change.

*Hermes Pensions Management is the principal investment manager for both the BT and Consignia (Post Office) pension funds. Its clients hold over 1 per cent of the value of nearly all of the largest 800 quoted companies on the London Stock Exchange and also have index and active holdings in over 2,000 public companies world-wide.*

> There is increasing emphasis on the need for closer relationships between non-executive directors and institutional shareholders, both to enable non-executive directors to gain a proper understanding of the issues and concerns of major shareholders and to provide institutions with a channel of communication with the board on issues of concern.

> Further, there is growing recognition of the obligation on institutions, as fiduciaries acting on behalf of underlying savers and investors, to exercise their voting powers actively and responsibly, when necessary by voting against board resolutions where companies have declined to address the legitimate concerns of shareholders.

# 14

# Constructive use of the AGM

> The board should use the AGM to communicate with investors and to encourage their participation.
>
> Main Principle D.2: Constructive use of the AGM

This chapter considers the existing requirements the circulation of the AGM notice and related information to shareholders and current proposals for improved timeliness and accessibility. It also discusses:

> ❭ the current arrangements for the circulation of resolutions proposed by directors and shareholders;
> ❭ proposed legal reforms to facilitate the requisitioning of shareholder resolutions;
> ❭ best practice for the open and constructive conduct of business at the AGM; and
> ❭ governance issues relating to voting in person and by proxy.

Company law identifies the annual general meeting (AGM) as the company's ultimate decision-making authority and confers on it a central role in the governance relationship between the shareholders, as the company's owners, and the directors, as their agents. As the emphasis in the revised Combined Code on constructive use of the AGM suggests, however, there is a perception that, in recent years, the meeting has too often failed to provide a genuine forum for accountability.

This perception has its origins in the pattern of share ownership now typical of large and listed companies. In many such companies, the great majority of shares, and hence voting rights, are held by a relatively small number of financial institutions, whose relationship with the company's management is frequently conducted as a continuing dialogue outside the forum of company meetings. Although institutions do increasingly vote on resolutions proposed at the AGM, they generally do so by proxy and their active participation in AGMs is comparatively rare.

Attendance and voting in person at the AGM is therefore dominated by private shareholders. These may be very numerous, especially in the privatised utilities and demutualised banks, but they represent, in aggregate, only a small percentage of the company's voting share capital. Despite their relative weakness in terms of voting rights, private shareholders clearly value the AGM as an opportunity – often the only one available to them – to meet the company's directors face to face and voice their opinions about the company's affairs. The AGM may not be equally valued by the company, however: in the knowledge that the shareholders present at the AGM do not exercise significant voting power, the directors may not approach the event as seriously as it deserves.

These considerations have led to a view in some quarters that the high cost and management time involved in holding the AGM may not be justified. Reflecting this, the Company Law Review Steering Group consulted on a proposal that listed companies should, with the consent of their shareholders, be permitted to dispense with the AGM altogether. Although this proposal attracted a measure of support, it does not appear to have been taken up by the Government. Moreover, at the time of writing, there were signs that the AGM had acquired fresh vitality thanks to the new requirement, introduced by the Directors' Remuneration Report Regulations 2002, for an 'advisory' vote on directors' remuneration at the AGMs of quoted companies. Further discussion on the Regulations can be found in *Chapter 9.*

The requirement for public and listed companies to hold AGMs will therefore remain for foreseeable future. It is unlikely, however, that active participation at AGMs by institutional investors will increase significantly, except in circumstances of extreme controversy. Attendance at the AGM will continue to be dominated by private shareholders. Although their capital may be insignificant from the company's perspective, such shareholders may have a substantial proportion of their personal wealth invested in the company. They have the same entitlement as larger shareholders to be informed about the company's performance and future intentions, and to participate in discussions and decision-making at general meetings. The question for corporate governance is, therefore, how to make the AGM an effective and meaningful forum for debate between private shareholders and the company's directors.

The key ingredients identified by the Company Law Review Steering Group were, first, timely shareholder access to high-quality information to enable them to assess company performance and the directors' stewardship of their assets. Second, shareholders must be able to act appropriately on the basis of this information, by questioning the directors, voting on the resolutions proposed by the directors and, where appropriate, proposing their own resolutions for discussion at the AGM.

While this chapter focuses on the AGM, other types of shareholder meeting, particularly extraordinary general meetings (EGMs) and Court meetings, are convened with increasing frequency in connection with corporate transactions. The legal and other technical arrangements for meetings of these types are outside the scope of this book, but the need for open, constructive and courteous debate is the same for all meetings between shareholders and directors.

## Giving notice of the AGM

### Basic requirements

CA 1985 specifies that a public company must hold an AGM in each calendar year, each AGM to be held within 15 months of the previous year's meeting. If the company is newly incorporated, its first AGM must be held within 18 months of incorporation, regardless of the calendar year. A private company is permitted to dispense with the requirement to hold an AGM provided that an explicit resolution to this effect has been approved by all shareholders, but there is no current intention to extend this provision to public companies.

The company's directors must ensure that all shareholders who have the right to attend and vote at general meetings are sent written notice of the AGM at least 21 clear days before the date of the meeting (or longer if required by the company's Articles). Listed companies are required by the revised Combined Code to ensure that the notice and related documents are sent to shareholders at least 20 *working* days before the meeting.

The AGM notice and accompanying documents, including the annual report and accounts, are usually despatched to shareholders by post. Where individual shareholders have consented to this method of delivery, documents may be sent to the shareholder's nominated electronic address or placed on a web-site with an e-mail notification to the shareholders concerned. In addition, the company is permitted to accept proxies sent by e-mail.

Further guidance on electronic communications with shareholders is provided in the ICSA's 25 points of recommended best practice on electronic communications with shareholders, a summary of which is given in *Appendix 22*.

## The contents of the AGM notice

The AGM notice must give the date, time and location of the meeting and specify the business to be conducted, identifying any special resolutions and giving details of shareholders' rights in respect of the meeting, including the right to appoint a proxy.

Items of routine business invariably include resolutions for the receipt of the annual report and accounts, the approval of any final dividend recommended by the directors, the reappointment and remuneration of the external auditors and the re-election of those directors who are retiring by rotation and of any new directors appointed by the board since the last AGM. The routine business of a quoted company's AGM now also includes a separate resolution for the receipt of the directors' remuneration report contained in the annual report and accounts.

Any necessary non-routine business can also be considered at the AGM, provided that appropriate notice is given and any shareholder approval, if obtained, will not expire before the action proposed by the directors has been completed. In public companies, such non-routine business will often include resolutions seeking new or renewed authority for the directors to allot shares and waiving existing shareholders' pre-emption rights over newly allotted shares.

## The AGM and the year-end reporting timetable

The resolution for receipt of the annual report and accounts is typically the main focus of discussion at the AGM. Although shareholders do not formally approve the annual report and accounts and are not entitled to reject or amend it, a vote declining to

## GOOD PRACTICE POINT

### Providing accessible information to shareholders

Beyond complying with statutory requirements, the AGM notice and accompanying documents must help shareholders to assess the performance of the company and its directors and encourage their constructive participation in the governance process. To this end, the directors and company secretary should consider:

- the need for the AGM notice to include clear explanations, in plain English, of the legal language of resolutions and any other technical aspects of the business of the AGM: such explanations could be given in the chairman's letter accompanying the notice, in separate explanatory notes, or both;

- the desirability of making the AGM notice and accompanying documents available in alternative formats, such as Braille, large print or audio tape, for the benefit of shareholders with special needs; and

- whether special arrangements are needed to ensure that investors who hold their shares indirectly receive information about the company and are able to exercise voting rights: such investors may include holders of American Depositary Receipts (ADRs) in the US, investors in Individual Savings Accounts (ISAs) and holders of shares in the company's own Corporate Sponsored Nominee.

receive the document would be interpreted as a vote of no confidence in the directors. Further information on the obligations of listed companies in respect of the form, content and publication of the annual report and accounts is given in *Chapter 10*.

Under current statutory requirements, the annual report and accounts must be laid at the AGM within seven months of the year-end for a public company, and within ten months of the year-end for a private company. Common practice is therefore to despatch the AGM notice, the related proxy voting materials and the annual report and accounts (or the annual review/SFS where relevant) as a single package, either as printed hard copy or electronically.

In listed companies, the timing of despatch of the AGM notice, and hence the date of the AGM itself, are closely linked to the timetable for the company's preliminary results announcement and the approval by directors of the annual report and accounts.

The Listing Rules require that the presentation of audited financial information in the annual report and accounts should be consistent with that in the preliminary results announcement and the annual report and accounts should be published as soon as practicable after approval by the directors. This dual requirement makes it desirable in most cases for both documents to be approved by the directors at much the same time and for the annual report and accounts (and annual review/SFS where relevant) to be published as quickly as possible thereafter. Where the company has a large number of shareholders, this may in practice take several weeks and require the coordination of numerous different parties inside and outside the company, including designers, printing and finishing plants, mailing houses, the company's share registrar and the Royal Mail.

## Proposals for reform

The Company Law Review Steering Group was critical of the current statutory reporting timetable for public companies on the grounds that it fails to take advantage of electronic communications to speed up the reporting process. The Steering Group pointed out also that the preliminary results announcement contains new and poten-

---

**GOOD PRACTICE POINT** ❯

## Despatching the AGM package to shareholders

Although the date of the AGM will be known months (or even years) in advance, the complex process of finalising the AGM package and sending it to shareholders is carried out in a matter of weeks and usually to tight deadlines. Advance planning and communication are therefore essential, as errors and delays may result in failure to give proper notice of the AGM, with potentially expensive and embarrassing consequences.

The company secretary should be responsible for the timetable and should ensure that all the parties involved, inside and outside the company, are aware of the key dates and of their own roles and responsibilities. These will include:

### Directors

- Take early decisions on the format and content of the documents making up the AGM package, including the annual report and accounts, the annual review/SFS where relevant and the AGM notice.
- Agree arrangements for final approval, usually by the full board, of all documents.
- Agree arrangements for signature, by the directors nominated by the board for this purpose, of the accounts and the directors' report.

### Auditors

- Agree arrangements for signature of the auditors' report.

### Share registrars (in-house or external)

- Advise the company secretary on the preferred format of proxy cards and the expected number of registered shareholders entitled to receive notice of the AGM.
- Agree arrangements for delivery to the printer/mailing house of shareholders' names and addresses for mailing purposes.
- Agree arrangements for reporting to the company secretary on the progress of proxy voting and producing the final count after expiry of the proxy deadline (usually 48 hours before the start of the AGM).
- Agree arrangements for the payment of any final dividend following approval at the AGM.

### Printer/mailing house

- Agree the posting date and other relevant arrangements – for example, whether first or second class post is to be used.
- Agree arrangements for receipt from the share registrars of shareholders' names and addresses for mailing purposes.
- Agree arrangements for final approval by the company secretary to commence bulk printing of documents.

tially price-sensitive information about the company's position and performance, but is not routinely made available to the generality of shareholders. Further, because the annual report and accounts is normally circulated to shareholders at the same time as the AGM notice, governance information is communicated to shareholders too late for them to take action by requisitioning their own resolutions for debate at the AGM.

To remedy these deficiencies, the Steering Group recommended significant changes to the year-end reporting timetable. The White Paper *Modernising Company Law* confirmed that the government had accepted the recommendations, but no timetable for their introduction has yet been announced.

The Steering Group's proposals envisage increased use of electronic communications to achieve equality between the capital markets and private shareholders through a more timely and structured flow of information. To this end, it is recommended that quoted companies should post their preliminary results announcements on their websites immediately after release to the market, with e-mail notifications to those shareholders who have requested this. Thereafter, the annual report and accounts should be published separately from the AGM notice, such that:

> ❯ the annual reports and accounts should be posted on the company's web-site, with e-mail notifications to shareholders, as soon as practicable after approval by the directors and no later than 120 days after year-end; and
> ❯ there should then be a 'holding period' of at least 15 clear days, during which shareholders can consider the contents of the annual report and accounts and, if they so wish, requisition AGM resolutions.

On expiry of the 15-day holding period, the AGM notice could be finalised and circulated to shareholders with the annual report and accounts, subject to a new requirements for the annual report and accounts to be laid before the AGM within six months of year end. The year-end reporting timetable in listed companies table summarises the recommended changes and compares these with the current requirements of CA 1985 and the Listing Rules and the existing practices of listed companies.

## AGM resolutions

In normal circumstances, the resolutions proposed at the AGM of a public company will fall into two categories: ordinary and special resolutions.

### Ordinary resolutions

Most resolutions proposed at the AGM are in the form of ordinary resolutions. These are sufficient for most of the routine business of the meeting, including, for example, receipt of the annual report and accounts and the directors' remuneration report; the appointment and reappointment of directors and auditors; approval of any recommended final dividend; and authorising the directors to allot shares.

If proposed at an EGM at which no special resolution is to be discussed, only 14 clear days' notice need be given of an ordinary resolution, but if proposed at an AGM, the normal AGM notice period of 21 clear days (20 working days for listed companies)

## Year-end reporting timetable in listed companies

| | Current | | CLRSG recommendation |
|---|---|---|---|
| *Event* | *Formal requirement* | *Typical practice* | |
| **Preliminary results announcement** | Within 120 days after year-end | 6–7 weeks after year-end | No change to timing, but preliminary results announcement must be published immediately on web-site, with e-mail notification to shareholders who have requested this |
| **Annual report and accounts published** | As soon as possible after approval | 12–13 weeks after year end – usually with AGM notice | Web-site publication and e-mail notification as soon as practicable after approval but no later than 120 days after year-end |
| **Holding period** | Not required | Not applicable | At least 15 clear days |
| **Notice of AGM despatched to shareholders** | Not less than 21 clear days before AGM (20 working days for listed companies) | 12–13 weeks after year-end | On expiry of holding period |
| **Annual report laid before AGM** | Within 7 months after year end | 16–17 weeks after year end | Not less than 21 clear days after despatch of AGM notice (20 working days for listed companies) but not more than 6 months after year-end |

continues to apply. To be passed, an ordinary resolution requires the approval of a simple majority of shareholders entitled to attend and vote at the meeting.

## Special resolutions

Special resolutions are required for proposals involving significant changes to the company's constitution or the rights of existing shareholders, including:

> alterations to the Memorandum or Articles;
> a change in the company's name;
> a reduction of share capital; or
> purchase of the company's own shares.

At least 21 clear days' written notice must be given of any meeting at which a special resolution to be proposed. A special resolution must be identified as such in the notice and, to be passed, must be approved by 75 per cent of shareholders entitled to attend and vote at the meeting.

Currently, the directors originate the great majority of the resolutions discussed at the AGM. They must ensure that special resolutions are identified at such in the AGM notice and that all resolutions passed by appropriate majorities.

In addition, the Combined Code requires that each substantially separate issue should be the subject of a separate resolution and be voted on separately. This is intended to prevent the practice of combining in a single resolution two or more issues, one popular and one contentious, in the hope that the contentious issue will be carried 'under cover' of the more popular proposal.

## Shareholder resolutions

A key purpose of the timetable changes recommended by the Company Law Review Steering Group is to make it easier for shareholders to take action on the governance information contained in the annual report and accounts by requisitioning their own resolutions for consideration at the AGM.

Currently, a shareholder resolution can be requisitioned by either (a) 100 or more shareholders each holding shares with average paid-up value of not less than £100, or (b) shareholders holding 5 per cent or more of the company's voting share capital. Shareholders wishing to requisition a resolution must lodge a written requisition, accompanied by the appropriate signatures, with the company not less than six weeks before the general meeting at which it is intended that the resolution should be discussed. On receipt of a valid requisition, the company is obliged to circulate with the AGM notice the resolution and a statement of not more than 1,000 words, at the requisitionists' expense. The Steering Group proposals in respect of shareholder resolutions would leave unchanged the current requirements in respect of the timing and shareholder support for the requisitioning of a resolution, but would require the company, on receipt of a valid requisition, to circulate the resolution and accompanying statement at its own expense.

Despite the apparently onerous nature of the requirements, there has been a steady increase in recent years in the use made by shareholders of the requisition provisions. A number of prominent companies, including BP, Shell, Balfour Beatty and Rio Tinto, have been the subject of shareholder resolutions. In most cases, these have been promoted by pressure groups with the intention of drawing wider attention to aspects of company conduct in respect of human rights and the environment. Notable exceptions are the shareholder resolutions requisitioned by the financial institution Laxey Partners, which have sought to oblige British Land to improve its corporate governance performance, specifically by separating the offices of chairman and CEO and appointing independent non-executive directors.

## The conduct of the meeting

### Formal requirements

As a minimum, the directors and the company secretary must ensure that the business of the AGM is conducted in compliance with statutory requirements and the provisions of the company's Articles so that the validity of the meeting and of the resolutions, once approved, is not open to challenge. However, compliance with formal

**GOOD PRACTICE POINT** ◗

### Responding to shareholder resolutions

A company may be relieved of its obligation to circulate a shareholder resolution where the court is satisfied that that its purpose is to secure publicity for defamatory material. Otherwise, there are no formal restrictions on the subject matter of shareholder resolutions, provided that they are requisitioned on time and with the appropriate level of shareholder support.

Some companies have declined, or attempted to decline, to circulate shareholder resolutions on the grounds that they were imprecise or otherwise invalid, or that the requisitionists included investors, such as holders of American Depositary Receipts (ADRs) and ISAs, who held their shares indirectly.

From the company's point of view, there is an obvious danger that the use of technicalities to avoid discussion on shareholder resolutions will be portrayed externally as censorship, with adverse effects on the reputation of the company and its directors. Unless a shareholder resolution is blatantly defamatory, vexatious or irrelevant, it may be better for the directors to accept it gracefully and to

concentrate instead on presenting an effective case at the AGM.

The directors and company secretary should therefore:

- ensure that the dates of forthcoming AGMs are published well in advance in company documents and web-sites so that the appropriate deadlines are clear to prospective requisitionists;
- decide in principle whether requisitions will be accepted from indirect investors or only from registered shareholders, communicate this decision to the company's share registrars and apply it consistently to all requisitions;
- agree arrangements with the share registrars for timely validation of all requisitions received;
- decide in principle whether the company will waive its right to demand that successful requisitionists should pay for the circulation of their resolution and accompanying statement: given the White Paper proposal that shareholder resolutions should in future be circulated at the company's expense, it may be preferable for the company to absorb the costs involved.

requirements may be insufficient by itself to enable the AGM to function effectively as a forum for debate between the shareholders and directors.

Thus, the July 2003 Combined Code emphasises the need to keep shareholders informed and enable them to comment on the work of the main board committees and issues of corporate governance generally. To this end, it recommends that the chairmen of the audit, remuneration and nomination committees should attend the AGM, where the opportunity should be given to shareholders to put questions to them.

In practice, many public and listed companies have expanded the business of the AGM beyond the basic statutory requirements, for example, by opening the meeting with a presentation, often by the chairman, on the company's performance over the past year and by inviting questions from shareholders. While such developments are clearly in the spirit of the July 2003 Combined Code recommendations, care must be taken to ensure that there is no inadvertent disclosure, in presentations or answers to shareholders' questions, of price-sensitive information which has not already been announced to the market.

Further information on the obligations of listed companies identify and manage price-sensitive information is given in *Chapter 13*.

## The role of the chairman

The role of the chairman, supported as necessary by the company secretary, is critical to the proper conduct of the AGM. Although it is possible in principle for another person – another director or, in the absence of any directors, one of the shareholders present – to chair the AGM, it is customary for chairman of the board of company to chair the meeting.

This involves a potential conflict of interest: as a director of the company, the chairman has a vested interest in securing the shareholders' approval for the resolutions proposed by the board. Against this, as the chairman of the meeting, he or she is responsible to the shareholders present for ensuring that AGM is conducted fairly and openly and that there is opportunity for all shades of opinion, including those critical of the directors, to be expressed. It is important for the chairman to recognise that, although the voting rights of different shareholders vary with the size of their respective ownership interests in the company, all shareholders are equally entitled to attend and participate in the AGM. These rights extend to pressure groups with token holdings and companies are not entitled to discriminate against them.

In this context, the directors of public companies should consider whether speaking rights should be extended to proxies attending the AGM on behalf of shareholders who are not able to be present in person. Proxies have no formal right to speak (although they may demand or join in a demand for a poll) but may be permitted to do so if the chairman of the meeting so determines. A decision on the speaking rights of proxies should be taken in advance of the AGM and applied consistently at the meeting.

## The order of business

At the advertised time for the start of the AGM, the company secretary should check that the necessary quorum is present: unless the company's Articles specify a different quorum, the meeting is quorate when two shareholders are present. The chairman should then propose that the AGM notice be taken as read, although the company secretary should be ready to read out the notice of AGM if the meeting so determines.

Once these formalities have been concluded, the chairman will normally explain the procedures to be adopted for the conduct of the meeting. In addition, he or she will often make an opening statement on the company's performance and prospects, handing over as appropriate to the CEO or any other director who is to make a presentation to shareholders or explain a particular aspect of the company's business. As a general rule, the chairman will then invite shareholders' questions and comments on each of the resolutions appearing in the AGM notice. The chairman may answer shareholders' questions in person, or may hand over to one or more of the other directors for reply.

The chairman must ensure that any ensuing debate between shareholders and directors is properly and fairly conducted and that an opportunity is provided for shareholders present to express their opinions. While all shareholders have a right to speak at the AGM, this does not necessarily imply that everyone who wishes to must be allowed to address the meeting: however, it does mean that the business of the meeting must not be rushed or unduly curtailed, perhaps to avoid discussion on matters which the directors regard as inconvenient.

After a reasonable period for debate on each resolution, the chairman should wind up the discussion, formally propose the resolution and invite the shareholders present to vote on it as described in 'Voting at the AGM', below.

### Dealing with interruptions

The chairman's responsibility for ensuring the orderly and businesslike conduct of the AGM may involve a requirement to adjudicate, with the help of the company secretary, on points of order and a variety of other potential interruptions to the flow of business. The company secretary should therefore have ready procedural notes covering all reasonably foreseeable types of event and may also find it helpful to have a telephone link to assistants backstage.

In a small number of cases, protests and other forms of deliberate disruption to the AGM have led to the forcible removal of individual shareholders, or even to the adjournment or abandonment of the meeting. While it is, of course, essential for the chairman and company secretary to ensure the orderly conduct of business and the safety of everyone present, it is also important to distinguish between genuine disruption and persistent but proper questioning of the directors and to avoid an inappropriately heavy-handed response.

## Voting at the AGM

### Formal requirements

The company's Articles will define the voting rights of shareholders and persons attending the AGM on behalf of shareholders. Typically:

## Organising the AGM

Holding the AGM is complex and expensive, involving time-consuming preparations, which are generally the responsibility of the company secretary. Key tasks include:

*Advance preparation:*

- ensuring that the date of the AGM is included in the programme of board meetings and the financial calendar in the annual report and accounts and on the company's web-site;
- booking the venue for the AGM – usually several months or even years in advance – ensuring that the venue is big enough and has adequate overflow facilities, with appropriate audio-visual links, in case of unexpectedly large shareholder attendance.

*Between the posting of the AGM notice and the date of the meeting:*

- monitoring the progress of proxy voting, with particular attention to proxy votes lodged against resolutions proposed by the directors;
- collating any manuscript comments written on returned proxy cards – these can be a valuable source of intelligence on the questions shareholders are likely to ask at the AGM;
- considering with the directors possible shareholder questions and how to deal with them;

- preparing the chairman's opening address and other presentations by directors;
- finalising venue arrangements, including shareholder registration, catering, marshalling and security;
- arranging facilities for shareholders with special needs, including sign language interpreters and wheelchair access.

*In the 48 hours before the meeting:*

- checking all venue arrangements;
- running through possible shareholders' questions with directors – if possible as part of a full dress rehearsal at the meeting venue;
- preparing poll cards and identification cards for shareholders and corporate representatives, proxies and non-voting observers and arranging with the share registrar for these to be handed to attendees on arrival at the meeting;
- arranging for the register of members, directors' service contracts and other documents for inspection to be available at the venue and other designated locations;
- arranging for the announcement, via a designated Regulatory Information Service, of any potentially price-sensitive information to be disclosed at AGM, including the outcome of voting on resolutions where appropriate.

› Shareholders attending in person are entitled to speak at the meeting, to demand or join in a demand for a poll and to participate in any vote, whether by show of hands or by poll.
› Corporate representatives appointed by institutional investors and other corporate shareholders are also entitled to speak, demand or join in a demand for a poll and to participate in any vote; however, only one representative is permitted

from each corporate shareholder and the directors need to ensure that this number is not exceeded, for example in voting by show of hands.

> Proxies attending the meeting on behalf of a shareholder are entitled to demand or join in a demand for a poll and to participate in a vote on a poll; however, proxies are not permitted to vote by show of hands under any circumstances, nor are they entitled to speak at the meeting unless permitted to do so by the chairman of the meeting.

The credentials of shareholders and corporate representatives, proxies and others attending the meeting must be checked on arrival at the meeting, usually by the company's share registrars. If the meeting is expected to be well attended, arrangements must also be made to ensure that the chairman and company secretary can identify shareholders, corporate representatives and proxies once the meeting has started. This can be achieved by handing voting cards of different colours to each group on arrival at the meeting, then asking for cards to be raised when a show of hands is necessary.

## At the meeting

The Articles also typically give the chairman of the meeting specific authorities in respect of the conduct of voting at the AGM. These include powers to declare the result of any vote taken by show of hands and to demand that a poll be taken. The chairman will normally have a casting vote in the event of an equality of votes for and against a resolution and have authority to rule on any question of the validity of votes cast at the meeting.

### Voting by show of hands

On a show of hands, every shareholder present in person and every corporate representative has one vote, irrespective of the number of shares held. Proxies have no right to vote on show of hands; similarly, proxy votes lodged by post are not counted towards the result of a vote by show of hands.

The chairman of the meeting will normally ask for those present at the meeting to indicate whether they are for or against each resolution by raising the voting card handed to them on arrival at the meeting. With the help of the company secretary, he or she will then visually assess the votes for and against each resolution and declare the outcome immediately.

It is not usually necessary for a formal count to be made of a show of hands on an ordinary resolution, where a visual check alone should be sufficient to establish whether there is a simple majority for or against a resolution. However, it may be necessary to account a show of hands on a special resolution, which must be passed by a 75 per cent majority, or otherwise if a show of hands is very close. Where a count on a show of hands is needed, it is generally carried out by scrutineers appointed by the company's share registrars.

### Voting by poll

The chairman of the meeting must call for a poll if the outcome of a show of hands is unclear, and will probably also wish to call for poll if a resolution proposed by the directors has been lost on a show of hands. Shareholders, corporate representatives and proxies present at the meeting may also call for a poll, which must be held if the demand is supported by not less than five shareholders entitled to vote. On a poll, every shareholder, whether voting in person of by proxy, has one vote for each share held, giving great (and often overwhelming) power to institutional shareholders. As a consequence, the outcome of a show of hands will often be overturned on a poll.

Once the validity of a demand for a poll has been established, the process is usually managed by the company's share registrars at the direction of the chairman or company secretary. The poll may be taken immediately following the discussion on the resolution to which it relates or, if more than one poll is anticipated, may be left until the end of the meeting. Where poll cards have be handed to shareholders, corporate representatives and proxies on arrival at the meeting, they can be asked to complete them; otherwise, poll cards will need to be distributed to those entitled to vote. The completed poll cards (including any poll cards held by chairman and other directors as proxies for shareholders) are then collected by the share registrars' representatives and taken away for verification and counting. On completion of the count, the share registrars produce a certificate recording the outcome of the poll. If the poll has been held during the course of the meeting, the chairman can declare the result immediately. If one or more polls have been held at the end of the meeting, it is customary for the company to publish the result on its web-site and in a national newspaper.

## Disclosing proxy votes

The Combined Code recommends that the company should count and record all proxy votes lodged by post in advance of the meeting and that, after a resolution has been dealt with on a show of hands, the level of proxy votes lodged for and against should be announced. This is intended to give recognition to the views of shareholders not present at the meeting and to ensure that the company is not able to push through controversial resolutions on the basis of a show of hands of the small minority of shareholders actually present.

The numbers of proxy votes lodged can be disclosed at the AGM in various ways, including an oral announcement by the chairman, the screening of a slide showing the relevant numbers or the production of a printed slip which can be given to interested shareholders at the end of the meeting. Irrespective of the method used at the meeting, the company should also publish on its web-site the details of the proxy votes lodged. See ICSA's Guidance Note: Disclosing proxy votes, reproduced in *Appendix 23*.

It should be noted that, on occasion, the disclosure of proxy votes may have the opposite effect to that envisaged by the July 2003 Combined Code, in that it may bring home to the private shareholders present at the meeting that their combined votes are massively outweighed by the proxy votes controlled by institutional shareholders. Even where the proxy votes merely confirm the outcome of voting by show of hands, private shareholders can gain the impression that institutional shareholders comprise a block vote in favour of the directors, by comparison with which their own influence over company decisions is insignificant.

The perceptions of the shareholders actually present at the AGM must therefore be handled tactfully. The chairman and directors must demonstrate that shareholders' opinions are valued and taken seriously. Conversely, they must not exhibit impatience with shareholders' questions or give the impression that their views can be ignored because the institutional proxy vote is 'in the bag'.

## Chapter summary

> Institutional shareholders control the great majority of voting shares in most large and public companies, but typically vote by proxy and rarely participate actively in discussions at the AGM.

> The value of the AGM as a forum for accountability thus lies less in its decision-making functions than in the opportunity it provides for private shareholders to question the directors about the company's performance and the directors' stewardship of their assets and to express their own opinions.

> Constructive use of the AGM therefore depends on careful advance planning to ensure that all shareholders receive high quality and timely information about the company and the business of the AGM, followed by sensitive chairing of the meeting itself to facilitate an atmosphere of openness and mutual respect in which all shades of shareholder opinion can be debated.

# Source materials

**PART**

**3**

Part Three of the Handbook contains the text of the relevant reports, documents and Codes referred to in Parts One and Two.

# Appendix I

## THE COMBINED CODE OF CORPORATE GOVERNANCE
## (July 2003)

### PREAMBLE

1   This Code supersedes and replaces the Combined Code issued by the Hampel Committee on Corporate Governance in June 1998. It derives from a review of the role and effectiveness of non-executive directors by Derek Higgs[1] and a review of audit committees[2] by a group led by Sir Robert Smith.

2   The Financial Services Authority has said that it will replace the 1998 Code that is annexed to the Listing Rules with the revised Code and will seek to make consequential Rule changes. There will be consultation on the necessary Rule changes but not further consultation on the Code provisions themselves.

3   It is intended that the new Code will apply for reporting years beginning on or after 1 November 2003.

4   The Code contains main and supporting principles and provisions. The existing Listing Rules require listed companies to make a disclosure statement in two parts in relation to the Code. In the first part of the statement, the company has to report on how it applies the principles in the Code. In future this will need to cover both main and supporting principles. The form and content of this part of the statement are not prescribed, the intention being that companies should have a free hand to explain their governance policies in the light of the principles, including any special circumstances applying to them which have led to a particular approach. In the second part of the statement the company has either to confirm that it complies with the Code's provisions or – where it does not – to provide an explanation. This 'comply or explain' approach has been in operation for over ten years and the flexibility it offers has been widely welcomed both by company boards and by investors. It is for shareholders and others to evaluate the company's statement.

5   While it is expected that listed companies will comply with the Code's provisions most of the time, it is recognised that departure from the provisions of the Code may be justified in particular circumstances. Every company must review each provision carefully and give a considered explanation if it departs from the Code provisions. Smaller listed companies, in particular those new to listing, may judge that some of the provisions are disproportionate or less relevant in their case. Some of the provisions do not apply to companies below FTSE 350. Such companies may nonetheless consider that it would be appropriate to adopt the approach in the Code and they are encouraged to consider this.

---

1 'Review of the role and effectiveness of non-executive directors', published January 2003.
2 'Audit Committees Combined Code Guidance', published January 2003.

Investment companies typically have a different board structure, which may affect the relevance of particular provisions.

7   Whilst recognising that directors are appointed by shareholders who are the owners of companies, it is important that those concerned with the evaluation of governance should do so with common sense in order to promote partnership and trust, based on mutual understanding. They should pay due regard to companies' individual circumstances and bear in mind in particular the size and complexity of the company and the nature of the risks and challenges it faces. Whilst shareholders have every right to challenge companies' explanations if they are unconvincing, they should not be evaluated in a mechanistic way and departures from the Code should not be automatically treated as breaches. Institutional shareholders and their agents should be careful to respond to the statements from companies in a manner that supports the 'comply or explain' principle. As the principles in Section 2 make clear, institutional shareholders should carefully consider explanations given for departure from the Code and make reasoned judgements in each case. They should put their views to the company and be prepared to enter a dialogue if they do not accept the company's position. Institutional shareholders should be prepared to put such views in writing where appropriate.

8   Nothing in this Code should be taken to override the general requirements of law to treat shareholders equally in access to information.

9   This publication includes guidance on how to comply with particular parts of the Code: first, 'Internal Control: Guidance for Directors on the Combined Code',[3] produced by the Turnbull Committee, which relates to Code provisions on internal control (C.2 and part of C.3 in the Code); and, second, 'Audit Committees: Combined Code Guidance', produced by the Smith Group, which relates to the provisions on audit committees and auditors (C.3 of the Code). In both cases, the guidance suggests ways of applying the relevant Code principles and of complying with the relevant Code provisions.

10  In addition, this volume also includes suggestions for good practice from the Higgs report.

11  The revised Code does not include material in the previous Code on the disclosure of directors' remuneration. This is because 'The Directors' Remuneration Report Regulations 2002'[4] are now in force and supersede the earlier Code provisions. These require the directors of a company to prepare a remuneration report. It is important that this report is clear, transparent and understandable to shareholders.

3  'Internal Control: Guidance for Directors on the Combined Code', published by the Institute of Chartered Accountants in England and Wales in September 1999.
4  The Directors' Remuneration Report Regulations 2002, S.I. no. 1986.

# CODE OF BEST PRACTICE
## Section 1 Companies

## A. DIRECTORS

### A.1 The Board

### MAIN PRINCIPLE

**Every company should be headed by an effective board, which is collectively responsible for the success of the company.**

### Supporting Principles

The board's role is to provide entrepreneurial leadership of the company within a framework of prudent and effective controls which enables risk to be assessed and managed. The board should set the company's strategic aims, ensure that the necessary financial and human resources are in place for the company to meet its objectives and review management performance. The board should set the company's values and standards and ensure that its obligations to its shareholders and others are understood and met.

All directors must take decisions objectively in the interests of the company.

As part of their role as members of a unitary board, non-executive directors should constructively challenge and help develop proposals on strategy. Non-executive directors should scrutinise the performance of management in meeting agreed goals and objectives and monitor the reporting of performance. They should satisfy themselves on the integrity of financial information and that financial controls and systems of risk management are robust and defensible. They are responsible for determining appropriate levels of remuneration of executive directors and have a prime role in appointing, and where necessary removing, executive directors, and in succession planning.

### Code Provisions

A.1.1 The board should meet sufficiently regularly to discharge its duties effectively. There should be a formal schedule of matters specifically reserved for its decision. The annual report should include a statement of how the board operates, including a high level statement of which types of decisions are to be taken by the board and which are to be delegated to management.

A.1.2 The annual report should identify the chairman, the deputy chairman (where there is one), the chief executive, the senior independent director and the chairmen and members of the nomination, audit and remuneration committees. It should also set out the number of meetings of the board and those committees and individual attendance by directors.

A.1.3 The chairman should hold meetings with the non-executive directors without the executives present. Led by the senior independent director, the non-executive directors should meet without the chairman present at least annually to appraise the chairman's performance (as described in A.6.1) and on such other occasions as are deemed appropriate.

A.1.4  Where directors have concerns which cannot be resolved about the running of the company or a proposed action, they should ensure that their concerns are recorded in the board minutes. On resignation, a non-executive director should provide a written statement to the chairman, for circulation to the board, if they have any such concerns.

A.1.5  The company should arrange appropriate insurance cover in respect of legal action against its directors.

## A.2 Chairman and chief executive

### MAIN PRINCIPLE

**There should be a clear division of responsibilities at the head of the company between the running of the board and the executive responsibility for the running of the company's business. No one individual should have unfettered powers of decision.**

### Supporting Principle

The chairman is responsible for leadership of the board, ensuring its effectiveness on all aspects of its role and setting its agenda. The chairman is also responsible for ensuring that the directors receive accurate, timely and clear information. The chairman should ensure effective communication with shareholders. The chairman should also facilitate the effective contribution of non-executive directors in particular and ensure constructive relations between executive and non-executive directors.

### Code Provisions

A.2.1  The roles of chairman and chief executive should not be exercised by the same individual. The division of responsibilities between the chairman and chief executive should be clearly established, set out in writing and agreed by the board.

A.2.2[5]  The chairman should on appointment meet the independence criteria set out in A.3.1 below. A chief executive should not go on to be chairman of the same company. If exceptionally a board decides that a chief executive should become chairman, the board should consult major shareholders in advance and should set out its reasons to shareholders at the time of the appointment and in the next annual report.

## A.3 Board balance and independence

### MAIN PRINCIPLE

**The board should include a balance of executive and non-executive directors (and in particular independent non-executive directors) such that no individual or small group of individuals can dominate the board's decision taking.**

---

5  Compliance or otherwise with this provision need only be reported for the year in which the appointment is made.

## Supporting Principles

The board should not be so large as to be unwieldy. The board should be of sufficient size that the balance of skills and experience is appropriate for the requirements of the business and that changes to the board's composition can be managed without undue disruption.

To ensure that power and information are not concentrated in one or two individuals, there should be a strong presence on the board of both executive and non-executive directors.

The value of ensuring that committee membership is refreshed and that undue reliance is not placed on particular individuals should be taken into account in deciding chairmanship and membership of committees.

No one other than the committee chairman and members is entitled to be present at a meeting of the nomination, audit or remuneration committee, but others may attend at the invitation of the committee.

## Code Provisions

A.3.1 The board should identify in the annual report each non-executive director it considers to be independent.[6] The board should determine whether the director is independent in character and judgement and whether there are relationships or circumstances which are likely to affect, or could appear to affect, the director's judgement. The board should state its reasons if it determines that a director is independent notwithstanding the existence of relationships or circumstances which may appear relevant to its determination, including if the director:
- has been an employee of the company or group within the last five years;
- has, or has had within the last three years, a material business relationship with the company either directly, or as a partner, shareholder, director or senior employee of a body that has such a relationship with the company;
- has received or receives additional remuneration from the company apart from a director's fee, participates in the company's share option or a performance-related pay scheme, or is a member of the company's pension scheme;
- has close family ties with any of the company's advisers, directors or senior employees;
- holds cross-directorships or has significant links with other directors through involvement in other companies or bodies;
- represents a significant shareholder; or
- has served on the board for more than nine years from the date of their first election.

A.3.2 Except for smaller companies,[7] at least half the board, excluding the chairman, should comprise non-executive directors determined by the board to be independent. A smaller company should have at least two independent non-executive directors.

A.3.3 The board should appoint one of the independent non-executive directors to be the senior independent director. The senior independent director should be available to shareholders if they have concerns which contact through the normal channels of chairman, chief executive or finance director has failed to resolve or for which such contact is inappropriate.

6 A.2.2 states that the chairman should, on appointment, meet the independence criteria set out in this provision, but thereafter the test of independence is not appropriate in relation to the chairman.
7 A smaller company is one that is below the FTSE 350 throughout the year immediately prior to the reporting year.

## A.4 Appointments to the Board

### MAIN PRINCIPLE

**There should be a formal, rigorous and transparent procedure for the appointment of new directors to the board.**

### Supporting Principles

Appointments to the board should be made on merit and against objective criteria. Care should be taken to ensure that appointees have enough time available to devote to the job. This is particularly important in the case of chairmanships.

The board should satisfy itself that plans are in place for orderly succession for appointments to the board and to senior management, so as to maintain an appropriate balance of skills and experience within the company and on the board.

### Code Provisions

A.4.1   There should be a nomination committee which should lead the process for board appointments and make recommendations to the board. A majority of members of the nomination committee should be independent non-executive directors. The chairman or an independent non-executive director should chair the committee, but the chairman should not chair the nomination committee when it is dealing with the appointment of a successor to the chairmanship. The nomination committee should make available[8] its terms of reference, explaining its role and the authority delegated to it by the board.

A.4.2   The nomination committee should evaluate the balance of skills, knowledge and experience on the board and, in the light of this evaluation, prepare a description of the role and capabilities required for a particular appointment.

A.4.3   For the appointment of a chairman, the nomination committee should prepare a job specification, including an assessment of the time commitment expected, recognising the need for availability in the event of crises. A chairman's other significant commitments should be disclosed to the board before appointment and included in the annual report. Changes to such commitments should be reported to the board as they arise, and included in the next annual report. No individual should be appointed to a second chairmanship of a FTSE 100 company.[9]

A.4.4   The terms and conditions of appointment of non-executive directors should be made available for inspection.[10] The letter of appointment should set out the expected time commitment. Non-executive directors should undertake that they will have sufficient time to meet what is expected of them. Their other significant commitments should be disclosed to the board before appointment, with a broad indication of the time involved and the board should be informed of subsequent changes.

---

8   The requirement to make the information available would be met by making it available on request and by including the information on the company's web-site.

9   Compliance or otherwise with this provision need only be reported for the year in which the appointment is made.

10   The terms and conditions of appointment of non-executive directors should be made available for inspection by any person at the company's registered office during normal business hours and at the AGM (for 15 minutes prior to the meeting and during the meeting).

A.4.5　The board should not agree to a full time executive director taking on more than one non-executive directorship in a FTSE 100 company nor the chairmanship of such a company.

A.4.6　A separate section of the annual report should describe the work of the nomination committee, including the process it has used in relation to board appointments. An explanation should be given if neither an external search consultancy nor open advertising has been used in the appointment of a chairman or a non-executive director.

## A.5 Information and professional development

### MAIN PRINCIPLE

**The board should be supplied in a timely manner with information in a form and of a quality appropriate to enable it to discharge its duties. All directors should receive induction on joining the board and should regularly update and refresh their skills and knowledge.**

### Supporting Principles

The chairman is responsible for ensuring that the directors receive accurate, timely and clear information. Management has an obligation to provide such information but directors should seek clarification or amplification where necessary.

The chairman should ensure that the directors continually update their skills and the knowledge and familiarity with the company required to fulfil their role both on the board and on board committees. The company should provide the necessary resources for developing and updating its directors' knowledge and capabilities. Under the direction of the chairman, the company secretary's responsibilities include ensuring good information flows within the board and its committees and between senior management and non-executive directors, as well as facilitating induction and assisting with professional development as required.

The company secretary should be responsible for advising the board through the chairman on all governance matters.

### Code Provisions

A.5.1　The chairman should ensure that new directors receive a full, formal and tailored induction on joining the board. As part of this, the company should offer to major shareholders the opportunity to meet a new non-executive director.

A.5.2　The board should ensure that directors, especially non-executive directors, have access to independent professional advice at the company's expense where they judge it necessary to discharge their responsibilities as directors. Committees should be provided with sufficient resources to undertake their duties.

A.5.3　All directors should have access to the advice and services of the company secretary, who is responsible to the board for ensuring that board procedures are complied with. Both the appointment and removal of the company secretary should be a matter for the board as a whole.

## A.6 Performance evaluation

### MAIN PRINCIPLE

**The board should undertake a formal and rigorous annual evaluation of its own performance and that of its committees and individual directors.**

### Supporting Principle

Individual evaluation should aim to show whether each director continues to contribute effectively and to demonstrate commitment to the role (including commitment of time for board and committee meetings and any other duties). The chairman should act on the results of the performance evaluation by recognising the strengths and addressing the weaknesses of the board and, where appropriate, proposing new members be appointed to the board or seeking the resignation of directors.

### Code Provision

A.6.1   The board should state in the annual report how performance evaluation of the board, its committees and its individual directors has been conducted. The non-executive directors, led by the senior independent director, should be responsible for performance evaluation of the chairman, taking into account the views of executive directors.

## A.7 Re-election

### MAIN PRINCIPLE

**All directors should be submitted for re-election at regular intervals, subject to continued satisfactory performance. The board should ensure planned and progressive refreshing of the board.**

### Code Provisions

A.7.1   All directors should be subject to election by shareholders at the first annual general meeting after their appointment, and to re-election thereafter at intervals of no more than three years. The names of directors submitted for election or re-election should be accompanied by sufficient biographical details and any other relevant information to enable shareholders to take an informed decision on their election.

A.7.2   Non-executive directors should be appointed for specified terms subject to re-election and to Companies Acts provisions relating to the removal of a director. The board should set out to shareholders in the papers accompanying a resolution to elect a non-executive director why they believe an individual should be elected. The chairman should confirm to shareholders when proposing re-election that, following formal performance evaluation, the individual's performance continues to be effective and to demonstrate commitment to the role. Any term beyond six years (e.g. two three-year terms) for a non-executive director should be subject to particularly rigorous review, and should take into account the need for progressive refreshing of the board. Non-executive directors may serve longer than nine years (e.g. three three-year terms), subject to annual re-election. Serving more than nine years could be relevant to the determination of a non-executive director's independence (as set out in provision A.3.1).

## B. REMUNERATION

### B.1 The Level and Make-up of Remuneration[11]

#### MAIN PRINCIPLES

**Levels of remuneration should be sufficient to attract, retain and motivate directors of the quality required to run the company successfully, but a company should avoid paying more than is necessary for this purpose. A significant proportion of executive directors' remuneration should be structured so as to link rewards to corporate and individual performance.**

#### Supporting Principle

The remuneration committee should judge where to position their company relative to other companies. But they should use such comparisons with caution, in view of the risk of an upward ratchet of remuneration levels with no corresponding improvement in performance.

They should also be sensitive to pay and employment conditions elsewhere in the group, especially when determining annual salary increases.

#### Code Provisions

*Remuneration policy*

B.1.1   The performance-related elements of remuneration should form a significant proportion of the total remuneration package of executive directors and should be designed to align their interests with those of shareholders and to give these directors keen incentives to perform at the highest levels. In designing schemes of performance-related remuneration, the remuneration committee should follow the provisions in Schedule A to this Code.

B.1.2   Executive share options should not be offered at a discount save as permitted by the relevant provisions of the Listing Rules.

B.1.3   Levels of remuneration for non-executive directors should reflect the time commitment and responsibilities of the role. Remuneration for non-executive directors should not include share options. If, exceptionally, options are granted, shareholder approval should be sought in advance and any shares acquired by exercise of the options should be held until at least one year after the non-executive director leaves the board. Holding of share options could be relevant to the determination of a non-executive director's independence (as set out in provision A.3.1).

B.1.4   Where a company releases an executive director to serve as a non-executive director elsewhere, the remuneration report[12] should include a statement as to whether or not the director will retain such earnings and, if so, what the remuneration is.

---

11  Views have been sought by the Department of Trade and Industry by 30 September 2003 on whether, and if so how, further measures are required to enable shareholders to ensure that compensation reflects performance when directors' contracts are terminated: See 'Rewards for Failure': Directors' Remuneration – Contracts, performance and severance, June 2003.

12  As required under the Directors' Remuneration Report Regulations.

## Service Contracts and Compensation

B.1.5   The remuneration committee should carefully consider what compensation commitments (including pension contributions and all other elements) their directors' terms of appointment would entail in the event of early termination. The aim should be to avoid rewarding poor performance. They should take a robust line on reducing compensation to reflect departing directors' obligations to mitigate loss.

B.1.6   Notice or contract periods should be set at one year or less. If it is necessary to offer longer notice or contract periods to new directors recruited from outside, such periods should reduce to one year or less after the initial period.

## B.2 Procedure

### MAIN PRINCIPLE

**There should be a formal and transparent procedure for developing policy on executive remuneration and for fixing the remuneration packages of individual directors. No director should be involved in deciding his or her own remuneration.**

### Supporting Principles

The remuneration committee should consult the chairman and/or chief executive about their proposals relating to the remuneration of other executive directors. The remuneration committee should also be responsible for appointing any consultants in respect of executive director remuneration. Where executive directors or senior management are involved in advising or supporting the remuneration committee, care should be taken to recognise and avoid conflicts of interest.

The chairman of the board should ensure that the company maintains contact as required with its principal shareholders about remuneration in the same way as for other matters.

### Code Provisions

B.2.1   The board should establish a remuneration committee of at least three, or in the case of smaller companies[13] two, members, who should all be independent non-executive directors. The remuneration committee should make available[14] its terms of reference, explaining its role and the authority delegated to it by the board. Where remuneration consultants are appointed, a statement should be made available[15] of whether they have any other connection with the company.

B.2.2   The remuneration committee should have delegated responsibility for setting remuneration for all executive directors and the chairman, including pension rights and any compensation payments. The committee should also recommend and monitor the level and structure of remuneration for senior management. The definition of 'senior management' for this purpose should be determined by the board but should normally include the first layer of management below board level.

13  See footnote 8.
14  See footnote 9.
15  See footnote 9.

B.2.3 The board itself or, where required by the Articles of Association, the shareholders should determine the remuneration of the non-executive directors within the limits set in the Articles of Association. Where permitted by the Articles, the board may however delegate this responsibility to a committee, which might include the chief executive.

B.2.4 Shareholders should be invited specifically to approve all new long-term incentive schemes (as defined in the Listing Rules) and significant changes to existing schemes, save in the circumstances permitted by the Listing Rules.

## C. ACCOUNTABILITY AND AUDIT

### C.1 Financial Reporting

#### MAIN PRINCIPLE

**The board should present a balanced and understandable assessment of the company's position and prospects.**

#### Supporting Principle

The board's responsibility to present a balanced and understandable assessment extends to interim and other price-sensitive public reports and reports to regulators as well as to information required to be presented by statutory requirements.

#### Code Provisions

C.1.1 The directors should explain in the annual report their responsibility for preparing the accounts and there should be a statement by the auditors about their reporting responsibilities.

C.1.2 The directors should report that the business is a going concern, with supporting assumptions or qualifications as necessary.

### C.2 Internal Control[16]

#### MAIN PRINCIPLE

**The board should maintain a sound system of internal control to safeguard shareholders' investment and the company's assets.**

#### Code Provision

C.2.1 The board should, at least annually, conduct a review of the effectiveness of the group's system of internal controls and should report to shareholders that they have done so. The review should cover all material controls, including financial, operational and compliance controls and risk management systems.

16 The Turnbull guidance suggests means of applying this part of the Code.

## C.3 Audit Committee and Auditors[17]

### MAIN PRINCIPLE

**The board should establish formal and transparent arrangements for considering how they should apply the financial reporting and internal control principles and for maintaining an appropriate relationship with the company's auditors.**

### Code Provisions

C.3.1  The board should establish an audit committee of at least three, or in the case of smaller companies[18] two, members, who should all be independent non-executive directors. The board should satisfy itself that at least one member of the audit committee has recent and relevant financial experience.

C.3.2  The main role and responsibilities of the audit committee should be set out in written terms of reference and should include:
- to monitor the integrity of the financial statements of the company, and any formal announcements relating to the company's financial performance, reviewing significant financial reporting judgements contained in them;
- to review the company's internal financial controls and, unless expressly addressed by a separate board risk committee composed of independent directors, or by the board itself, to review the company's internal control and risk management systems;
- to monitor and review the effectiveness of the company's internal audit function;
- to make recommendations to the board, for it to put to the shareholders for their approval in general meeting, in relation to the appointment, re-appointment and removal of the external auditor and to approve the remuneration and terms of engagement of the external auditor;
- to review and monitor the external auditor's independence and objectivity and the effectiveness of the audit process, taking into consideration relevant UK professional and regulatory requirements;
- to develop and implement policy on the engagement of the external auditor to supply non-audit services, taking into account relevant ethical guidance regarding the provision of non-audit services by the external audit firm; and
- to report to the board, identifying any matters in respect of which it considers that action or improvement is needed and making recommendations as to the steps to be taken.

C.3.3  The terms of reference of the audit committee, including its role and the authority delegated to it by the board, should be made available.[19] A separate section of the annual report should describe the work of the committee in discharging those responsibilities.

C.3.4  The audit committee should review arrangements by which staff of the company may, in confidence, raise concerns about possible improprieties in matters of financial reporting or other matters. The audit committee's objective should be to ensure that

---

17  The Smith guidance suggests means of applying this part of the Code.
18  See footnote 7.
19  See footnote 8.

arrangements are in place for the proportionate and independent investigation of such matters and for appropriate follow-up action.

C.3.5 The audit committee should monitor and review the effectiveness of the internal audit activities. Where there is no internal audit function, the audit committee should consider annually whether there is a need for an internal audit function and make a recommendation to the board, and the reasons for the absence of such a function should be explained in the relevant section of the annual report.

C.3.6 The audit committee should have primary responsibility for making a recommendation on the appointment, reappointment and removal of the external auditors. If the board does not accept the audit committee's recommendation, it should include in the annual report, and in any papers recommending appointment or re-appointment, a statement from the audit committee explaining the recommendation and should set out reasons why the board has taken a different position.

C.3.7 The annual report should explain to shareholders how, if the auditor provides non-audit services, auditor objectivity and independence is safeguarded.

## D. RELATIONS WITH SHAREHOLDERS

### D.1 Dialogue with Institutional Shareholders

**MAIN PRINCIPLE**

**There should be a dialogue with shareholders based on the mutual understanding of objectives. The board as a whole has responsibility for ensuring that a satisfactory dialogue with shareholders takes place.[20]**

**Supporting Principles**

Whilst recognising that most shareholder contact is with the chief executive and finance director, the chairman (and the senior independent director and other directors as appropriate) should maintain sufficient contact with major shareholders to understand their issues and concerns. The board should keep in touch with shareholder opinion in whatever ways are most practical and efficient.

**Code Provisions**

D.1.1 The chairman should ensure that the views of shareholders are communicated to the board as a whole. The chairman should discuss governance and strategy with major shareholders. Non-executive directors should be offered the opportunity to attend meetings with major shareholders and should expect to attend them if requested by major shareholders. The senior independent director should attend sufficient meetings with a range of major shareholders to listen to their views in order to help develop a balanced understanding of the issues and concerns of major shareholders.

---

20 Nothing in these principles or provisions should be taken to override the general requirements of law to treat shareholders equally in access to information.

D.1.2  The board should state in the annual report the steps they have taken to ensure that the members of the board, and in particular the non-executive directors, develop an understanding of the views of major shareholders about their company, for example through direct face-to-face contact, analysts' or brokers' briefings and surveys of shareholder opinion.

## D.2 Constructive Use of the AGM

### MAIN PRINCIPLE

**The board should use the AGM to communicate with investors and to encourage their participation.**

### Code Provisions

D.2.1  The company should count all proxy votes and, except where a poll is called, should indicate the level of proxies lodged on each resolution, and the balance for and against the resolution and the number of abstentions, after it has been dealt with on a show of hands. The company should ensure that votes cast are properly received and recorded.

D.2.2  The company should propose a separate resolution at the AGM on each substantially separate issue and should in particular propose a resolution at the AGM relating to the report and accounts.

D.2.3  The chairman should arrange for the chairmen of the audit, remuneration and nomination committees to be available to answer questions at the AGM and for all directors to attend.

D.2.4  The company should arrange for the Notice of the AGM and related papers to be sent to shareholders at least 20 working days before the meeting.

## Section 2 Institutional Shareholders

## E. INSTITUTIONAL SHAREHOLDERS[21]

### E.1  Dialogue with companies

### MAIN PRINCIPLE

**Institutional shareholders should enter into a dialogue with companies based on the mutual understanding of objectives.**

---

21  Agents such as investment managers, or voting services, are frequently appointed by institutional shareholders to act on their behalf and these principles should accordingly be read as applying where appropriate to the agents of institutional shareholders.

## Supporting Principles

Institutional shareholders should apply the principles set out in the Institutional Shareholders' Committee's 'The Responsibilities of Institutional Shareholders and Agents – Statement of Principles',[22] which should be reflected in fund manager contracts.

## E.2 Evaluation of Governance Disclosures

### MAIN PRINCIPLE

When evaluating companies' governance arrangements, particularly those relating to board structure and composition, institutional shareholders should give due weight to all relevant factors drawn to their attention.

### Supporting Principle

Institutional shareholders should consider carefully explanations given for departure from this Code and make reasoned judgements in each case. They should give an explanation to the company, in writing where appropriate, and be prepared to enter a dialogue if they do not accept the company's position. They should avoid a box-ticking approach to assessing a company's corporate governance. They should bear in mind in particular the size and complexity of the company and the nature of the risks and challenges it faces.

## E.3 Shareholder Voting

### MAIN PRINCIPLE

**Institutional shareholders have a responsibility to make considered use of their votes.**

### Supporting Principles

Institutional shareholders should take steps to ensure their voting intentions are being translated into practice.

Institutional shareholders should, on request, make available to their clients information on the proportion of resolutions on which votes were cast and non-discretionary proxies lodged.

Major shareholders should attend AGMs where appropriate and practicable. Companies and registrars should facilitate this.

## Schedule A: Provisions on the design of performance-related remuneration

1   The remuneration committee should consider whether the directors should be eligible for annual bonuses. If so, performance conditions should be relevant, stretching and designed to enhance shareholder value. Upper limits should be set and disclosed. There may be a case for part payment in shares to be held for a significant period.

2   The remuneration committee should consider whether the directors should be eligible for benefits under long-term incentive schemes. Traditional share option schemes should

22   Available at web-site: www.investmentuk.org.uk/press/2002/20021021-01.pdf.

be weighed against other kinds of long-term incentive scheme. In normal circumstances, shares granted or other forms of deferred remuneration should not vest, and options should not be exercisable, in less than three years. Directors should be encouraged to hold their shares for a further period after vesting or exercise, subject to the need to finance any costs of acquisition and associated tax liabilities.

3   Any new long-term incentive schemes which are proposed should be approved by shareholders and should preferably replace any existing schemes or at least form part of a well considered overall plan, incorporating existing schemes. The total rewards potentially available should not be excessive.

4   Payouts or grants under all incentive schemes, including new grants under existing share option schemes, should be subject to challenging performance criteria reflecting the company's objectives. Consideration should be given to criteria which reflect the company's performance relative to a group of comparator companies in some key variables such as total shareholder return.

5   Grants under executive share option and other long-term incentive schemes should normally be phased rather than awarded in one large block.

6   In general, only basic salary should be pensionable.

7   The remuneration committee should consider the pension consequences and associated costs to the company of basic salary increases and any other changes in pensionable remuneration, especially for directors close to retirement.

## Schedule B: Guidance on liability of non-executive directors: care, skill and diligence

1   Although non-executive directors and executive directors have as board members the same legal duties and objectives, the time devoted to the company's affairs is likely to be significantly less for a non-executive director than for an executive director and the detailed knowledge and experience of a company's affairs that could reasonably be expected of a non-executive director will generally be less than for an executive director. These matters may be relevant in assessing the knowledge, skill and experience which may reasonably be expected of a non-executive director and therefore the care, skill and diligence that a non-executive director may be expected to exercise.

2   In this context, the following elements of the Code may also be particularly relevant.

(i) In order to enable directors to fulfil their duties, the Code states that:
- The letter of appointment of the director should set out the expected time commitment (Code provision A.4.4); and
- The board should be supplied in a timely manner with information in a form and of a quality appropriate to enable it to discharge its duties. The chairman is responsible for ensuring that the directors are provided by management with accurate, timely and clear information. (Code principles A.5).

(ii)   Non-executive directors should themselves:
- Undertake appropriate induction and regularly update and refresh their skills, knowledge and familiarity with the company (Code principle A.5 and provision A.5.1)
- Seek appropriate clarification or amplification of information and, where necessary, take and follow appropriate professional advice. (Code principle A.5 and provision A.5.2)

- Where they have concerns about the running of the company or a proposed action, ensure that these are addressed by the board and, to the extent that they are not resolved, ensure that they are recorded in the board minutes (Code provision A.1.4).
- Give a statement to the board if they have such unresolved concerns on resignation (Code provision A.1.4)

3   It is up to each non-executive director to reach a view as to what is necessary in particular circumstances to comply with the duty of care, skill and diligence they owe as a director to the company. In considering whether or not a person is in breach of that duty, a court would take into account all relevant circumstances. These may include having regard to the above where relevant to the issue of liability of a non-executive director.

## Schedule C: Disclosure of corporate governance arrangements

The Listing Rules require a statement to be included in the annual report relating to compliance with the Code, as described in the preamble. For ease of reference, the specific requirements in the Code for disclosure are set out below:

The annual report should record:
- a statement of how the board operates, including a high level statement of which types of decisions are to be taken by the board and which are to be delegated to management (A.1.1);
- the names of the chairman, the deputy chairman (where there is one), the chief executive, the senior independent director and the chairmen and members of the nomination, audit and remuneration committees (A.1.2);
- the number of meetings of the board and those committees and individual attendance by directors (A.1.2);
- the names of the non-executive directors whom the board determines to be independent, with reasons where necessary (A.3.1);
- the other significant commitments of the chairman and any changes to them during the year (A.4.3);
- how performance evaluation of the board, its committees and its directors has been conducted (A.6.1);
- the steps the board has taken to ensure that members of the board, and in particular the non-executive directors, develop an understanding of the views of major shareholders about their company (D.1.2).

The report should also include:
- a separate section describing the work of the nomination committee, including the process it has used in relation to board appointments and an explanation if neither external search
- consultancy nor open advertising has been used in the appointment of a chairman or a non-executive director (A.4.6);
- a description of the work of the remuneration committee as required under the Directors' Remuneration Reporting Regulations 2002, and including, where an executive director serves as a non-executive director elsewhere, whether or not the director will retain such earnings and, if so, what the remuneration is (B.1.4);
- an explanation from the directors of their responsibility for preparing the accounts and a statement by the auditors about their reporting responsibilities (C.1.1);

- a statement from the directors that the business is a going concern, with supporting assumptions or qualifications as necessary (C.1.2);
- a report that the board has conducted a review of the effectiveness of the group's system of internal controls (C.2.1);
- a separate section describing the work of the audit committee in discharging its responsibilities (C.3.3);
- where there is no internal audit function, the reasons for the absence of such a function (C.3.5);
- where the board does not accept the audit committee's recommendation on the appointment, reappointment or removal of an external auditor, a statement from the audit committee explaining the recommendation and the reasons why the board has taken a different position (C.3.6); and
- an explanation of how, if the auditor provides non-audit services, auditor objectivity and independence is safeguarded (C.3.7).

**The following information should be made available (which may be met by making it available on request and placing the information available on the company's web-site):**

- the terms of reference of the nomination, remuneration and audit committees, explaining their role and the authority delegated to them by the board (A.4.1, B.2.1 and C.3.3);
- the terms and conditions of appointment of non-executive directors (A.4.4) (see footnote 10 on page 9); and
- the terms of reference of any remuneration consultants, together with a statement of whether they have any other connection with the company (B.2.1).
- The board should set out to shareholders in the papers accompanying a resolution to elect or re-elect:
- sufficient biographical details to enable shareholders to take an informed decision on their election or re-election (A.7.1).
- why they believe an individual should be elected to a non-executive role (A.7.2).
- on re-election of a non-executive director, confirmation from the chairman that, following formal performance evaluation, the individual's performance continues to be effective and to demonstrate commitment to the role, including commitment of time for board and committee meetings and any other duties (A.7.2).

**The board should set out to shareholders in the papers recommending appointment or reappointment of an external auditor:**

- if the board does not accept the audit committee's recommendation, a statement from the audit committee explaining the recommendation and from the board setting out reasons why they have taken a different position (C.3.6).

# Appendix 2

OECD PRINCIPLES OF CORPORATE GOVERNANCE

## Part One

## I  THE RIGHTS OF SHAREHOLDERS

*The corporate governance framework should protect shareholders' rights.*

A  Basic shareholder rights include the right to:
1) secure methods of ownership registration;
2) convey or transfer shares;
3) obtain relevant information on the corporation on a timely and regular basis;
4) participate and vote in general shareholder meetings;
5) elect members of the board; and
6) share in the profits of the corporation.

B  Shareholders have the right to participate in, and to be sufficiently informed on, decisions concerning fundamental corporate changes such as:
1) amendments to the statutes, or articles of incorporation or similar governing documents of the company;
2) the authorisation of additional shares; and
3) extraordinary transactions that in effect result in the sale of the company.

C  Shareholders should have the opportunity to participate effectively and vote in general shareholder meetings and should be informed of the rules, including voting procedures, that govern general shareholder meetings:
1  Shareholders should be furnished with sufficient and timely information concerning the date, location and agenda of general meetings, as well as full and timely information regarding the issues to be decided at the meeting.
2  Opportunity should be provided for shareholders to ask questions of the board and to place items on the agenda at general meetings, subject to reasonable limitations.
3  Shareholders should be able to vote in person or in absentia, and equal effect should be given to votes whether cast in person or in absentia.

D  Capital structures and arrangements that enable certain shareholders to obtain a degree of control disproportionate to their equity ownership should be disclosed.

E  Markets for corporate control should be allowed to function in an efficient and transparent manner.
1  The rules and procedures governing the acquisition of corporate control in the capital markets, and extraordinary transactions such as mergers, and sales of substantial portions of corporate assets, should be clearly articulated and disclosed so that investors understand their rights and recourse. Transactions should occur at transparent prices and under fair conditions that protect the rights of all shareholders according to their class.

2   Anti-take-over devices should not be used to shield management from accountability.

F   Shareholders, including institutional investors, should consider the costs and benefits of exercising their voting rights.

## II  THE EQUITABLE TREATMENT OF SHAREHOLDERS

*The corporate governance framework should ensure the equitable treatment of all shareholders, including minority and foreign shareholders. All shareholders should have the opportunity to obtain effective redress for violation of their rights.*

A   All shareholders of the same class should be treated equally.
  1   Within any class, all shareholders should have the same voting rights. All investors should be able to obtain information about the voting rights attached to all classes of shares before they purchase. Any changes in voting rights should be subject to shareholder vote.
  2   Votes should be cast by custodians or nominees in a manner agreed upon with the beneficial owner of the shares.
  3   Processes and procedures for general shareholder meetings should allow for equitable treatment of all shareholders. Company procedures should not make it unduly difficult or expensive to cast votes.

B   Insider trading and abusive self-dealing should be prohibited.

C   Members of the board and managers should be required to disclose any material interests in transactions or matters affecting the corporation.

## III  THE ROLE OF STAKEHOLDERS IN CORPORATE GOVERNANCE

*The corporate governance framework should recognise the rights of stakeholders as established by law and encourage active co-operation between corporations and stakeholders in creating wealth, jobs, and the sustainability of financially sound enterprises.*

A   The corporate governance framework should assure that the rights of stakeholders that are protected by law are respected.

B   Where stakeholder interests are protected by law, stakeholders should have the opportunity to obtain effective redress for violation of their rights.

C   The corporate governance framework should permit performance-enhancing mechanisms for stakeholder participation.

D   Where stakeholders participate in the corporate governance process, they should have access to relevant information.

## IV  DISCLOSURE AND TRANSPARENCY

*The corporate governance framework should ensure that timely and accurate disclosure is made on all material matters regarding the corporation, including the financial situation, performance, ownership, and governance of the company.*

A  Disclosure should include, but not be limited to, material information on:
1  The financial and operating results of the company.
2  Company objectives.
3  Major share ownership and voting rights.
4  Members of the board and key executives, and their remuneration.
5  Material foreseeable risk factors.
6  Material issues regarding employees and other stakeholders.
7  Governance structures and policies.

B  Information should be prepared, audited, and disclosed in accordance with high quality standards of accounting, financial and non-financial disclosure, and audit.

C  An annual audit should be conducted by an independent auditor in order to provide an external and objective assurance on the way in which financial statements have been prepared and presented.

D  Channels for disseminating information should provide for fair, timely and cost-efficient access to relevant information by users.

## V  THE RESPONSIBILITIES OF THE BOARD

*The corporate governance framework should ensure the strategic guidance of the company, the effective monitoring of management by the board, and the board's accountability to the company and the shareholders.*

A  Board members should act on a fully informed basis, in good faith, with due diligence and care, and in the best interest of the company and the shareholders.

B  Where board decisions may affect different shareholder groups differently, the board should treat all shareholders fairly.

C  The board should ensure compliance with applicable law and take into account the interests of stakeholders.

D  The board should fulfil certain key functions, including:
1  Reviewing and guiding corporate strategy, major plans of action, risk policy, annual budgets and business plans; setting performance objectives; monitoring implementation and corporate performance; and overseeing major capital expenditures, acquisitions and divestitures.
2  Selecting, compensating, monitoring and, when necessary, replacing key executives and overseeing succession planning.
3  Reviewing key executive and board remuneration, and ensuring a formal and transparent board nomination process.
4  Monitoring and managing potential conflicts of interest of management, board members and shareholders, including misuse of corporate assets and abuse in related party transactions.

5   Ensuring the integrity of the corporation's accounting and financial reporting systems, including the independent audit, and that appropriate systems of control are in place, in particular, systems for monitoring risk, financial control, and compliance with the law.

6   Monitoring the effectiveness of the governance practices under which it operates and making changes as needed.

7   Overseeing the process of disclosure and communications.

E   The board should be able to exercise objective judgement on corporate affairs independent, in particular, from management.

1   Boards should consider assigning a sufficient number of non-executive board members capable of exercising independent judgement to tasks where there is a potential for conflict of interest. Examples of such key responsibilities are financial reporting, nomination and executive and board remuneration.

2   Board members should devote sufficient time to their responsibilities.

F   In order to fulfil their responsibilities, board members should have access to accurate, relevant and timely information.

# Appendix 3

## PROPOSED LEGISLATIVE STATEMENT OF DIRECTORS' DUTIES

**COMPANIES BILL SCHEDULE 2:**

### General Principles by Which Directors Are Bound

*Obeying the constitution and other lawful decisions*

1   A director of a company must act in accordance with –
    (a)   the company's constitution; and
    (b)   decisions taken under the constitution (or by the company, or any class of members, under any enactment or rule of law as to means of taking company or class decisions),
    and must exercise his powers for their proper purpose.

*Promotion of company's objectives*

2   A director of a company must in any given case -
    (a)   act in the way he decides, in good faith, would be most likely to promote the success of the company for the benefit of its members as a whole (excluding anything which would breach his duty under paragraph 1 or 5); and
    (b)   in deciding what would be most likely to promote that success, take account in good faith of all the material factors that it is practicable in the circumstances for him to identify.

**Notes**

(1)   In this paragraph, 'the material factors' means -
      (a)   the likely consequences (short and long term) of the actions open to the director, so far as a person of care and skill would consider them relevant; and
      (b)   all such other factors as a person of care and skill would consider relevant, including such of the matters in Note (2) as he would consider so.
(2)   Those matters are -
      (a)   the company's need to foster its business relationships, including those with its employees and suppliers and the customers for its products and services;
      (b)   its need to have regard to the impact of its operations on the communities affected and on the environment;
      (c)   its need to maintain a reputation for high standards of business conduct;
      (d)   its need to achieve outcomes that are fair as between its members.
(3)   In Note (1), a 'person of care and skill' means a person exercising the care, skill and diligence required by paragraph 4.
(4)   A director's decision as to what constitutes the success of the company for the benefit of its members as a whole must accord with the constitution and any decisions as mentioned in paragraph 1.

### Delegation and independence of judgement

3  A director of a company must not, except where authorised to do so by the company's constitution or any decisions as mentioned in paragraph 1 -
   (a)  delegate any of his powers; or
   (b)  fail to exercise his independent judgement in relation to any exercise of his powers.

   **Note**
   Where a director has, in accordance with this schedule, entered into an agreement which restricts his power to exercise independent judgement later, this paragraph does not prevent him from acting as the agreement requires where (in his independent judgement, and according to the other provisions of this Schedule) he should do so.

### Care, skill and diligence

4  A director of a company must exercise the care, skill and diligence which would be exercised by a reasonably diligent person with both -
   (a)  the knowledge, skill and experience which may reasonably be expected of a director in his position; and
   (b)  any additional knowledge, skill and experience which he has.

### Transactions involving conflict of interest

5  A director of a company must not -
   (a)  in the performance of his functions as a director, authorise, procure or permit the company to enter into a transaction; or
   (b)  enter into a transaction with the company
      if he has an interest in the transaction which he is required by this Act to disclose to any persons and has not disclosed the interest to them to the extent so required.

### Personal use of the company's property, information or opportunity

6  A director or former director of a company must not use for his own or anyone else's benefit any property or information of the company, or any opportunity of the company which he became aware of in the performance of his functions as a director, unless -
   (a)  the use has been proposed to the company and the company has consented to it by ordinary resolution; or
   (b)  the company is a private company, the use has been proposed to and authorised by the board, and nothing in the constitution invalidates that authorisation; or
   (c)  the company is a public company, its constitution includes provision enabling the board to authorise such use if proposed, and the use has been proposed to and authorised by the board in accordance with the constitution.

   **Notes**
   (1)  In this paragraph, 'the board' means the board of directors acting without the participation of any interested director.
   (2)  This paragraph does not apply to a use to which a director has a right under a contract or other transaction that he has entered into with the company, or that he has in the performance of his functions authorised, procured or permitted the company to enter into.

### Benefits from third parties

7   A director or former director of a company must not accept any benefit which is conferred because of the powers which he has as a director or by way of reward for any exercise of his powers as a director, unless the benefit is conferred by the company or -

(a)   acceptance of the benefit has been proposed to the company and the company has consented to it by ordinary resolution; or

(b)   the benefit is necessarily incidental to the proper performance of any of his functions as a director.

*Source:* Companies Bill (Cm 5553 – II, July 2002).

# Appendix 4

## ASSOCIATION OF BRITISH INSURERS: DISCLOSURE GUIDELINES ON SOCIALLY RESPONSIBLE INVESTMENT

### 1  Background and introduction

Public interest in corporate social responsibility has grown to the point where it seems helpful for institutional shareholders to set out basic disclosure principles, which will guide them in seeking to engage with companies in which they invest.

In drawing up guidelines for this purpose they are mindful of statements made at multilateral level through the Guidelines for Multinational Corporations published in 2000 by the Organisation for Economic Cooperation and Development, as well as by the European Union and UK Government. These, coupled with legal disclosure obligations on UK pension funds and local authority investments, point to clear responsibilities both for companies and for institutions that invest in them.

Institutional shareholders are also anxious to avoid unnecessary prescription or the imposition of costly burdens, which can unnecessarily restrict the ability of companies to generate returns. Indeed, by focusing on the need to identify and manage risks to the long and short-term value of the business from social, environmental and ethical matters, the guidelines highlight an opportunity to enhance value through appropriate response to these risks.

It is not the intention of these guidelines to set a limit on the amount of information companies should provide on their response to social, environmental and ethical matters. Some shareholders with specific ethical investment objectives may seek more specific information. Some companies may choose to make additional information available in order to enhance their appeal to investors.

The ABI hopes that in elaborating these guidelines it will provide a helpful basic benchmark for companies seeking to develop best practice in this area..

### The Disclosure Guidelines

The guidelines take the form of disclosures, which institutions would expect to see included in the annual report of listed companies. Specifically they refer to disclosures relating to Board responsibilities and to policies, procedures and verification.

With regard to the board, the company should state in its annual report whether:

1.1    The Board takes regular account of the significance of social, environmental and ethical (SEE) matters to the business of the company.

1.2 The Board has identified and assessed the significant risks to the company's short and long term value arising from SEE matters, as well as the opportunities to enhance value that may arise from an appropriate response.

1.3 The Board has received adequate information to make this assessment and that account is taken of SEE matters in the training of directors.

1.4 The Board has ensured that the company has in place effective systems for managing significant risks, which, where relevant, incorporate performance management systems and appropriate remuneration incentives.

With regard to policies, procedures and verification, the annual report should:

2.1 Include information on SEE-related risks and opportunities that may significantly affect the company's short and long term value, and how they might impact on the business.

2.2 Describe the company's policies and procedures for managing risks to short and long term value arising from SEE matters. If the annual report and accounts states that the company has no such policies and procedures, the Board should provide reasons for their absence.

2.3 Include information about the extent to which the company has complied with its policies and procedures for managing risks arising from SEE matters.

2.4 Describe the procedures for verification of SEE disclosures. The verification procedure should be such as to achieve a reasonable level of credibility.

## Towards best practice

Institutional shareholders consider that adherence to the principles outlined above will help companies to develop appropriate policies on corporate social responsibility.

The principles should also provide a constructive basis for engagement between companies and their shareholders. Over time this will allow both parties jointly to develop a clear joint understanding of best practice in the handling of social, environmental and ethical matters which will help preserve and enhance value. It is the intention of the ABI to continue regular contact with companies and stakeholders with a view to refining the concept of best practice.

Current understanding of best practice leads to the following conclusions and indications as to how the guidelines should operate:

1 The guidelines are intended to apply to all companies, including small and medium companies.

2 The cost of managing risks should be proportionate to their significance. Ideally, procedures should be integrated into existing management structures and systems.

3 Statements relating to the guidelines should be made in the annual report, and not separately as part of the summary accounts or on a web site dedicated to social responsibility. In view of the close philosophical linkage between these guidelines and Turnbull reporting, it would make sense to include a brief statement in the Internal Control section of the annual report, although this would not preclude a cross reference

to other parts of the report where more detailed disclosure of the type of risks involved and systems for managing those risks may also fit with other content.

4   With regard to the implementation, shareholders are anxious to leave leeway for companies to establish their own systems best suited to their business. However, they believe that, with regard to clause 1.1, best practice would require the full Board to consider the issues on a regular basis, although some on-going detailed work might be delegated to a committee. Disclosure should include a brief description of the process undertaken by the Board for identifying significant risks and indicate which risks are the most significant in terms of their impact on the business.

5   Examples of initiatives for reducing and managing risks (see 1.4 and 2.2) include regular contact with stakeholders and mechanisms to ensure that appropriate standards are maintained in the supply chain. Evidence of such initiatives would be viewed positively by shareholders.

6   Reporting on performance over time in complying with policies to reduce risk will help shareholders monitor improvement in compliance.

7   Independent external verification of SEE disclosures would be regarded by shareholders as a highly significant advantage. Credible verification may also be achieved by other means, including internal audit. It would assist shareholders in their assessment of SEE policies if the reason for choosing a particular method of verification were explained in the annual report.

## Appendix 1: Questions on social, environmental and ethical matters

Disclosure could be addressed by response in the annual report to the following questions:

1   Has the company made any reference to social, environmental and ethical matters? If so, does the board take these regularly into account?

2   Has the company identified and assessed significant risks and opportunities affecting its long- and short-term value arising from its handling of SEE matters?

3   Does the company state that it has adequate information for identification and assessment?

4   Are systems in place to manage the SEE risks?

5   Are any remuneration incentives relating to the handling of SEE risks included in risk management systems?

6   Does Directors' training include SEE matters?

7   Does the company disclose significant short and long term risks and opportunities arising from SEE issues? If so, how many different risks/opportunities are identified?

8   Are policies for managing risks to the company's value described?

9   Are procedures for managing risk described? If not, are reasons for non-disclosure given?

10 Does the Company report on the extent of its compliance with its policies and procedures?

11 Are verification procedures described?

## Appendix 2: Questions for investment trusts

1 Is the voting policy of the trust publicly available?

2 Does the voting policy make reference to SEE matters?

3 Is the manager encouraged actively to engage with companies to promote better SEE practice?

# Appendix 5

## ICSA GUIDANCE NOTE: MATTERS RESERVED FOR THE BOARD (DECEMBER 2003)

No matter how effective a board of directors may be it is not possible for the directors to have hands-on involvement in every area of the company's business. An effective board controls the business but delegates day-to-day responsibility to the executive management. That said there are a number of matters which are required, or that should in the interests of the company, only be decided by the board of directors as a whole.

It is incumbent upon the board to make it clear what these Matters Reserved for the Board are.

The Combined Code states that 'There should be a formal schedule of matters specifically reserved for [the Board's] decision'[1] and that the annual report should contain a 'high level statement of which types of decisions are to be taken by the Board and which are to be delegated to management'.

The Combined Code also states that 'The Board's role is to provide entrepreneurial leadership of the company within a framework of prudent and effective controls which enables risk to be assessed and managed. The Board should set the company's strategic aims, ensure that the necessary financial and human resources are in place for the company to meet its objectives and review management performance. The Board should set the company's values and standards and ensure that its obligations to its shareholders and others are understood and met.'[2]

ICSA has produced this Guidance Note to aid directors and company secretaries in drawing up such a schedule of Matters Reserved for the Board. The original version of this document was first published in the February 1993 edition of The Company Secretary and has been adopted as a precedent by a number of writers on corporate governance. It has been updated to incorporate more recent developments in best practice.

The relative importance of some matters included in this Guidance Note will vary according to the size and nature of the company's business. For example all companies will have a different view on the establishment of the financial limits for transactions which should be referred to the board. Equally, there may well be items not mentioned in the Guidance Note which some companies (eg those subject to additional forms of external regulation) would wish to include in their own schedule.

### Multiple signatures

In drawing up a schedule of Matters Reserved for the Board, companies should clarify which transactions require multiple board signatures on the relevant documentation.

---

1 *The Combined Code on Corporate Governance – July 2003*, A1.1
2 *The Combined Code on Corporate Governance – July 2003*, A.1, first supporting principle

## Delegation

Certain of the matters included in this Guidance Note should, under the recommendations of the Cadbury Committee and/or Combined Code, be the responsibility of the audit, nomination or remuneration committee. However, full delegation is not permitted in these cases as the final decision on the matter is required to be taken by the whole board.

## Urgent matters

In drawing up a schedule of Matters Reserved for the Board it is important to establish procedures for dealing with matters which often have to be dealt with urgently, often between board meetings. It is recommended that a telephone or video conference meeting should be held in which as many directors as possible participate. This allows directors the opportunity to discuss the matter and ask any questions. Any director who cannot attend should still be sent the relevant papers and have the opportunity to give their views to the chairman, another director or the Company Secretary before the meeting. If the matter is routine and discussion is not necessary the approval of all the directors may be obtained by means of a written resolution. In all cases however the procedures should balance the need for urgency with the overriding principle that each director should be given as much information as possible, the time to consider it properly and an opportunity to discuss the matter prior to the commitment of the company.

The following schedule has been produced to assist boards of directors and company secretaries in preparing a schedule of Matters Reserved for the Board in accordance with good Corporate Governance.

Items marked * are not considered suitable for delegation to a committee of the board, for example because of Companies Act requirements or because, under the recommendations of the Combined Code, they are the responsibility of an audit, nomination or remuneration committee, with the final decision required to be taken by the board as a whole.

## SCHEDULE OF MATTERS RESERVED FOR THE BOARD

*CA refers to the Companies Act 1985*
*CC refers to the Combined Code*
*LR refers to the UKLA Listing Rules*
*References to Audit, Nomination or Remuneration refer to the Board committee which will consider the item and make recommendations to the board for its final decision.*

1    Strategy and Management

    1.1   Responsibility for the overall management of the group.          CC A.1

    1.2   Approval of the group's long term objectives and commercial
           strategy.          CC A.1

    1.3   Approval of the annual operating and capital expenditure
           budgets and any material changes to them.

    1.4   Oversight of the group's operations ensuring:
- competent and prudent management
- sound planning
- an adequate system of internal control

- adequate accounting and other records
- compliance with statutory and regulatory obligations.

1.5  Review of performance in the light of the group's strategy, objectives, business plans and budgets and ensuring that any necessary corrective action is taken.                                    CC A.1

1.6  Extension of the group's activities into new business or geographic areas.

1.7  Any decision to cease to operate all or any material part of the group's business.

## 2    Structure and capital

2.1  Changes relating to the group's capital structure including reduction of capital, share issues (except under employee share plans), share buy backs [including the use of treasury shares].

2.2  Major changes to the group's corporate structure.

2.3  Changes to the group's management and control structure.

2.4  Any changes to the company's listing or its status as a plc.

## 3    Financial reporting and controls

3.1*  Approval of preliminary announcements of interim and     CC C.1
final results.                                              Audit

3.2*  Approval of the annual report and accounts, [including the    CA s233, s234C
corporate governance statement and remuneration report].[3]   LR 9.35
CC C.1
Audit

3.3*  Approval of the dividend policy.

3.4*  Declaration of the interim dividend and recommendation of    LR 9.35
the final dividend.

3.5*  Approval of any significant changes in accounting policies or
practices.                                                 Audit

3.6  Approval of treasury policies [including foreign currency exposure andthe use of financial derivatives].

## 4    Internal controls

4.1  Ensuring maintenance of a sound system of internal control and    CC C.2, C.2.1
risk management including:                                     Audit
- receiving reports on, and reviewing the effectiveness of, the group's risk and control processes to support its strategy and objectives
- undertaking an annual assessment of these processes
- approving an appropriate statement for inclusion in the annual report.

3 These items are often considered by the whole Board but with the final formal decision being delegated to a committee (set up solely for that purpose).This allows time for any changes requested at the Board meeting to be incorporated into the final document before publication.

5    Contracts

5.1   Major capital projects.
5.2   Contracts which are material strategically or by reason of size, entered into by the company [or any subsidiary] in the ordinary course of business, for example bank borrowings [above £xx million] and acquisitions or disposals of fixed assets [above £xx million].
5.3   Contracts of the company [or any subsidiary] not in the ordinary course of business, for example loans and repayments [above £xx million]; foreign currency transactions [above £xx million]; major acquisitions or disposals [above £xx million].
5.4   Major investments [including the acquisition or disposal of interests of more than (5) percent in the voting shares of any company or the making of any takeover offer].

6    Communication

6.1   Approval of resolutions and corresponding documentation to be put forward to shareholders at a general meeting.                    LR 14.1
6.2*  Approval of all circulars and listing particulars [approval of routine documents such as periodic circulars about scrip dividend procedures or exercise of conversion rights could be delegated to a committee].                    LR 14.1, 16.1, 5.2
6.3*  Approval of press releases concerning matters decided by the Board.

7    Board membership and other appointments

7.1*  Changes to the structure, size and composition of the Board, following recommendations from the nomination committee.                    Nomination
7.2*  Ensuring adequate succession planning for the Board and senior management.                    CC A.4, A.7.
7.3*  Appointments to the Board, following recommendations by the nomination committee.                    CA s282 Nomination
7.4*  Selection of the Chairman of the Board and the Chief Executive.                    Nomination
7.5*  Appointment of the Senior Independent Director.                    CC A.3.3 Nomination
7.6*  Membership and Chairmanship of Board committees.                    Nomination
7.7*  Continuation in office of directors at the end of their term of office, when they are due to be re-elected by shareholders at the AGM and otherwise as appropriate.                    Nomination
7.8*  Continuation in office of any director at any time, including the suspension or termination of service of an executive director as an employee of the company, subject to the law and their service contract.                    Nomination
7.9*  Appointment or removal of the company secretary.                    CA s283, s286 CC A.5.3

7.10* Appointment, reappointment or removal of the external
auditor to be put to shareholders for approval, following the
recommendation of the audit committee.

CA s384<br>CC C.3.2<br>Audit

7.11  Appointments to boards of subsidiaries.

## 8   Remuneration

8.1*  Determining the remuneration policy for the directors, company
secretary and other senior executives.

Remuneration

8.2  Determining the remuneration of the non-executive directors,
subject to the articles of association and shareholder approval
as appropriate.

CC B.2.3

8.3*  The introduction of new share incentive plans or major changes
to existing plans, to be put to shareholders for approval.

Remuneration

## 9   Delegation of Authority

9.1*  The division of responsibilities between the chairman, the chief
executive [and other executive directors,] which should be in
writing.

9.2*  Approval of terms of reference of Board committees.

CC A.2.1<br>CC A.4.1,<br>B.2.1, C.3.1

9.3*  Receiving reports from Board committees on their activities.

## 10   Corporate governance matters

10.1* Undertaking a formal and rigorous review [annually] of its
own performance, that of its committees and individual directors.

10.2* Determining the independence of directors.

CC A.6<br>CC A.3.1.

10.3* Considering the balance of interests between shareholders,
employees, customers and the community.

10.4  Review of the group's overall corporate governance arrangements.

10.5* Receiving reports on the views of the company's shareholders.

CC D.1.1

## 11   Policies

11.1 Approval of policies, including:

CC A.1

- Code of Conduct
- Share dealing code
- Health and safety policy
- Environmental policy
- Communications policy [including procedures for the
release of price sensitive information].
- Corporate social responsibility policy
- Charitable donations policy.

## 12   Other

12.1  The making of political donations.

12.2  Approval of the appointment of the group's principal
professional advisers.

12.3 Prosecution, defence or settlement of litigation [involving above £xx million or being otherwise material to the interests of the group].

12.4 Approval of the overall levels of insurance for the group including Directors' & Officers' liability insurance [and indemnification of directors].

12.5 Major changes to the rules of the group's pension scheme, or changes of trustees or [when this is subject to the approval of the company] changes in the fund management arrangements.

12.6 This schedule of matters reserved for Board decisions.

Matters which the Board considers suitable for delegation are contained in the terms of reference of its Committees.

In addition, the Board will receive reports and recommendations from time to time on any matter which it considers significant to the Group.

# Appendix 6

## ICSA GUIDANCE NOTE: DUE DILIGENCE FOR DIRECTORS

**A guide to the due diligence process that prospective directors should undertake before joining a company**

### Why undertake due diligence?

The review carried out by Derek Higgs and published in January 2003 as the Review of the role and effectiveness of non-executive directors, recommended that before accepting an appointment, the prospective non-executive director should undertake their own thorough examination of the company to satisfy themselves that it is an organisation in which they can have faith and in which they will be well suited to working.

The Institute of Chartered Secretaries and Administrators assisted in the compilation of a list of questions for this purpose and undertook to keep them up to date. The questions as seen below are more or less as per the original Higgs report and as repeated in the Financial Reporting Council's re-issue of the Combined Code in July 2003. The order has, however, been re-arranged slightly and sub-headings added.

The following questions are not intended to be exhaustive, but are intended to be a helpful basis for the pre-appointment due diligence process that all non-executive directors should undertake. By making the right enquiries, asking the right questions and taking care to understand the replies, a prospective director can reduce the risk of nasty surprises and dramatically increase the likelihood of success.

### Questions to ask

#### The business

What is the company's current financial position and what has its financial track record been over the last three years?

What are the exact nature and extent of the company's business activities?

What is the company's competitive position and market share in its main business areas?

What are the key dependencies (e.g. regulatory approvals, key licences)?

#### Governance and investor relations

What record does the company have on corporate governance issues?

Does the company have sound and effective systems of internal controls?

Who are the current executive and non-executive directors, what is their background and record and how long have they served on the board?

What is the size and structure of the board and board committees and what are the relationships between the chairman and the board, the chief executive and the management team?

Who owns the company i.e. who are the company's main shareholders and how has the profile changed over recent years?

What is the company's attitude towards, and relationship with, its shareholders?

## The role of the non-executive director

Is the company clear and specific about the qualities, knowledge, skills and experience that it needs to complement the existing board?

If the company is not performing particularly well is there potential to turn it round and do I have the time, desire and capability to make a positive impact?

Am I satisfied that the size, structure and make-up of the board will enable me to make an effective contribution?

Would accepting the non-executive directorship put me in a position of having a conflict of interest?

Do I have the necessary knowledge, skills, experience and time to make a positive contribution to the board of this company?

How closely do I match the job specification and how well will I fulfil the board's expectations?

## Risk management

Is there anything about the nature and extent of the company's business activities that would cause me concern both in terms of risk and any personal ethical considerations?

Is any material litigation presently being undertaken or threatened, either by the company or against it?

Am I satisfied that the internal regulation of the company is sound and that I can operate effectively within its stated corporate governance framework?

What insurance cover is available to directors and what is the company's policy on indemnifying directors?

## Sources of information

- Company report and accounts, and/or any listing prospectus, for the recent years.
- Analysts' reports.
- Press reports.
- Company web site.

- Any Corporate Social Responsibility or Environmental Report issued by the company.

- Rating agency reports.

- Voting services reports.

Published material is unlikely to reveal wrongdoing, however a lack of transparency may be a reason to proceed with caution.

Further information may be obtained from discussions with existing directors, senior management, employees, suppliers and customers although care should be taken to preserve confidentiality especially considering that, in itself, the fact that an approach has been made will undoubtedly be deemed to be price-sensitive information

# Appendix 7

## ICSA GUIDANCE NOTE: DIRECTORS' AND OFFICERS' INSURANCE (October 2003)

In 2002, at the request of the Secretary of State, Derek Higgs undertook a review of the role and effectiveness of non-executive directors. One point identified as causing concern related to the perceived inadequacies and high costs of Directors' and Officers' Liability cover (D&O). Following publication of the Report,[1] and at the request of the Higgs team, ICSA convened a meeting of representatives of:

- City of London Law Society;

- ICSA;

- The Association of British Insurers;

- British Insurance Brokers Association; and

- The ICSA Company Secretaries Forum

to produce guidance on this topic.

It was agreed that, given the wide variety of organisations, the range of industries in which they operate and the differing everyday business risks, it would not be practical to draft a 'specimen policy'. This note is therefore:

- a checklist of just some of the major issues that prospective directors (whether executive or non-executive) should consider, both to help them understand D&O insurance and also to evaluate the cover provided by companies they are considering joining; and

- a useful aide-mémoire for existing directors and for organisations when considering their own requirements for such cover.

The Guidance is **not** intended to be a comprehensive summary of the topic and should **not** be considered a substitute for specific advice from a good broker or legal adviser.

It should be remembered that D&O insurance is only one of the methods by which risk is transferred from directors. They may also, for example, have an indemnity from the company, but this will undoubtedly be restricted, either by its specific terms or by law.

D&O insurance is not compulsory. Although Section 310 of the Companies Act 1985 permits companies to take out insurance on behalf of their directors and to pay the premiums, it is not mandatory. However the newly published Combined Code[2] includes a provision (A.1.5) that 'The company should arrange appropriate insurance cover in respect of legal action against its directors'.

---

1  *Review of the role and effectiveness of non-executive directors*, DTI January 2003.
2  *The Combined Code on Corporate Governance* issued by the Financial Reporting Council, July 2003.

D&O insurance is normally taken out in one of three formats:

- A policy which is taken out by the company (and most usually the policy schedule will be in the name of that company) and which provides cover for indemnifiable risks under one section and non-indemnifiable risks under another – commonly referred to as sections A and B;

- A policy which is taken out by the company (again most usually the policy schedule will be in the name of that company) and which provides cover only for non-indemnifiable risks. This type of policy is particularly popular for companies that wish to provide significant limits of indemnity for directors and officers when the company does not, cannot or will not indemnify. Particular care and attention must be paid to the wording of the operative clause in such policies (ie regarding when indemnity can be provided);

- A policy covering an individual named person, e.g. Mr David Smith, who may have one and/or a number of directorships, executive and/or non-executive positions which he wishes to insure under his 'own personal policy'.

From this it is clear that individuals may find themselves covered by more than one policy which can cause major difficulties between parties. It is therefore important that due cognisance is made of potential overlap and/or gaps in cover.

The headings in this note are for general guidance; many of the issues raised overlap between areas.

## Who does it cover?

Unless written as an 'individual' policy, the company itself, parent and/or subsidiary companies may be covered to the extent that they in turn have to indemnify their directors and officers. Associated companies[3] may not be included at all.

The policy normally covers the directors, the company secretary(ies) and any other nominated officers of the insured company(ies).

**Those seeking to join a company as a director or officer should seek written confirmation that they will be included in the company's D&O insurance and notified of any changes in cover that might affect them.** This may be particularly important when considering the sufficiency of the amount of cover provided – see section headed 'Amount of cover'.

**From the individual's point of view it is also important to check that the policy covers 'past and present directors' to ensure that cover continues after 'retirement'[4]** – at least in respect of situations occurring during their period of office. There are examples where those who ceased to be directors prior to the inception of the policy were not covered, even where the claim arose after the policy's inception – see section headed 'Automatic conversion to run-off'.

---

3  Whilst different insurers may define 'associated companies' differently, the Financial Reporting Standard FRS 9 defines it as 'An entity (other than a subsidiary) in which another entity (the investor) has a participating interest and over whose operating and financial policies the investor exercises significant influence.'
4  'Retirement' is used here in its broadest sense and covers a director leaving the company for whatever reason.

## Outside directors

Standard policies will not automatically cover directors and officers sitting on unconnected boards, i.e. boards outside the insured group, where the director sits at the request of the group. In such cases, 'Outside Directors' cover will be required. This will often only be available on different, more restricted terms, than the basic D&O cover. Typical wording of such an inclusion may read:

> 'a past, present or future director of an outside entity who has become or became a director of the entity at the specific request of the company'.

Care will be needed to ensure that the particular needs of the company and individual are correctly catered for, e.g. **Directors or officers seconded to, or given an additional role in, an Associated or unrelated company should check that they will be covered either under the main or the Associated/unrelated company's policies.**

## Acquisitions

As with many issues in D&O insurance different insurers deal with acquisitions in differing ways. Some will cover acquisitions automatically, but this could be on any one of a number of different bases. It is essential to check. A typical clause may read:

> 'The benefit of the insurance cover provided by this policy shall extend automatically to all newly acquired or created subsidiaries of the company, other than those which have or have had a listing of any of its securities on any exchange in the USA or Canada; such extension to apply solely in respect of WRONGFUL ACTS alleged to have been committed whilst the newly acquired or created company was a subsidiary of the company'.

Note the exclusion of US and Canadian listed companies. If such an organisation is involved, the insurer would undoubtedly seek to clarify the risk involved and quote specific terms and conditions for such an inclusion.

## Period of cover

Cover will normally start from the date of appointment, but there may be a requirement to notify the insurer of the appointment. Frequently, the only obligation is to update the list of directors and officers at annual renewal. **Directors should ask the company to confirm that the appropriate notifications have been or will be made.** In any event, companies would be wise to play safe and notify the insurer/broker of changes – especially in circumstances such as the appointment of a new US based director which may fundamentally alter the risk.

Care should be taken to ensure that the insurer will be or has been notified of the appointment within any prevailing time limits.

## Basis of cover

D&O policies are almost exclusively written on a 'claims made' basis. Cover will normally cease when the appointment comes to an end, but an individual's liability may continue for some time in respect of actions or inactions occurring during the period of appointment. To cover this a policy can be extended to include 'run-off' cover.

**Directors should obtain clear guidance on the extent of 'run-off' cover that is provided under the policy and what, if any, action is required to ensure that they are /will be included under such provision.** Although there are examples of run-off cover being provided for up to six years, there are also examples where it has been restricted to just six months.

This can pose particular problems for 'retiring' directors and officers or where divisions or parts of businesses are disposed of, and the continuity of cover is broken.

## Automatic conversion to run-off

Some policies have an 'automatic run-off' option. More often, this will come under the condition of 'Extended Discovery Period'. Either approach usually involves payment of an additional premium, which varies in amount. It can be as little as 25% or up to 100% of the most recent annual premium, depending on the duration of the run-off period and the insurer's willingness to extend the policy on this basis.

> It is vital to remember that indemnity contracts do not have any automatic extensions or 'periods of grace'. If renewal is required, the insurer must be advised long before the expiry of the existing contract otherwise continuity[5] of cover will be broken and then backdating the start of the cover can become a serious issue.

## What is a 'claim'?

A 'claim' is usually defined quite narrowly e.g. 'a demand made in writing'. Anything else, such as a threat of legal action, has to be notified as a 'Circumstance' (which may give rise to a claim). As a 'Circumstance', if accepted by the insurer, will lodge in the year it is registered regardless of when the eventual claim may materialise insurers, are generally reluctant to accept them.

## Duty of disclosure

As with all insurances, the policy will incorporate a duty of disclosure whether or not specifically mentioned. **A director will therefore be obliged to disclose to the insurer any claims or circumstances which may give rise to a claim.**

Some policies contain clauses which can be quite helpful to the insured e.g severability clauses whereby one insured's knowledge, or facts pertaining to one insured, are not ascribed to other insureds. In addition, insurers will sometimes agree not to void a policy for non-disclosure or misrepresentation if the insured can establish that such non-disclosure or misrepresentation was entirely innocent.

---

5  We understand that the word 'continuity ' may have a specific meaning within the realms of D&O insurance however in this text the word is used in its everyday sense.

## Extent of cover

Policy wording, and the extent of cover, can vary widely and care should be taken to understand what is (and – more importantly – what is not) covered, and any areas of risk that may remain.

It is usual and/or highly desirable to include the following:

- **Damages** awarded against an insured person;
- **Out-of-court settlements** – care should be taken to ensure that these are also specifically included;
- **Costs,** including fees, professional costs and expenses resulting from the investigation and /or defence or settlement of a claim will normally be covered. However, material or information may come to light during a claim which causes the insurer to cease paying the defence costs half way through. In such cases the insurer may also seek to recover costs already paid out;
- **Libel and slander** – may be included, but not always;
- **Wrongful Acts** which can be defined as any error, misstatement, misleading statement, act, omission, neglect or breach of duty committed or attempted or any matter claimed against the individual *solely by reason of their serving in a capacity as a Director or Officer of the company.* Whilst the definition of Wrongful Acts can vary and be very widely construed it is of vital importance to recognise that the act must be something done in the capacity of director or officer.

The following are common restrictions and/or exclusions:

- **Fines, penalties and punitive damages** levied by regulators or criminal courts. (Note that the Financial Services Authority has recently suggested that it will, in any event, ban insurance cover for regulatory fines);
  **Criminal defence costs** can apply in respect of criminal proceedings, but only to the point of conviction/release. No cover is given for appeal costs in the event of a conviction – the premise of innocent until proven guilty applies only to a limited extent; Note
- **Loss of earnings or expenses** incurred by the insured themselves, such as PR expenses to preserve reputations;
- **Personal injury or property damage** are also frequently excluded (this will typically be covered elsewhere – see below);
- **Fraudulent, dishonest or illegal acts.** Cover will not extend to deliberate dishonesty or the deliberate committing of fraudulent or illegal acts as to do so would be against the public interest;
- **Legal jurisdiction.** Some policies may restrict cover to certain geographical areas or exclude specific jurisdictions, eg the highly litigious USA. **Directors and potential directors should consider carefully the possibility of a claim arising in any area excluded under the policy;**
- **Taxes** are rarely covered. It should also be noted that premiums may not be tax deductible by the insuring company but, if structured properly, they may not be taxable as a benefit in kind to the director or officer.

- **Directors and potential directors should obtain confirmation of the tax treatment in relation to the policy and their personal position.** Premiums paid by an individual where cover is taken out personally will, on the other hand, usually be tax deductible;

- **Existing conditions.** Cover will normally exclude any loss or liability arising from an action or inaction occurring prior to the commencement of the cover. Careful attention should be paid to 'Conditions precedent' clauses which can be quite onerous;

- **Liabilities covered elsewhere** – e.g. liabilities normally covered under Employer's or Public Liability policies or Prospectus Liability policies. **Those who may find themselves covered by more than one policy should make a point of clarifying the precise position.** Some policies, for example, will cover executive directors in non-executive positions of other companies who may also have their own cover;

- **Insured v. insured.** Some policies will not cover actions between parties covered by the same policy, often now described as the 'Equitable Life Claim scenario'. This might be an action taken by the company against a director or one director against another covered by the same policy. This can be particularly complicated when one policy covers a Group of companies including directors and officers of the parent and various subsidiary companies. Policies differ widely in the wording here but it is critical that directors and potential directors recognise whether the policy would cover them against claims from the company itself and /or another director covered by the same policy;

- **Additional services.** D&O policies are designed to cover liabilities arising from the insured services as a director or officer and will not extend to services, e.g. professional services, outside the scope of their role as directors or officers of the company. Similarly D&O cover will not normally extend to personal guarantees and undertakings given by directors and officers. Although they may be given in connection with the role, e.g. personal guarantees to lenders, they do not arise out of the role itself;

- **Service Companies.** Additional complications can arise where a director may provide his/her services through a service company. **If a director intends to act through a service company, care should be taken to clarify the position.**

## 'Basis of contract' clause

The proposal form for the policy may include a 'basis of contract' clause. This seemingly innocuous phrase can have far-reaching consequences – its legal effect is to give every statement in the proposal form the status of a warranty so that a trivial error can be used by the insurer to avoid the policy. This has been upheld by UK courts despite criticism of the potentially severe consequences it can have for the insured – while the Statement of General Insurance Practice issued by the ABI recommends that personal lines insurance is not written on this basis, Directors' & Officers' Liability cover is treated as corporate insurance and may still include a 'basis of contract' clause. Companies should therefore seek to have this removed in renewal negotiations and a director who hopes to benefit from cover under a D&O policy should establish whether the policy contains this clause, given its potential to negate the cover provided by the policy.

## Amount of cover

Policies are usually written with a specific monetary limit but how this limit is applied may vary:

- **Per claim** – the policy will normally have a limit per claim or incident and may have sub-limits for different heads of claim;

- **Per year** – cover will frequently have an overall limit per year, often including defence costs. This can be particularly problematic where a number of companies or individuals are covered by the same policy. If the overall limit is exhausted by one or two claims, the unfortunate subject of a third claim may find they have no cover at all. This situation is often exacerbated when Policy cover for one area is extended without due consideration to the impact on the overall or other parts of the Policy. **Directors and potential directors should clarify the amount of cover provided.**

## Automatic re-instatement of sums insured

This extension, if available, can be particularly useful in guarding against the using up of cover. Clauses vary between insurers. Many take the position that they would seek a higher initial sum insured – for example, several hundreds of millions. In the UK, the tendency has been to err on the side of caution, which sees the vast majority of limits in the tens of millions.

More recently, many new companies coming into the market have found it difficult to obtain this type of extension. Insurers are becoming more concerned over the complications of providing a 'top up' of sums insured – but existing policies with this cover built in may still be able to renew with the extension.

In the current market, the availability of cover has been restricted – but the hope is that it will become easier as the liability market settles down in the coming months.

## Deductibles

Any deductible will be a matter of commercial negotiation, and can vary from nil to quite a high 'excess'. Different deductibles will apply to different sections of a policy **and directors should be clear when or whether a deductible applies and, if so, in which circumstances this will be paid by the company and when it might be for their own account.** If, for example, deductibles apply 'per event' it is essential to be clear on what constitutes a single event. For example, was 9/11 a single act of terrorism or a series of separate hijackings?

## Conditions

All D&O policies will have fairly strict conditions attached. These may cover such things as:

- notification of appointments or other changes in the list of insured persons;

- notification of potential or actual claims;

- what actually constitutes a 'claim' in the terms of the policy;

- admission of liability;

- the actual conduct of any claims; and

- an obligation to make oneself available to defend a claim;

- most of which are dealt with individually within this Guidance Note.

The general point, however, is that the exact wording in some of these clauses can be critical. For example, where there is an obligation to 'notify', the language might refer to circumstances which 'may' or 'are likely' to give rise to a claim. Clearly the two situations are significantly different. It can however be a double-edged sword; if the duty is to notify 'promptly' or within a specified time limit then there is a greater risk of breaching the 'may' condition than there is if the threshold is 'likely to'.

If there is simply an obligation to notify (without a time limit) then 'may' reduces the prospect of insurers alleging that a claim is not sufficiently probable. Further difficulties can then arise because, in the ordinary way, the matter giving rise to concern would have to be disclosed to the next insurer for the following period and the new insurer might insist on an exclusion in respect of that particular matter.

As with all insurance policies, it is a contract of 'utmost good faith'. Additionally there will be a requirement to mitigate losses wherever possible. It may, for example, be financially beneficial to settle a claim out of court rather than bear the costs of a protracted and complicated defence, especially if advice is that the defence is unlikely to succeed – even though this may be damaging to the reputation of the individual concerned.

## Right of litigation

The insurer will almost invariably have the right to act on behalf of the insured although, unlike most insurance policies, with D&O insurance it is the duty of the company/director actually to defend a claim. **This can be an extremely onerous experience for the individual.**

Whilst the choice of legal adviser might be agreed between the insured and insurer there will be a tendency to appoint a legal firm who will have a good degree of insurance knowledge – which is all well and good in major centres like London, Birmingham etc. but might raise problems in more remote areas.

## Summary

The July 2003 Combined Code contains a specimen appointment letter for new non-executive directors and suggests that a copy of the D&O policy is provided. Clearly this is a pragmatic and reasonable practice.

Potential directors should make every effort to understand the D&O policy, what it does and does not cover and the manner in which cover operates when joining, serving or leaving the company. It may also be prudent to understand the company's procedures for renewing or amending the cover to ensure that the cover cannot be diluted without the knowledge of those affected. If anything is unclear, clarification should be sought from the Company Secretary.

Given the complexity of the topic we make no apologies for repeating the earlier warning. The purpose of this Guidance Note is to alert, particularly new, directors to some of the issues involved with D&O insurance. It is not intended to be, nor in just a few pages can it be, a comprehensive guide. For those requiring more detailed information there are some authoritative books available on the subject. The risks and extent of cover available are however changing all the time and anyone contemplating taking out D&O insurance are advised to seek good professional advice.

It has been suggested that a short guide such as this is likely to raise more questions than it answers. If that is what happens, then it may be that this Guide has served its purpose.

# Appendix 8

## ICSA GUIDANCE NOTE: INDUCTION OF DIRECTORS

Since the publication of the ICSA Best Practice Guide *The Appointment and Induction of Directors*, it has become apparent that some newly appointed directors have been completely overwhelmed with the sheer volume of documents and other papers provided by the well meaning company secretary to such an extent that some have been completely put off by it.

The objective of induction is to inform the director such that he or she can become as effective as possible in their new role as soon as possible. The provision of reams of paper in one go is, obviously, not conducive to this process. It is therefore recommended that, on appointment, a new director be provided with certain key, essential information together with a comprehensive list of other information that will be made available subsequently.

More recently we have seen the publication of the Higgs Report on the role and effectiveness of non-executive directors. That report includes various recommendations including, as Annex I, an induction checklist. ICSA worked closely with the Higgs Review team on the creation of that checklist and, in order to enable it to be kept brief and to the point, undertook to produce this Guidance Note providing more comprehensive details of the material that should be considered for inclusion in an induction pack provided to new directors on, or during the weeks immediately following their appointment.

The following list is divided into three parts. The first includes the essential material that should be provided immediately and the second, material that should be provided over the first few weeks following the appointment, as and when deemed most appropriate. The director should, however, be provided immediately with a comprehensive list of the material being made available in total, together with an undertaking to provide it earlier if required.

The third list covers items which the company secretary might consider making the director aware of.

Note that some information may have already been provided during the director's due diligence process prior to appointment, or along with the appointment letter. Whilst duplication should be avoided, care should be taken to provide any updates that may be necessary.

The topics contained within this note should be supplied to all newly appointed directors, both executive and non-executive, however the secretary will need to gauge the level of previous knowledge and adjust them accordingly, particularly in regard to the appointment of executive directors.

### Essential information to be provided immediately

*The following information is felt to be essential and needs to be given to the director prior to the first board meeting.*

*Methods of delivery vary. Some of the information needs to be sent to the director with his appointment letter; but some could be deferred until a meeting after the board papers have been issued, so that the company secretary can review the board pack with the director before the first meeting highlighting any relevant issues.*

## Directors' Duties

Brief outline of the role of a director and a summary of his/her responsibilities and ongoing obligations under legislation, regulation and best practice.

Copy of UKLA Model Code, and details of the company's procedure regarding directors' share dealings and the disclosure of price sensitive information.

The company's guidelines on:

- Matters reserved for the board;
- Delegated Authorities;
- The policy for obtaining independent professional advice for directors;
- Other standing orders, policies and procedures of which the director should be aware.
- 'Fire Drill' procedures (the procedures in place to deal with such as hostile takeover bids).

## The Company's Business

Current strategic/business plan, market analysis and budgets for the year with revised forecast, and three-/five-year plan.

Latest annual report and accounts, and interims as appropriate.

Explanation of key performance indicators.

List of major domestic and overseas subsidiaries, associated companies and joint ventures, including any parent company(ies).

Summary details of major group insurance policies including D&O liability insurance.

Details of any major litigation, either current or potential, being undertaken by the company or against the company.

Treasury issues:

- Funding position and arrangements;
- Dividend policy.

The corporate brochure, mission statement and any other reports issued by the company such as an environmental report, with a summary of the main events (such as mergers, divestments, introductions of new products, diversification into new areas, restructuring, etc.) over the last three years.

## Board Issues

Up to date copy of the company's Memorandum and Articles of Association/Constitution, with a summary of the most important provisions.

Minutes of the last 3–6 board meetings.

Schedule of dates of future board meetings and board subcommittees if appropriate.

Description of board procedures covering details such as when papers are sent out, the normal location of meetings, how long they last and an indication of the routine business transacted.

Brief biographical and contact details of all directors of the company, the company secretary and other key executives. This should include any executive responsibilities of directors, their dates of appointment and any board committees upon which individual directors sit.

Details of board subcommittees together with terms of reference and, where the director will be joining a committee, copies of the minutes of meetings of that committee during the previous 12 months.

## Additional material to be provided during the first few months

*The following information is crucial to assist the director to develop his/her knowledge of the company, its operations and staff, but is not necessary for him/her to commence his/her involvement. It is suggested, however, that a detailed schedule of the information available is provided to him/her, and the information is supplied either on request or within three months of appointment. It would also be appropriate to involve senior members of staff in the induction programme, for example the Investor Relations Manager could give a presentation on the IR programme, so that the non-executive director begins to get a view of the depth of management available and the executive director is exposed to areas of the business he/she has less previous knowledge of.*

Copies of the company's main product/service brochures.

Copies of recent press cuttings, reports and articles concerning the company.

Details of the company's advisers (lawyers, bankers, auditors, registrars etc.), both internal and external, with the name of the partner dealing with the company's affairs.

The company's risk management procedures and relevant disaster recovery plans.

An outline of the provisions of the Combined Code as appended to the UK Listing Rules together with details of the company's corporate governance guidelines and any Investor's corporate governance guidelines which the company seeks to follow.

Brief history of the company including when it was incorporated and any significant events during its history.

Notices of any general meetings held in the last 3 years, and accompanying circulars as appropriate.

Company organisation chart and management succession plans.

Copy of all management accounts prepared since the company's last audited accounts.

The company's investor relations policy and details of the major shareholders.

Details of the five largest customers with the level of business done over the last five years.

Details of the five largest suppliers to the company.

Policies as regards:

- Health & Safety;
- Environmental;
- Ethics and Whistleblowing;
- Charitable & Political donations.

Internal company telephone directory (including any overseas contact numbers and names).

## Additional information which the company secretary might consider making the director aware of

*The final section includes information which will differ for all companies depending on the sector and the company secretary will need to use his/her experience and knowledge to pass on information to allow the director to feel accustomed to the business as soon as possible.*

Protocol, procedures and dress code for:

- Board meetings;
- General meetings;
- Formal dinners, staff social events, site visits etc. including the involvement of partners where appropriate.

Procedures for:

- Accounts sign off;
- Results announcements;
- Items requiring approval outside of board meetings.

Expenses policy and method of reimbursement.

# Appendix 9

## ICSA CODE OF GOOD BOARDROOM PRACTICE

1  The board should establish written procedures for the conduct of its business which should include the matters covered in this Code. A copy of these written procedures should be given to each director. Compliance should be monitored, preferably by an audit committee of the board, and breaches of the procedures should be reported to the board.

2  The board should ensure that each director is given on appointment sufficient information to allow him or her to perform his or her duties. In particular, guidance for non-executive directors should cover the procedures:
   - for obtaining information concerning the company; and
   - for requisitioning a meeting of the board.

3  In the conduct of board business, two fundamental concepts should be observed:
   - each director should receive the same information at the same time; and
   - each director should be given sufficient time in which to consider such information.

4  The board should identify matters which require the prior approval of the board and lay down procedures to be followed when, exceptionally, a decision is required before its next meeting on any matter not required by law to be considered at board level.

5  As a basic principle, all material contracts, and especially those not in the ordinary course of business, should be referred to the board for decision prior to the commitment of the company.

6  The board should approve definition of the terms 'material' and 'not in the ordinary course of business' and these definitions should be brought to the attention of all relevant persons.

7  Where there is any doubt about the materiality or nature of a contract, it should normally be assumed that the contract should be brought before the board.

8  Decisions regarding the content of the agenda for individual meetings of the board and concerning the presentation of agenda items should be taken by the chairman in consultation with the company secretary.

9  The company secretary should be responsible to the chairman for the proper administration of the meetings of the company, the board and any committees of the board. To carry out this responsibility, the company secretary should be entitled to be present at, or represented at, all such meetings and should be responsible for preparing, or arranging for the preparation of, the minute of the proceedings of all such meetings.

10 The minutes of meetings should record the decisions taken and provide sufficient background to those decisions. All papers presented at meetings should be clearly identified in the minutes and retained for reference. Procedures for the approval and circulation of minutes should be established.

11 Where the articles of association allow the board to delegate any of its powers to a committee, the board should give its prior approval to:
- the membership and quorum of any such committee;
- its terms of reference; and
- the extent of any powers delegated to it.

12 The minutes of all meetings of committees of the board (or a written summary thereof) should be circulated to the board prior to its next meeting and the opportunity should be given at that meeting for any member of the board to ask questions thereon.

13 Notwithstanding the absence of a formal agenda item, the chairman should permit any director or the company secretary to raise at any board meeting any matter concerning the company's compliance with this Code of Practice, with the company's Memorandum and Articles of association and with any other legal or regulatory requirement.

## Notes

If it is practicable, the approval of all of the directors for matters reserved to the board should be obtained by means of a written resolution. In all cases, however, the procedures should balance the need for urgency with the overriding principle that each director should be given as much information as possible and have an opportunity to requisition an emergency meeting of the board to discuss the matter prior to the commitment of the company.

Different definitions of the term 'material' should be established for 'contracts not in the ordinary course of business'. Financial limits should be set where appropriate.

# Appendix 10

## COMMONWEALTH ASSOCIATION FOR CORPORATE GOVERNANCE: FRAMEWORK FOR BOARD AND INDIVIDUAL DIRECTOR PERFORMANCE EVALUATION

### Background

The Board is appointed to guide, lead, monitor, and conduct all aspects of business and to supervise or control business activities. There are considerable benefits in appointing directors from the wider community but there is a definite level of risk. Risk can be considerably reduced and performance enhanced if appointees are briefed at the outset as part of the selection and appointment process. Risk is further reduced if directors are obliged to take part in a formal evaluation of directors and Board performance each year. The information obtained from the evaluation provides a basis for the appointment and reappointment. A formal evaluation ensures that the Board is adding value to the organisation and fulfilling its responsibilities to the organisation and to the stakeholders.

### Board Evaluation

Performance measurement enhances the effectiveness of the Director and thus further reduces the risk to the organisation. The obligation to have an annual formal evaluation ensures that the Board takes time to evaluate its own performance. The primary purpose is not only to enhance the performance, effectiveness and contribution of each director, but also to improve the effectiveness of the Board as a whole in fulfilling its role. Formal evaluation once a year should not replace informal feedback on performance on an ongoing basis, although establishing a formal evaluation methodology provides an objective framework for analytical feedback to the Board and members for the appointment processes. The framework provides a mechanism for ensuring that the Chairman is accountable when giving advice about Board members to the Board [and Chief Executive] and fully responsible for the effective performance of the Board. Directors are sensitive about Board evaluation. Some directors believe there is an element of voluntary devoted service, they believe their contribution should be gratefully received and not questioned. Other Directors are grateful for an objective framework in which to compare their performance with others or to improve their contribution around the Board table. Within this framework, experienced Directors can offer practical support to first-time Directors. So that experienced Directors do not find the process insulting, the purpose of the evaluation should be clearly communicated. Chief Executives are increasingly under scrutiny, with their pay package being dependent on their performance. Peer review is an integral part of professionals monitoring their own performance. It is equally relevant that Directors also have a performance evaluation. Through this process, members and stakeholders can ensure that the Board is adding value to the organisation and fulfilling its legal obligations. Director evaluations are achieving greater importance in the Corporate Sector with introduction of codes of best governance practice.

## Skills Mix

The successful dynamics of a Board depends on a combination of skills. The evaluation process identifies individual Directors' special attributes and their particular contribution to Board deliberations. The self-appraisal of Board effectiveness and evaluation of individual Directors will identify any skills gaps in the composition of the Board, providing important input into the selection and appointment process.

## Letter of Appointment

The obligation to take part in director and Board evaluations will be referred to in the Letter of Appointment and the accompanying terms of reference. Acceptance by all appointees will remove the suspicion that only some Directors are being evaluated. Board Training and Re-appointments.

A formal mechanism for evaluating individuals' contributions to the Board provides valuable input to selection procedures. Some Directors might not 'score' well simply due to inexperience, but training needs can be identified resulting in a bigger pool of capable Directors. Often new Directors such as those from the management ranks of corporate bodies, though capable as managers, are not familiar with the role of corporate governance. The formality of an evaluation process provides a framework for identifying the training needs in a professional way and, where necessary, to explain where re-appointment is not appropriate.

## Board Goals

The evaluation process is completed by a full Board discussion to identify key objectives for the functioning of the Board for the subsequent year.

## Confidentiality

Evaluation material about Directors should be sought on the express basis of confidentiality. Those responding should be advised that the information they give is received on a confidential basis and that their identity will be protected as far as the law allows. This should allow free expression of views.

## Methodology

Evaluation can involve self-evaluation by peers or by a 'consultant', the former relying on the Board members themselves, the latter providing an external viewpoint. Board evaluation by peers can be based on checklists for the Directors and the Chairman. The more detailed and explicit the checklists, the easier it will be to execute and to generate transparent, comparable, written information.

## Chairman

The Chairman's own performance is linked both to the performance of each director as well as the functioning of the Board as a whole. Each director will assess the Chairman based on a checklist relating specifically to the Chairman's duties. Should the Chairman's performance be considered unsatisfactory, the Deputy Chairman will have a discussion with the Board members to determine whether members or appointing authority or the shareholders should be alerted.

## Directors

The Chairman assesses Directors in a one-on-one interview set annually, or more frequently if necessary, with reference to a director's checklist. Directors are encouraged to complete a self-evaluation questionnaire prior to the Chair's discussion. Should a director's performance not be satisfactory, the Chairman should identify training needs or indicate areas to be addressed or, if necessary, indicate that recommendation to reappoint will be forthcoming. The director takes the opportunity to report back on their assessment of the Chairman during this interview.

## Functioning of the Board

Although this is partly covered within the performance of the Chairman, a separate Board discussion, included as an agenda item at least once a year will focus on the effectiveness of the Board as a team and the way it functions e.g. input into strategic planning, monitoring of the Chief Executive, relations with stakeholders and the servicing of the Board, that is, information supplied, time frames, information conveyed between Board meetings.

## A. BOARD SELF-APPRAISAL

### Key issues to be addressed

1   *Shareholders*

- How well do company objectives reflect shareholder expectations?
- Is there full and accurate reporting on company affairs to the shareholders?
- What is the state of relationship with the shareholders?
- What are the board's relationships with monitoring agencies?

2   *Stakeholders*

- Has the board identified key stakeholders?
- What is the state of the relationship with the key stakeholders?

3   *The company*

- Is the level of strategic planning of sufficient quality and content?
- How accurately is the strategic plan reflected at an operational level in the business plan?
- Does the board review the company's performance against the business plan?

4   *Legal/ethical duties*

- Are all legal/ethical requirements met satisfactorily?
- Is the company a good employer?

## 5  *The direction of the company*

- How satisfactory is the board's monitoring of the company?
- Are the important issues being identified?
- How well are these analysed and discussed?

## 6  *The CEO*

- How well is the CEO's job description defined?
- Is the CEO satisfactorily supported by counsel from the board?
- Is the CEO's performance monitored and appraised satisfactorily?
- Is the board avoiding excessive intrusion in the CEO and/or management's responsibilities?

## 7  *Board meetings*

- Is information supplied to the board appropriate and relevant?
- Is preparation and planning for board meetings satisfactory?
- Is the frequency and style of meetings appropriate?
- Is board attendance and participation working well?
- Is the board and committee structure still appropriate?
- Are accurate and timely minutes made and maintained?
- Is there follow up on actions necessary and/or reports to the board on actions taken?

## 8  *Individual board member contributions*

- Is the chairman carrying out the role satisfactorily?
- Is there recognition and use of individual board members' particular skills?
- Is the board contributing contacts and generating business?
- Is the board making other special contributions to the success of the company as a whole?

## 9  *Other*

- Does the board have a working knowledge of other providers or competitors in their sector?
- Does the board play a role in social accountability or the wider responsibility of the company?

## Functions of the board

- The board understands, agrees, defines and promulgates its functions on an annual basis.
- The board knows and understands the company's beliefs, values, philosophy, mission and vision and reflects this understanding on key issues throughout the year.

- Such beliefs, values, philosophy, mission and vision are set and consistent with company's status.
- The board devotes significant time and serious thought to the organisation's long- term objectives and to the strategic options available to achieve them.
- The board has defined and communicated to management the scope and powers, roles and responsibilities to be adhered to by management to meet routine and exceptional circumstances.
- The majority of the board's time is not spent on issues of day-to-day management.
- the board is involved in formulating long-range strategy from the beginning of the planning cycle.
- The board ensures that the organisation has sufficient and appropriate resources to achieve its strategic goals.
- Proposals from management are analysed and debated vigorously before being approved by the board. a proposal that is considered inappropriate is declined.
- The board has an operating plan that specifies its functions, activities and objectives.
- The board has reviewed its needs in terms of skills and has these skills.
- When appropriate the board seeks counsel from professional advisors.
- The chief executive officer's remuneration and performance is reviewed and determined by the board.
- The board determines, annually, the objectives and measurement criteria for the chief executive officer.
- A broad range of appropriate performance indicators are used to monitor the performance of management.
- Reliability is not placed solely on the financial statements provided by management.
- The board has identified the groups to which it is (a) accountable (b) responsible
- The board understands and agrees that its first duty is to (a) the company (b) members and shareholders (c) others.
- Board activities are conducted in an atmosphere of creative tension.
- The board has procedures in place to ensure that the organisation is meeting its legal responsibilities.
- Formal review of the board's performance has become an integral part of the culture of the board.
- The board ensures that key members of management are brought into the board meetings so that they can participate and add value to their deliberations and work on behalf of the board.
- The board ensures all conflicts of interest are (a) declared (b) resolved
- Every board member has been supplied with a letter of appointment.

- The letter of appointment defines the roles and functions of the board and the specific role of each director.

## Board meeting management and procedures

- Every board member has been supplied with a board manual and a copy of standing orders and regulations governing conduct of board meetings.

- Every board member was supplied with a calendar of meetings showing dates of board meetings, committee meetings etc and key or critical events of the company.

- Board meetings are conducted in a manner that encourages open communication, meaningful participation, and timely resolution of issues.

- Sufficient time is provided during board meetings for thoughtful discussion in addition to management dialogue.

- Board time is used effectively so that the board adds value to management.

- Formal meeting and reporting procedures have been adopted by the board.

- Board members receive timely and accurate minutes, advance written agendas and meeting notices; and clear and concise background material to prepare in advance of meetings.

- All board members are fully informed of relevant matters and there are never any surprises.

- Absenteeism from board meetings is the exception rather than the rule.

- Board meetings are facilitated, but not overtly influenced by the chairman.

- All board members are permitted to add items to the meeting agenda.

- All board members receive detailed board papers copies of draft minutes and agenda papers in advance.

- All proceedings and resolutions of the board are recorded accurately, adequately and on a timely basis.

## Appointment, selection, induction, training development, succession and removal of directors

- The board is involved with the selection of appointed directors.

- The selection process considers any deficiencies in the skills of current board members.

- The composition of the board fairly represents the diversity of stakeholders.

- The board actively encourages good candidates to stand for board appointments.

- New board members are introduced to their duties with an appropriate induction process.

- Board members understand the extent of their relationship with management and the separation of stewardship and management.

- Board members evaluate their individual and overall board performance formally on an annual basis.

- The performance of the chief executive officer is reviewed formally on an annual basis.

- Encouragement is given for board members to continue their study of corporate governance and improve the skills they need.

- Directors understand the extent of their personal liability for the affairs of the company.

- A succession plan is in place for the chairman, chief executive officer, board members and senior management and is reviewed regularly.

- Directors who have not been contributing to the governance of the organisation, and are uninterested in improving their performance are asked to terminate.

- Where the ethical or professional conduct of any director is called into question such director is suspended pending investigations.

- Board members bind themselves to uphold, honour and respect the code of ethics of the organisation on first appointment and to resign where their actions are called into question.

### Board structure

- The board has a balanced mix of executive, non-executive and independent non-executive directors.

- The roles of chairman of the board and chief executive officer are separated and held by different persons.

- The board has established and appointed committees with defined terms of reference, composition and reporting requirements, all of which are formally recorded.

- The committees have been established and appointed in light of the need to increase the effectiveness of the board by utilizing the specialized skills of board members, the need to provide support and guidance to management and the to ensure effective and independent professional consideration of issues e.g. audit reports, finance issues, etc.

- The board has established and appointed (a) an executive committee (b) an audit committee (c) a board appointment and remuneration committee and the terms of reference of each committee are restricted and defined

### Information and communication

- Every board member was supplied with all establishment instrument, all legal documents, mission statement, vision and strategy documents of the company on first appointment.

- Every board member receives a copy of the board manual together with a letter of appointment on first appointment.

- Every board member receives copies of all policy documents including organisation policy documents, personnel and financial manuals on first appointment and every time these are reviewed.

- Board members are encouraged to discuss matters with members of management after gaining the approval of the chairman or the chief executive.

- The board receives sufficient information from management in an appropriate format as determined by the board from management.
- The board's information requirements are communicated to management on a regular basis and requested information is received in a timely fashion.
- The board is proactive in developing an effective communication strategy for the company.
- The company secretary advises board members regularly on matters of governance and the applicable law.

## B. CHAIRMAN OF THE BOARD

### Shareholder relations

- Managing relations with shareholders.
- Facilitating advisory and monitoring processes between shareholder and company
- ensuring that shareholders are pre-warned of announcements or policy changes ('no surprises').

### Leadership

- Providing leadership to the board in planning and direction.
- Representing the company with the CEO in the community.

### Management relations

- Monitoring company planning and operations.
- Bbuilding relationships.
- Guiding strategy.
- Helping define problems.
- Monitoring and evaluating the performance of the CEO and Senior Officers.
- Representing shareholders and board to management.
- Representing management to the board and shareholders.
- Maintaining accountability.
- Ensuring succession plans are in place at a senior management level.
- Meetings, as requested by CEO, with financial analysts.
- Meetings, as requested by CEO, with potential sources of debt and equity capital.

### Board management

- Chairing meetings of the board.
- Managing directors' performance.

- Communications with directors between meetings.

- Setting meeting schedules.

- Setting meeting agendas.

- Controlling meeting attendance.

- Determining board information packages.

- Ensuring all board papers are distributed, i.e. advance of the meeting to enhance the knowledge base and ensure an informed level of debate.

- Helping appoint committees and define terms of reference.

- Aattending committee meetings where appropriate.

- Determining director compensation.

- Optimising use of the board's resource.

## Board effectiveness

- Encouraging all board members to contribute.

- Planning board composition and succession.

- Establishing and working towards a shared vision.

## Liaison with stakeholders

- In conjunction with the CEO, representing the company to the staff, the public, the media, suppliers and customers.

- Iin conjunction with the CEO, representing the company in developing relationships with government representatives and government agencies.

## Summary of questions for evaluation of chairman by chief executive officer and individual board members

### 1    Shareholder relationships

*Does the chairman:*

- Manage shareholder relationships and meets with shareholders?

- Actively meet with potential sources of equity and debt capital?

- Manage shareholder meetings effectively and promotes a sense of participation in all shareholders?

- Promote shareholder confidence in the board?

### 2    Leadership

- Is the chairman an effective board leader?

- Does he/she promote effective participation of all board members in the decision-making process?

- Does the chairman promote the image of the company, portraying the requisite leadership in the community?

## 3 Management relationships

*How effective is the chairman in:*

- Monitoring planning and operations?
- Building relationships?
- Influencing strategy?
- Helping define problems?
- Monitoring and evaluation performance of the CEO and senior officers?
- Representing shareholders and board to the management?
- Representing management to the board and shareholders?
- Maintaining accountability?
- Ensuring succession plans are in place at senior management level?

## 4 Managing the board

*How effective is the chairman in:*

- Chairing meetings of the board?
- Managing directors' performance?
- Communicating with directors between meetings?
- Setting meeting schedules?
- Setting meeting agendas?
- Controlling meeting attendance?
- Determining board information packages?
- Helping appoint committees?
- Attending committee meetings where appropriate?
- Determining director compensation?
- Promoting the training and development of directors?

## 5 Developing a more effective board

*How effective is the chairman in:*

- Encouraging board contribution?
- Planning board composition and succession?
- Establishing and working towards a vision?
- Promoting effective good corporate governance?

### 6   Relationship with other stakeholders

*How effective is the chairman in:*

- In conjunction with the CEO representing company to public, suppliers, customer and staff?
- In conjunction with the CEO developing relationships and representing the company with regulators and government agencies?
- Working with competitors in industry sector problems?
- In liaison with CEO and management, leading the company in charitable, educational and cultural activities?

In your view, should the chairman continue in office?

## C: INDIVIDUAL DIRECTOR PERFORMANCE

### 1   Strategic Thought

- Contribution to the strategic planning process.
- Ability to contribute at a strategic level in board debate.

### 2   Corporate Governance

- Understanding of the role of the board (governance versus management).
- Acceptance of collective responsibility and board room confidentiality.
- Level of understanding with regard to the legal and ethical responsibilities of the board.

### 3   Competence

- Contribution to the board: strengths, abilities, experience and judgement.
- Understanding the financial structure of the business.
- Understanding of the business as a whole.
- Level of understanding of the relevant sector.
- Communication with fellow board members, CEO and shareholders.
- Level of understanding of the market, the customer and quality focus.

### 4   Independence

- Confidence and courage of thinking, speaking and acting.
- Ability to constructively debate in a reasoned manner.
- Willingness to take an independent viewpoint.

### 5   Preparedness as a director

- Preparation for meetings.

- Contribution to committee work.
- Willingness to give extra time with chairman/CEO on relevant matters between meetings.
- Knowledge of company's key officers, managers and facilities.

### 6 Personal attributes

- Special attributes or skills brought to the board.
- Understanding of socio-economic issues facing the community and the business.
- Level of ethical and moral judgement.
- Preparedness to keep abreast with latest developments in the sector and in their corporate responsibilities.

### 7 Awareness of stakeholders

- Awareness of shareholders' expectations.
- Understanding of sectoral reform.
- Level of understanding of the boards obligations to staff, the media and the community with respect to board policy.
- Understanding the relationships between other key players in the sector.

## Summary of questions for chairman's review of individual director performance

### 1 Attendance at meetings

(a) Number of board/relevant committee meetings held since date of appointment.

(b) Number of board/relevant committee meetings attended by director.

(c) Attendance at meetings: eg (i) attends in time and stays for full duration of meeting (ii) attends briefly (iii) etc.

### 2 Preparation for meetings

(a) How well does the director prepare for meetings?

(b) Chairman's comments.

### 3 Participation at meetings

(a) What level of effective participation does the director have in meetings.

(b) Chairman's comments.

### 4 Additional roles

(a) Does the director make other contributions (e.g. chair of a board committee, completion of special board assignments).

(b)   Chairman's comments.

## 5   Personal attributes

- The chairman's assessment of a director's attributes with comment, in particular, on:
- The director's understanding of socio-economic issues facing the community and the business.
- The level of ethical and moral judgement.
- Preparedness to keep abreast of the latest developments in the sector and in their corporate responsibilities.
- Relationship with the stakeholders.

## 6   Professional attributes

- The chairman's assessment of a director's professional attributes with comment on:
- The director's strategic awareness.
- Independence.
- Understanding of governance.
- Technical competence.
- Industrial relations.
- Director responsibilities.

# Appendix 11

## ICSA GUIDANCE NOTE: TERMS OF REFERENCE OF THE NOMINATION COMMITTEE

Following the publication of the Higgs Review[1] the Financial Reporting Council has indicated its intention of introducing the revised Combined Code with effect from 1 July 2003. This Guidance Note advises on best practice in light of the Higgs recommendations and has been drafted referring to the provisions in the suggested code.

The Combined Code states as one of its principles that:

'*There should be a formal, rigorous and transparent procedure for the appointment of new directors to the board.*'[2]

Previous guidance has permitted smaller listed companies to allow the Board to act as a Nomination Committee. This is no longer the case, and although the Higgs Review recognised that it may take time for time for smaller companies to comply, it states '*there should be no differentiation in the Code's provision for larger and smaller companies*'.

The recommendation is that companies should go through a formal process of reviewing the balance and effectiveness of its Board, identifying the skills needed and those individuals who might best provide them. In particular the committee must assess the time commitments of the Board posts and ensure that the individual has sufficient available time to undertake them.

As with most aspects of Corporate Governance, however, the company must be seen to be doing so in a fair and thorough manner. It is, therefore, essential that a Nomination Committee be properly constituted with a clear remit and identified authority.

The Combined Code states that the majority of members of a Nomination Committee should be independent non-executive directors.[3] The Chairman of the Board may be a member but, as he or she is not deemed to be independent under the revised definition, the Committee, should be chaired by another independent non-executive director. It is, however, recognised in some companies, that there may be a valid reason for the Chairman of the company to chair the Nomination Committee if only for a period of time. In this case we would draw attention to the 'comply or explain' principle behind the Combined Code and suggest that, in such a case the matter be discussed with major shareholders and a full explanation for the company's decision to be included in the company's Annual Report.

The Code gives no guidance on the overall size of the Committee, we have recommended a Committee of three but companies with larger Boards should consider increasing this to four or five.

---

1  *Review of the role and effectiveness of non-executive directors*, published January 2003
2  Principles of Good Governance and Code of Best Practice, (The Combined Code), A.4.
3  The definition of independence is given in Code Provision A.3.4.

Although not a provision in the Code, the Higgs Review states as good practice, in its Non-Code Recommendations, that the Company Secretary (or their nominee) should act as Secretary to the Committee. It is the Company Secretary's responsibility to ensure that the Board and its Committees are properly constituted and advised. There also needs to be a clear co-ordination between the main Board and the various Committees where the Company Secretary would normally act as a valued intermediary.

The frequency with which the Committee needs to meet will vary considerably from company to company and will no doubt change from time to time. It is, however, clear that it must meet at least once each year prior or close to the year-end if only to consider whether or not directors retiring by rotation or reaching a pre-determined age limit should be put forward for re-appointment at the next the Annual General Meeting (AGM).

The list of duties we have proposed are those contained in the Summary of The Principal Duties of the Nomination Committee which ICSA drew up for the Higgs Review, which we believe all Nomination Committees should consider. Some companies may wish to add to this list and some smaller companies may need to modify it in other ways.

The Chairman of the Committee should attend the AGM and be prepared to respond to any questions which may be raised by shareholders on matters within the Committee's area of responsibility.

The reporting requirements within the Annual Report suggested by Higgs, means that the following has to be disclosed by the Board each year:

● The Chairman and members of the Committee need to be identified;

● The terms of reference need to be explained, to an extent that the role and authority is clearly demonstrated;

● A statement, detailing the activities and process used for appointments to the Board, for both Executive and Non-Executive appointments, explaining the reasons why external advice (recruitment consultants) or open advertising were not used;

● The number of Committee meetings held and attendance levels by members; and

● The reasons why a director should be appointed by the shareholders at the forthcoming AGM.

These recommendations and explanations clearly indicate a need for a guiding document. Further, the provisions of the Combined Code also advocate terms of reference for a Nomination Committee. This has led the ICSA to produce this Guidance Note proposing model terms of reference for a Nomination Committee to support the Summary of Principal Duties of the Nomination Committee contained within the Higgs Review. The document draws on the experience of senior Company Secretaries and Best Practice as carried out in some of the country's leading companies.

*Reference to 'The Committee' shall mean The Nomination Committee.*

*Reference to 'The Board' shall mean The Board of Directors.*

*The square brackets contain recommendations which are in line with Best Practice but which may need to be changed to suit the circumstances of the particular organisation.*

## 1 Membership

1.1 The Committee shall be appointed by The Board and shall comprise of a Chairman and at least [2] other members.

1.2 A majority of members of The Committee shall be independent non-executive directors.

1.3 The Board shall appoint The Committee Chairman who should not be the Chairman of The Board. In the absence of The Committee Chairman and/or an appointed deputy, the remaining members present shall elect one of their number to chair the meeting.

1.4 If a regular member is unable to act due to absence, illness or any other cause, the Chairman of The Committee may appoint another director of the company to serve as an alternate member having due regard to maintaining the required balance of executive and independent non-executive members.

1.5 Care should be taken to minimise the risk of any conflict of interest that might be seen to give rise to an unacceptable influence. (It is recommended that, where possible, the Chairman and members of the Committee should be rotated on a regular basis.) No member of the Committee shall also be a member of both the Audit and Remuneration Committee.[4]

## 2 Secretary

2.1 The Company Secretary or their nominee shall act as the Secretary of The Committee.

## 3 Quorum

3.1 The quorum necessary for the transaction of business shall be [2] of whom at least [1] must be a non-executive director. A duly convened meeting of The Committee at which a quorum is present shall be competent to exercise all or any of the authorities, powers and discretions vested in or exercisable by The Committee.

## 4 Frequency of Meetings

4.1 The Committee shall meet [not less than once a year] [quarterly on the first Wednesday in each of January, April, July and October] and at such other times as the Chairman of The Committee shall require.[5]

## 5 Notice of Meetings

5.1 Meetings of The Committee shall be summoned by the Secretary of The Committee at the request of the Chairman of The Committee.dance Note

---

4 It is recognised that small companies who do not have sufficient NEDs may not always be able to comply with this rule. Although not stated in the Code, ICSA consider it best practice that no member of the Nomination Committee be a Member of the Remuneration Committee, so that no conflict of interest can arise following a new appointment.
5 The frequency and timing of meetings will differ according to the needs of the company. Meetings should be organised so that attendance is maximised (e.g. by timetabling them to coincide with Board meetings).

5.2    Unless otherwise agreed, notice of each meeting confirming the venue, time and date together with an agenda of items to be discussed, shall be forwarded to each member of The Committee no fewer than [5] working days prior to the date of the meeting.

## 6  Minutes of Meetings

6.1    The Secretary shall minute the proceedings and resolutions of all Committee meetings, including the names of those present and in attendance.

6.2    Minutes of Committee meetings shall be circulated to all members of The Committee and to the Chairman of The Board and made available on request to other members of The Board.

## 7  Annual General Meeting

7.1    The Chairman of The Committee shall attend the Annual General Meeting prepared to respond to any shareholder questions on The Committee's activities.

## 8  Duties

8.1    The Committee shall:

8.1.1   regularly review the structure, size and composition of The Board and make recommendations to The Board with regard to any adjustments that are deemed necessary;

8.1.2   prepare a description of the role and capabilities required for a particular appointment;

8.1.3   be responsible for identifying and nominating for the approval of The Board candidates to fill board vacancies as and when they arise;

8.1.4   satisfy itself with regard to succession planning, that the processes and plans are in place with regard to both Board and senior appointments;

8.1.5   assess and articulate the time needed to fulfil the role of Chairman, senior independent director and non executive director, and undertake an annual performance evaluation to ensure that the all members of the board have devoted sufficient time to their duties.

8.1.6   ensure on appointment that a candidate has sufficient time to undertake the role and review his commitments, ensuring that if he is an executive of another company this will be his sole non–executive appointment; and in the event that a candidate for chairman is being considered take note that he can not be a Chairman of more than one FTSE100 company or equivalent;[6] and

8.1.7   Ensure that the Secretary on behalf of the Board has formally written to any appointees, detailing the role and time commitments and proposing an induction plan produced in conjunction with the Chairman.dance

---

6  Combined Code Provision A.4.8.

8.2.   It shall also make recommendations to The Board:

8.2.1   with regard to the Chairman having assessed every three years whether the present incumbent shall continue in post, taking into account the needs of continuity versus freshness of approach;

8.2.2   as regards the re-appointment of any non-executive director at the conclusion of his or her specified term of office; especially when they have concluded their second term;[7]

8.2.3   for the continuation (or not) in service of any director who has reached the age of [70];

8.2.4   concerning the re-election by shareholders of any director under the 'retirement by rotation' provisions in the company's articles of association;

8.2.5   concerning any matters relating to the continuation in office as a director of any director at any time;

8.2.6   concerning the appointment of any director to executive or other office other than to the positions of Chairman and Chief Executive, the recommendation for which would be considered at a meeting of:

8.2.6.1   all the non-executive directors regarding the position of Chief Executive;

8.2.6.2   all the directors regarding the position of Chairman;[8]

8.2.7   detailing items that should be published in the company's Annual Report relating to the activities of The Committee; and

8.2.8   with regard to the membership and chairmanship of the Audit Committee.[9]

## 9  Authority

9.1   The Committee is authorised to seek any information it requires from any employee of the company in order to perform its duties.

9.2   The Committee is authorised to obtain, at the company's expense, outside legal or other professional advice on any matters within its terms of reference.

---

7  Combined Code Provision A.7.3 recommends only two terms of three years, where a third term is proposed for a NED, the reasons must be explained in the Annual Report. After nine years the NED must submit to annual re-election and The Board must continue to give its reasons.

8  The appointment of a chairman should be led by the senior independent director, leading a committee which will exclude the present incumbent and any potential candidates for the position.

9  *Audit Committees, Combined Code Guidance, A Report and Proposed Guidance* by an FRC appointed group chaired by Sir Robert Smith, published January 2003, clause 3.3.

# Appendix 12

## ICSA GUIDANCE NOTE: TERMS OF REFERENCE OF THE REMUNERATION COMMITTEE

Following the publication of the Higgs Review[1] the Financial Reporting Council has indicated its intention of introducing the revised Combined Code with effect from 1 July 2003. This Guidance Note advises on best practice in light of the recommendations contained in the Higgs Review and has been redrafted using the provisions in the suggested code.

The Combined Code states as one of its principles that:

> '*Companies should establish a formal and transparent procedure for developing policy on executive remuneration and for fixing the remuneration packages of individual directors. No director should be involved in deciding his or her own remuneration.*'[2]

As with most aspects of Corporate Governance, the above stated principle makes it clear that, not only should companies go through a formal process of considering executive remuneration, but also they must be seen to be doing so in a fair and thorough manner. It is, therefore, essential that the Remuneration Committee is properly constituted with a clear remit and identified authority.

The Combined Code recommends that the Remuneration Committee should consist of at least three independent[3] non-executive directors; larger companies may wish to increase the number. The Chairman should not be a member of the Committee but may be asked, as the Chief Executive may, to attend on occasion to assist in the discussions.

Although not a provision in the code, the Higgs review states as good practice in its Non-Code Recommendations, that the Company Secretary (or their nominee) should act as Secretary to the Committee. It is the Company Secretary's responsibility to ensure that the Board and its Committees are properly constituted and advised. There also needs to be a clear co-ordination between the main Board and the various Committees where the Company Secretary would normally act as a valued intermediary.

The frequency with which the Committee needs to meet will vary considerably from company to company and will no doubt change from time to time. It is, however, clear that it must meet at least once each year prior or close to the year-end; its purpose at this meeting should be to prepare the Remuneration Report which the Combined Code and now the Remuneration Report Regulations require to be submitted to shareholders with or as part of the company's Annual Report. The Remuneration Report must be put to the shareholders for approval at the AGM.[4]

---

1 *Review of the role and effectiveness of non-executive directors*, published January 2003.
2 Principles of Good Governance and Code of Best Practice, (The Combined Code),B.2.
3 An Independent non-executive director is one that satisfies Combined Code Provision A.3.4.
4 *Directors' Remuneration Report Regulations 2002.*

The reporting requirements suggested by Higgs and expanded on in Schedule B to the Combined Code, means that the following has to be disclosed by the Board each year within the Annual Report:

- The Chairman and members of the committee need to be identified.

- The terms of reference need to be explained, to an extent that the role and authority is clearly demonstrated.

- The number of committee meetings and attendance level by members.

- The Company's policy with regard to both executive and non-executive pay.

- The information required under Schedule B and the Directors' Remuneration Report Regulations 2002.

The list of duties we have proposed are those contained within the Summary of Principle Duties Of the Remuneration Committee which ICSA helped compile for the Higgs Review and which we believe all Remuneration Committees should consider. Some companies may wish to add to this list and some smaller companies may need to modify it in other ways. The Chairman of the Committee should attend the Annual General Meeting (AGM) and be prepared to respond to any questions which may be raised by shareholders on the Committee's report or other matters within the Committee's area of responsibility.

These recommendations and explanations clearly show the need for there to be a guiding document and the provisions of the Combined Code also advocate terms of reference for a Remuneration Committee. This has led the ICSA to produce this Guidance Note proposing model terms of reference for a Remuneration Committee. The document draws on the experience of senior Company Secretaries and Best Practice as carried out in some of the country's leading companies.

*References to 'The Committee' shall mean the Remuneration Committee.*

*References to 'The Board' shall mean the full Board of Directors.*

*The square brackets contain recommendations which are in line with Best Practice but which may need to be changed to suit the circumstances of the particular organisation.*

## 1 Membership

1.1 The Committee shall comprise of at least [3] members, each of whom shall be appointed by The Board.

1.2 All members of The Committee shall be non-executive directors who are independent of management and free from any business or other relationship which could interfere with the exercise of their independent judgement.

1.3 The Board should appoint The Committee Chairman and determine the period for which they shall hold office. The Chairman of the company shall not be eligible to be appointed as Chairman of The Committee.

1.4 Care should be taken to minimise the risk of any conflict of interest that might be seen to give rise to an unacceptable influence. (It is recommended that, where possible, the Chairman and members of The Committee should be rotated on a regular basis.) No member of The Committee shall also be a member of both the Audit and Nomination Committee.[5]

## 2  Secretary

2.1    The Company Secretary or their nominee shall act as the Secretary of The Committee.

## 3  Quorum

3.1    The quorum necessary for the transaction of business shall be [2]. A duly convened meeting of The Committee at which a quorum is present shall be competent to exercise all or any of the authorities, powers and discretions vested in or exercisable by The Committee.

## 4  Meetings

4.1    The Committee shall meet [not less than once a year] [quarterly on the first Wednesday in each of January, April, July and October] and at such other times as the Chairman of The Committee shall require.[6]

## 5  Notice of Meetings

5.1    Meetings of The Committee shall be summoned by the Secretary of The Committee at the request of any member thereof.

5.2    Unless otherwise agreed, Notice of each meeting confirming the venue, time and date together with an agenda of items to be discussed, shall be forwarded to each member of The Committee, any other person required to attend and all other non-executive directors, no fewer than [5] working days prior to the date of the meeting.

5.3    The Chief Executive [and Personnel Director] shall have the right to address any meeting of The Committee; others may be called upon or shall able to speak by prior arrangement with the Chairman of The Committee.

## 6  Minutes of Meetings

6.1    The Secretary shall minute the proceedings and resolutions of all Committee meetings, including the names of those present and in attendance.

6.2    Minutes of Committee meetings shall be circulated to all members of The Committee and to all members of The Board.

## 7  Annual General Meeting

7.1    The Chairman of The Committee shall attend the Annual General Meeting prepared to respond to any shareholder questions on The Committee's activities.

---

5 It is recognised that small companies who do not have sufficient NEDs may not always be able to comply with this rule. Although not stated in the Code, ICSA consider it best practice that no member of the Nomination Committee be a Member of the Remuneration Committee, so that no conflict of interest can arise following a new appointment.
6 The frequency and timing of meetings will differ according to the needs of the company. Meetings should be organised so that attendance is maximised (e.g.by timetabling them to coincide with Board meetings).

## 8 Duties

The Committee shall:

8.1 Determine and agree with The Board the framework or broad policy for the Remuneration of the Chief Executive, the Chairman of the company and such other members of the executive management as it is designated to consider.[7] The remuneration of non-executive directors shall be a matter for the executive members of the Board. No director or manager shall be involved in any decisions as to his or her own remuneration. In order to assure his independence, the Committee will also review and recommend to the Board the remuneration of the Company Secretary;

8.2 In determining such policy, take into account all factors which it deems necessary. The objective of such policy shall be to ensure that members of the executive management of the company are provided with appropriate incentives to encourage enhanced performance and are, in a fair and responsible manner, rewarded for their individual contributions to the success of the company. It shall also liase with the Nomination Committee to ensure that the remuneration of newly appointed executives is within the company's overall policy;[8]

8.3 Determine targets for any performance related pay schemes operated by the company and asking the Board, when appropriate, to seek shareholder approval for any long term incentive arrangements;[9]

8.4 Within the terms of the agreed policy, determine the total individual remuneration package of each executive director including, where appropriate, bonuses, incentive payments and share options;

8.5 Determine the policy for and scope of pension arrangements, service agreements for the executive director, termination payments and compensation commitments;

8.6 In determining such packages and arrangements, give due regard to the comments and recommendations of the Combined Code[10] as well as the UK Listing Authority's Listing Rules and associated guidance;

8.7 Review competitor companies but insure that automatic increases are not implemented, thereby avoiding the 'ratchet' effect;

8.8 Be aware of and oversee any major changes in employee benefit structures throughout the company or group;idance Note

---

7 Some companies require the Remuneration Committee to consider the packages of all executives at or above a specified level such as those reporting to a main Board Director whilst others require the Committee to deal with all packages above a certain figure.

8 Combined Code Provision B.1.10 specifically refers to termination provisions within a service contract, but the Higgs Review refers to an obligation to consider that all incentives are properly structured.

9 A long term incentive is defined as an arrangement, whereby a payment either in shares or in cash, is paid to an executive at least two years after he was invited into the scheme and is not based on that year's performance.

10 In particular Schedule A of the Combined Code which details Provisions on the Design of Performance-Related Remuneration.

8.9   Vet and authorise the reimbursement of any claims for expenses from the Chief Executive and Chairman of the company;[11]

8.10   Ensure that provisions regarding disclosure of remuneration including pensions, as listed in the Directors' Remuneration Report Regulations 2002, are fulfilled; and

8.11   Produce an annual report of The Committee's remuneration policy.

## 9  Authority

9.1   The Committee is authorised by The Board to seek any information it requires from any employee of the company in order to perform its duties.

9.2   In connection with its duties The Committee is required by The Board to select, set the terms of reference and appoint Remuneration Consultants, at the company's expense.

9.3   Although the Committee can seek the advice and assistance of any of the Company's executives, it needs to ensure that this role is clearly separated from their role within the business.

---

11 It is suggested that the more common arrangement is for the Chairman to vet and authorise the Chief Executive's expenses and for the Chairman of the Remuneration Committee to vet and authorise the Company Chairman's claim. Whilst this may be more appropriate where Remuneration Committees do not meet that frequently we believe that the recommended provision is preferable.

# Appendix 13

## ASSOCIATION OF BRITISH INSURERS: PRINCIPLES AND GUIDELINES ON EXECUTIVE REMUNERATION (December 2003)

### Executive Remuneration – Principles

1  Remuneration Committees should maintain a constructive and timely dialogue with their major institutional shareholders and the ABI about remuneration policies including but not only issues relating to share incentive schemes or changes to share incentive schemes any proposed departure from the stated remuneration policy should be subject to prior approval by shareholders.

2  Companies should ensure that Remuneration Committees are properly established with appropriate powers of authority delegated from Company Boards.

3  Boards should demonstrate that performance based remuneration arrangements are clearly aligned with business strategy and objectives and are regularly reviewed. They should ensure overall structures remain appropriate and that these arrangements accord with current best practice. Simple structures assist with motivation and enhance the prospects of successful communication with shareholders.

4  The Remuneration Report should set out principles which have been followed and describe the approach used when putting into place the different components of total remuneration. The description should be clear and accessible.

5  Remuneration should reflect market requirements and take business size, complexity and geographical location into account, when appropriate with justification for the chosen policy clearly demonstrated to shareholders.

6  Remuneration Committees should have regard to pay and conditions throughout the company. They should pay particular attention to arrangements for senior executives who are not board directors but have a significant influence over the company's ability to meet its strategic objectives. There should be appropriate disclosure, which may be best achieved through disclosing the number of executives with specified levels of remuneration on a banded basis.

7  All new share-based incentive schemes should be subject to approval by shareholders by means of a separate and binding resolution. Furthermore where the rules of share-based incentive schemes, or the basis on which the scheme was approved by shareholders, permits some degree of latitude as regards quantum of grant or performance criteria it is expected that any changes will be detailed in the Remuneration Report. Any substantive changes in practical operation of schemes resulting from policy changes or modifications of scheme rules as previously approved should be subject to prior shareholder approval.

8   Where there is any type of matching arrangement or performance-linked enhancement or matching arrangements in respect of shares awarded under deferred bonus arrangements, there should be a separate shareholder vote. (See paragraphs 6.6 and 14.4.)

9   There should be transparency on all matters relating to the remuneration of present and past directors and where appropriate other senior executives. Shareholders' attention should be drawn to any special arrangements and significant changes since the previous Remuneration Report.

## Guidelines for the Structure of Remuneration

1   Remuneration packages should achieve an appropriate balance between fixed and variable pay as well as between long and short-term incentives.

2   When setting salary levels Remuneration Committees should take into consideration the requirements of the market, bearing in mind competitive forces applicable to the sector in which the company operates and to the particular challenges facing the company. Disclosure of policy in this regard is helpful to shareholders. Remuneration Committees should be able to satisfy shareholders that the company is not paying more than is necessary to attract and retain directors needed to run the company successfully. It is also appropriate to evaluate other elements of the overall remuneration package, which are usually expressed by reference to base salary.

3   A policy of setting salary levels below the comparator group median can provide more scope for increasing the amount of variable performance based pay and incentive scheme participation. Where a company seeks to pay salaries at above median, justification is required.

4   Annual bonuses, normally payable in cash, can provide a useful means of short-term incentivisation, but should be related to performance. Both individual and corporate performance targets are relevant and should be tailored to the requirements of the business and reviewed regularly to ensure they remain appropriate.

5   The performance targets should generally be disclosed in the Remuneration Report, subject to commercial confidentiality considerations. Shareholders understand that commercial confidence may prevent disclosure of specific short-term targets, but they expect to be informed of the basic parameters adopted in the financial year being reported on. The maximum participation levels should be disclosed. As provided for under the Combined Code, annual bonuses should not be pensionable.

6   Shareholders are not supportive of transaction bonuses which reward directors and other executives for effecting transactions irrespective of their future financial consequences. Any material payments that may be viewed as being *ex-gratia* in nature should be subject to shareholder approval prior to payment.

7   Boards should review regularly the potential liabilities associated with all elements of remuneration including share incentive participation and pension arrangements and should make appropriate disclosures to shareholders.

8   Institutional shareholders recognise that pension entitlements accruing to directors represent a significant, and potentially costly, item of remuneration. There should be informative disclosure identifying incremental value accruing to pension scheme

participation or from any other superannuation arrangements, relating to service during the year in question. Pension costs should be clearly explained, any disproportionate costs and values identified, and the extent to which liabilities are funded and aggregate outstanding unfunded liabilities disclosed.

9   Remuneration Committees should have regard to outstanding dilution in accordance with Guideline limits (see Section 13) and where appropriate available dilution capacity should be disclosed so that this can be compared with previous years.

10  Shareholders do not expect directors to be paid compensation in relation to their pension entitlements on account of variation in their contract specifications consequent upon changes to tax treatment of retirement benefits.

11  Remuneration Committees should scrutinise all other benefits, including benefits in kind and other financial arrangements to ensure they are justified, appropriately valued and suitably disclosed.

## 1  Guidelines for Share Incentive Schemes

1.1   Institutional shareholders generally support share incentive schemes that link remuneration to performance and align the interests of participating directors and senior executives with those of shareholders.

1.2   The implementation of such schemes involves either the commitment of shareholder funds or the dilution of shareholders' equity. It is important, therefore, that they be objectively costed, well-designed and form a coherent part of the overall remuneration package.

1.3   Shareholders expect all share incentive schemes to follow the spirit of the Guidelines.

## 2  General Principles

2.1   Institutional shareholders rely on a number of principles when evaluating share incentive schemes and determining their voting intentions.

2.2   Share incentive schemes should emphasise the importance of linking remuneration to performance, limits on dilution and individual participation, and a structure that effectively aligns the long-term interests of management with those of shareholders, having due regard to the cost of the schemes, which should be disclosed.

2.3   Shareholders strongly encourage the adoption of phased grants and welcome the trend towards awards being applied on a sliding scale in relation to the achievement of demanding and stretching financial performance against a target group or other relevant benchmark

2.4   Dilution is a matter of particular concern to investors. These Guidelines re-affirm the basic principle that dilution should not exceed 10 per cent in any 10-year period with further limitations on discretionary schemes (see Section 13).

2.5   Schemes should be designed to encourage share retention so that directors and other senior executives build up and maintain shareholdings which are meaningful in the context of their remuneration.

## 3  Scope

3.1   These Guidelines apply to all share incentive schemes or arrangements sponsored by UK listed companies whether option-based or involving conditional awards of shares, and including arrangements whereby awards on vesting or exercise are made in cash, or the transfer of shares to the value of the imputed gain at vesting date. Other companies should have regard for them, whenever possible.

## 4  Remuneration Committees

4.1   Remuneration Committees should:
- regularly review share incentive schemes to ensure their continued effectiveness and compliance with current Guidelines and contribution to shareholder value
- obtain prior shareholder authorisation for any substantive or exceptional amendments to scheme rules and practice including changes to limits and changes which make it easier to achieve performance targets, also where significant exercise of discretion is proposed by the Remuneration Committee

## 5  Disclosure

5.1   Companies must make full and relevant disclosure in their Remuneration Reports and in new proposals regarding share incentive schemes. Their rationale should be fully explained in order to enable shareholders to make informed decisions. In the absence of clear disclosure, shareholders may not be able to take the informed decision that will enable them to give their support.

5.2   Scheme and individual participation limits must be fully disclosed in share incentive schemes. Disclosure should, *inter alia*, cover performance conditions and related costs and dilution limits as set out in the relevant sections below. The reasons for selecting the performance conditions and target levels, together with the overall policy for granting conditional share or option awards, should be fully explained to shareholders.

## 6  Performance Conditions

6.1   It is now widely recognised that the desired alignment of interests is best achieved through the vesting of awards under share incentive schemes being conditional on satisfaction of performance criteria. These should demonstrate the achievement of demanding and stretching financial performance over the incentivisation period.

6.2   Challenging performance conditions should govern the vesting of awards or the exercise of options under any form of long term share-based incentive scheme.

These should:

- relate to overall corporate performance
- demonstrate the achievement of a level of performance which is demanding in the context of the prospects for the company and the prevailing economic environment in which it operates
- be measured relative to an appropriate defined peer group or other relevant benchmark
- be disclosed and transparent.

The reasons for selecting the performance condition(s), together with the overall policy for granting conditional share or share option incentive awards, should be fully explained to shareholders.

6.3   Share-based performance awards should not be made for less than median performance. Initial vesting levels should not be significant in relation to annual salary.

6.4   The greater the level of potential reward to individual participants the more stretching and demanding the performance conditions should be. Companies should explain clearly how this is achieved, especially when annual grants of options in excess of one times salary, or equivalent long term share incentive awards, are made.

6.5   Sliding scales that correlate the reward potential with a performance scale that incorporates the provisions of these Guidelines are a useful way of ensuring that performance conditions are genuinely stretching. They generally provide a better motivator for improving corporate performance than a 'single hurdle'.

6.6   When Share Schemes provide for awards of matching shares in respect of annual bonuses further performance conditions should be satisfied before the matching shares are permitted to vest (see Paragraph 14.4).

## 7   Performance Criteria

7.1   Total shareholder return (TSR) relative to a relevant index or peer group is generally acceptable as a performance criteria. However, the Remuneration Committee should satisfy itself prior to vesting that the recorded TSR or other criterion is a genuine reflection of the company's underlying financial performance and explain its reasoning.

7.2   Innovative types of performance criteria will need to be fully explained. It should be demonstrated that they are robust and demanding, and linked clearly to the achievement of enhanced shareholder value.

7.3   Shareholders need to have sufficient data to judge the appropriate size of the award for any given performance level. They also expect a maximum level of grant to be disclosed.

7.4   Other than in exceptional circumstances, the setting of a premium exercise price is not of itself a substitute for the adoption of relative performance conditions in accordance with these Guidelines.

## 8   Retesting of Performance Conditions

8.1   It is increasingly recognised that retesting of performance conditions for all share-based incentive schemes is unnecessary and unjustified as is clearly the case for Long Term Incentive Plans (LITPs) and similar nil-priced option schemes. The stipulated performance conditions should not combine a fixed performance hurdle with measurement from a variable base date.

8.2   It is unlikely that the criteria described in 8.1 will be met for retesting proposals for Long Term Incentive Plans (LTIPs) and similar nil-priced option schemes.

## 9   Vesting of Awards

9.1   Performance conditions should be measured over a period of three or more years. Strong encouragement is given to use of longer performance measurement periods of more than 3 years and deferred vesting schedules, in order to motivate the achievement of sustained improvements in financial performance.

## 10   Performance on Grant

10.1   Where competitive factors genuinely make awards of performance-linked options impossible then shareholders will consider alternative proposals carefully and only in the most exceptional circumstances approve them. For example, Remuneration Committees may consider the application of challenging performance conditions to govern the grant instead of the vesting of options. However shareholders are likely only to consider such proposals in certain specific and exceptional circumstances, and in particular that the company has clearly demonstrated to the satisfaction of shareholders that it is operating in a global environment which genuinely requires it to pay attention to global remuneration practices. Shareholders will expect that at least the conditions (see Appendix A) have been met.

## 11   Change of Control Provisions

11.1   Scheme rules should state that there will be no automatic waiving of performance conditions either in the event of a change of control or where subsisting options and awards are 'rolled-over' in the event of a capital reconstruction, and/or the early termination of the participant's employment.

11.2   Shareholders expect that the underlying financial performance of a company that is subject to a change of control should be a key determinant of what share-based awards, if any, should vest for participants. In the event of change of control, share incentive awards should vest on a pro-rata basis i.e. taking into account the vesting period that has elapsed at the time of change of control, though making due allowance for the reduction in value resulting from truncation of the life of the option.

## 12  Cost

12.1  The cost of share incentive schemes (and any amendments to existing schemes) should be disclosed at the time shareholder approval is sought in order that shareholders can assess the benefits of the proposal against the total costs and award justification. The following information should be disclosed:

- The total cost of all incentive arrangements.
- The potential value of awards (see Note 1) due to individual scheme participants on full vesting. This should be expressed by reference to the face value of shares or shares under option at point of grant, and expressed as a multiple of base salary.
- The expected value (see Note 2) of the award at the outset, bearing in mind the probability of achieving the stipulated performance criteria.
- The maximum dilution which may arise through the issue of shares to satisfy entitlements.

12.2  There should be prudent and appropriate arrangements governing acquisition of shares, and financing thereof, to meet contingent obligations under share-based incentive schemes. 12.3 The use of phased grants of share options and restricted shares, and utilisation of both new and purchased shares to satisfy the vesting of awards, requires a comprehensive approach to valuation. Assessment should focus on expected value, which should be disclosed, and it should take account of the performance vesting schedule which is adopted as well as the existence of any 'retesting' and 'replacement option' facilities such as have been prevalent under traditional schemes. Shareholders are helped in this task by disclosure of face value of any share award or option grant as well as of expected value.

## 13  Dilution Limits

13.1  Where the terms of any incentive scheme provide that entitlements may be satisfied through the issue of new shares, then the rules of that scheme must provide that, when aggregated with awards under all of the company's other schemes, commitments to issue new shares must not exceed 10% of the issued ordinary share capital (adjusted for scrip/bonus and rights issues) in any rolling 10 year period. Remuneration Committees should ensure that appropriate policies regarding flow-rates exist in order to spread the potential issue of new shares over the life of relevant schemes in order to ensure the limit is not breached. As an alternative, Remuneration Committees may give consideration to market purchases of shares in order to meet share incentive scheme liabilities.

13.2  Commitments to issue new shares or reissue treasury shares under executive (discretionary) schemes should not exceed 5% of the issued ordinary share capital of the company (adjusted for scrip/bonus issues) in any rolling 10-year period. This may be exceeded where vesting is dependent on the achievement of more stretching performance criteria with full vesting typically requiring at least top quartile performance.

13.3  For small companies, up to 10% of the ordinary share capital may be utilised for executive (discretionary) schemes, provided that the total market value of the capital utilised for the scheme at the time of grant does not exceed £500,000.

## 14  Participation

14.1    Participation in share incentive schemes should be restricted to *bona-fide* employees and executive directors, and be subject to appropriate limits for individual participation which should be disclosed.

14.2    It is considered beneficial for non-executive directors to have shareholdings and this may be achieved through having their fees paid in the form of shares at the full market price. However they should not participate in any form of share incentive scheme.

14.3    Participation in more than one share incentive scheme must form part of a well-considered remuneration policy, and should not be part of a multiple arrangement designed to raise the prospects of payout.

14.4    Institutional shareholders are not supportive of arrangements whereby shares or options may, in effect, be granted at a discount. This principle applies in circumstances where Remuneration Committees provide for awards of matching shares in respect of annual bonuses payable in the form of shares where these are then held for a qualifying period of, say, 3 years. In these cases, institutional shareholders will generally expect that satisfaction of further performance criteria will be required in order for the matching element to vest. (see Paragraph 6.6)

## 15  Phasing of Awards and Grants

15.1    The regular phasing of share incentive awards and option grants, generally on an annual basis, is encouraged because:
- It reduces the risk of unanticipated outcomes that arise out of share price volatility and cyclical factors.
- It eliminates the perceived problem that a limit on subsisting options encourages early exercise.
- It allows the adoption of a single performance measurement period
- It lessens the possible incidence of 'underwater' options, where the share price falls below the exercise price.

The phased vesting of awards in specific tranches following the minimum three year performance measurement period is not an alternative to phased grants. However, it can help to enhance the linking of vesting of awards to sustained performance and maintain incentivisation.

## 16  Pricing of Options and Shares

16.1    The price at which shares are issued under a scheme should not be less than the mid-market price (or similar formula) immediately preceding grant of the shares under the scheme.

16.2    Options granted under executive (discretionary) schemes should not be granted at a discount to the prevailing mid-market price.

16.3    Re-pricing or surrender and re-grant of awards or 'underwater' share options is not appropriate.

## 17   Timing of Grant

17.1   The rules of a scheme should provide that share or option awards normally be granted only within a 42 day period following the publication of the company's results.

## 18   Life of Schemes and Incentive Awards

18.1   No awards should be made beyond the life of the scheme approved on adoption by shareholders, which should not exceed 10 years.

18.2   Shares and options should not vest or be exercisable within three years from the date of grant. In addition, options should not be exercisable more than 10 years from the date of grant.

18.3   Where a company is taken over (except where arrangements are made for a switch to options of the offeror company) or in the event of the death or cessation of employment of the option holder, outstanding options may be exercised (or lapse) within 12 months. Any performance conditions attaching to the exercise of options should normally be fulfilled prior to exercise.

18.4   Any shares or options that a company may grant in exchange for those released under the schemes of acquired companies should normally be taken into account for the purposes of dilution and individual participation limits determined in accordance with these Guidelines.

## 19   Retirement

19.1   Options or other conditional share awards should not be granted within 6 months of a participant's anticipated retirement date. In determining the size and other terms of a grant made within 3 years of the anticipated retirement date, Remuneration Committees should have regard to the executive's ability to contribute to the achievement of the performance conditions.

19.2   Any unvested options or other conditional share awards which are outstanding at a participant's retirement date should be subject to performance measurement over the original stipulated period. Where the rules of the scheme require early exercise on retirement, performance should be pro-rated over the shorter period. In any event options should vest no later than the end of the initial performance measurement period, and should be finally exercisable no later than 12 months following the date of vesting.

## 20   Personal Shareholding Requirements

20.1   Institutional shareholders are generally supportive of companies which encourage their senior executives to build up meaningful shareholdings in the companies for which they work. The rules of incentive schemes should incorporate the requirement to retain a significant proportion of shares to which participants become entitled and the targets for shareholding should relate to the reward potential. This is particularly important in the case of awards where performance conditions apply principally at the point of grant.

## 21   Subsidiary Companies and Joint Venture Companies

21.1   It is generally undesirable for options to be granted over the share capital in a joint venture company.

21.2   In normal circumstances grants over the shares in a subsidiary company should not be made. However shareholders may consider exceptions where the condition of exercise is subject to flotation or sale of the subsidiary company. In such circumstances, grants should be conditional so that vesting is dependent on a return on investment that exceeds the cost of capital and that the market value of the shares at date of grant is subject to external validation. Exceptions will apply in the case of an overseas subsidiary where required by local legislation, or in circumstances where at least 25% of the ordinary share capital of the subsidiary is listed and held outside the group.

## 22   All-Employee Schemes

22.1   All-Employee schemes, such as SAYE schemes and Share Incentive Plans (SIPs) – (formerly known as AESOPs), should operate within an appropriate best practice framework. If newly issued shares are utilised, the overall dilution limits for share schemes should be complied with. Guidelines relating to timing of grants (except for pre-determined regular appropriation of shares under SIPs) apply.

## 23   Employee Share Ownership Trusts– ESOTS

23.1   ESOTs should not hold more shares at any one time than would be required in practice to match their outstanding liabilities, nor should they be used as an anti-takeover or similar device. The prior approval of shareholders should be obtained before 5% or more of a company's share capital at any one time may be held within ESOTs.

### Appendix A

The following are the minimum criteria that shareholders will expect to be satisfied in respect of any share incentive scheme adopting performance at point of grant instead of performance criteria governing the vesting of awards or exercise of options. (See Paragraph 10.1)

The scheme should be tailored to executives who are exposed to global remuneration practices and the approach should not be applied automatically to UK-based participants. Comparisons with overseas companies should take account of the different practices for setting remuneration, including pension provision, when compared with UK practices.

Performance conditions covering the grant should refer to overall corporate performance as a reference, not just individual performance of the grantee.

The basis of performance criteria should be fully disclosed and explained.

Performance-linking at grant does not alter the requirement that the minimum period for exercise of options should be three years from the date of grant.

The dilution limits set out in Section 13 are adhered to.

Participants in schemes are expected by the Board to build up a significant and disclosed shareholding through retention of awards that vest. Holding share options is not a substitute for share ownership in meeting ownership targets.

Disclosure concerning the scheme should comply with the highest standards relevant to the other jurisdictions in which the company operates e.g. those applied by the US Securities and Exchange Commission.

## Appendix B
### Note 1: Potential Value of the Award

Shareholders are likely to have regard to the potential value of the award assuming full vesting. This should be expressed on the basis that a conditional award is made of shares, or options over shares, with a face value, at current prices, equal to a given percentage of base salary. However the potential value will also be a function of share price at the time of vesting and of illustrative disclosures of potential outcomes may also be helpful. Full vesting of awards of higher potential value should require the achievement of commensurately greater performance.

### Note 2: Expected Value

The concept of expected value (EV) should be central to assessment of share incentive schemes. Essentially, EV will be the present value of the sum of all the various possible outcomes at vesting or exercise of awards. This will reflect the probabilities of achieving these outcomes and also the future value implicit in these outcomes. The calculation of the EV of share schemes is often complex and relies on a range of assumptions, and reliance on this concept by Remuneration Committees will require a sufficient measure of disclosure to enable shareholders to make informed judgments about such arrangements.

The nature of performance hurdles governing exercise is also crucial to calculations of EV and it must also be recognised that any facility for 'retesting' will also increase the EV of the award whereas in contrast if the exercise price is set at a premium to the share price at the outset, this will reduce the value of the EV of the instrument.

Institutional investors welcome efforts towards ensuring that accounting for share options and other share-based payment awarded under incentive schemes fully reflects the true cost to shareholders.

# Appendix 14

ASSOCIATION OF BRITISH INSURERS AND THE
NATIONAL ASSOCIATION OF PENSION FUNDS:
JOINT STATEMENT ON BEST PRACTICE ON
EXECUTIVE CONTRACTS AND SEVERANCE
(December 2003)

## 1 Introduction

1.1 Institutional shareholders believe top executives of listed companies should be appropriately rewarded for the value they generate. However, they are also concerned to avoid situations where departing executives are rewarded for failure or under-performance. This is a matter of good governance, about which the ABI and NAPF have been concerned for many years.

1.2 It is unacceptable that failure, which detracts from the value of an enterprise and which can threaten the livelihood of employees, can result in large payments to its departing leaders. Executives, whose remuneration is already at a level which allows for the risk inherent in their role, should show leadership in aligning their financial interests with those of their shareholders.

1.3 Our two organisations, whose members are leading institutional investors in UK markets, are therefore publishing this statement of best practice, which sets out the expectations of shareholders that boards will give careful consideration to the risk that negotiation of inappropriate executive contracts can lead to situations where failure is rewarded.

1.4 If companies are to recruit executives of sufficient calibre, Boards must bear in mind the basic demands of the market. These require them to offer incoming executives a degree of protection against downside risk. Contract law also provides employees with certain rights that must be respected.

1.5 However, shareholders also believe it is the duty of Boards to develop and implement recruitment and remuneration policies which will prevent them being required to make payments that are not strictly merited. When companies recruit senior executives, they do so in a mood of optimism and expectation of success. They may therefore tend to overlook the consequences of failure, which is clearly inappropriate.

1.6 At the outset, Boards should calculate the potential cost of termination in monetary terms. This should cover all elements of the severance package, including any property liabilities the company may be required to assume on behalf of the departing executive. They must also consider and avoid the serious reputational risk of being obliged to make and disclose large payments to executives who have failed to perform.

1.7 Shareholders will hold Boards accountable for the design and implementation of appropriate contracts. The primary responsibility resides, however, with Remuneration Committees.

1.8 Remuneration Committees should have the leeway to design a policy appropriate to the needs and objectives of the company, but they must also have a clear understanding of their responsibility to negotiate suitable contracts and be able to justify severance payments to shareholders.

1.9 This statement provides a reference point, both to make companies aware of the reasonable expectations of shareholders and to inform voting decisions under the new legislation giving shareholders an annual vote on the remuneration report. We expect that this guidance will be reviewed periodically and refreshed as necessary to take account of changing market circumstances.

## 2  Basic Principles

2.1 The design of contracts should not commit companies to payment for failure. Shareholders expect Boards to pay attention to minimising this risk when drawing up contracts. They should bear in mind that it may be in the interest of incoming executives and their personal advisers to exaggerate their potential loss on dismissal. Boards should resist consequent pressure to concede overly generous severance conditions.

2.2 Choices made when the contract is agreed have an important bearing on subsequent developments. Companies should have a clear, considered policy on directors' contracts which should be clearly stated in the remuneration report. Boards should calculate and take account of all the material commitments which the company would face in the event of severance for failure or underperformance. The Nomination Committee needs to see through the process of appointment by working with the Remuneration Committee to ensure that the contract is fair to all parties.

2.3 Objectives set for executives by the Board should be clear. The more transparent the objectives, the easier it is to determine whether an executive has failed to perform and therefore to prevent payment for failure. Wherever possible, objectives against which performance will be measured should be made public.

2.4 It should be clearly understood that investors do not expect executives to be automatically entitled to bonuses. Bonuses should be cut or eliminated when individual performance is poor. From the outset, Boards should therefore establish a clear link between performance and bonus as well as other aspects of variable pay.

2.5 Compensation for risks run by senior executives is already implicit in the absolute level of remuneration. Boards should ensure that there is an appropriate balance between contractual protection and total remuneration and be able to justify their policies to shareholders. Shareholders prefer short contracts of one year or less, and Boards must be able to justify the length agreed. The one-year period provided for under the Combined Code best practice should thus not be seen as a floor. Shorter periods would be appropriate if other remuneration conditions would mean that a one-year contract period would lead to excessive severance payment.

2.6     In highly exceptional circumstances – for example, where a new chief executive is being recruited to a troubled company – a longer initial notice period may be appropriate. These cases should be justified to shareholders and the longer notice period should apply to the initial term only with reversion to best practice at the earliest opportunity.

2.7     Experience suggests that courts take account of some elements of variable pay, such as bonuses, when making awards to departing executives. This can be limited through the attachment of clear performance conditions to variable pay. Boards may also wish to specify that a proportion of the bonus is for retaining the executive and this should fall away in the event of severance. A remuneration policy that favours relatively low base pay and a higher proportion of variable pay is a good way of linking remuneration to performance.

## 3  Contract Setting

3.1     There is no standard form of contract that can apply in all circumstances. Companies have taken a number of different approaches to severance in the past. These include phased payments, liquidated damages, and reliance on mitigation. It is important that Boards consider the relative merits of different approaches as they apply to their own company's situation, follow their chosen approach consequentially and are able to justify it to shareholders.

3.2     A welcome recent innovation has been the use of phased payments, which involve continued payment, eg on a normal monthly basis to the departing executive for the outstanding term of his or her contract. Payments cease when and if the executive finds fresh employment. Shareholders believe this approach has considerable advantages, which deserve the active consideration of Boards, but this approach does need to be specifically provided for in the contract and specific reference made to the legal obligation to miligate. It does not involve payment of large lump sums, which cannot be recovered. In many cases, executives will wish to seek further employment rather than remain idle till the monthly payments lapse. Allowing the contract to run off may also obviate the need for pension enhancement (see below).

3.3     The liquidated damages approach involves agreement at the outset on the amount that will be paid in the event of severance. It is clear from the beginning how much will be paid, but the amount cannot be varied to reflect under-performance. Shareholders do not believe the liquidated damages approach is generally desirable. Boards, which adopt it, should justify their decision, and should therefore consider a modified approach. This would involve reaching agreement in advance that, in the event of severance, the parties would go to arbitration to decide how much should be paid. This approach needs to take account of the likely cost of arbitration.

3.4     The concept of mitigation refers to the legal obligation on the part of the outgoing director to mitigate the loss incurred through severance, for example by seeking other employment and reducing the need for compensation. Where this is the sole approach, shareholders expect reassurance that the Board has taken steps to ensure that the full benefit is obtained. As with liquidated damages, boards need to have considered at the outset what the cost of severance would be under the proposed contract as well as the relative merits of arbitration as opposed to litigation.

3.5 An essential problem is that it is not normally possible for under-performance to be established as a ground for summary dismissal without compensation. Under the Employment Act 2002, however, a statutory disciplinary procedure will be implied into every employment contract, including those of executive directors. Boards should be aware of this and be prepared to use disciplinary procedures if warranted.

3.6 In the wake of this legislation contracts should also make clear that, if a director is dismissed in the wake of a disciplinary procedure, a shorter notice period than that given in the contract would apply. A reasonable period would be the statutory period, comprising one week for each year's service up to a maximum of 12 weeks. Without such a provision the full notice period would continue to apply even after dismissal following a disciplinary procedure.

3.7 Companies should also consider including in contracts a safeguard for more extreme cases, for example, that compensation would not be payable in case of dismissal for financial failure such as a very significant fall of the share price relative to the sector.

3.8 Other than in highly exceptional circumstances, such as the recruitment of a new chief executive of a troubled company, contracts should not provide additional protection in the form of compensation for severance as a result of change of control. Where exceptional circumstances apply, any additional protection should relate to the initial contract term only and not be a rolling provision.

3.9 Companies may consider other options, including a provision for compensation to be paid by reference to shares with the amount of shares set at the outset of employment. Where such an option is proposed it should, however, be clearly explained both as to purpose and to the details of its operation. Remuneration committees should satisfy themselves that it is workable and will yield advantages greater than the phased payment and other approaches outlined above. Compensation paid by reference to shares should be paid in cash rather than directly in shares to prevent unmerited windfall gains.

3.10 The use of shareholding targets for senior executives and directors is likely to be a powerful and therefore more effective means of aligning the financial interests of executives with those of shareholders.

## 4 Pension Arrangements and Other Remuneration Issues

4.1 Pension enhancements can represent a large element of severance pay and involve heavy cost to shareholders, the full extent of which may not be immediately evident. It is important that Boards state the full economic cost for pension enhancement at the earliest opportunity. Boards should not support enhanced pension payments without making themselves fully aware of the costs.

4.2 A large liability looms in the future where companies choose not to fund an enhanced pension liability but to pay it as it arises. In all cases, whether the pension is funded or not, Boards must disclose the cost, justify their choice to shareholders and demonstrate that they have chosen a route that involves the least overall cost to the company.

4.3   An important principle with regard to pensions is that Boards should distinguish between the amount that is a contractual entitlement and the amount of discretionary enhancement agreed as part of a severance package. Contracts should state clearly that the pension would not be enhanced in the event of early retirement unless the board was satisfied that the objectives set for the executive had been met or that the enhancement was merited. Shareholders are likely to question enhancement decisions when they are doubtful of the merit and, if not satisfied with the board's justification, they may vote against the remuneration report.

## 5   General Considerations and Conclusion

5.1   Boards should have a clear and explicit policy on contracts and on how Remuneration Committees will play a primary role. It should include calculation of the cost of severance at the time the contract is drawn up and an approach to implementation which ensures that all payments made on severance take account of performance in relation to objectives set for the departing executive by the board.

5.2   Companies should fulfil their legal obligations to make contracts readily available for shareholders to inspect, together with any side letters relating to severance terms and pension arrangements. Shareholders will take account of contracts and the way they are implemented in considering their vote on the remuneration report.

# Appendix 15

ACCOUNTING STANDARDS BOARD: STATEMENT ON
OPERATING AND FINANCIAL REVIEW
(January 2003)

## Introduction

1    The Accounting Standards Board originally issued the Statement 'Operating and
Financial Review' in 1993. The Statement built on the foundations of existing best
practice by providing a framework within which directors could discuss the main factors
underlying the company's performance and financial position. This revised statement has
been issued to reflect later improvements in narrative reporting. It has persuasive rather
than mandatory force and is not an accounting standard.

2    The Operating and Financial Review (OFR) should set out the directors' analysis of the
business, in order to provide to investors a historical and prospective analysis of the
reporting entity "through the eyes of management". It should include discussion and
interpretation of the performance of the business and the structure of its financing, in the
context of known or reasonably expected changes in the environment in which it
operates.

3    For many companies, the OFR is already an important element of their communication
with the capital markets, complementing as well as supplementing the financial
statements. This Statement has been developed as a broad framework rather than a set of
rules or requirements. It is for the directors to decide how best to interpret this
framework in the particular circumstances of their business. The principles set out in
paragraph 6 below should be regarded as essential to the preparation of a good OFR. The
guidance in the remainder of the Statement indicates how those principles can be
applied.

4    Directors should develop the presentation of their OFR in a way that complements the
format of their annual report as a whole. The guidance is not intended to result in the
duplication of information provided elsewhere in the annual report. The directors are
encouraged to include at least the key features of the OFR in a separate, stand-alone
section. However, they may decide that, in the context of their annual report, it would be
more appropriate to incorporate some of the detailed discussion within the structure of
one or more sections such as the Chairman's report, corporate governance statement or
environmental report.

## Scope

5    This Statement has been drafted with listed companies in mind, but it is also applicable to
other large entities where there is a legitimate public interest in their financial statements.

## Principles

6   The directors should apply the following principles when preparing the Operating and Financial Review (OFR):

(i) *Purpose*

The OFR should assist the user's assessment of the future performance of the reporting entity by setting out the directors' analysis of the business. It should include discussion of:

- the nature of the business, its objectives and the strategies adopted to achieve those objectives;
- the performance of the business in the period and the main influences on performance, including the expected effect of known trends and the potential effect of risks facing the business; and
- the financial position, including capital structure and treasury policy, and the factors affecting, and likely to affect, that position.

The OFR should focus on those matters the directors consider to be significant in the circumstances of their business as a whole.

(ii) *Audience*

The OFR will normally be of interest to a wide range of users; however, it should focus on matters that are relevant to investors. It should not assume that users have a detailed prior knowledge of the business, nor of the significant features of its operating environment. The OFR should be written in a clear and readily understandable style.

(iii) *Time frame*

The OFR should discuss the performance of the period, identifying those trends and factors relevant to the user's assessment of the future performance of the business and the achievement of long-term business objectives. The particular factors identified and discussed should be those that have affected performance in the period and those that are expected to have an effect on the future performance and financial position of the business. The discussion should comment on the impact of future operations of significant post-balance sheet events. The OFR should also discuss predictive comments made in previous statements where these have not been borne out by events.

(iv) *Reliability*

Information and analysis contained in the OFR should be neutral, free from bias and complete, dealing even-handedly with both good and bad aspects.[1] Where a significant matter is not discussed in the OFR, for example where it is discussed elsewhere in the annual report, the directors should ensure that the OFR retains balance and that the user is not misled as a result of the omission. Cross-references to other sections of the annual report will assist the users.

---

1  Note that paragraph 9.3A of the Listing Rules states that 'A company must take all reasonable care to ensure that any statement or forecast or any other information it notifies to the Company Announcements Office or makes available through the UK Listing Authority is not misleading, false or deceptive and does not omit anything likely to affect the import of such statement, forecast or other information'.

(v) *Comparability*

It will be appropriate for the approach adopted for the presentation of the OFR to evolve over time, or to differ from that adopted by other entities. However, disclosure should be sufficient for the user to be able to compare the information presented with similar information about the entity for previous periods and with information about other entities in the same industry or sector. The OFR should highlight accounting policies that are key to an understanding of the performance and financial position of the entity, focusing on those which have required the exercise of judgement in their application and to which the results are most sensitive. In addition, it should draw attention to the accounting policies which have changed during the year.

(vi) *Measures*

The OFR will typically include a range of financial and non-financial measures. Comparability will be enhanced if the measures disclosed are accepted and widely used, either within the industry sector or more generally.

When disclosing these measures in the OFR:

- they should be defined and calculation measures explained;
- the source of underlying data should be disclosed and, where relevant, assumptions explained. Where information from the financial statements has been adjusted for inclusion in the OFR, that fact should be highlighted and a reconciliation provided;
- comparative amounts should be disclosed; and
- changes in the measures disclosed and calculation methods used compared to previous periods, including significant changes in the underlying accounting policies applied in the financial statements, should be identified and explained. Comparative amounts should be restated on the new basis.

Wherever possible, the OFR should identify and comment on the measures that are used by the directors as key performance indicators in managing the business.

## Guidance

The following sections indicate how the principles set out above can be applied. Not all of the items listed will be relevant to all businesses, nor should the guidance be regarded as a comprehensive list of all matters that might be considered by the directors to be relevant to an appreciation of their business. The OFR should focus on those matters that are of greatest significance to that business as a whole.

### The business, its objectives and strategy

8   The OFR should include a description of the business as context for the directors' discussion and analysis of performance and financial position. Depending on the nature of the business, this might cover areas such as:

- the industries in which the business operates
- its main products and services, business processes and distribution methods
- its major markets and competitive position within those markets
- the structure of the business, including an overview of the main operating facilities and their location
- the significant features of the legal and regulatory environment that influence the business

- key dependencies, including significant strategic alliances and relationships with customers, suppliers, financiers and key employees.

This description would normally be enhanced by the disclosure of non-financial and physical measures that give an insight into the scale of the business, its position in the market and the key relationships on which it is currently dependent.

9   The OFR should discuss the objectives of the business and management's strategy for achieving those objectives. Objectives will often be defined in terms of financial performance; however, objectives in other areas should also be discussed where relevant. For example, the directors might define business objectives that relate to total shareholder return, market position, net cash flow (or cash flow return on investment), or in the area of corporate responsibility (environmental performance, for example).

10  The related measures that are used by management to assess the achievement of objectives should be identified. These measures may be financial (for example, profit, turnover or net cash flow) or non-financial (for example, customer satisfaction, productivity or emission levels). It will often be helpful to identify any milestones and benchmarks (including peer-group comparators) against which the achievement of objectives is assessed.

## Operating review

11  The principal aim of the operating review is to enable the user to understand the dynamics of the various lines of the business undertaken – that is, the main influences on the performance of the business, and how these interrelate. Hence the OFR should identify and explain the main factors that underlie the business, and in particular those that either have varied in the past or are expected to change in the future.

## Performance in the period

12  The OFR should discuss the significant features of performance in the period covered by the financial statements, focusing on those business segments that are relevant to an understanding of the performance as a whole. Trends in performance suggested by an analysis of the current and previous periods should be highlighted. Performance should be discussed in the context of the long-term objectives of the business and related measures (including any milestones and benchmarks disclosed in previous periods).

13  The discussion should cover all aspects of the performance statements, including the profit and loss account and the statement of recognised gains and losses. However, as indicated by paragraph 9 above, other aspects of performance should be discussed where relevant.

14  The OFR should set out the directors' analysis of the effect on current and future performance of changes in the industry or the environment in which the business operates and of developments within the business. For example:

- changes in market conditions
- the introduction, or announcement, of new products and services
- changes in exchange rates and inflation rates
- new activities, discontinued activities and other acquisitions and disposals.

15 In the case of material acquisitions, the discussion should comment on the extent to which the expectations at the time of acquisition have been realised. Where a seasonal business has been acquired in the period under review, and the results of the acquisition included are not indicative of those for a full year, this should be indicated.

16 The analysis should cover any other special factors that have affected performance in the year under review; this includes influences whose effect cannot be quantified, as well as any specific 'exceptional items' reported in the financial statements.

## Returns to shareholders

17 The OFR should discuss returns to shareholders, including distributions and share repurchases. Any discussion of the performance of the company in terms of the increase or decrease in its share price in the period should be in comparison to that of its peers. The OFR should also include a commentary on the comparison between profit for the financial year and dividends, both in total and in per share terms, indicating the directors' overall dividend policy.

18 Where the directors have shown in the financial statements alternative measures of earnings – for example, as providing a more useful indication of future trends – these measures should be discussed. In such situations, basic and diluted earnings per share, as defined by FRS 14 'Earnings per share', should also be discussed.

## Dynamics of the business

19 The OFR should analyse the main factors and influences that may have an effect on future performance, whether or not they were significant in the period under review.

20 This should include a discussion identifying the principal risks facing the business, together with a commentary on the directors' approach to managing them[2] and, in qualitative terms, the nature of their potential impact on performance. Examples of matters that may be relevant, depending on the nature of the business, are:
- scarcity of raw materials
- skill shortages and expertise of uncertain supply
- technological change
- dependence on major suppliers or customers
- risks related to environmental issues
- access to markets
- product liability
- regulatory issues
- changes in demographic, political or macro-economic conditions (exchange rate fluctuations, for example)
- other reputational risks

2 'Internal Control: Guidance for Directors on the Combined Code' deals with the disclosure of the directors' approach to risk management. This disclosure would often be included within a separate corporate governance statement.

21 The OFR should also give a commentary on the strengths and resources of the business that should assist it in the pursuit of its objectives and, in particular, those items that are not reflected in the balance sheet. Such items might include:

- corporate reputation and brand equity
- intellectual capital
- licences, patents, copyrights and trademarks
- research and development
- customer/supplier relationships
- proprietary business processes
- web-sites and databases
- market position/dominance

22 The use of relevant financial or non-financial measures will often assist the user's understanding of the potential value of such items. However, it is not intended that an overall valuation of the business be given, nor, in the case of listed companies, for net asset value to be reconciled to market capitalisation.

## Investment for the future

23 Directors should comment in the OFR on how they have sought to maintain and improve future performance. Many types of activity and expenditure can be regarded, to a greater or lesser extent, as a form of investing in the future (activities and expenditure designed to maintain or enhance the strengths and resources of the business, referred to in paragraph 21 above, would fall into this category.) By their very nature, the definition of such items will vary from one business to another, and particularly from one business to another. Examples might include:

- human capital policies and practices, including employee training
- pure and applied research which may lead to potential new products, services or processes
- development of new products and services
- investment in brand equity, through advertising and other marketing activities for example
- technical support to customers
- refurbishment and maintenance programmes

24 Capital expenditure may also be an important element, both because of the amounts involved and the long lead time in implementing projects. The OFR should discuss the current level of capital expenditure together with planned future expenditure.

25 Information should be given on the benefits expected from such activities and expenditure. This should cover both those benefits arising in the period under review as a result of previous activities, and the future benefits expected. The OFR should explain how investment is directed to assist the achievement of business objectives.

26 It is often difficult to split such expenditure between that benefiting the current period and that benefiting future periods; nor is the level of activity always measured meaningfully by the expenditure involved. Hence, the absolute level of expenditure will often be less relevant to the user than the directors' analysis of the impact on performance of changes in the levels of such activities and expenditure, and of management policies in these areas.

### Financial review

27 The principal aim of the financial review is to explain to the users of the annual report the capital structure of the business, its treasury policy and the dynamics of its financial position – its sources of liquidity and their application, including the implications of the financing requirements arising from its investment plans.[3]

28 The discussion should concentrate on matters of significance to the position of the business as a whole. It should be a narrative commentary, supported by figures that assist the users' understanding of the policies and their effect in practice. The following paragraphs indicate specific matters that should be addressed where these are important to an understanding of the business.

## Capital structure and dividend policy

29 The OFR should contain a discussion of the capital structure of the business, in terms of the maturity profile of type, type of capital instruments used, currency and interest rate structure. This should include comments on relevant rations such as interest cover and debt/equity ratios, as well as short- and longer-term funding plans.

30 The discussion should state the capital funding and treasury policies and objectives. These will include the management of interest rate risk, the maturity profile of borrowings, and the management of currency risk. The OFR should also discuss the implementation of these policies in the period under review, in terms of:
- the manner in which treasury activities are controlled
- the currencies in which borrowings are made and in which cash and cash equivalents are held
- the extent to which borrowings are at fixed interest rates
- the use of financial instruments, for hedging purposes and otherwise
- the extent to which foreign currency net investments are hedged by currency borrowings and other hedging instruments.

31 The purpose and effect of major financing transactions undertaken up to the date of approval of the financial statements should be explained. The effect of interest costs on profits and the potential impact of interest rate changes should also be discussed.

## Cash flows

32 Cash inflows and outflows during the period under review should be discussed. The principal sources of cash inflows should be identified, highlighting the relative contribution from customers and other sources. Similarly, the principal destinations of cash outflows in the period should be identified. The OFR should comment on any special factors that have influenced cash flows in the current period and those that may have a significant effect on future cash flows.

---

3 FRS 13 'Derivatives and other Financial Instruments: Disclosures' requires the financial statements to include disclosure relating to the risks arising from the use of financial instruments in the business. It is envisaged that the discussion required by FRS 13 would usually be presented in the context of the OFR's wider disclosures.

33 Although segmental analysis of profit may be indicative of the cash flow generated by each segment, this will not always be so – for example, because of fluctuations in capital expenditure. Where segmental cash flows are significantly out of line with segmental profits, this should be indicated and explained.

## Current liquidity

34 The business's liquidity at the end of the period under review should be discussed, including a commentary on the level of borrowings, the seasonality of borrowing requirements (indicated by the peak level of borrowings during that period) and the maturity profile of both borrowings and undrawn committed borrowing facilities.

35 Reference should be made to the funding requirements for investment commitments and authorisations.

36 The discussion should cover internal sources of liquidity, referring to any restrictions on the ability to transfer funds from one part of the group to meet the obligations of another part of the group, where these represent, or might foreseeably come to represent, a significant restraint on the group. Such constraints would include exchange controls and taxation consequences of transfers.

37 Where the business has entered into covenants with lenders which could have the effect of restricting the use of credit facilities, and negotiations with the lenders on the operation of these covenants are taking place or are expected to take place, this fact should be indicated in the OFR. Where a breach of covenant has occurred or is expected to occur, the OFR should give details of the measures taken or proposed to remedy the situation.

## Going concern

38 Provision D.1.3 of the Combined Code states that the directors of listed companies should report that the business is a going concern. 'Going Concern and Financial Reporting'[4] gives directors guidance on how this should be done. This confirmation may appropriately be made as part of the OFR discussion of financial position.

## Statement of compliance

39 As this is a statement of voluntary best practice, directors are not expected to include in the annual report any formal confirmation that that they have complied with the principles set out in this Statement, although the inclusion of some comment on the extent to which the Statement has been followed may be helpful to the user. Where it is implied, through the use of the words 'operating and financial review' or otherwise, that the directors have endeavoured to follow these principles, they should signal any fundamental departure from them.

4  Guidance developed by a Joint Working Group comprising members of the accountancy profession and preparers of accounts (published in November 1994).

# Appendix 16

## COMBINED CODE OF CORPORATE GOVERNANCE: SMITH GUIDANCE ON AUDIT COMMITTEES

### The Smith Guidance on Audit Committees

### 1 Introduction

1.1 This guidance is designed to assist company boards in making suitable arrangements for their audit committees, and to assist directors serving on audit committees in carrying out their role.

1.2 The paragraphs in bold are taken from the Combined Code (Section C3). Listed companies that do not comply with those provisions should include an explanation as to why they have not complied in the statement required by the Listing Rules.

1.3 Best practice requires that every board should consider in detail what arrangements for its audit committee are best suited for its particular circumstances. Audit committee arrangements need to be proportionate to the task, and will vary according to the size, complexity and risk profile of the company.

1.4 While all directors have a duty to act in the interests of the company the audit committee has a particular role, acting independently from the executive, to ensure that the interests of shareholders are properly protected in relation to financial reporting and internal control.

1.5 Nothing in the guidance should be interpreted as a departure from the principle of the unitary board. All directors remain equally responsible for the company's affairs as a matter of law. The audit committee, like other committees to which particular responsibilities are delegated (such as the remuneration committee), remains a committee of the board. Any disagreement within the board, including disagreement between the audit committee's members and the rest of the board, should be resolved at board level.

1.6 The Code provides that a separate section of the annual report should describe the work of the committee. This deliberately puts the spotlight on the audit committee and gives it an authority that it might otherwise lack. This is not incompatible with the principle of the unitary board.

1.7 The guidance contains recommendations about the conduct of the audit committee's relationship with the board, with the executive management and with internal and external auditors. However, the most important features of this relationship cannot be drafted as guidance or put into a code of practice: a frank, open working relationship and a high level of mutual respect are essential, particularly between the audit committee chairman and the board chairman, the chief executive and the finance director. The audit committee must be prepared to take a robust stand, and all parties must be prepared to make information freely available to the audit committee, to listen to their views and to talk through the issues openly.

1.8   In particular, the management is under an obligation to ensure the audit committee is kept properly informed, and should take the initiative in supplying information rather than waiting to be asked. The board should make it clear to all directors and staff that they must cooperate with the audit committee and provide it with any information it requires. In addition, executive board members will have regard to their common law duty to provide all directors, including those on the audit committee, with all the information they need to discharge their responsibilities as directors of the company.

1.9   Many of the core functions of audit committees set out in this guidance are expressed in terms of 'oversight', 'assessment' and 'review' of a particular function. It is not the duty of audit committees to carry out functions that properly belong to others, such as the company's management in the preparation of the financial statements or the auditors in the planning or conducting of audits. To do so could undermine the responsibility of management and auditors. Audit committees should, for example, satisfy themselves that there is a proper system and allocation of responsibilities for the day-to-day monitoring of financial controls but they should not seek to do the monitoring themselves.

1.10   However, the high-level oversight function may lead to detailed work. The audit committee must intervene if there are signs that something may be seriously amiss. For example, if the audit committee is uneasy about the explanations of management and auditors about a particular financial reporting policy decision, there may be no alternative but to grapple with the detail and perhaps to seek independent advice.

1.11   Under this guidance, audit committees have wide-ranging, time-consuming and sometimes intensive work to do. Companies need to make the necessary resources available. This includes suitable payment for the members of audit committees themselves. They – and particularly the audit committee chairman – bear a significant responsibility and they need to commit a significant extra amount of time to the job. Companies also need to make provision for induction and training for new audit committee members and continuing training as may be required.

1.12   This guidance applies to all companies to which the Code applies – i.e. UK listed companies. For groups, it will usually be necessary for the audit committee of the parent company to review issues that relate to particular subsidiaries or activities carried on by the group. Consequently, the board of a UK-listed parent company should ensure that there is adequate cooperation within the group (and with internal and external auditors of individual companies within the group) to enable the parent company audit committee to discharge its responsibilities effectively.

## 2   Establishment and role of the audit committee; membership, procedures and resources

### Establishment and role

2.1   The board should establish an audit committee of at least three, or in the case of smaller companies two, members.

2.2 The main role and responsibilities of the audit committee should be set out in written terms of reference and should include: to monitor the integrity of the financial statements of the company and any formal announcements relating to the company's financial performance, reviewing significant financial reporting judgements contained in them; to review the company's internal financial controls and, unless expressly addressed by a separate board risk committee composed of independent directors or by the board itself, the company's internal control and risk management systems; to monitor and review the effectiveness of the company's internal audit function; to make recommendations to the board, for it to put to the shareholders for their approval in general meeting, in relation to the appointment of the external auditor and to approve the remuneration and terms of engagement of the external auditor; to review and monitor the external auditor's independence and objectivity and the effectiveness of the audit process, taking into consideration relevant UK professional and regulatory requirements; to develop and implement policy on the engagement of the external auditor to supply non-audit services, taking into account relevant ethical guidance regarding the provision of non-audit services by the external audit firm; and to report to the Board, identifying any matters in respect of which it considers that action or improvement is needed, and making recommendations as to the steps to be taken.

### *Membership and appointment*

2.3 All members of the committee should be independent non-executive directors. The board should satisfy itself that at least one member of the audit committee has recent and relevant financial experience.

2.4 The chairman of the company should not be an audit committee member.

2.5 Appointments to the audit committee should be made by the board on the recommendation of the nomination committee (where there is one), in consultation with the audit committee chairman.

2.6 Appointments should be for a period of up to three years, extendable by no more than two additional three-year periods, so long as members continue to be independent.

### *Meetings of the audit committee*

2.7 It is for the audit committee chairman, in consultation with the company secretary, to decide the frequency and timing of its meetings. There should be as many meetings as the audit committee's role and responsibilities require. It is recommended there should be not fewer than three meetings during the year, held to coincide with key dates within the financial reporting and audit cycle.[1] However, most audit committee chairmen will wish to call more frequent meetings.

2.8 No one other than the audit committee's chairman and members is entitled to be present at a meeting of the audit committee. It is for the audit committee to decide if non-members should attend for a particular meeting or a particular agenda item. It is to be expected that the external audit lead partner will be invited regularly to attend meetings as well as the finance director. Others may be invited to attend.

---

1 For example, when the audit plans (internal and external) are available for review and when interim statements, preliminary announcements and the full annual report are near completion.

2.9   Sufficient time should be allowed to enable the audit committee to undertake as full a discussion as may be required. A sufficient interval should be allowed between audit committee meetings and main board meetings to allow any work arising from the audit committee meeting to be carried out and reported to the board as appropriate.

2.10  The audit committee should, at least annually, meet the external and internal auditors, without management, to discuss matters relating to its remit and any issues arising from the audit.

2.11  Formal meetings of the audit committee are the heart of its work. However, they will rarely be sufficient. It is expected that the audit committee chairman, and to a lesser extent the other members, will wish to keep in touch on a continuing basis with the key people involved in the company's governance, including the board chairman, the chief executive, the finance director, the external audit lead partner and the head of internal audit.

### Resources

2.12  The audit committee should be provided with sufficient resources to undertake its duties.

2.13  The audit committee should have access to the services of the company secretariat on all audit committee matters including: assisting the chairman in planning the audit committee's work, drawing up meeting agendas, maintenance of minutes, drafting of material about its activities for the annual report, collection and distribution of information and provision of any necessary practical support.

2.14  The company secretary should ensure that the audit committee receives information and papers in a timely manner to enable full and proper consideration to be given to the issues.

2.15  The board should make funds available to the audit committee to enable it to take independent legal, accounting or other advice when the audit committee reasonably believes it necessary to do so.

### Remuneration

2.16  In addition to the remuneration paid to all non-executive directors, each company should consider the further remuneration that should be paid to members of the audit committee to recompense them for the additional responsibilities of membership. Consideration should be given to the time members are required to give to audit committee business, the skills they bring to bear and the onerous duties they take on, as well as the value of their work to the company. The level of remuneration paid to the members of the audit committee should take into account the level of fees paid to other members of the board. The chairman's responsibilities and time demands will generally be heavier than the other members of the audit committee and this should be reflected in his or her remuneration.

### Skills, experience and training

2.17  It is desirable that the committee member whom the board considers to have recent and relevant financial experience should have a professional qualification from one of the professional accountancy bodies. The need for a degree of financial literacy among the other members will vary according to the nature of the company, but experience of corporate financial matters will normally be required. The availability of appropriate financial expertise will be particularly important where the company's activities involve specialised financial activities.

2.18 The company should provide an induction programme for new audit committee members. This should cover the role of the audit committee, including its terms of reference and expected time commitment by members; and an overview of the company's business, identifying the main business and financial dynamics and risks. It could also include meeting some of the company staff.

2.19 Training should also be provided to members of the audit committee on an ongoing and timely basis and should include an understanding of the principles of and developments in financial reporting and related company law. In appropriate cases, it may also include, for example, understanding financial statements, applicable accounting standards and recommended practice; the regulatory framework for the company's business; the role of internal and external auditing and risk management.

2.20 The induction programme and ongoing training may take various forms, including attendance at formal courses and conferences, internal company talks and seminars, and briefings by external advisers.

## 3 Relationship with the board

3.1 The role of the audit committee is for the board to decide and to the extent that the audit committee undertakes tasks on behalf of the board, the results should be reported to, and considered by, the board. In doing so it should identify any matters in respect of which it considers that action or improvement is needed, and make recommendations as to the steps to be taken.

3.2 The terms of reference should be tailored to the particular circumstances of the company.

3.3 The audit committee should review annually its terms of reference and its own effectiveness and recommend any necessary changes to the board.

3.4 The board should review the audit committee's effectiveness annually.

3.5 Where there is disagreement between the audit committee and the board, adequate time should be made available for discussion of the issue with a view to resolving the disagreement. Where any such disagreements cannot be resolved, the audit committee should have the right to report the issue to the shareholders as part of the report on its activities in the annual report.

## 4 Role and responsibilities

### Financial reporting

4.1 The audit committee should review the significant financial reporting issues and judgements made in connection with the preparation of the company's financial statements, interim reports, preliminary announcements and related formal statements.

4.2   It is management's, not the audit committee's, responsibility to prepare complete and accurate financial statements and disclosures in accordance with financial reporting standards and applicable rules and regulations. However the audit committee should consider significant accounting policies, any changes to them and any significant estimates and judgements. The management should inform the audit committee of the methods used to account for significant or unusual transactions where the accounting treatment is open to different approaches. Taking into account the external auditor's view, the audit committee should consider whether the company has adopted appropriate accounting policies and, where necessary, made appropriate estimates and judgements. The audit committee should review the clarity and completeness of disclosures in the financial statements and consider whether the disclosures made are set properly in context.

4.3   Where, following its review, the audit committee is not satisfied with any aspect of the proposed financial reporting by the company, it shall report its views to the board.

4.4   The audit committee should review related information presented with the financial statements, including the operating and financial review, and corporate governance statements relating to the audit and to risk management. Similarly, where board approval is required for other statements containing financial information (for example, summary financial statements, significant financial returns to regulators and release of price sensitive information), whenever practicable (without being inconsistent with any requirement for prompt reporting under the Listing Rules) the audit committee should review such statements first.

### Internal controls and risk management systems

4.5   The audit committee should review the company's internal financial controls (that is, the systems established to identify, assess, manage and monitor financial risks); and unless expressly addressed by a separate board risk committee comprised of independent directors or by the board itself, the company's internal control and risk management systems.

4.6   The company's management is responsible for the identification, assessment, management and monitoring of risk, for developing, operating and monitoring the system of internal control and for providing assurance to the board that it has done so. Except where the board or a risk committee is expressly responsible for reviewing the effectiveness of the internal control and risk management systems, the audit committee should receive reports from management on the effectiveness of the systems they have established and the conclusions of any testing carried out by internal and external auditors.

4.7   Except to the extent that this is expressly dealt with by the board or risk committee, the audit committee should review and approve the statements included in the annual report in relation to internal control and the management of risk.

### Whistleblowing

4.8   The audit committee should review arrangements by which staff of the company may, in confidence, raise concerns about possible improprieties in matters of financial reporting or other matters. The audit committee's objective should be to ensure that arrangements are in place for the proportionate and independent investigation of such matters and for appropriate follow-up action.

### The internal audit process

4.9 The audit committee should monitor and review the effectiveness of the company's internal audit function. Where there is no internal audit function, the audit committee should consider annually whether there is a need for an internal audit function and make a recommendation to the board, and the reasons for the absence of such a function should be explained in the relevant section of the annual report.

4.10 The audit committee should review and approve the internal audit function's remit, having regard to the complementary roles of the internal and external audit functions. The audit committee should ensure that the function has the necessary resources and access to information to enable it to fulfil its mandate, and is equipped to perform in accordance with appropriate professional standards for internal auditors.[2]

4.11 The audit committee should approve the appointment or termination of appointment of the head of internal audit.

4.12 In its review of the work of the internal audit function, the audit committee should, *inter alia*:
- ensure that the internal auditor has direct access to the board chairman and to the audit committee and is accountable to the audit committee;
- review and assess the annual internal audit work plan;
- receive a report on the results of the internal auditors' work on a periodic basis;
- review and monitor management's responsiveness to the internal auditor's findings and recommendations;
- meet with the head of internal audit at least once a year without the presence of management; and
- monitor and assess the role and effectiveness of the internal audit function in the overall context of the company's risk management system.

### The external audit process

4.13 The audit committee is the body responsible for overseeing the company's relations with the external auditor.

### Appointment

4.14 The audit committee should have primary responsibility for making a recommendation on the appointment, reappointment and removal of the external auditors. If the board does not accept the audit committee's recommendation, it should include in the annual report, and in any papers recommending appointment or reappointment, a statement from the audit committee explaining its recommendation and should set out reasons why the board has taken a different position.

4.15 The audit committee's recommendation to the board should be based on the assessments referred to below. If the audit committee recommends considering the

---

2  Further guidance can be found in the Institute of Internal Auditors' Code of Ethics and the International Standards for the Professional Practice of Internal Auditing Standards.

selection of possible new appointees as external auditors, it should oversee the selection process.

4.16 The audit committee should assess annually the qualification, expertise and resources, and independence (see below) of the external auditors and the effectiveness of the audit process. The assessment should cover all aspects of the audit service provided by the audit firm, and include obtaining a report on the audit firm's own internal quality control procedures.

4.17 If the external auditor resigns, the audit committee should investigate the issues giving rise to such resignation and consider whether any action is required.

### Terms and remuneration

4.18 The audit committee should approve the terms of engagement and the remuneration to be paid to the external auditor in respect of audit services provided.

4.19 The audit committee should review and agree the engagement letter issued by the external auditor at the start of each audit, ensuring that it has been updated to reflect changes in circumstances arising since the previous year. The scope of the external audit should be reviewed by the audit committee with the auditor. If the audit committee is not satisfied as to its adequacy it should arrange for additional work to be undertaken.

4.20 The audit committee should satisfy itself that the level of fee payable in respect of the audit services provided is appropriate and that an effective audit can be conducted for such a fee.

### Independence, including the provision of non-audit services

4.21 The audit committee should have procedures to ensure the independence and objectivity of the external auditor annually, taking into consideration relevant UK professional and regulatory requirements. This assessment should involve a consideration of all relationships between the company and the audit firm (including the provision of non-audit services). The audit committee should consider whether, taken as a whole and having regard to the views, as appropriate, of the external auditor, management and internal audit, those relationships appear to impair the auditor's judgement or independence.

4.22 The audit committee should seek reassurance that the auditors and their staff have no family, financial, employment, investment or business relationship with the company (other than in the normal course of business). The audit committee should seek from the audit firm, on an annual basis, information about policies and processes for maintaining independence and monitoring compliance with relevant requirements, including current requirements regarding the rotation of audit partners and staff.

4.23 The audit committee should agree with the board the company's policy for the employment of former employees of the external auditor, paying particular attention to the policy regarding former employees of the audit firm who were part of the audit team and moved directly to the company. This should be drafted taking into account the relevant ethical guidelines governing the accounting profession. The audit committee should monitor application of the policy, including the number of former employees of the external auditor currently employed in senior positions in the company, and consider whether in the light of this there has been any impairment, or appearance of impairment, of the auditor's judgement or independence in respect of the audit.

4.24 The audit committee should monitor the external audit firm's compliance with applicable United Kingdom ethical guidance relating to the rotation of audit partners, the level of fees that the company pays in proportion to the overall fee income of the firm, office and partner, and other related regulatory requirements.

4.25 The audit committee should develop and recommend to the board the company's policy in relation to the provision of non-audit services by the auditor. The audit committee's objective should be to ensure that the provision of such services does not impair the external auditor's independence or objectivity. In this context, the audit committee should consider:
- whether the skills and experience of the audit firm make it a suitable supplier of the non audit service;
- whether there are safeguards in place to ensure that there is no threat to objectivity and independence in the conduct of the audit resulting from the provision of such services by the external auditor;
- the nature of the non-audit services, the related fee levels and the fee levels individually and in aggregate relative to the audit fee; and
- the criteria which govern the compensation of the individuals performing the audit.

4.26 The audit committee should set and apply a formal policy specifying the types of non-audit work:
- from which the external auditors are excluded;
- for which the external auditors can be engaged without referral to the audit committee; and
- for which a case-by-case decision is necessary.
In addition, the policy may set fee limits generally or for particular classes of work.

4.27 In the third category, if it is not practicable to give approval to individual items in advance, it may be appropriate to give a general pre-approval for certain classes for work, subject to a fee limit determined by the audit committee and ratified by the board. The subsequent provision of any service by the auditor should be ratified at the next meeting of the audit committee.

4.28 In determining the policy, the audit committee should take into account relevant ethical guidance regarding the provision of non-audit services by the external audit firm, and in principle should not agree to the auditor providing a service if, having regard to the ethical guidance, the result is that:
- the external auditor audits its own firm's work;
- the external auditor makes management decisions for the company;
- a mutuality of interest is created; or
- the external auditor is put in the role of advocate for the company.
The audit committee should satisfy itself that any safeguards required by ethical guidance are implemented.

4.29 The annual report should explain to shareholders how, if the auditor provides non-audit services, auditor objectivity and independence is safeguarded.

*Annual audit cycle*

4.30 At the start of each annual audit cycle, the audit committee should ensure that appropriate plans are in place for the audit.

4.31 The audit committee should consider whether the auditor's overall work plan, including planned levels of materiality, and proposed resources to execute the audit plan appears consistent with the scope of the audit engagement, having regard also to the seniority, expertise and experience of the audit team.

4.32 The audit committee should review, with the external auditors, the findings of their work. In the course of its review, the audit committee should:
- discuss with the external auditor major issues that arose during the course of the audit and have subsequently been resolved and those issues that have been left unresolved;
- review key accounting and audit judgements; and
- review levels of errors identified during the audit, obtaining explanations from management and, where necessary the external auditors, as to why certain errors might remain unadjusted.

4.33 The audit committee should also review the audit representation letters before signature by management and give particular consideration to matters where representation has been requested that relate to non-standard issues[3]. The audit committee should consider whether the information provided is complete and appropriate based on its own knowledge.

4.34 As part of the ongoing monitoring process, the audit committee should review the management letter (or equivalent). The audit committee should review and monitor management's responsiveness to the external auditor's findings and recommendations.

4.35 At the end of the annual audit cycle, the audit committee should assess the effectiveness of the audit process. In the course of doing so, the audit committee should:
- review whether the auditor has met the agreed audit plan and understand the reasons for any changes, including changes in perceived audit risks and the work undertaken by the external auditors to address those risks;
- consider the robustness and perceptiveness of the auditors in their handling of the key accounting and audit judgements identified and in responding to questions from the audit committees, and in their commentary where appropriate on the systems of internal control;
- obtain feedback about the conduct of the audit from key people involved, e.g. the finance director and the head of internal audit; and
- review and monitor the content of the external auditor's management letter, in order to assess whether it is based on a good understanding of the company's business and establish whether recommendations have been acted upon and, if not, the reasons why they have not been acted upon.

---

3 Further guidance can by found in the Auditing Practices Board's Statement of Auditing Standard 440 'Management Representations'.

## 5 Communication with shareholders

5.1 The terms of reference of the audit committee, including its role and the authority delegated to it by the board, should be made available. A separate section in the annual report should describe the work of the committee in discharging those responsibilities.

5.2 The audit committee section should include, *inter alia*:
- a summary of the role of the audit committee;
- the names and qualifications of all members of the audit committee during the period;
- the number of audit committee meetings;
- a report on the way the audit committee has discharged its responsibilities; and
- the explanation provided for in paragraph 4.29 above.

5.3 The chairman of the audit committee should be present at the AGM to answer questions, through the chairman of the board, on the report on the audit committee's activities and matters within the scope of audit committee's responsibilities.

# Appendix 17

## ICSA GUIDANCE NOTE: TERMS OF REFERENCE OF THE AUDIT COMMITTEE

Following the publication of the Higgs Review and the Report of the Smith Group, the Financial Reporting Council has indicated its intention of introducing the revised Combined Code with effect from 1 July 2003. This Guidance Note advises on best practice in light of the Higgs Review and has been drafted referring to the provisions in the suggested code.

The Combined Code states:

> *'The board should establish formal and transparent arrangements for considering how they should apply the financial reporting and internal control principles and for maintaining an appropriate relationship with the company's auditors.'*

The Combined Code goes on to state that the Audit Committee should have 'written terms of reference which deal clearly with its authority and duties'. Such statements express a clear need for an Audit Committee, the requirement for which is also supported by other influential organisations such as the Commonwealth Association for Corporate Governance and the International Corporate Governance Network.

As with most aspects of Corporate Governance, the above stated principle makes it clear that, not only should companies go through a formal process of considering its internal auditing and control procedures and evaluating its relationship with its external auditors, but it must be seen to be doing so in a fair and thorough manner. It is, therefore, essential that the Audit Committee is properly constituted with a clear remit and identified authority.

As regards the make up of the Committee, we have followed the Combined Code and recommend a minimum of three non-executive directors who should be clearly independent of management and, as far as possible, free from any conflicts of interest. Although it may seem obvious, we would, for example, suggest that members of the Committee should have no links with the external auditors. We have made specific recommendations that others may be required to assist the Committee from time to time, according to the particular items being considered and discussed.

Although not a provision in the Code, the Higgs Review, states as good practice, in its Non-Code Recommendations, the Company Secretary (or their nominee) should act as Secretary to the Committee. The Smith Report states that the Company Secretary should attend the Audit Committee. It is the Company Secretary's responsibility to ensure that the Board and its Committees are properly constituted and advised. There also needs to be a clear co-ordination between the main Board and the various Committees where the Company Secretary would normally act as a valued intermediary. In addition, although the responsibility for internal controls clearly remains with the Board as a whole, the Company Secretary would normally have the day-to-day task of reviewing the internal control procedures of the company and responsibility for drafting the governance report.

The frequency with which the Committee needs to meet will vary considerably from company to company and will no doubt change from time to time. As a general rule, most Audit Committees would be expected to meet quarterly, however, it is clear that it must meet at least three times each year, prior to the publication of financial statements, and again close to the year-end for the purpose of considering the relationship with the external auditors and to recommend whether or not they should be put forward for re-appointment at the next Annual General Meeting (AGM).

The list of duties we have proposed are those contained in the Smith Report which we believe all Audit Committees should consider. Some companies may wish to add to this list and some smaller companies may need to modify it in other ways.

The Audit Committee should compile a brief report for shareholders which should be included in the company's Annual Report, and will need to disclose the following:

- Role and main responsibilities of the Audit committee;

- Composition of committee, including relevant qualifications and experience; the appointment process; and any fees paid in respect of membership;

- Number of meetings and attendance levels;

- A description of the main activities of the year to:
    - Monitor the integrity of the financial statements;
    - Review the integrity of the internal financial control and risk management systems;
    - Review the independence of the external auditors, and the provision of non audit services;
    - Describe the oversight of the external audit process, and how its effectiveness was assessed;
    - Explain the recommendation to the Board on the appointment of auditors.

The Chairman of the Committee should attend the AGM prepared to respond to any questions that may be raised by shareholders on matters within the Committee's area of responsibility.

The above recommendations and explanations clearly show the need for there to be a guiding document. Furthermore, the provisions of the Combined Code also advocate terms of reference for an Audit Committee. This has led the ICSA to produce this Guidance Note proposing model terms of reference for an Audit Committee. The document draws on the experience of senior Company Secretaries and Best Practice as carried out in some of the country's leading companies.

Companies who have a US listing may need to amend these terms in light of the requirements of the recently introduced rules following the Sarbanes-Oxley Act.

Whilst this Guidance Note is aimed primarily at the corporate sector, the doctrine of good governance, including the introduction of Audit Committees, is increasingly being recognised and adopted by other organisations particularly in the public and not for profit sectors. The principles underlying the content of this Guidance Note are applicable regardless of the size or type of organisation and we trust that it will be to be found useful across all sectors.

*Reference to 'The Committee' shall mean The Audit Committee.*

*Reference to 'The Board' shall mean The Board of Directors.*

*The square brackets contain recommendations which are in line with Best Practice but which may need to be changed to suit the circumstances of the particular organisation.*

## 1   Membership and attendance

1.1   The Committee shall be appointed by The Board, on the recommendation of the Nomination Committee, and shall comprise of a Chairman and at least [2] other members.

1.2   All members of The Committee shall be independent non-executive directors. The Chairman of the Board shall not be a member of The Committee. At least one member of The Committee should have recent relevant financial knowledge.

1.3   Care should be taken to minimise the risk of any conflict of interest that might be seen to give rise to an unacceptable influence. (It is recommended that, where possible, the Chairman and members of The Committee should be rotated on a regular basis.) No committee member shall also be a member of both the Nomination and Remuneration Committees.

1.4   The Board, on the recommendation of the Nomination Committee, shall appoint The Committee Chairman who shall be an independent non-executive director. In the absence of The Committee Chairman and/or an appointed deputy, the remaining members present shall elect one of their number present to chair the meeting.

1.5   The Committee may ask the Chairman, Chief Executive, Finance Director and any relevant senior management to attend meetings either regularly or by invitation, but the invitees have no right of attendance.

1.6   The Committee shall ask a representative of the external auditors and the head of internal audit to attend all meetings. The Committee should have at least one meeting, or part thereof, with the external auditor without management being present.

## 2   Secretary

2.1   The Company Secretary or their nominee shall act as the Secretary of The Committee.

## 3   Quorum

3.1   The quorum necessary for the transaction of business shall be [2]. A duly convened meeting of The Committee at which a quorum is present shall be competent to exercise all or any of the authorities, powers and discretions vested in or exercisable by The Committee.

## 4   Frequency of Meetings

4.1   The Committee shall meet [*not less than once a year*] [*quarterly on the first Wednesday in each of January, April, July and October*] and at such [*other*] times as the Chairman of The Committee shall require.

4.2 Meetings will be arranged to tie in with the publication of the company's financial statements, allowing at least [3] working days prior to a Board Meeting where accounts or financial statements are to be approved.

4.3 Meetings can be requested by the external or internal auditors if they consider one is necessary.

## 5 Notice of Meetings

5.1 Meetings of The Committee shall be summoned by the Secretary of The Committee at the request of any member thereof.

5.2 Unless otherwise agreed, Notice of each meeting confirming the venue, time and date together with an agenda of items to be discussed, shall be forwarded to each member of The Committee, any other person required to attend and all other non-executive directors, no fewer than [5] working days prior to the date of the meeting.

## 6 Minutes of Meetings

6.1 The Secretary shall minute the proceedings and resolutions of all meetings of The Committee, including recording the names of those present and in attendance.

6.2 The Secretary should ascertain, at the beginning of each meeting, the existence of any conflicts of interest and minute them accordingly.

6.3 Minutes of Committee meetings shall be circulated promptly to all members of The Committee and to the Chairman and all members of The Board.

## 7 Annual General Meeting

7.1 The Chairman of The Committee shall attend the Annual General Meeting prepared to respond to any shareholder questions on The Committee's activities.

## 8 Duties

### 8.1 Internal Control and Risk Assessment

8.1.1 The Committee shall keep under review the effectiveness of the company's financial reporting and internal control policies and procedures for the identification, assessment and reporting of risks.

### 8.2 Internal Audit

8.2.1 The Committee shall consider applications for the post of and [appoint]/[approve the appointment of] the head of the internal audit function; any dismissal of the post holder should be considered by The Committee.

8.2.2 The Committee shall consider and approve the terms of reference of the internal audit function, and shall be advised of the planned programme of audits and the reason for any change or delay in the programme.

8.2.3 The Committee shall review the management of financial matters and focus upon the freedom allowed to the internal auditors.

8.2.4   The Committee shall review promptly all reports on the company from the internal auditors.

8.2.5   The Head of Internal Audit shall be given the right of direct access to the Chairman of The Committee.

## 8.3   External Audit

8.3.1   The Committee shall consider and make recommendations to The Board as regards the appointment and re-appointment of the company's external auditors, and shall ensure that key partners within the appointed firm are rotated from time to time.

8.3.2   The Committee shall meet with the external auditors at least twice each year, once at the planning stage, where the scope of the audit will be considered, and once post audit at the reporting stage, and shall ensure that any auditor's management letters and management's responses are reviewed.

8.3.3   The Committee shall keep under review the relationship with external auditors including (but not limited to):

8.3.3.1   the independence and objectivity of the external auditors;

8.3.3.2   the consideration of audit fees which should be paid as well as any other fees which are payable to auditors in respect of non-audit activities; and

8.3.3.3   discussions with the external auditors concerning such issues as compliance with accounting standards and any proposals which the external auditors have made vis-à-vis the company's internal auditing standards.

## 8.4   Financial Statements

8.4.1   The Committee shall keep under review the consistency of accounting policies both on a year to year basis and across the company/group.

8.4.2   The Committee shall review and challenge where necessary the company's financial statements taking into account:

8.4.2.1   decisions requiring a major element of judgement;

8.4.2.2   the extent to which the financial statements are affected by any unusual transactions;

8.4.2.3   the clarity of disclosures;

8.4.2.4   significant adjustments resulting from the audit;

8.4.2.5   the going concern assumption;

8.4.2.6   compliance with accounting standards;

8.4.2.7   compliance with stock exchange and other legal requirements; and

8.4.2.8 reviewing the company's statement on internal control systems prior to endorsement by The Board and to review the policies and process for identifying and assessing business risks and the management of those risks by the company.

The Committee shall review the annual financial statements of the pension funds where not reviewed by The Board as a whole.

## 8.5 Reporting Responsibilities

8.5.1 The Committee or its Chairman shall meet formally with the Board of Directors at least [once] a year to discuss such matters as the Annual Report and the relationship with the external auditors.

8.5.2 In the light of its other duties, the Committee shall make whatever recommendations to The Board it deems appropriate and shall compile a report to shareholders to be included in the company's Annual Report and Accounts.

## 8.6 Other Matters

8.6.1 The Committee shall give due consideration to the requirements of the UK Listing Authority's Listing Rules.

8.6.2 The Committee shall be responsible for co-ordination of the internal and external auditors.

8.6.3 The Committee will review the company's procedures for handling allegations from whistleblowers.

8.6.4 The Committee shall oversee any investigation of activities, which are within its terms of reference and act as a court of the last resort.

8.6.5 The Committee should, on a regular basis, review its own performance, constitution and terms of reference to ensure it is operating at maximum effectiveness.

## 9 Authority

The Committee is authorised:

9.1 to seek any information it requires from any employee of the company in order to perform its duties;

9.2 to obtain, at the company's expense, outside legal or other professional advice on any matters within its terms of reference; and

9.3 to call any member of staff to be questioned at a meeting of The Committee as and when required.

# Appendix 18

## SMITH REPORT: OUTLINE REPORT TO SHAREHOLDERS ON THE ACTIVITIES OF THE AUDIT COMMITTEE

1  **Role of the audit committee**
   - Main responsibilities of the audit committee

2  **Composition of the audit committee**
   - Members and secretary – names and appointment/resignation dates
   - Appointment process
   - The relevant qualifications, expertise and experience of each member

3  **Resources**
   - Any dedicated resources available to the committee, internal or bought-in

4  **Meetings**
   - Number of meetings, and attendance

5  **Remuneration of the members of the audit committee**
   - Describe the specific policies in relation to the members of the audit committee (or cross refer to the Directors' Remuneration Report)

**Main activities of the committee in the year to xxxx**

6  **Financial statements**
   - Describe the activities carried out in order to monitor the integrity of the financial statements

7  **Internal financial control and risk management systems**
   - Describe the activities carried out in order to review the integrity of the company's internal financial control and risk management systems

8  **External auditors**
   - Describe the procedures adopted to review the independence of the external auditors, including disclosure of the policy on the provision of non-audit services and an explanation of how the policy protects auditor independence
   - Describe the oversight of the external audit process and confirm that an assessment of the effectiveness of the external audit was made
   - Explain the recommendation to the board on the appointment of the auditors and, if applicable, the process adopted to select the new auditor

9  **Internal audit function**
   - Confirm that a review of the plans and work of the department was carried out. If there is no function explain the committee's consideration of whether there is a need for an internal audit function in accordance with the recommendations of the Turnbull Report.

# Appendix 19

## TURNBULL GUIDANCE FOR DIRECTORS ON INTERNAL CONTROL PROVISIONS OF THE COMBINED CODE

### INTRODUCTION

#### Internal control requirements of the Combined Code

1   When the Combined Code of the Committee on Corporate Governance (the Code) was published, the Institute of Chartered Accountants in England & Wales agreed with the London Stock Exchange that it would provide guidance to assist listed companies to implement the requirements in the Code relating to internal control.

2   Principle D.2 of the Code states that 'The board should maintain a sound system of internal control to safeguard shareholders' investment and the company's assets'.

3   Provision D.2.1 states that 'The directors should, at least annually, conduct a review of the effectiveness of the group's system of internal control and should report to shareholders that they have done so. The review should cover all controls, including financial, operational and compliance controls and risk management'.

4   Provision D.2.2 states that 'Companies which do not have an internal audit function should from time to time review the need for one'.

5   Paragraph 12.43A of the London Stock Exchange Listing Rules states that 'in the case of a company incorporated in the United Kingdom, the following additional items must be included in its annual report and accounts:
   (a)   a narrative statement of how it has applied the principles set out in Section 1 of the Combined Code, providing explanation which enables its shareholders to evaluate how the principles have been applied;
   (b)   a statement as to whether or not it has complied throughout the accounting period with the Code provisions set out in Section 1 of the Combined Code. A company that has not complied with the Code provisions, or complied with only some of the Code provisions or (in the case of provisions whose requirements are of a continuing nature) complied for only part of an accounting period, must specify the Code provisions with which it has not complied, and (where relevant) for what part of the period such non-compliance continued, and give reasons for any non-compliance'.

6   The Preamble to the Code, which is appended to the Listing Rules, makes it clear that there is no prescribed form or content for the statement setting out how the various principles in the Code have been applied. The intention is that companies should have a free hand to explain their governance policies in the light of the principles, including any special circumstances which have led to them adopting a particular approach.

7  The guidance in this document should be followed by boards of listed companies in:
   - assessing how the company has applied Code principle D.2;
   - implementing the requirements of Code provisions D.2.1 and D.2.2; and
   - reporting on these matters to shareholders in the annual report and accounts.

## Objectives of the guidance

8  This guidance is intended to:
   - reflect sound business practice whereby internal control is embedded in the business processes by which a company pursues its objectives;
   - remain relevant over time in the continually evolving business environment; and
   - enable each company to apply it in a manner which takes account of its particular circumstances.

   The guidance requires directors to exercise judgement in reviewing how the company has implemented the requirements of the Code relating to internal control and reporting to shareholders thereon.

9  The guidance is based on the adoption by a company's board of a risk-based approach to establishing a sound system of internal control and reviewing its effectiveness. This should be incorporated by the company within its normal management and governance processes. It should not be treated as a separate exercise undertaken to meet regulatory requirements.

## The importance of internal control and risk management

10 A company's system of internal control has a key role in the management of risks that are significant to the fulfilment of its business objectives. A sound system of internal control contributes to safeguarding the shareholders' investment and the company's assets.

11 Internal control (as referred to in paragraph 20) facilitates the effectiveness and efficiency of operations, helps ensure the reliability of internal and external reporting and assists compliance with laws and regulations.

12 Effective financial controls, including the maintenance of proper accounting records, are an important element of internal control. They help ensure that the company is not unnecessarily exposed to avoidable financial risks and that financial information used within the business and for publication is reliable. They also contribute to the safeguarding of assets, including the prevention and detection of fraud.

13 A company's objectives, its internal organisation and the environment in which it operates are continually evolving and, as a result, the risks it faces are continually changing. A sound system of internal control therefore depends on a thorough and regular evaluation of the nature and extent of the risks to which the company is exposed. Since profits are, in part, the reward for successful risk-taking in business, the purpose of internal control is to help manage and control risk appropriately rather than to eliminate it.

## Groups of companies

14 Throughout this guidance, where reference is made to 'company' it should be taken, where applicable, as referring to the group of which the reporting company is the parent company. For groups of companies, the review of effectiveness of internal control and the report to the shareholders should be from the perspective of the group as a whole.

## 1 The Appendix

15 The Appendix to this document contains questions which boards may wish to consider in applying this guidance.

## MAINTAINING A SOUND SYSTEM OF INTERNAL CONTROL

### Responsibilities

16 The board of directors is responsible for the company's system of internal control. It should set appropriate policies on internal control and seek regular assurance that will enable it to satisfy itself that the system is functioning effectively. The board must further ensure that the system of internal control is effective in managing risks in the manner which it has approved.

17 In determining its policies with regard to internal control, and thereby assessing what constitutes a sound system of internal control in the particular circumstances of the company, the board's deliberations should include consideration of the following factors:
- the nature and extent of the risks facing the company;
- the extent and categories of risk which it regards as acceptable for the company to bear;
- the likelihood of the risks concerned materialising;
- the company's ability to reduce the incidence and impact on the business of risks that do materialise; and
- the costs of operating particular controls relative to the benefit thereby obtained in managing the related risks.

18 It is the role of management to implement board policies on risk and control. In fulfilling its responsibilities, management should identify and evaluate the risks faced by the company for consideration by the board and design, operate and monitor a suitable system of internal control which implements the policies adopted by the board.

19 All employees have some responsibility for internal control as part of their accountability for achieving objectives. They, collectively, should have the necessary knowledge, skills, information and authority to establish, operate and monitor the system of internal control. This will require an understanding of the company, its objectives, the industries and markets in which it operates, and the risks it faces.

### Elements of a sound system of internal control

20 An internal control system encompasses the policies, processes, tasks, behaviours and other aspects of a company that, taken together:
- facilitate its effective and efficient operation by enabling it to respond appropriately to significant business, operational, financial, compliance and other risks to achieving the company's objectives. This includes the safeguarding of assets from inappropriate use or from loss and fraud, and ensuring that liabilities are identified and managed;
- help ensure the quality of internal and external reporting. This requires the maintenance of proper records and processes that generate a flow of timely, relevant and reliable information from within and outside the organisation;
- help ensure compliance with applicable laws and regulations, and also with internal policies with respect to the conduct of business.

21  A company's system of internal control will reflect its control environment which encompasses its organisational structure. The system will include:
- control activities;
- information and communications processes; and
- processes for monitoring the continuing effectiveness of the system of internal control.

22  The system of internal control should:
- be embedded in the operations of the company and form part of its culture;
- be capable of responding quickly to evolving risks to the business arising from factors within the company and to changes in the business environment; and
- include procedures for reporting immediately to appropriate levels of management any significant control failings or weaknesses that are identified together with details of corrective action being undertaken.

23  A sound system of internal control reduces, but cannot eliminate, the possibility of poor judgement in decision-making; human error; control processes being deliberately circumvented by employees and others; management overriding controls; and the occurrence of unforeseeable circumstances.

24  A sound system of internal control therefore provides reasonable, but not absolute, assurance that a company will not be hindered in achieving its business objectives, or in the orderly and legitimate conduct of its business, by circumstances which may reasonably be foreseen. A system of internal control cannot, however, provide protection with certainty against a company failing to meet its business objectives or all material errors, losses, fraud, or breaches of laws or regulations.

## REVIEWING THE EFFECTIVENESS OF INTERNAL CONTROL

### Responsibilities

25  Reviewing the effectiveness of internal control is an essential part of the board's responsibilities. The board will need to form its own view on effectiveness after due and careful enquiry based on the information and assurances provided to it. Management is accountable to the board for monitoring the system of internal control and for providing assurance to the board that it has done so.

26  The role of board committees in the review process, including that of the audit committee, is for the board to decide and will depend upon factors such as the size and composition of the board; the scale, diversity and complexity of the company's operations; and the nature of the significant risks that the company faces. To the extent that designated board committees carry out, on behalf of the board, tasks that are attributed in this guidance document to the board, the results of the relevant committees' work should be reported to, and considered by, the board. The board takes responsibility for the disclosures on internal control in the annual report and accounts.

### The process for reviewing effectiveness

27  Effective monitoring on a continuous basis is an essential component of a sound system of internal control. The board cannot, however, rely solely on the embedded monitoring processes within the company to discharge its responsibilities. It should regularly receive

and review reports on internal control. In addition, the board should undertake an annual assessment for the purposes of making its public statement on internal control to ensure that it has considered all significant aspects of internal control for the company for the year under review and up to the date of approval of the annual report and accounts.

28 The reference to 'all controls' in Code Provision D.2.1 should not be taken to mean that the effectiveness of every internal control (including controls designed to manage immaterial risks) should be subject to review by the board. Rather it means that, for the purposes of this guidance, internal controls considered by the board should include all types of controls including those of an operational and compliance nature, as well as internal financial controls.

29 The board should define the process to be adopted for its review of the effectiveness of internal control. This should encompass both the scope and frequency of the reports it receives and reviews during the year, and also the process for its annual assessment, such that it will be provided with sound, appropriately documented, support for its statement on internal control in the company's annual report and accounts.

30 The reports from management to the board should, in relation to the areas covered by them, provide a balanced assessment of the significant risks and the effectiveness of the system of internal control in managing those risks. Any significant control failings or weaknesses identified should be discussed in the reports, including the impact that they have had, could have had, or may have, on the company and the actions being taken to rectify them. It is essential that there be openness of communication by management with the board on matters relating to risk and control.

31 When reviewing reports during the year, the board should:
- consider what are the significant risks and assess how they have been identified, evaluated and managed;
- assess the effectiveness of the related system of internal control in managing the significant risks, having regard, in particular, to any significant failings or weaknesses in internal control that have been reported;
- consider whether necessary actions are being taken promptly to remedy any significant failings or weaknesses; and
- consider whether the findings indicate a need for more extensive monitoring of the system of internal control.

32 Additionally, the board should undertake an annual assessment for the purpose of making its public statement on internal control. The assessment should consider issues dealt with in reports reviewed by it during the year together with any additional information necessary to ensure that the board has taken account of all significant aspects of internal control for the company for the year under review and up to the date of approval of the annual report and accounts.

33 The board's annual assessment should, in particular, consider:
- the changes since the last annual assessment in the nature and extent of significant risks, and the company's ability to respond to changes in its business and the external environment;
- the scope and quality of management's ongoing monitoring of risks and of the system of internal control, and, where applicable, the work of its internal audit function and other providers of assurance;

- the extent and frequency of the communication of the results of the monitoring to the board (or board committee(s)) which enables it to build up a cumulative assessment of the state of control in the company and the effectiveness with which risk is being managed;
- the incidence of significant control failings or weaknesses that have been identified at any time during the period and the extent to which they have resulted in unforeseen outcomes or contingencies that have had, could have had, or may in the future have, a material impact on the company's financial performance or condition; and
- the effectiveness of the company's public reporting processes.

34 Should the board become aware at any time of a significant failing or weakness in internal control, it should determine how the failing or weakness arose and re-assess the effectiveness of management's ongoing processes for designing, operating and monitoring the system of internal control.

## THE BOARD'S STATEMENT ON INTERNAL CONTROL

35 In its narrative statement of how the company has applied Code principle D.2, the board should, as a minimum, disclose that there is an ongoing process for identifying, evaluating and managing the significant risks faced by the company, that it has been in place for the year under review and up to the date of approval of the annual report and accounts, that it is regularly reviewed by the board and accords with the guidance in this document.

36 The board may wish to provide additional information in the annual report and accounts to assist understanding of the company's risk management processes and system of internal control.

37 The disclosures relating to the application of principle D.2 should include an acknowledgement by the board that it is responsible for the company's system of internal control and for reviewing its effectiveness. It should also explain that such a system is designed to manage rather than eliminate the risk of failure to achieve business objectives, and can only provide reasonable and not absolute assurance against material misstatement or loss.

38 In relation to Code provision D.2.1, the board should summarise the process it (where applicable, through its committees) has applied in reviewing the effectiveness of the system of internal control. It should also disclose the process it has applied to deal with material internal control aspects of any significant problems disclosed in the annual report and accounts.

39 Where a board cannot make one or more of the disclosures in paragraphs 35 and 38, it should state this fact and provide an explanation. The Listing Rules require the board to disclose if it has failed to conduct a review of the effectiveness of the company's system of internal control.

40 The board should ensure that its disclosures provide meaningful, high-level information and do not give a misleading impression.

41 Where material joint ventures and associates have not been dealt with as part of the group for the purposes of applying this guidance, this should be disclosed.

## INTERNAL AUDIT

42  Provision D.2.2 of the Code states that companies which do not have an internal audit function should from time to time review the need for one.

43  The need for an internal audit function will vary depending on company-specific factors including the scale, diversity and complexity of the company's activities and the number of employees, as well as cost/benefit considerations. Senior management and the board may desire objective assurance and advice on risk and control. An adequately resourced internal audit function (or its equivalent where, for example, a third party is contracted to perform some or all of the work concerned) may provide such assurance and advice. There may be other functions within the company that also provide assurance and advice covering specialist areas such as health and safety, regulatory and legal compliance and environmental issues.

44  In the absence of an internal audit function, management needs to apply other monitoring processes in order to assure itself and the board that the system of internal control is functioning as intended. In these circumstances, the board will need to assess whether such processes provide sufficient and objective assurance.

45  When undertaking its assessment of the need for an internal audit function, the board should also consider whether there are any trends or current factors relevant to the company's activities, markets or other aspects of its external environment, that have increased, or are expected to increase, the risks faced by the company. Such an increase in risk may also arise from internal factors such as organisational restructuring or from changes in reporting processes or underlying information systems. Other matters to be taken into account may include adverse trends evident from the monitoring of internal control systems or an increased incidence of unexpected occurrences.

46  The board of a company that does not have an internal audit function should assess the need for such a function annually having regard to the factors referred to in paragraphs 43 and 45 above. Where there is an internal audit function, the board should annually review its scope of work, authority and resources, again having regard to those factors.

47  If the company does not have an internal audit function and the board has not reviewed the need for one, the Listing Rules require the board to disclose these facts.

## APPENDIX

### Assessing the effectiveness of the company's risk and control processes

Some questions which the board may wish to consider and discuss with management when regularly reviewing reports on internal control and carrying out its annual assessment are set out below. The questions are not intended to be exhaustive and will need to be tailored to the particular circumstances of the company.

This Appendix should be read in conjunction with the guidance set out in this document.

### 1  *Risk assessment*

●  Does the company have clear objectives and have they been communicated so as to provide effective direction to employees on risk assessment and control issues? For example, do objectives and related plans include measurable performance targets and indicators?

- Are the significant internal and external operational, financial, compliance and other risks identified and assessed on an ongoing basis? (Significant risks may, for example, include those related to market, credit, liquidity, technological, legal, health, safety and environmental, reputation, and business probity issues.)

- Is there a clear understanding by management and others within the company of what risks are acceptable to the board?

## 2   Control environment and control activities

- Does the board have clear strategies for dealing with the significant risks that have been identified? Is there a policy on how to manage these risks?

- Do the company's culture, code of conduct, human resource policies and performance reward systems support the business objectives and risk management and internal control system?

- Does senior management demonstrate, through its actions as well as its policies, the necessary commitment to competence, integrity and fostering a climate of trust within the company?

- Are authority, responsibility and accountability defined clearly such that decisions are made and actions taken by the appropriate people? Are the decisions and actions of different parts of the company appropriately co-ordinated?

- Does the company communicate to its employees what is expected of them and the scope of their freedom to act? This may apply to areas such as customer relations; service levels for both internal and outsourced activities; health, safety and environmental protection; security of tangible and intangible assets; business continuity issues; expenditure matters; accounting; and financial and other reporting.

- Do people in the company (and in its providers of outsourced services) have the knowledge, skills and tools to support the achievement of the company's objectives and to manage effectively risks to their achievement?

- How are processes/controls adjusted to reflect new or changing risks, or operational deficiencies?

## 3   Information and communication

- Do management and the board receive timely, relevant and reliable reports on progress against business objectives and the related risks that provide them with the information, from inside and outside the company, needed for decision-making and management review purposes? This could include performance reports and indicators of change, together with qualitative information such as on customer satisfaction, employee attitudes etc.

- Are information needs and related information systems reassessed as objectives and related risks change or as reporting deficiencies are identified?

- Are periodic reporting procedures, including half-yearly and annual reporting, effective in communicating a balanced and understandable account of the company's position and prospects?

- Are there established channels of communication for individuals to report suspected breaches of laws or regulations or other improprieties?

### 4 *Monitoring*

- Are there ongoing processes embedded within the company's overall business operations, and addressed by senior management, which monitor the effective application of the policies, processes and activities related to internal control and risk management? (Such processes may include control self-assessment, confirmation by personnel of compliance with policies and codes of conduct, internal audit reviews or other management reviews).

- Do these processes monitor the company's ability to re-evaluate risks and adjust controls effectively in response to changes in its objectives, its business, and its external environment?

- Are there effective follow-up procedures to ensure that appropriate change or action occurs in response to changes in risk and control assessments?

- Is there appropriate communication to the board (or board committees) on the effectiveness of the ongoing monitoring processes on risk and control matters? This should include reporting any significant failings or weaknesses on a timely basis.

- Are there specific arrangements for management monitoring and reporting to the board on risk and control matters of particular importance? These could include, for example, actual or suspected fraud and other illegal or irregular acts, or matters that could adversely affect the company's reputation or financial position?

# Appendix 20

## INSTITUTIONAL SHAREHOLDERS' COMMITTEE: THE RESPONSIBILITIES OF INSTITUTIONAL SHAREHOLDERS AND AGENTS – STATEMENT OF PRINCIPLES

### 1 Introduction and Scope

This Statement of Principles has been drawn up by the Institutional Shareholders' Committee.[1] It develops the principles set out in its 1991 statement 'The Responsibilities of Institutional Shareholders in the UK' and expands on the Combined Code of Corporate Governance of June 1998. It sets out best practice for institutional shareholders and/or agents in relation to their responsibilities in respect of investee companies in that they will:

- set out their policy on how they will discharge their responsibilities – clarifying the priorities attached to particular issues and when they will take action – see 2 below;

- monitor the performance of, and establish, where necessary, a regular dialogue with investee companies – see 3 below;

- intervene where necessary – see 4 below;

- evaluate the impact of their activism – see 5 below; and

- report back to clients/beneficial owners – see 5 below.

In this statement the term 'institutional shareholder' includes pension funds, insurance companies, and investment trusts and other collective investment vehicles. Frequently, agents such as investment managers are appointed by institutional shareholders to invest on their behalf.

This statement covers the activities of both institutional shareholders and those that invest as agents, including reporting by the latter to their institutional shareholder clients. The actions described in this statement in general apply only in the case of UK listed companies. They can be applied to any such UK company, irrespective of market capitalisation, although institutional shareholders' and agents' policies may apply *de minimis* limits for reasons of cost-effectiveness or practicability. Institutional shareholders and agents should keep under review how far the principles in this statement can be applied to other equity investments.

The policies of activism set out below do not constitute an obligation to micro-manage the affairs of investee companies, but rather relate to procedures designed to ensure that shareholders derive value from their investments by dealing effectively with concerns over

---

1 In 1991 the members of the Institutional Shareholders' Committee were: the Association of British Insurers; the Association of Investment Trust Companies; the British Merchant Banking and Securities Houses Association; the National Association of Pension Funds; and the Unit Trust Association. In 2002, the members are: the Association of British Insurers; the Association of Investment Trust Companies; the National association of Pension Funds; and the Investment Management Association.

under-performance. Nor do they preclude a decision to sell a holding, where this is the most effective response to such concerns.

Fulfilling fiduciary obligations to end-beneficiaries in accordance with the spirit of this statement may have implications for institutional shareholders' and agents' resources. They should devote appropriate resources, but these should be commensurate with the benefits for beneficiaries. The duty of institutional shareholders and agents is to the end beneficiaries and not to the wider public.

## 2 Setting out their policy on how they will discharge their responsibilities

Both institutional shareholders and agents will have a clear statement of their policy on activism and on how they will discharge the responsibilities they assume. This policy statement will be a public document. The responsibilities addressed will include each of the matters set out below.

- How investee companies will be monitored. In order for monitoring to be effective, where necessary, an active dialogue may need to be entered into with the investee company's board and senior management.

- The policy for requiring investee companies' compliance with the core standards in the Combined Code.

- The policy for meeting with an investee company's board and senior management.

- How situations where institutional shareholders and/or agents have a conflict of interest will be minimised or dealt with.

- The strategy on intervention.

- An indication of the type of circumstances when further action will be taken and details of the type of action that may be taken.

- The policy on voting.

Agents and their institutional shareholder clients should agree by whom these responsibilities are to be discharged and the arrangements for agents reporting back.

## 3 Monitoring performance

Institutional shareholders and/or agents, either directly or through contracted research providers, will review Annual Reports and Accounts, other circulars, and general meeting resolutions. They may attend company meetings where they may raise questions about investee companies' affairs. Also investee companies will be monitored to determine when it is necessary to enter into an active dialogue with the investee company's board and senior management. This monitoring needs to be regular, and the process needs to be clearly communicable and checked periodically for its effectiveness. Monitoring may require sharing information with other shareholders or agents and agreeing a common course of action.

As part of this monitoring, institutional shareholders and/or agents will:

- seek to satisfy themselves, to the extent possible, that the investee company's board and sub-committee structures are effective, and that independent directors provide adequate oversight; and

- maintain a clear audit trail, for example, records of private meetings held with companies, of votes cast, and of reasons for voting against the investee company's management, for abstaining, or for voting with management in a contentious situation.

In summary, institutional shareholders and/or agents will endeavour to identify problems at an early stage to minimise any loss of shareholder value. If they have concerns and do not propose to sell their holdings, they will seek to ensure that the appropriate members of the investee company's board are made aware of them. It may not be sufficient just to inform the Chairman and/or Chief Executive. However, institutional shareholders and/or agents may not wish to be made insiders. Institutional shareholders and/or agents will expect investee companies and their advisers to ensure that information that could affect their ability to deal in the shares of the company is not conveyed to them without their agreement.

## 4   Intervening when necessary

Institutional shareholders' primary duty is to those on whose behalf they invest, for example, the beneficiaries of a pension scheme or the policyholders in an insurance company, and they must act in their best financial interests. Similarly, agents must act in the best interests of their clients. Effective monitoring will enable institutional shareholders and/or agents to exercise their votes and, where necessary, intervene objectively and in an informed way. Where it would make intervention more effective, they should seek to engage with other shareholders.

Many issues could give rise to concerns about shareholder value. Institutional shareholders and/or agents should set out the circumstances when they will actively intervene and how they propose to measure the effectiveness of doing so. Intervention should be considered by institutional shareholders and/or agents regardless of whether an active or a passive investment policy is followed. In addition, being underweight is not, of itself, a reason for not intervening. Instances when institutional shareholders and/or agents may want to intervene include when they have concerns about:

- the company's strategy;

- the company's operational performance;

- the company's acquisition/disposal strategy;

- independent directors failing to hold executive management properly to account;

- internal controls failing;

- inadequate succession planning;

- an unjustifiable failure to comply with the Combined Code;

- inappropriate remuneration levels/incentive packages/severance packages; and

- the company's approach to corporate social responsibility.

If boards do not respond constructively when institutional shareholders and/or agents intervene, then institutional shareholders and/or agents will consider on a case-by-case basis whether to escalate their action, for example, by:

- holding additional meetings with management specifically to discuss concerns;

- expressing concerns through the company's advisers;

- meeting with the Chairman, senior independent director, or with all independent directors;

- intervening jointly with other institutions on particular issues;

- making a public statement in advance of the AGM or an EGM;

- submitting resolutions at shareholders' meetings; and

- requisitioning an EGM, possibly to change the board.

Institutional shareholders and/or agents should vote all shares held directly or on behalf of clients wherever practicable to do so. They will not automatically support the board; if they have been unable to reach a satisfactory outcome through active dialogue then they will register an abstention or vote against the resolution. In both instances it is good practice to inform the company in advance of their intention and the reasons why.

## 5  Evaluation and reporting

Institutional shareholders and agents have responsibility for monitoring and assessing the effectiveness of their activism. Those that act as agents will regularly report to their clients details of how they have discharged their responsibilities. This should include a judgement on the impact and effectiveness of their activism. Such reports will be likely to comprise both qualitative as well as quantitative information. The particular information reported, including the format in which details of how votes have been cast will be presented, will be a matter for agreement between agents and their principals as clients.

Transparency is an important feature of effective shareholder activism. Institutional shareholders and agents should not however be expected to make disclosures that might be counterproductive. Confidentiality in specific situations may well be crucial to achieving a positive outcome.

## 6  Conclusion

The Institutional Shareholders' Committee believes that adoption of these principles will significantly enhance how effectively institutional shareholders and/or agents discharge their responsibilities in relation to the companies in which they invest. To ensure that this is the case, the Institutional Shareholders' Committee will monitor the impact of this statement with a view to reviewing and refreshing it, if needs be, within two years in the light of experience and market developments.

# Appendix 21

## ASSOCIATION OF BRITISH INSURERS: STATEMENT OF POLICY ON VOTING AT COMPANY GENERAL MEETINGS

### Introduction and background

Institutional investors wield significant influence over companies through their voting rights at general meetings. ABI members, who control some 20 per cent of shares listed in the UK, believe it is important that this right be exercised responsibly. This is an essential part of their duty to the millions of savers who place their money with life insurance companies or in pension funds managed by them.

In the light of recent developments, including agreement on the new Higgs Code of corporate governance, the Company Law debate over the role of institutions, the launch of the European Corporate Governance Action Plan and questions over the reliability of the system of registering votes, it is appropriate to set out the views of the Association on best practice in voting.

These views have been endorsed by the ABI Board and Investment Committee. They rest on the over-arching principle that institutions should make active but considered use of their voting power with the aim of securing value over the longer term for those whose money they are investing. This means they should aim to use their votes wherever practicable.

### The voting decision and companies

Members are guided in their voting decisions by their support for the Combined Code on corporate governance and by the ABI's own guidelines,[1] including those on share capital management, remuneration and social responsibility.

Fulfilment of voting responsibilities will involve considering the particular circumstances of the investee company and careful assessment of any explanations for departure from best governance practice set out in the Combined Code. Dialogue with companies is an important part of the process

In keeping with the Institutional Shareholders' Committee (ISC) statement on shareholder responsibilities published in October 2002,[2] the ABI recommends that its members should raise concerns directly with investee companies in the hope of resolving them privately before any critical vote.

---

1 Full guideline details are available on our web-site www.abi.org.uk and on that of our Institutional Voting Information Service www.ivis.co.uk
2 See also web-site references above.

Where companies have declined to address legitimate concerns of investors, the latter should be prepared to vote against the board on relevant resolutions. In these cases they should inform companies of the reasons for their decision.

Investors should seek to make a clear decision to vote in favour of or against each resolution, in preference to the use of an abstention. However, if a decision to abstain is taken, it should represent a warning signal of the extent of shareholder concern, and this message should be conveyed to the company.

Institutions should use their best efforts to ensure that votes cast are properly recorded and collaborate with others as necessary to ensure that the voting process goes smoothly.

## The voting decision and beneficiaries

Institutions should aim for a high level of transparency on voting policy, consistent with the overall aim of generating value for beneficiaries.

Insurance companies should have a clear policy on voting which is approved at board level, publicly available and easily accessible to retail customers and investee companies, preferably via their web-site.[3]

The boards of life companies should monitor implementation of this policy through regular reports from fund managers conducting investment business on their behalf whether in-house or externally.

Such reports should include details of how votes were cast in individual cases. For example, they may highlight instances where the institution abstained or voted against the board and the action taken to convey concerns to the company concerned.

In keeping with the ISC statement, insurance companies conducting business for institutional third parties such as pension funds should have similar report-back arrangements with trustees or those in a similar position of accountability. They should follow the wishes of trustees or beneficial owners in executing votes and where this leads to an adverse voting decision, they should explain the circumstances to the investee company.

The ABI does not believe that there should be a legal requirement to disclose specific voting records to the general public. Some members do so now on a voluntary basis. All are, however, encouraged to monitor demand for such disclosure from retail customers and respond accordingly, taking account of the need to ensure that the context in which decisions were taken is properly explained and understood.

---

3 Such a statement might cover, *inter alia*, the institution's approach to engagement with companies, voting, attendance at annual meetings, board composition, directors' remuneration, audit committee accountability, social responsibility and takeovers.

# Appendix 22

## ICSA: RECOMMENDED BEST PRACTICE ON ELECTRONIC COMMUNICATIONS WITH SHAREHOLDERS

The Companies Act 1985 (Electronic Communications) Order 2000 allows documents which the Companies Act had previously required a company to send out in writing to be sent to shareholders electronically e.g. by e-mail or placed on a website, where shareholders agree.

The Order also makes appropriate amendments to Table A of CA 1985, one of which, an amendment to Regulation 115 (when notices given) reads:

After the words 'notice was given' insert

> 'Proof that a notice contained in an electronic communication was sent in accordance with guidance issued by the Institute of Chartered Secretaries and Administrators shall be conclusive evidence that notice was given'.

The guidance referred to is contained in ICSA's publication *Electronic Communications with Shareholders – A Guide to Recommended Best Practice*: this includes 25 points of recommended best practice (set out below), together with other points that companies should consider before offering the facility to shareholders and a specimen invitation to shareholders to use electronic communications. Detailed guidance on such issues as:

- Offering the facility to shareholders and maintaining an appropriate register

- What to do if electronic communications obviously fail

- Records necessary to establish 'proof of sending'

- Security, use of a unique identifier, encryption, etc.

- Identification of audited material on a web-site

- Electronic delivery of proxy form

### The ICSA's 25 Points of Recommended Best Practice

It is recommended best practice that:

1 a company takes steps to amend its Articles specifically to facilitate the use of electronic communications as soon as is practical. (para 2.2)

2 the invitation to shareholders to use electronic communications includes full details of any particular software or equipment specifications which will be required to enable the shareholder to take advantage of the options being made available. (para 3.10)

3 shareholders electing to use computer based electronic communications are warned that any electronic communication, including the filing of an electronic proxy form, found to contain a computer virus will not be accepted by the company. (para 3.15)

4 the offer and provision of a facility to communicate with shareholders electronically should not discriminate between shareholders of the same class and should include a statement reassuring shareholders of that fact. The invitation to participate and provision of the facility should be made available to all shareholders on equal terms and in such a way as to make it as simple as possible for shareholders to participate. (para 4.3)

5 the initial invitation to use electronic means of communications should be sent by post to each member of the company. The invitation should detail which documents will be available by which means and explain the procedures that will be adopted in each case. (para 4.4)

6 the list of alternative delivery mechanisms offered by the company should specifically include an option to continue to receive all material in hard copy by post. (para 4.5)

7 the company should, at least once each year, repeat the invitation to use electronic communications to those shareholders who continue to receive hard copy material. Such an offer should be included at the latest with the Notice of the Annual General Meeting unless the company has elected not to hold an AGM. (para 4.8)

8 the invitation to opt to use electronic communications should include clear advice on how to register an election. This should include any dedicated telephone number, fax number or e-mail address provided for the purpose and/or the address of an Internet web-site page where the election form may be completed on-line. (para 5.1)

9 where a company is offering shareholders the opportunity to use electronic communications all newly registered shareholders should, within 3 months of registration, be provided with a statement as to the company's policy on electronic shareholder communications together with a copy of the facility letter providing the shareholder with the opportunity to register his/her choice. (para 5.3)

10 the company's web-site should include fax and telephone numbers and an 'on-line' facility to enable shareholders to notify the company of any change in their choice of communication medium or contact details. (para 6.2)

11 where the information being made available on a web-site includes a notice of a general meeting, the 'notification of availability' should:
   - Draw specific attention to that fact;
   - Indicate the date, time and place of the meeting;
   - Highlight any applicable deadlines e.g. for the return of proxy forms; and
   - include any special or non-routine business (such as proposed amendments to the Articles or Members' (s.376) resolutions) that may be on the Agenda (para 7.2)

12 an e-mail notifying a shareholder that information is being made available on a web-site should contain a hyperlink direct to the appropriate pages of the web-site to enable the information to be accessed as simply as possible. (para 7.3)

13 when notices are delivered by telephone, the company should compile and retain a suitable evidential record of all those contacted with the date and time of the call. (para 8.6)

14 when information or notifications of availability are sent by fax a comprehensive transaction report or log generated by the fax machine should be suitably certified and retained by or on behalf of the company as 'proof of sending'. (para 8.7)

15  when information or notifications of availability are sent by e-mail the company should ensure that it uses a system which produces either confirmation of the total number of recipients sent to or, preferably, a record of each recipient to whom the message has been sent. A copy of such record and any notices of any failed transmissions and subsequent re-sending, suitably certified, should be retained by or on behalf of the company as 'proof of sending'. (para 8.8)

16  the company should alert those shareholders electing to receive communications electronically that the company's obligation is satisfied when it transmits an electronic message and that it cannot be held responsible for a failure in transmission beyond its control. (para 8.9)

17  the company should where it is aware of the failure in delivery of an electronic communication (and subsequent attempts do not remedy the situation) revert to sending a hard copy of the communication by mail to the recipient's last known postal address. This should be done within 48 hours of the original attempt. The company should include a standard notice advising the shareholder why he/she is being sent a copy by post and should take the opportunity of asking him/her to confirm his contact details. (para 8.10)

18  electronic proxy forms should contain:
- Clear instructions as to the address to which the proxy form should be returned;
- A warning that a proxy lodged electronically will only be valid if lodged at the address supplied by the company; and
- Where applicable, a notice that proxy appointments may, subject to a specified verification procedure, be made by telephone (para 10.2)

19  each shareholder is allocated a discrete identifier which should be required to be entered on the proxy form, used when logging on to the company's website to complete a proxy 'on-line' or as part of the verification procedure in the case of proxy appointments lodged by telephone (para 10.4)

20  where no poll is demanded, electronically lodged proxy forms should be retained until one month after the meeting. Where a poll is held records should be retained for a period of one year after the meeting. (para 14.3)

21  any e-mail or other electronic address provided by the shareholder for the purposes of electronic communication should not be recorded as part of the publicly available part of the company's register of members. (para 14.4)

22  the company liaises closely with and obtain clearance from its auditors prior to the display of audited information and the Audit Report on a company web-site. (para 15.3)

23  the company should clearly identify 'statutory' information on its web-site and to indicate when the information being viewed forms part of the audited accounts. (para 15.4)

24  the company establishes a routine system of checking that statutory or audited information made available via a web-site has not been tampered with and that the home page of the statutory section of the web-site contains a message indicating the time and date when the contents of that section of the site were last verified. (para 15.8)

25  the company gives serious thought to arranging a form of back up facility for its own web-site. (para 19.6)

# Appendix 23

## ICSA GUIDANCE NOTE: DISCLOSING PROXY VOTES

Following the publication of the Combined Code it has become common practice for companies to disclose proxy instructions lodged 'for' and 'against' each resolution being considered on a show of hands at a General meeting. For ease of explanation, this guide refers to 'proxy votes', but recognizes that it is the proxy appointment that is lodged and that the total voting figure reflecting the proxy instructions may actually change if a poll is declared and the results scrutinized. ICSA have always cautioned that the disclosure of 'proxy votes' should not be made prior to a vote by show of hands as it might be seen as an attempt to influence the vote.

It should be noted that the Combined Code only requires that companies 'except where a poll is called, should indicate the level of proxies lodged on each resolution, and the balance for and against the resolution, after it has been dealt with on a show of hands'[1]. The Hampel Report goes on to explain 'This will indicate publicly the proportion of total votes in respect of which proxies were lodged and the weight of shareholder opinion revealed by those proxy votes. Publication is thus likely to encourage an increase in shareholder voting'[2]. A strict interpretation of this rule means that a reading-out of the figure or the display on a screen is sufficient. This however, as mentioned below, usually means that attendees cannot make a note of the figures and the information is not available to non-attendees. Although such an announcement satisfies the Combined Code, ICSA believes that only publication meets the spirit of the rules.

We also recommend that it be made clear to attendees and the recipients of the published results that the breakdown being provided gives the position as at a given point in time (usually 36–48 hours prior to the meeting). The point being that shareholders may have subsequently amended the instructions to their proxy or, having lodged a proxy form, may have subsequently attended the meeting and, having heard the debate, voted in person thus overriding the proxy instruction.

Several companies project the balance of 'proxy votes' on to a screen immediately following a vote by show of hands but, as mentioned above, some investors have indicated that the information is not always displayed long enough for them to take note of the details. Some companies also publish the information on the company's web-site after the close of the meeting, a practice we strongly support.

Whether or not the 'proxy votes' are displayed or announced during the meeting, ICSA recommends that companies provide a written summary of the 'proxy votes' to be available for shareholders to collect at the end of the meeting as they leave, specifically including and drawing attention to the caveats and notes mentioned above and below.

---

1 Combined Code provision C.2.1.
2 *Committee on Corporate Governance. Final report, January 1998* para.5.14(b).

One of the reasons for publishing the 'proxy votes' is to encourage institutional shareholders into exercising the voting rights attached to their holdings. Notwithstanding the fact that an abstention is not a vote at all, many institutional shareholders would consider an instruction to their proxies to abstain from voting on a resolution as meeting the obligation to 'vote' their shares. ICSA has, therefore, recommended that proxy forms, particularly electronic versions that cannot be altered by hand, should include a 'vote withheld' option (see separate Guidance Note: *Proxy Instructions – Abstentions*).

Another reason for publishing 'proxy votes', is to reassure shareholders that a vote taken by a show of hands has not produced a result at odds with the overall weight of shareholders' opinion.[3] As only 'for' and 'against' votes are taken into account when calculating whether or not a resolution has been passed, it is only necessary to publish the proxy votes cast for and against each resolution. Where the chairman has been appointed proxy with discretion as to how to vote it is suggested that the summary of proxy votes also includes a note to indicate how those votes have been cast (which will, presumably, normally be in favour of management).

Companies should, however, be aware that many investors and other 'interested parties' may also request details of abstentions or 'votes withheld' on the basis that these are considered to be a 'warning shot across the bows'. The problem here though is being able to distinguish between those votes that have been deliberately withheld for the purpose of providing such a 'warning shot' and those where shareholders have, for whatever reason, simply not bothered to vote. There is therefore a danger that providing such information without detailed clarification, which may not always be available, may actually be misleading.

## Proxy Appointment Disclosure Specimen Pro Forma

At the AGM of XYZ PLC held on DD/MM/YYYY, the following levels of proxy appointments and associated voting instructions were received prior to the meeting. Any resolutions that were to be decided by a poll are excluded from the schedule.

| Resolution number | Proxy votes for the resolution | Proxy votes against the resolution |
|---|---|---|
| 1 | 125,056 | 10,215 |
| 2 | 120,004 | 15,267 |

### Notes to the disclosure

1   Any proxy appointments which gave discretion to the Chairman have been included in the 'for' total.[4]

---

3  See Guidance Note on *Polls and Proxies – The Chairman's Obligation*.

4  If however the general meeting has received a resolution from a shareholder, this statement might need to be changed to reflect the board's decision to recommend that the shareholders vote against the resolution, and therefore it will need to state 'that the proxy votes given to the discretion of the Chairman have been voted against the resolution'. This is a complicated area and attention is drawn to the separate guidance note *Polls and Proxies – The Chairman's obligations*.

2   It should be noted that the appointment of a proxy is not an unequivocally precise
    indicator of the way that the shareholder would have voted on a poll, it merely reflects
    their intention at the time the instruction was given. Voting instructions can be changed
    at any time prior to a poll being demanded, and a shareholder having lodged a proxy is
    still entitled to attend the meeting and having heard/participated in the debate vote their
    shares themselves as they see fit.

# Appendix 24

## NAPF: CORPORATE GOVERNANCE POLICY (December 2003)

### Introduction

The members of the National Association of Pension Funds (NAPF) have a clear interest in promoting the success of the Companies in which they invest either directly, in the case of pension funds, or on behalf of their pension fund clients, in the case of investment management firms.

As a consequence of this, the NAPF has long considered that one of its prime functions is to represent these interests on behalf of its membership. This representation takes many forms including, among others, involvement with the Accounting Standards Board and the Financial Reporting Council, membership of the Institutional Shareholders' Committee and representation on the Panel on Takeovers and Mergers and on various Government-appointed committees and investigative bodies.

Throughout all that the NAPF does in the area of investment there are four clear strands:

- The **first** is that the NAPF should assist its members in promoting the success of the Companies in which they invest.

- The **second** is holding the management of these Companies accountable to shareholders.

- The **third** is that the NAPF's efforts should be directed towards maximising the long-term benefit of its membership, irrespective of the potential for short-term discomfort.

- The **fourth** is that the NAPF investment staff, rather than making policy themselves, must take and accept direction from the seasoned practitioners who are elected to the Investment Council by their peers in recognition of their experience and knowledge.

In its work over the years, the NAPF has developed a set of corporate governance policies, codes and working practices which have developed and grown. In 2003 it was decided that these should be re-examined in their entirety and in great detail. The approach that was taken was that every principle, sub-principle and detail should be meticulously examined and tested for its logic and consistency with other parts of our practice. In each area we aspired to determine Good Practice[1] and the hope was that we would thus build a broad and coherent framework of Good Practice in corporate governance.

This major task has now been completed and has benefited from the conscientious scrutiny of the NAPF's Shareholder Affairs Committee and of its Investment Council.

---

1 Throughout this document, the term 'Good Practice' is used to identify the standard which the NAPF considers that its members expect from the Boards and management of the Companies they own.

The NAPF's Corporate Governance Policy comprises the:

- Statement of Underlying Principles and Additional Issues (pages 3–5)

- Voting Guidelines and Appendices (pages 6–58)

Readers of the NAPF's Policy and the Combined Code will be able to determine the likely actions of the NAPF and many of its members and will generally be able to anticipate voting recommendations and decisions derived from the application of the NAPF's Corporate Governance Policy.

Ken Ayers
Chairman, NAPF Investment Council

## Statement of Underlying Principles

1  The welfare of pension fund investors is an economic and social benefit from which society as a whole derives value.

2  The welfare of pension fund investors is no different from the welfare of other long-term investors and this alignment of interest is beneficial to wealth-creation for all participants in society.

3  The interests of management should be aligned with the long-term interests of investors. This principle dictates that managers should hold shares in the business for which they are responsible.

4  It should be clearly recognised that shareholders in aggregate are the owners of Companies and that Boards are their agents.

5  It is essential that shareholders as owners recognise that they have responsibilities to monitor and normally to support the work of the management of the Companies in which they invest. Good corporate governance is about dialogue and the promotion of success. Confrontation is a sign of failure by owners or Boards or, sometimes, both.

6  One of the duties of owners is to allow Company Boards to manage the businesses which have been entrusted to their care without excessive interference. The NAPF robustly supports the Combined Code in its entirety and wishes to add minimal requirements to that body of work. However the NAPF will keep this under review.

7  It is the duty of Boards, as the agents of the owners of the Companies they manage, to set out their interpretation of the objectives, aspirations and culture of the Company in order that the shareholders, as owners, can let it be known whether they share and accept these views.

8  At all times the Board and management should be mindful of the wider perception of the Company in society, bearing in mind that maximisation of short-term gain in a manner which is deemed unacceptable by society as a whole, can seriously damage the longer-term prospects of a Company.

9  The NAPF considers the ownership rights of shareholders to be a principle of fundamental importance. For that reason the NAPF supports the principle underlying pre-emption rights and will not countenance any material erosion of this principle unless a clear case is made for it in the context of the best interests of the owners of the Company concerned. For the same reason the NAPF will generally oppose the creation of any "poison pill" provisions.

The above Principles, together with the principles and detail of the Combined Code, set the framework for the bulk of the NAPF's detailed policies and voting guidelines.

## Additional Issues

There are additional Issues which the NAPF would wish readers to bear in mind.

a   The NAPF considers that the informed use of votes is an obligation (although not a legal duty) of owners and an implicit fiduciary duty of Trustees and of Investment Managers to whom Trustees may delegate this function. In recognition of this, the NAPF policy will recommend active voting, in support of management wherever possible, but will recommend a vote against where appropriate. Recommendations of abstention will rarely be made and, whenever such a recommendation occurs, it will be carefully explained why the NAPF considers that this is the appropriate course of action.

b   Engagement with Companies is a necessary part of good ownership. The NAPF and its associates will engage with Companies at various levels on routine and more serious matters. In addition the NAPF is prepared to facilitate confidential Case Committees for members who have concerns about particular issues and/or about the strategic direction of Companies. Equally, Companies should take great care to ensure that their messages are clearly understood by shareholders and that the concerns of the shareholders are clearly understood by the Board. The roles of the Chairman and the Senior Independent Director in these regards are of the greatest importance.

c   The NAPF expects Boards to show that they accept the terms of the Combined Code by observing its requirements wherever appropriate. Non-compliance must be accompanied by clear and valid explanation. The NAPF policy will be to recommend to its members whenever appropriate that they should not accept "boiler-plate" explanations which provide no valid insights into the reason for a Board choosing to ignore the clearly argued case for the provisions of the Code. Non-acceptance by the NAPF of the reasons for non-compliance will frequently result in the recommendation of a vote against. Notwithstanding this, the NAPF recognises that special circumstances dictate special actions and will go to great lengths to listen to Boards which believe it is appropriate not to comply. Good corporate governance is a matter of principle and nuance, not dogma. Similarly, the NAPF expects Boards to listen to the NAPF and its members in their wish to achieve Good Practice.

d   In all the key areas of Good Practice (as opposed to explicit requirements) identified by the Combined Code the NAPF expects Boards to state unequivocally in the Annual Report that they have met the standard and how they have done so. If they have not done so, clear and valid explanations should be set out which will allow shareholders to determine whether or not they accept the reasoning. The absence of adequate information to reach an informed conclusion will lead the NAPF to conclude that the required standards are not being met and could lead to a recommendation of a vote against the Board, where appropriate.

e   The status of Independent Non-Executive Directors is a bastion of security for shareholders. This has been NAPF policy for some time and more recently has been reinforced by the Higgs report. The NAPF will not accept a dilution of this principle and will monitor the position carefully.

f   Whenever a significant change is made (for example, between the roles of Executive and Non-Executive Director or to an element of remuneration policy) the NAPF expects the matter to be brought before shareholders for a vote of approval at the first possible AGM or EGM. Failure to do this could result in a recommendation of a vote against the Board on a comparable issue.

g   The balance and structure of the Board are of crucial importance to the NAPF and its members. The NAPF has consistently supported the concept of the unitary Board with a healthy balance of Executive Directors and independent Non-Executive Directors. The NAPF sees no contradiction in this statement. All the Directors in a unitary Board are responsible for the strategy and governance of the Company. The Executive Directors are responsible and accountable for the successful implementation of that strategy. The independent Non-Executive Directors have a special responsibility for the oversight of the performance of the Executive Directors and have a key role in managing conflicts in certain of the Board Committees as set out in the Combined Code.

h   The balance and structure of the Board and the role of the Company Secretary in serving the Board as defined in the Combined Code are crucial issues. The NAPF does not believe that the role of Company Secretary can normally be effectively fulfilled by an Executive Director with another role. Furthermore the NAPF expects the resignation of a Non-Executive Director or of a Company Secretary to be announced on a regulatory information service together with a full explanation, at the earliest opportunity.

i   The NAPF expects Nomination Committees to anticipate change by ensuring the proper planning of succession. This is part of the process of refreshing the Board to which reference is made in the Combined Code. Inadequate succession planning could lead the NAPF policy to recommend a vote against the Chairman of the Nomination Committee or another member of that Committee.

j   The Remuneration Committee has a particular responsibility to ensure that Executive Directors and senior management are appropriately rewarded. This is a complex area which, unfortunately, tends to attract a great deal of adverse and, often, uninformed comment. The NAPF supports the principle that the remuneration of Executive Directors should be set at a level which makes it possible to recruit, retain and motivate the right individuals. As a corollary, it should be clear that shareholders' funds should not be squandered by paying more than is deemed to be necessary to achieve these objectives.

Furthermore, the Remuneration Committee must be mindful of the reputational damage which can be caused both externally and within the ranks of the employees of the Company if apparently unjustifiable payments, particularly 'payments for failure', are made to Executive Directors. A system of remuneration should be established which clearly aligns the interests of Executive Directors with those of shareholders. Such a system should be readily explicable and transparent. This can best be achieved by establishing a system of incentives which are harmonised with the stated objectives of the Company as set out in Principle 7 above.

The Principles and Issues, together with the Combined Code, form the basis of the NAPF's Corporate Governance Voting Guidelines. These Principles, Issues and Voting Guidelines will be regularly reviewed by the NAPF.

# Glossary

**accountability:** the requirement for a person in a position of authority to justify, explain and take responsibility for the exercise of his or her performance or actions. Accountability is owed to the person or persons from whom the authority is derived.

**Accounting Standards Board (ASB):** a subsidiary body of the Financial Reporting Council established under the terms of Companies Act 1989 with responsibility for making, amending and withdrawing accounting standards.

**active fund:** an investment fund whose objective is to outperform the market average by actively seeking out stocks that are forecast to provide superior total return.

**agency problem:** the potential for conflicts of interest which arise where an agent (in the context of this book, a director as manager of a company's business) acts and takes decisions on behalf of a principal (in the context of this book, a shareholder as part-owner of a company).

**agent:** a person authorised to carry out business transactions on behalf of another (the principal), who is thereby bound by such actions.

**allotment:** the issue of shares by a company.

**American Depositary Receipt (ADR):** a certificate representing a specified number of shares in a non-US company. The share certificates themselves are held by a US bank (known as a depositary bank) which issues the ADRs, then collects dividends and distributes them to ADR holders after converting them into dollars. The holders of ADRs normally have all the rights of normal shareholders, including voting rights. ADRs are tradable instruments in their own right.

**analyst:** a financial professional working for a bank, fund manager or broker, whose job is to study key industry sectors (e.g. retail, oil, pharmaceuticals), forecast the prospects for the companies operating in them, and make buy and sell recommendations in respect of their shares.

**annual accounts:** financial accounts prepared in fulfilment of the directors' duty to present audited accounts to shareholders in respect of each financial year. Annual accounts of limited companies must be filed with the Registrar of Companies.

**annual general meeting:** a general meeting of a company's shareholders, which must normally be held in each calendar year within 15 months of the previous AGM. A company's first AGM need not be held in the year of incorporation, but must be held within 18 months of incorporation.

**annual report:** a narrative statement prepared in fulfilment of the directors' duty to report to shareholders on the performance of the company over the previous financial year and to disclose specified non-financial information. Annual reports of listed companies typically incorporate the annual accounts.

**annual return:** a form filed each year with the Registrar of Companies containing specified information about a company's directors, secretary, registered office, shareholders, share capital, etc.

**anti-takeover defence:** a measure designed to impede or prevent an unwelcome takeover, for example by increasing the prospective purchaser's costs by issuing new shares carrying severe redemption provisions.

**Articles of Association:** a constitutional document setting out the internal regulations of a company; unless modified or excluded by consent of the shareholders, the specimen Articles in Table A of CA 1985 have effect in public and private companies limited by shares.

**Association of British Insurers (ABI):** the trade association for the UK insurance industry, the members of which account for approximately 20 per cent of shares listed on the London Stock Exchange. The ABI recommends responsible voting within the framework of a considered corporate governance policy but does not make specific recommendations on how its members should vote at company general meetings.

**audit committee:** a committee of the board of directors responsible for a range of audit-related issues, in particular the conduct of the external audit and the company's relationship with its external auditor. The July 2003 version of the Combined Code recommends that the audit committees of listed companies should consist of a least three (or, in the case of smaller companies, two) independent non-executive directors, at least one of whom should have recent and relevant financial experience.

**audit independence:** the ability of external auditors to exercise independent professional judgement without being influenced by the closeness of the relationship with the client company or by considerations of self-interest.

**audit report:** a report to shareholders prepared by the company's external auditors on completion of the statutory audit and included in the company's published annual report and accounts.

**audit:** a process of independent systematic examination, especially of a company's financial accounts.

**auditors:** *See* external auditors, internal auditors.

**authorised share capital:** the maximum amount of share capital (by nominal value and number of shares) that a company is permitted to issue. A company's authorised share capital is stated in its Memorandum of Association and can be increased only with the agreement of shareholders, normally (in the case of public companies) by ordinary resolution in a general meeting.

**balance sheet:** one of the main components of a company's accounts, the balance sheet provides a snapshot of the company's assets and liabilities on a specified date (usually the end of its financial year) and is thus an indicator of the financial health of the company.

**beneficial owner:** the individual who benefits from ownership of a share or other property registered in the name of another person or corporate body (for example, a nominee company, pension fund or other investment body).

**board:** the group of individuals elected by the shareholders of a company to manage its affairs.

**'box-ticking':** the adoption, by listed companies or their shareholders, of a slavish or unreflective approach to corporate governance in which companies' compliance with best practice is assessed on the basis of prescriptive rules rather than by reference to qualitative measures and outcomes.

**Cadbury Code of Best Practice:** a voluntary code of corporate governance applicable to UK listed companies based on the recommendations of the Committee on the Financial Aspects of Corporate Governance chaired by Sir Adrian Cadbury. The Cadbury Code was appended to the Listing Rules in 1993 and remained in effect until its replacement by the Combined Code of Corporate Governance in 1998.

**case law:** the principles and rules of law established by judicial decisions. Under this system the decision reached in a particular case creates a precedent – that is, it is regarded as exemplifying rules of broader application, which must be followed in subsequent cases, except by higher courts.

**chairman:** the director nominated by a company's board to chair its meetings and take the lead in discussions with shareholders. It is established best practice in the UK that the positions of chairman and chief executive officer (CEO) should not be held by the same person.

**chief executive officer (CEO):** the director (usually a full-time employee of the company) nominated by the board to lead the company's executive management team. It is established best practice in the UK that the positions of chief executive officer and chairman should not be held by the same person.

**City Code (or Takeover Code):** rules written and enforced by the Panel on Takeover and Mergers and governing the management and timing of takeover bids involving listed companies. The objective of the City Code is to ensure that high standards of integrity and fairness are maintained, and that shareholders in both the bidding and target company are treated equitably.

**Combined Code of Corporate Governance:** a voluntary code of corporate governance applicable to UK listed companies, which are required by the Listing Rules to disclose whether they comply with the Code and to explain any areas of non-compliance. The original Combined Code introduced in 1998 was replaced by a revised version in July 2003.

**common law:** a body of law based on custom and usage and decisions reached in previous cases. The principles and rules of common law derive from judgments and judicial opinions delivered in response to specific circumstances, not from written legislation.

**company secretary:** an officer of the company with statutory duties (e.g. to sign the annual return and accompanying documents) and charged with a range of duties relating to the company's statutory books and records, filing requirements, etc. Every company must have a secretary who, in the case of a public company, must meet the qualification requirements laid down in the Companies Act.

**company:** an association of persons which, on incorporation, becomes a legal entity entirely separate from the individuals comprising its membership. In the Companies Act 1985, 'company' is restricted to companies registered under that Act or previous Companies Acts.

**comply or explain:** the approach adopted in the UK to compliance by listed companies with best practice in corporate governance. Under this approach, successive codes of corporate governance have been appended to the Listing Rules, with a requirement on listed companies to disclose in their annual reports whether or not they have complied with Code recommendations and, to the extent that they have not, to give reasons for the areas of non-compliance. While the company is under no formal obligation to comply with best practice recommendations, the disclosure obligation ensures that its shareholders can monitor the extent of its compliance, consider the explanations provided by the directors for any areas of non-compliance and, if dissatisfied, express their concerns through their voting behaviour at the AGM.

**concentration of ownership:** a situation, prevalent in some economies, in which a large proportion of the shares in a listed company are held by a single shareholder or a small group of shareholders connected by family ties, cross-shareholdings or other mutual interests.

**conflict of interest:** a situation in which an individual or corporate body is in a position of trust which requires them to exercise judgement on behalf of others, but also has self-interests which interfere with the exercise of their independent judgement.

**connected person:** any person with whom a director is connected, including the spouse, child or stepchild of a director; or any business partner or company associated with a director in which he or she has 20 per cent of the equity share capital (CA 1985, s. 346).

**Co-ordinating Group on Audit and Accounting Issues (CGAA):** a group established by the UK Government to review arrangements for audit and accountancy regulation following the collapse of Enron and other major US corporations. The CGAA produced its interim report in July 2002 and its final report in January 2003.

**corporate social responsibility (CSR):** the recognition by a company of its responsibilities to parties other than shareholders, usually including employees, customers, suppliers, local communities and the environment.

**cross-directorship:** a situation (also known as a 'board interlock') in which the boards of two or more listed companies have directors in common. Cross-directorships are considered to have a detrimental effect on corporate governance by impairing the independence of the directors concerned.

**cross-shareholding:** the holding of shares between two or more publicly listed companies that gives each company involved an equity stake in the other. Prevalent in economies in insider systems, where cross-shareholdings reinforce concentration of ownership; may also be employed as a means of preventing unsolicited takeovers.

**de facto director:** any person occupying the position of a director, even if their appointment or qualifications prove to be invalid.

**debenture:** a bond issued by a company to providers of long-term borrowing, whereby the company agrees to pay a fixed rate of interest ('coupon') to debenture holders each year until maturity, when the loan will be repaid. If the company fails to pay either the interest or the principal amount of the loan at maturity, debenture holders can force the company into liquidation and recover their money from a sale of its assets.

**demutualisation:** in the UK, the process by which building societies have converted from being mutual organisations owned by their members to profit-making companies which distribute profits to their shareholders.

**Department of Trade and Industry (DTI):** The UK Government department responsible for the administration of company law. The Companies Act confers certain powers on the Secretary of State for Trade and Industry.

**director:** an officer of a company responsible for determining policy, supervising the management of the company's business and exercising the powers of the company. Directors must generally carry out these responsibilities collectively as a board.

**directors' report:** a statement attached to the annual accounts containing certain information laid down in the Companies Act 1985.

**distribution:** the transfer of some or all of a company's assets (usually in cash) to its shareholders in proportion to their shareholdings, generally by way of dividend or on a winding up.

**dividend:** the distribution of part of a company's earnings to shareholders, usually twice a year in the form of a main dividend and an interim dividend. The directors of a company have discretion as to the size of a dividend or whether to pay a dividend at all.

**due diligence:** a systematic investigation into a company's financial position, past performance, legal liabilities, etc. before a deal is done to ensure that no unexpected problems emerge afterwards. Due diligence is generally carried out by companies or their advisers before acquiring or merging with another company. The July 2003 version of the Combined Code of Corporate Governance recommends that prospective directors should also carry out a process of due diligence before joining the board of a company with which they have no prior involvement.

**elective resolution:** a resolution, of which 21 days' notice must be given, requiring unanimous approval at a general meeting of a private company.

**equity:** the amount which shareholders own in a publicly quoted company. Equity is the risk-bearing part of the company's capital and contrasts with debt capital which is usually secured in some way and which has priority over shareholders if the company becomes insolvent and its assets are distributed. For most companies there are two types of equity: ordinary shares, which have voting rights, and preference shares, which do not. Owners of preference shares rank ahead of ordinary shareholders in a liquidation.

**executive director:** a member of a company's board of directors who is also an employee of the company.

**'exit':** the ability of shareholders to maintain, increase or dispose of their shareholdings in a company according to their opinion of the performance of the business and the quality of the directors.

**external auditors:** firms, or partners and staff of such firms, which provide financial audit (and often other consultancy) services to client companies, particularly in association with the statutory audit.

**extraordinary general meeting (EGM):** any general meeting of the company's members that is not an annual general meeting. An EGM is required to approve certain special resolutions, e.g. for a takeover or merger or break-up of the company. For such resolutions to be passed, 75 per cent of more of the shareholders have to vote for it.

**extraordinary resolution:** a resolution requiring a 75 per cent majority at a general meeting.

**fiduciary duties:** the duties of a trustee: the directors of a company are given their powers in trust by the company and therefore have fiduciary duties towards it, obliging them to act always in good faith and not to derive a personal profit from their position.

**Financial Reporting Council (FRC):** a body established under the terms of Companies Act 1989 to promote good financial reporting by UK companies.

**Financial Reporting Review Panel (FRRP):** a subsidiary body of the FRC established under the terms of Companies Act 1989 to examine departures from accounting requirements by public and large private companies and if necessary to seek an order from the court to remedy them.

**FTSE 100:** one of the Financial Times Stock Exchange indices designed to give investors an idea of the overall value and general movement of the stock market. The FTSE 100 is an index of the share prices of the 100 largest companies (by market capitalisation) in the UK and is updated throughout the trading day in real time.

**fund manager:** a financial professional employed by an investment trust, unit trust, pension fund or other investing institution to decide how its funds should be invested. Fund managers have considerable influence over the prices of company shares because of the large amounts of money for which they are responsible.

**general meeting:** a meeting of the company which all members (subject to any restrictions in the company's Articles) are entitled to attend.

**Greenbury Code of Best Practice:** a voluntary code of best practice on remuneration policy and the setting of individual directors' remuneration applicable to UK listed companies and based on the recommendations of the Study Group on Directors' Remuneration chaired by Sir Richard Greenbury. The Cadbury Code was appended to the Listing Rules in 1995 and remained in effect until its replacement by the Combined Code of Corporate Governance in 1998.

**Hampel Committee:** a Committee on Corporate Governance chaired by Sir Ronald Hampel and established in 1995 to review the implementation and effectiveness of the Cadbury Code of Corporate Governance and the Greenbury Code of Best Practice on directors' remuneration. In line with the Hampel Committee's findings, a Combined Code of Corporate Governance was appended to the Listing Rules in 1998.

**Higgs Report:** the report on the role and effectiveness of non-executive directors produced by Derek Higgs and published in January 2003.

**hostile takeover:** an unsolicited takeover not supported by the board of directors of the target company.

**independence:** in general terms, the state of being free from the influence of another individual or individuals and free from any conflict of interest. In the specific context of the July 2003 Combined Code, an independent non-executive director is one who is independent in character and judgement and who has no relationships or circumstances which are likely to affect, or could appear to affect, his or her judgement. A non-executive director may be considered not to be independent if he or she has been an employee of the company or group within the last five years; has, or has had within the last three years, a material business relationship with the company either directly, or as a partner, shareholder, director or senior employee of a body that has such a relationship with the company; has received or receives additional remuneration from the company apart from a director's fee; participates in the company's share option or a performance-related pay scheme, or is a member of the company's pension scheme; has close family ties with any of the company's advisers, directors or senior employees; holds cross-directorships or has significant links with other directors through involvement in other companies or bodies; represents a significant shareholder; or has served on the board for more than nine years from the date of their first election.

**insider dealing:** share dealings by employees of a company or other individuals who use price-sensitive information not available to the market for personal gain or the gain of their associates. Insider dealing is a criminal offence under Part V of the Criminal Justice Act 1993.

**insider trading:** the term used in the US for the criminal offence known in the UK as insider dealing.

**institutional shareholder:** a financial institution, such as a pension fund or insurance company, which invests money in the share, bond and other financial markets on behalf of underlying investors and savers.

**internal audit:** employees of a company with responsibility for evaluating and providing assurance on the integrity and effectiveness of the company's system of internal controls.

**investor relations:** the process by which a company communicates with its shareholders and the wider investment community; used particularly in relation to the company's contacts with institutional shareholders and analysts.

**issued share capital:** the nominal value of the shares that a company has actually issued. The company's issued share capital must not exceed its authorised share capital.

*keiretsu:* in Japan, an alliance among suppliers and other companies that operate vertically and horizontally, centred on a bank or other financial institution.

**limited company:** a company in which the liability of members for the debts of the company is limited, either to the amount of share capital for which they have subscribed (a company limited by shares) or to a specific amount guaranteed in the event of a winding up (a company limited by guarantee).

**limited liability:** a legal arrangement whereby the potential liability of members for the debts of a company is limited either to the nominal value of their shares (in the case of a company limited by shares) or to a specific amount guaranteed in the event of a winding up (in the case of a company limited by guarantee). In either case, the personal assets of members are not at risk if the company becomes insolvent and is liquidated.

**liquidation:** the process by which a company ceases to trade and realises its assets for distribution to creditors and then shareholders. Also known as a 'winding up'.

**liquidity:** in financial markets, the ease of dealing in a particular share or other financial instrument, measured by the readiness with which shares can be bought and sold without significantly affecting their price. Broadly speaking, liquidity is achieved where companies have large numbers of shares in issues and available for trading on stock markets in which there are many potential buyers and sellers. In contrast, markets tend to be illiquid where companies have few shares in issue and where there are few potential buyers and sellers.

**listed company:** in the UK, a company whose shares are listed by the UKLA and admitted for trading on the London Stock Exchange.

**listing:** the process by which a company's shares become tradable on a stock exchange.

**listing particulars:** details which a company is obliged to publish about itself and its securities before it can obtain a listing on a recognised stock exchange.

**Listing Rules:** rules published by the UKLA setting out the conditions for admission to listing and specifying the ongoing obligations of listed companies, particularly in respect of disclosure of information.

**London Stock Exchange (LSE):** the principal UK stock exchange.

**majority shareholder(s):** a shareholder, or alliance of shareholders, holding a majority of the voting shares in a company and so having a controlling interest over its affairs.

**management board:** in a two-tier board structure, a board comprising executive managers of the company and having responsibility for the operational performance of the business. A management board will typically be chaired by the chief executive officer and report to the company's supervisory board.

**market abuse:** a civil offence created by FSMA 2000 for which an individual can be fined by the FSA. Market abuse occurs when an individual distorts a market in investments, creates a false or misleading impression of the value or price of an investment, or otherwise misuses relevant information before it is published.

**market capitalisation:** the market value of a listed company, calculated by multiplying its current share price by the number of shares in issue.

**median:** the value of the middle item when all the items in a data set are arranged from lowest to highest: the median is the value halfway through the ordered data set, below and above which there lies an equal number of data values.

**Memorandum of Association:** a constitutional document stating the company's name, domicile, objects, limitations of liability (where applicable) and authorised share capital.

**minority shareholders:** shareholders whose combined shareholdings in a company are insufficient to enable them to influence the outcome of votes at a general meeting.

**Model Code:** a code for transactions in the securities of listed companies by directors, certain employees and persons connected with them. The Model Code is promulgated by the UKLA and incorporated within the Listing Rules.

**Myners Report:** a report of a review of institutional investment carried out on behalf of the UK government by Paul Myners and published in March 2001.

**Nasdaq:** (US) the National Association of Securities Dealers Automated Quotations system, an electronic stock market established by the National Association of Securities Dealers.

**National Association of Pension Funds (NAPF):** an umbrella body representing 75 per cent of occupational pension funds in the UK, accounting for some 20 per cent of shares listed on the London Stock Exchange. Through its Voting Issues Service (VIS), NAPF monitors the corporate governance practices of listed companies and makes recommendations to its members on the exercise of their voting powers at company general meetings.

**New York Stock Exchange (NYSE):** the largest stock exchange in the US.

**nominal value:** the 'face value' of a share, expressed as the proportion of the company's issued share capital represented by each of the shares in issue. The nominal value of a share defines the extent of the shareholder's liability to contribute to the company's debts at liquidation, but generally bears no relation to the share's market price.

**nomination committee:** a committee of the board of directors responsible for leading the process for board appointments. The July 2003 Combined Code recommends that the nomination committees of listed companies should consist of non-executive directors, a majority of whom should be independent, and should be chaired by the chairman of the company or the senior independent director.

**non-audit services:** services other than the statutory audit performed by a firm of auditors on behalf of an audit client. From the point of view of corporate governance, there are concerns that the performance of non-audit services by an external auditor may compromise the auditor's objectivity and independence, particularly where the fees payable are substantial in relation to the statutory audit fee.

**non-executive director:** a member of a company's board of directors who is not an employee of the company and who has no involvement in the day-to-day management of its operations.

**objects:** the purpose for which the company was incorporated, as set out in the objects clause of its Memorandum of Association. Most companies are formed with general trading objects rather than specific objects.

**Official List:** the main exchange of the London Stock Exchange whose members tend to be the larger quoted or listed companies.

**Operating and Financial Review (OFR):** a narrative statement intended to provide shareholders and other users with systematic and objective information on which to base their assessment of the business, including qualitative disclosures on the key dependencies of the business, the company's relationships with customers, suppliers and employees, and the factors and influences likely to affect future performance. Currently, preparation of an OFR is voluntary, but proposals for a mandatory OFR for major companies have been accepted by the UK Government.

**ordinary resolution:** a resolution proposed at a general meeting of shareholders, which may be carried by a simple majority of votes actually cast.

**ordinary shares:** the most common form of shares in a company, conferring on holders the right to share in the company's profits in proportion to their holdings and (with occasional exceptions) the right to vote at general meetings.

**OECD:** The Organisation for Economic Co-operation and Development, the member countries of which are Australia, Austria, Belgium, Canada, Czech Republic, Denmark, Finland, France, Germany, Greece, Hungary, Iceland, Ireland, Italy, Japan, Korea, Luxembourg, the Netherlands, New Zealand, Mexico, Norway, Poland, Portugal, Spain, Sweden, Switzerland, Turkey, the UK and US.

**outside director (US):** a member of a corporation's board of directors who is not an employee of the corporation and who has no involvement in the day-to-day management of its operations.

**pension fund:** a fund set up by a company, union, government entity or other organisation to invest the pension contributions of members and employees, and pay out pensions to those people when they reach retirement age. Pension funds accumulate huge pools of capital, which they invest in the stock markets. As a result, they exert considerable influence on the markets, and their decisions on which shares to hold in which sectors have a substantial impact on prices.

**Pensions Investments Research Consultants Ltd (PIRC):** a company which produces investment advice and voting recommendations for its clients, mainly local authority and other public sector pension funds. PIRC is in some respects the most radical of the institutional investor bodies and is active in the public policy debate on issues of corporate governance and socially responsible investment.

**preference shares:** shares which give their holders the right to payment of a fixed dividend out of profits before the payment of an ordinary dividend or the preferential return of capital or both, but which do not usually carry voting rights.

**price-sensitive information:** information which, if made public, is likely to have a significant effect on the price of a company's securities. Such information must, in connection with a listed company, be reported via the London Stock Exchange so that it can be released to the market in a manner that is fair to all investors.

**privatisation:** in the UK, the sale of government-owned equity in nationalised industries or other commercial enterprises to private investors.

**profit and loss account:** a set of accounts, prepared annually, which depicts a company's trading performance. It is normally read in conjunction with the balance sheet and cash flow data.

**profits warning:** an announcement issued via the London Stock Exchange in circumstances where a listed company's directors expect its profits to be lower than forecast by analysts and other market participants. The warning is released to ensure that all investors have access to the news at the same time.

**prospectus:** a document published in accordance with the Listing Rules in the form of a notice, circular, investment advertisement or other invitation to the public to subscribe for or purchase a company's shares or debentures.

**proxy:** a person authorised by a shareholder to vote on his or her behalf at a general meeting.

**Public Accounting Oversight Board (US):** a regulatory body established under the terms of the Sarbanes-Oxley Act with responsibility for registration, inspection and discipline of public accounting firms, including the establishment of auditing, quality control, ethical, independence and other standards relating to the preparation of audit reports.

**public company:** a company which meets specified requirements as to its minimum share capital and which is registered as a public company. Only public companies are allowed to offer shares and debentures to the public.

**Public Interest Disclosure Act 1998:** UK legislation which protects from victimisation or discrimination workers who report known or suspected wrongdoings in their workplaces in relation to criminal acts; failure to comply with legal duties (such as negligence or breach of contract); miscarriages of justice; danger to health and safety; damage to the environment; and deliberate cover-up of any of these.

**quoted companies:** for purposes of UK legislation and regulation, companies listed in any state of the European Economic Area (the EU plus Iceland, Norway and Liechtenstein) and on NYSE and Nasdaq.

**'rational apathy':** an economic theory which states that, where share ownership in large publicly quoted companies is widely dispersed, it may not be worthwhile for individual shareholders to devote time, effort and resources to trying to change unacceptable management behaviour. Traditionally used by institutional investors to justify reluctance to exercise voting powers, the concept of rational apathy is increasingly being challenged by reference to the fiduciary duties of institutions to act responsibly on behalf of underlying beneficiaries.

**registered office:** the address at which legal documents may be served on the company and at which its statutory books are normally kept. The registered office need not be the company's place of business and may be changed freely so long as it remains in the company's country of origin.

**Registrar of Companies:** the official responsible for maintaining the company records filed under the requirements of the Companies Acts.

**remuneration committee:** a committee of the board of directors responsible for determining the company's remuneration policy and setting the remuneration of individual executive directors. The July 2003 Combined Code recommends that the remuneration committees of listed companies should consist exclusively of independent non-executive directors.

**resolution:** a decision reached by a requisite majority of the shareholders of a company voting in person or by proxy at a general meeting of shareholders; in the case of a written resolution, a decision approved in writing by all shareholders.

**rewards for failure:** the perception, currently prevalent in the UK, that the severance terms paid to directors leaving their positions for reasons of under-performance fail to take account of poor performance and disappointing results for shareholders.

**rights issue:** an offer made by a listed company to its shareholders to enable them to buy new shares in the company at a discount to the market price. Existing shareholders are usually offered shares in proportion to their existing holding. Because the new shares are offered at a discount to the current market price, the rights have a value in themselves and can be separately sold.

**risk management:** the process of analysing a company's exposure to financial and non-financial risk and determining how to best handle such exposure.

**Sarbanes-Oxley Act** (formally the Public Company Accounting Reform and Investor Protection Act of 2002): US legislation adopted in the light of Enron and other major corporate failures. Significant provisions include measures intended to restore investor confidence in company financial reports, safeguard the integrity of the audit process and strengthen audit regulation.

**Securities and Exchange Commission (SEC):** the US federal agency empowered to regulate US financial markets in order to protect investors. All US quoted companies have to comply with SEC rules and regulations, including the filing of quarterly results statements.

**senior independent director:** the recognised senior member of the non-executive element on a company's board, other than the chairman.

**shadow director:** any person, including a corporate body such as a bank, in accordance with whose directions or instructions the other directors of the company are accustomed to act.

**share:** a unit of ownership of a company, representing a fraction of the share capital and usually conferring rights to participate in distributions. There may be several kinds of shares each carrying different rights. Shares are issued at a fixed nominal value, although the company may actually receive a larger amount, the excess representing share premium. Shareholders may not be required to subscribe the full amount immediately, in which case the shares are partly paid. The shareholders then await calls, which require them to pay further amounts until the shares are fully paid.

**share capital:** the proportion of the company's capital which is contributed by shareholders on the issue of ordinary shares and preference shares.

**share option:** an incentive given to company directors and employees in the form of an option to buy shares in the company at a fixed price at a defined future date.

**share registrar:** an organisation which maintains the register of shareholders on behalf of a client company. Registrars are generally responsible for the issue of share certificates, the despatch of company communications to shareholders and the processing of proxy voting returns and other shareholder responses.

**shareholder:** as defined by s. 22 of the Companies Act 1985, a member of a company limited by shares who has both agreed to become a member of the company (whether by subscription to the Memorandum, by acquisition, by way of allotment or transfer or by transmission) and has been registered as such in the company's register of members.

**Smith Report:** the report and proposed guidance on audit committees by a group chaired by Sir Robert Smith and published by the Financial Reporting Council in January 2003.

**socially responsible investing (SRI):** an investment strategy that seeks to achieve a balance between financial returns and wider social benefits, usually by investing in companies which are judged to operate to appropriate standards of social, ethical and environmental responsibility.

**special resolution:** a resolution of which 21 clear days' notice must be given and which must be approved by 75 per cent of the votes cast in general meeting.

**stakeholder:** an individual or group with a direct interest in a company's performance or conduct, either because of a financial or non-financial investment in the company or because of the impact of the company's activities; stakeholders may include shareholders, employees, customers, suppliers, competitors, local communities, government and regulators and proxies for the natural environment.

**statute law:** the body of law represented by legislation and thus occurring in authoritative written form. Statute law contrasts with common law, over which it takes precedence.

**statutory audit:** independent examination of, and expression of expert professional opinion on, the published financial statements of a company on behalf of its shareholders.

**statutory books:** a general term applied to the registers and minute books etc. that a company is required by the Companies Act to maintain.

**Summary Financial Statement (SFS):** a short-form version of the annual report and accounts which UK listed companies are permitted by the Companies (Summary Financial Statement) Regulations 1995 (SI 1995/2092) to send to shareholders and other recipients who do not specifically elect to receive a copy of the full document. The minimum content of the SFS is specified in the Regulations.

**supervisory board:** in a two-tier board structure, a board comprising non-executive directors of the company and having responsibility for oversight of the management board.

**sustainability:** the ability of a community or society to develop a strategy of economic growth and development that continues to function indefinitely within the limits set by ecology and is beneficial to all stakeholders and the environment.

**Table A:** the specimen Articles of Association for a company limited by shares set out in Table A of the Companies (Tables A to F) Regulations 1985. Unless specifically modified or excluded, the Articles set out in the version of Table A in force at the time of a company's incorporation automatically apply.

**Takeover Code:** *see* City Code.

**takeover:** the acquisition of one company by another, on either an agreed or a hostile basis. There are strict rules in the UK about the conduct and timing of a takeover bid.

**Total Shareholder Return (TSR):** a measure of the returns to shareholders over a defined period, increasingly used as the performance measure against which directors' rewards under performance-related remuneration arrangements are determined. TSR measures the percentage increase in the value of a given holding of the company's shares over a specified period, taking account of the increase or fall in the market share price of the company's shares over the period and assuming that all dividends received on the holding are reinvested in the company's shares.

**tracker fund:** an investment fund of which the objective is to achieve the same returns as a chosen share index, and which does this by investing in all the companies in the index according to a market value weighting.

**transparency:** in the context of company reporting, the provision of information in a manner which ensures that the company's position and prospects can be assessed on the basis of complete, reliable and meaningful data; otherwise, the existence of clear and visible procedures for the making of decisions.

**Turnbull Report:** the report *Internal Control: Guidance for Directors on the Combined Code* produced by a working party chaired by Nigel Turnbull and published in September 1999 by the Institute of Chartered Accountants in England and Wales.

**two-tier board:** a board structure in which the management and supervisory functions of the board are formally separated and allocated between a management board of full-time executives and a supervisory board of part-time external directors. Two-tier boards are the norm in a small number of Continental European countries, notably Germany, the Netherlands, Denmark and Austria.

**Tyson Report:** the report on the recruitment and development of non-executive directors produced by a task force chaired by Laura D'Andrea Tyson and published in June 2003.

**unitary board:** the most common board structure worldwide, in which the management and supervisory functions of the board are discharged by a single body comprising both executive and non-executive directors.

**United Kingdom Listing Authority (UKLA):** the Financial Services Authority (FSA) in its capacity as the competent authority in the UK for the listing of company shares and other securities for trading on public stock exchanges. The UKLA promulgates and enforces the Listing Rules, which require companies, as a condition of listing, to prepare listing particulars and comply with ongoing disclosure obligations.

**'voice':** the ability of shareholders to exercise the voting powers attaching to shares to appoint and dismiss the directors and to give or withhold approval for proposals affecting their interests.

**voting cap:** a limit on the number of votes permitted to be cast by a shareholder or group of shareholders irrespective of the number of shares held. Voting caps may be used to secure for controlling shareholders voting powers in excess of their investment and are therefore considered to be detrimental to effective corporate governance.

**voting rights:** rights attaching to shares in a company which confer on their holder the entitlement to vote at general meetings of the company's shareholders.

**whistleblower:** an individual (usually an employee) who draws attention to concerns about suspected misconduct on the part of a colleague or superior or the organisation itself. Where no whistleblowing procedure has been established, a whistleblower may consider it necessary raise concerns with a senior individual inside the company or with an external regulator or the media.

**whistleblowing procedure:** an internal procedure whereby employees with concerns about suspected misconduct on the part of a colleague or superior or the organisation itself can report them in confidence in the knowledge that they will not be subject to retaliatory action.

**written resolution:** a means by which a private company may obtain shareholder approval for a proposal without needing to convene a general meeting. To be passed, the written resolution must be signed by all members entitled to vote.

**wrongful trading:** a civil offence established in insolvency law which occurs where a company continues to trade when the directors are aware that the company had gone into (or would shortly go into) insolvent liquidation. A liquidator of the company can apply to the court for a director or shadow director to be held liable to contribute to the assets of the company.

# Bibliography

## ICSA Publications

available from ICSA Publishing: www.icsapublishing.co.uk

Armour D. (2002) *The ICSA Company Secretary's Checklists*, 4th edition
Armour, D. (2003) *The ICSA Company Secretary's Handbook*, 4th edition
Bruce, M. (2003) *The ICSA Directors' Guide*
Walmsley, K. *Company Secretarial Practice*

## ICSA Best Practice Guides and Guidance Notes

Available from The Information Centre, ICSA, 16 Park Crescent, London W1B 1AH, UK.

The ICSA Policy Unit produces a range of Best Practice Guides and Guidance Notes to support company secretaries.

All relevant Guidance Notes are reproduced on the CSP CD-Rom. Copies are also available via the ICSA web-site at www.icsa.org.uk/news/guidance.php. This area of the site also offers and e-mail alert service whereby users register to receive notification of any new Guidance Note published.

Appointment and Induction of Directors
Duties of the Company Secretary
Duties of the Company Secretary in Ireland
Electronic Communications with Shareholders
Establishing a Whistleblowing Procedure
Good Boardroom Practice: A Code for Directors and Company Secretaries
Guide to Best Practice at Annual General Meetings
Guide to the Statement of Compliance
Matters Reserved for the Board
Short Guide to the Retention of Documents
Specimen job description: the corporate governance role of the company
Terms of Reference of the Audit Committee
Terms of Reference of the Nominations Committee
Terms of Reference of the Remuneration Committee

## Codes, guidelines and reports

Association of British Insurers (1996) *Guidelines on Long-Term Remuneration for Senior Executives* (available at www.abi.org.uk)
Association of British Insurers (1999) *Statement of Principles on Share Incentive Schemes* (available at www.abi.org.uk)
Association of British Insurers (2001) *Disclosure Guidelines on Socially Responsible Investment* (available at www.abi.org.uk)
Association of British Insurers (2002) *Guidelines on Executive Remuneration* (available at www.abi.org.uk)

Association of British Insurers/National Association of Pension Funds (1999) *Statement on Responsible Voting* (available at www.abi.org.uk)

Cadbury Committee on the Financial Aspects of Corporate Governance (1992) *Report of the Committee on the Financial Aspects of Corporate Governance: The Code of Best Practice*, Gee Publishing

Combined Code on Corporate Governance (July 2003) Financial Reporting Council (available at www.frc.org.uk or in hard copy from CCH Information)

Commonwealth Association for Corporate Governance (1999) *Principles for Corporate Governance in the Commonwealth: Towards Global Competitiveness and Economic Accountability*

GoodCorporation/Institute of Business Ethics (2001) *The Good Corporation Charter* London, Institute of Business Ethics (available at www.goodcorporation.com)

Greenbury Study Group (1995) *Report on Directors' Remuneration*, Gee Publishing

Hampel Committee on Corporate Governance (1998) *Committee on Corporate Governance: Final Report*, Gee Publishing

Hermes Pensions Management (1998, updated 2001) *Statement on Corporate Governance and Voting Policy* (available at www.hermes.co.uk)

Hermes Pensions Management (2002) *The Hermes Principles* (available at www.hermes.co.uk)

Higgs Review (2003) *The Role and Effectiveness of Non-Executive Directors* Department of Trade and Industry (available at www.dti.gov.uk)

Institute of Social and Ethical Accountability (1999) *AccountAbility 1000 (AA1000) Foundation Standard in Social and Ethical Accounting, Auditing and Reporting*, AccountAbility Ltd

Institutional Shareholders Committee (2002) *Responsibilities of Institutional Shareholders and Agents – Statement of Principles* (available at www.abi.org.uk)

Myners, Paul (2001) *Institutional Investment in the UK: A Review*, HM Treasury

National Association of Pension Funds (2001) *Corporate Governance Policy* (available at www.napf.co.uk)

Organisation for Economic Cooperation and Development, *OECD Guidelines for Multinational Companies* (available at www.oecd.org)

Organisation for Economic Cooperation and Development (1999) *OECD Principles of Corporate Governance* (available at www.oecd.org)

Pensions Investments Research Consultants Ltd (2003) *Shareholder Voting Guidelines* (available at www.pirc.co.uk)

Smith Review Panel (2003) *Audit Committees: Combined Code Guidance* Financial Reporting Council (original version available at www.frc.org.uk; updated version included in the July 2003 Combined Code)

South African Institute of Directors (1994) *King Report on Corporate Governance*

South African Institute of Directors (2002) *King II Report on Corporate Governance for South Africa*

Turnbull Working Party (1999) *Internal Control: Guidance for Directors on the Combined Code* Croner CCH (available in pdf format via www.icaew.co.uk and also included in the July 2003 Combined Code)

## Additional reading

Bingham, K. (2001) *The Professional Board*, Gee Publishing

Bruce, M. *Rights and Duties of Directors* 5th edition, Tolley

Cadbury, A. (2002) *Corporate Governance and Chairmanship: A Personal View*, Oxford University Press

Chambers, A (2003) *Corporate Governance Handbook*, Tolley

Charkham, J. and Simpson, A. (1999) *Fair Shares: The Future of Shareholder Power and Responsibility*. Oxford University Press

Charkham, Jonathan P. (1994) *Keeping Good Company: A Study of Accountability in Five Countries*, Clarendon Press

Cheffins, B. (1997) *Company Law: Theory, Structure and Operation*, Oxford University Press

Cowe, R. (2001) *Investing in Social Responsibility: Risks and Opportunities*, Association of British Insurers

Davies, Paul L. (ed.) (1997) *Gower's Principles of Modern Company Law*, 6th edition, Sweet & Maxwell

Department of Trade and Industry (2002) *White Paper: Modernising Company Law* Cm 5553-I, The Stationery Office

Dunne, P. (1997) *Running Board Meetings*, Kogan Page

Low Chee Keong (ed.) (2002) *Corporate Governance: An Asia-Pacific Critique*, Sweet & Maxwell Asia

Monks, A.G. and Minow, N. (2001) *Corporate Governance*, Blackwell

Parkinson, J.E. (1993) *Corporate Power and Corporate Responsibility*, Clarendon Press

Smith, Deborah (2002) *Demonstrating Corporate Values*, Institute of Business Ethics

Stiles, P. and Taylor, B. (2001) *Boards at Work*, Oxford University Press

Tricker, R.I. (1984) *Corporate Governance*, Gower

Wheeler, D. and Sillanpaa, M. (1997) *The Stakeholder Corporation*, Pitman Publishing

Zadek, S. Pruzan, P. and Evans, R. (1997) *Building Corporate Accountability*, Earthscan

## Web resources

Association of British Insurers: www.abi.org.uk

Business for Social Responsibility: www.bsr.org

Council of Institutional Investors (US): www.cii.org

Department of Trade and Industry: www.dti.gov.uk

Financial Reporting Council:  www.frc.org.uk

Financial Services Authority: www.fsa.gov.uk

Global Corporate Governance Forum: www.gcgf.org

Institute for Business Ethics: www.ibe.org.uk

Institute of Chartered Secretaries and Administrators: www.icsa.org.uk

Institute of Directors: www.iod.co.uk

International Corporate Governance Network: www.icgn.org

Investor Relations Society: www.ir-soc.org.uk

London Stock Exchange: www.londonstockexchange.com

National Association of Pension Funds: www.napf.co.uk and www.votingissues.com

New York Stock Exchange: www.nyse.com

Organisation for Economic Cooperation and Development: www.oecd.org

Panel on Takeovers and Mergers: www.thetakeoverpanel.org.uk

Pensions Investments Research Consultants Limited: www.pirc.co.uk/

Public Concern at Work (whistleblowing): www.pcaw.co.uk

The Corporate Library: www.thecorporatelibrary.com

US Securities and Exchange Commission: www.sec.gov

# Index